Pulling Together or Pulling Apart?

NATIONALISMS ACROSS THE GLOBE
VOL. 21

SERIES EDITORS

Dr Tomasz Kamusella
(University of St Andrews, Scotland, UK)

Dr Krzysztof Jaskułowski
(University of Social Sciences and Humanities, Poland)

EDITORIAL BOARD

Balázs Apor (Dublin)
Peter Burke (Cambridge)
Monika Baár (Groningen)
Andrea Graziosi (Naples)
Akihiro Iwashita (Sapporo)
Sławomir Łodziński (Warsaw)
Alexander Markarov (Yerevan)
Elena Marushiakova and Veselin Popov (Sofia)
Alexander Maxwell (Wellington)
Anastasia Mitrofanova (Moscow)
Michael Moser (Vienna)
Frank Lorenz Müller (St Andrews)
Sabelo J. Ndlovu-Gatsheni (Pretoria)
Balázs Trencsényi (Budapest)
Sergei Zhuk (Muncie, Indiana)

PETER LANG
Oxford · Bern · Berlin · Bruxelles · New York · Wien

Susana Bayó Belenguer and Nicola Brady
(editors)

Pulling Together or Pulling Apart?

Perspectives on Nationhood, Identity
and Belonging in Europe

PETER LANG
Oxford · Bern · Berlin · Bruxelles · New York · Wien

Bibliographic information published by Die Deutsche Nationalbibliothek.
Die Deutsche Nationalbibliothek lists this publication in the Deutsche National-
bibliografie; detailed bibliographic data is available on the Internet at
http://dnb.d-nb.de.

A catalogue record for this book is available from the British Library.

Library of Congress Control Number: A CIP catalog record for this book has been applied for at the Library of Congress.

 An electronic version of this book is freely available, thanks to the support of libraries working with Knowledge Unlatched. KU is a collaborative initiative designed to make high quality books Open Access for the public good. More information about the initiative and links to the Open Access version can be found at www.knowledgeunlatched.org

Cover design by Peter Lang Ltd.

ISSN 2235-1809
ISBN 978-1-78707-304-3 (print) • ISBN 978-1-78997-674-8 (ePDF)
ISBN 978-1-78997-675-5 (ePub) • ISBN 978-1-78997-676-2 (mobi)

Open Access: This work is licensed under a Creative Commons Attribution CC-BY 4.0 license. To view a copy of this license, visit https://creativecommons.org/licenses/by/4.0/

© Peter Lang AG 2020

Published by Peter Lang Ltd, International Academic Publishers,
52 St Giles, Oxford, OX1 3LU, United Kingdom
oxford@peterlang.com, www.peterlang.com

All rights reserved.
All parts of this publication are protected by copyright.
Any utilisation outside the strict limits of the copyright law, without
the permission of the publisher, is forbidden and liable to prosecution.
This applies in particular to reproductions, translations, microfilming,
and storage and processing in electronic retrieval systems.

This publication has been peer reviewed.

Nationalism's kingdom is frankly of this world, and its attainment involves tribal selfishness and vainglory, a particularly ignorant and tyrannical intolerance [...] nationalism brings not peace but the sword.
— Carlton J. H. Hayes

Identity is revealed to us only as something to be invented rather than discovered; as a target of an effort, 'an objective'; as something one still needs to build from scratch or to choose from alternative offers and then to struggle for and then to protect through yet more struggle.
— Zigmunt Bauman

The disappearance of nations would have impoverished us no less than if all men had become alike, with one personality and one face. Nations are the wealth of mankind, its collective personalities; the very least of them wears its own special colours and bears within itself a special facet of divine intention.
— Aleksandr Solzhenitsyn

Contents

List of Tables   ix

Preface   xi

SUSANA BAYÓ BELENGUER AND NICOLA BRADY

Introduction   1

LEYRE ARRIETA ALBERDI

The Basque Country within Spain and Europe: Basque Nationalist Party Proposals during the Spanish Transition to Democracy (1975–1980)   29

Nationalism and Identity: An Interview with Professor Xosé M. Núñez Seixas   55

EMMANUEL DALLE MULLE

Enlargement from Within? Secession and EU Membership   61

GORKA ETXEBARRIA DUEÑAS

Flagging the Nation in the Basque Country: The Flag War   91

KATERINA GARCIA

Al tyempo del kuechko dulse: History, Language and Identity in Enrique Saporta y Beja's Account of Jewish Life in Salonika   119

RICHARD GOW

Patria and Citizenship: Miguel Primo de Rivera, *Caciques* and Military *Delegados*, 1923–1924   147

MARK FRIIS HAU
Becoming Catalan: Narrative Cultivation of Self among Catalan Nationalists   177

CARLES JOVANÍ GIL
Russian Geopolitical Thinking and the Ukrainian Crisis: Neo-Imperialist Aspirations or Merely a Survival Strategy?   203

DANIEL PURCELL
Contested Unionism along the Irish Border at the Time of Partition   223

JUAN ROMERO, JOAQUÍN MARTÍN CUBAS, MARGARITA SOLER SÁNCHEZ, JOSÉ MARÍA VIDAL BELTRÁN, AND CARLES JOVANÍ GIL
Rebuilding Bridges: Nations and State in Present-Day Spain   253

ROBERT A. SAUNDERS
Separatism in the New Millennium: Looking Back to See Forward   283

MARÇAL SINTES OLIVELLA, JOSEP-LLUÍS MICÓ-SANZ, AND FRANCESC-MARC ÁLVARO VIDAL
The Pro-Independence Movement in Catalonia: Impact on the International Agenda and Media Pluralism   303

SORINA SOARE
Romania: The Challenges of Contested Identities   339

IÑIGO URRUTIA
The Constitutional Crossroads in Spain   379

ERIC VANDERHEYDEN
Ethical Nationalism: Social Citizenship in Multi-National States   399

Notes on Contributors   423

Index   431

Tables

Table 8.1:	Signatories of the Ulster Covenant and Women's Declaration as a percentage of the adult non-Catholic population in 1911 census. Source: Fitzpatrick (2014: 243).	228
Table 8.2:	Membership of the UVF and Ulster Clubs as a percentage of estimated adult non-Catholic population. Source: Fitzpatrick (2014: 244).	229
Table 8.3:	Arms held by the UVF in each county. Source: Mac Giolla Choille (1966: 34).	230
Table 8.4:	First World War enlistments per 1,000 non-agricultural males and percentage of non-agricultural males listed as non-Catholic in the 1911 census. Source: Unpublished figures provided by David Fitzpatrick.	231
Table 11.1:	Number of journal pieces	333
Table 11.2:	Number of front-page or table-of-contents pieces	333
Table 11.3:	Most common genres in printed press (%)	333
Table 11.4:	Most common genres in broadcast media (%)	333
Table 11.5:	Most common genres in online media (%)	334
Table 11.6:	Opinion articles typology (%)	334
Table 11.7:	Main subjects in printed press headlines (%)	334
Table 11.8:	Main subjects in broadcasting media (%)	334
Table 11.9:	Main subjects in online media (%)	335
Table 11.10:	Typology of headlines (%)	335
Table 11.11:	Typology of international headlines (%)	335

Table 11.12:	Ideology of print media contributors (%)	335
Table 11.13:	Ideology of online media contributors (%)	336
Table 11.14:	Ideology of radio talk-show guests (%)	336
Table 11.15:	Ideology of television talk-show guests (%)	336

Preface

The editors, Susana Bayó Belenguer and Nicola Brady, have put together a penetrating and stimulating collection of studies on the subject of nationhood and identity on Europe's multi-ethnic peripheries, with the main focus on the case of Spain. How Spain has addressed and is addressing the challenges of diversity are explored from a variety of disciplines, including politics, history, law, international relations, sociology, anthropology, media studies, and even literature. The scope and methodology of chapters vary even more widely, from a broad-ranging interview with Professor Xosé M. Núñez Seixas on the subject of nationalism to the analysis of an account of Jewish life in Salonika in the language of Judeo-Spanish.

A theme that runs through the volume and which is implicit even in the chapters with a particular historical focus is that Spain's pluri-national constitution remains a work in progress, as is evident in the analysis of both the Basque and Catalan cases. The larger emphasis on Catalan nationalism reflects changing contemporary priorities, with the waning of violence in the Basque Country. Still relevant to both cases is the issue of national identification: to what extent do people in these regions identify as both Basque and Spanish or as both Catalan and Spanish? Or is there a trend to identify exclusively with one or the other? This issue has been addressed in line with an innovative methodology that Luis Moreno developed as far back as 1986. He designed a self-identification scale that asked respondents what weight they gave to different national identities. For example, did they feel more Basque than Spanish or vice-versa? Or did they attach equal importance to both identities? The Moreno question continues to be asked in many different countries and to yield significant results that chart changes in sentiment over time. The rise of the politics of identity, as well as that of status, has meant that for many voters, these issues have become more salient than the bread and butter concerns that previously dominated their political preferences.

A corollary is that from a policy perspective, the accommodation of different identities looms large in the governance of European states. In states in which ethnic minorities within a country are associated with particular regions in which they constitute a majority of the population, the granting of regional autonomy is an obvious step. However, it is rarely the end of the matter, as arguments between the region and the centre over the exercise of their respective powers are likely to remain a source of friction, even under the most carefully designed constitutions. Further, dissatisfaction over the terms of autonomy and demands for their radical modification short of full independence may generate practically as much heat as the original push for autonomy and in the process increase support for secession. As a number of chapters in this volume underline, this is precisely what has happened in Spain.

The inclusion of other cases of multi-national and bi-national states gives further weight to the comparative approach to the analysis of these issues, with chapters on Russia and the Ukrainian crisis, Ulster Unionism during the partition of Ireland, sub-state nationalism in Scotland and Flanders, Romania's relations with its kin-state of Moldova, and separatism as a phenomenon across Europe. One chapter compares the cases of Scotland and Catalonia, examining in forensic detail their prospects of achieving independence within Europe. Hitherto, the European Union has been unwilling to accept the legitimacy of secession within any member state, but has been ready to accept as members, states that emerged as a result of the collapse of communism and the break-up of states in Eastern Europe, i.e. that involved secession outside of the European Union. Whether the European Union would be ready to accept Scotland as a member after Brexit remains a fascinating question, as does the attitude of the Spanish government to such a possibility.

Even while broadly discouraging the flow of refugees from outside of Europe, the European Union has played a generally constructive role in the promotion of the accommodation of diversity within Europe. That is one reason why Brussels has been a target of populists of a nativist bent. But, as the editors point out, the European project has by no means eliminated ethnic fault lines, nor should populism and the reaction against immigration and multi-culturalism simply be seen as manifestations of nationalism, even majoritarian nationalism. The multiple angles from which these issues are addressed in this volume provide a valuable addition to our understanding of the processes of both integration and disintegration.

Adrian Guelke

SUSANA BAYÓ BELENGUER AND NICOLA BRADY

Introduction

> Our present world is simultaneously moving towards the opposing dystopias of hyper centralisation and endless fragmentation.
>
> — Francis Fukuyama (2018)

This publication has its origins in a multi-disciplinary conference of the same name hosted by the Department of Hispanic Studies in Trinity College, Dublin University, which, at a time when many Western democracies are being pulled apart by identity politics, brought together academics from around the world to explore themes of nationhood and belonging. In addressing multiple issues within identity formation, this volume assembles comparative and single-area case studies from different academic disciplines which enable an holistic view of the evolution of identity-based conflict in Europe, and situate contemporary challenges in their historical context.

It is appropriate therefore to set the scene by outlining the conceptual and contextual notions that underlie its themes, looking at what is understood by terms like 'nation' and 'nationalism' in the search for socio-political identity. And as our setting is Europe, it also seems apt to consider briefly the problems of an embattled EU at a time when Brexit is spearheading a general rising of dissent among its members.

The Resilience of Nationalism as a Sociopolitical Force

Experts recognize that, in divisive power, nationalism in the present western world has come to occupy the place once held by faiths, both prompting a visceral adherence and defying rational conceptualizations. As Arthur M. Schlesinger, Jr noted: 'Nationalism remains […] the most vital political emotion in the world – far more vital than social ideologies such as communism or fascism or even democracy' (1998: 53). Years earlier, in the aftermath of the First World War, Carlton Hayes had made much the same point, asking 'why apostles of nationalism are characterised by a missionary zeal that is fiery and why its multitudinous disciples are possessed of a love that is consuming' and linking the question to the assertion that 'it is the latest and nearest approach to a world-religion' (1926: 6).

Nationalisms and their associated phenomena have continued to defy precise definition because they possess perhaps too many dimensions, too many facets, too many subjectivities to pin down.[1] But, although whatever we may measure and quantify of the brain contributes only marginally to an understanding of what our thoughts are 'made of', we continue to observe that which is as yet definitionally out of reach. In much the same way we may note that common to all our understandings of identity, of nationalism and of nation are (equally indefinable) emotions, beliefs and desires that continue to confound debate. Spain's internal divides provide a clear example, as perfectly sound arguments from one region are refuted by perfectly valid arguments from another, while all concerned are aware that debate is futile without a common understanding of what is meant by 'nation'.

Definitions are elusive also because, as Ernest Renan (1882) long ago realized, nationalism and nation are often compounds of the worst and best aspirations of communities, who call upon an 'imagined' past in support of demands for a future that will cater for present ambitions of 'national' identity. It is clear that to belong (however understood) and specifically, for the purposes of our present concern, to belong to a place, to a definable space, remains among the most powerful needs of human beings, and thus nationalism has the potential to arouse in us what Schlesinger identifies as '[t]he hostility of one tribe for another' (1998: 12). This oldest of tribal instincts, still engendering among even the most advanced societies a drive to exclude from belonging, and the urge to cast out whatever is perceived as not belonging, is implicit in what Alain Touraine maintained: 'Society

1   Among the perspectives from which they may be viewed, in no particular order, are: ethnic, geographic, religious, linguistic, historical, socio-biological, instrumentalist, modernist and postmodernist.

is not merely a system of norms or a system of domination: it is a system of social relations, of debates and conflicts, of political initiatives and claims, of ideologies and alienation' (1977: 30). Identity, that inherent heart of belonging, whatever its subjective and objective components, is realized as a social phenomenon, with the person finding expression only in terms of a society, and society having meaning only in terms of the person. Thus the ability of nationalism to (re)surface and adapt to the times depends substantially on its offering a perennially utopian vision of one's roots, of one's tribal identity within a recognizable community of kindred people. In the words of Anthony D. Smith: 'Just as "the nation" is felt and willed and acted out, as well as imagined, so do many of the members of today's nations feel that their own interests, needs and welfare are bound up with the welfare and destiny of "their" nation' (2009: 14).[2]

But understandings of precisely what is meant by their nation may be as many and as varied as the members, and – just as significantly – the non-members, of it. In 1913 Joseph Stalin defined the nation along the lines of a community of language, territory, economic life and psychological make-up.[3] Not too differently, but from a non-Marxist perspective, Ernest Gellner (1983), asserting that without nationalism there would not exist

2   As well as Smith (1971), for other earlier works on nationalism see, for example, Deutsch (1953); Rustow (1967). Apart from the 1983 contributions of Gellner and also Anderson, the 1980s and 1990s saw a wealth of offerings, among them, again, Smith (1995). Publications in the twenty-first century proliferate, with Smith (2009) this time challenging modernist and post-modernist views of the birth of the nation and nationalism. There are innovative takes on nationalism by, for example, Malesevic (2013); Berger and Conrad (2015); Brubaker (2015); edited books by Jensen (2016), and by Tierney (2018); and relevant to nationalisms in Spain (the topic area of several contributors to the present volume), see García (2018) and the edited book by Sepúlveda Muñoz (2018).

3   While early Marxist thinkers naturally perceived a link between the rise of capitalism and nationalism, maintaining that the latter would disappear as it was supplanted by worldwide class consciousness, the same view, that capitalism is largely responsible for nationalism is still held by, for example, Craig Calhoun (1997); and Bernadette McAliskey, addressing a meeting in (London)Derry to commemorate the 50th anniversary of the rioting in Northern Ireland that became known as the 'Battle of the Bogside' claimed both that 'the capitalist classes of Ireland [...] extol the virtues of the European Union' and that 'a focus on nationalism will "sooner or later" take Ireland towards fascism' (McClements 2019).

the nation, gave two down-to-earth exemplifications of what constitutes a nation:

> Two men are of the same nation if and only if they share the same culture, where culture in turn means a system of ideas and signs and associations and ways of behaving and communicating.
> [...]
> A mere category of persons (say, occupants of a given territory, or speakers of a given language, for example) becomes a nation if and when the members of the category firmly recognize certain mutual rights and duties to each other in virtue of their shared membership of it. It is their recognition of each other as fellows of this kind which turns them into a nation, and not the other shared attributes, whatever they might be, which separate that category from non-members. (Gellner 1983: 6, 7)[4]

But whereas in the past a shared culture and ethnicity (however indefinable or smudged by history) over a sufficient period of time might have made it relatively easy to identify, and to identify with, one's fellow nationals, Europe is increasingly experiencing an era not unlike that of the later Roman Empire in the West (itself long hybrid), when movements of people, many of them motivated by threats from other groupings, obliged overwhelming hegemonic shifts in a remix of cultures and communities that would take centuries to resolve into what we today understand as 'Europe'. Similarly, today from a different direction, a new wave of migration is beginning to force a reconsideration of what constitutes a national identity, and to oblige a recognition of challenges to the traditional state (see, for example, Guibernau and Rex, 2010, 'Introduction').

And to muddy even further the already murky waters, Benedict Anderson, in taking a conceptual approach, suggested that the nation

> is an imagined political community – and imagined as both inherently limited and sovereign [...] The nation is imagined as limited because even the largest of them [...] has finite, if elastic, boundaries, beyond which lie other nations [...] It is imagined as sovereign because the concept was born in an age in which Enlightenment and Revolution were destroying the legitimacy of the divinely ordained, hierarchical dynastic realm [...] Finally, it is imagined as a community, because, regardless of the actual inequality and exploitation that may prevail in each, the nation is always

---

4   For a discussion of Gellner's thought see Breuilly (2006).

conceived as a deep, horizontal comradeship. Ultimately it is this fraternity that makes it possible, over the past two centuries, for so many millions of people, not so much to kill, as willingly to die for such limited imaginings. (Anderson 1983: 49–50)

Hayes had similarly equated nationalism with 'an emotional loyalty to the idea or the fact of the national state, a loyalty so intensely emotional that it motivates all sorts of people and causes them to subordinate all other human loyalties to national loyalty' (1926: 3). And present-day nationalisms have familiar echoes of a past which tore Europe apart in wars between 'nations' whose claim to that title might be no more than the possession of frontiers established by a ruling dynasty, or whose political elite were prepared to have millions of people slaughtered over territorial hegemonies disguised as ideological value disputes and 'home' defence. On all sides, a common call to arms was bolstered by appeal to the solidarity of a people, motivated then as now by what Victor Orbán has recently put in these terms: 'This is our homeland, our life, and since we don't have another one, we will fight for it until the very end and we will never give it up.'[5]

As historian Xosé M. Núñez Seixas (2012: 14) has noted, questions about nationalism might be asked about regionalism and regional identity (local or sub-national identities), and a better understanding of both might be arrived at by considering to what extent regionalisms are 'complementary' or 'opposed' to national identities and what differentiates them from nations, nationalism and 'separatism.'[6] He has claimed that regionalism and nationalism share common traits, that regionalist aspirations

---

[5] Viktor Orbán (2018), 'Ceremonial Speech on the 170th Anniversary of the Hungarian Revolution of 1848'. Website of the Hungarian government: <https://www.kormany.hu/en/the-prime-minister/the-prime-minister-s-speeches/orban-viktor-s-ceremonial-speech-on-the-170th-anniversary-of-the-hungarian-revolution-of-1848> accessed 16 December 2018.

[6] Particularly relevant in a European context to the current demands of Andalusian, Basque, Bavarian, Catalan, Flemish, Galician, Québécois and Scottish nationalisms. And, given the recent rapid rise of pro-independence numbers in Catalonia, an interesting speculation on the formation, post-Brexit, of a new Celtic state (Celtonia) quotes the latest available census figures (2011) as showing that '21pc of Northern Irish identified themselves as, just that, Northern Irish, as against British or Irish', Dorcha Lee, *Irish Independent*, 15 August 2019, p. 30.

'generally precede or even accompany sub-state nationalisms.' It is widely perceived that these aspirations may turn into claims when a confluence of economic and socio-political circumstances coincides with emotional reactions to what is considered disregard for a collective regional identity by the nation-state;[7] these reactions may include what Wendy Brown (1995) identified as a sense of 'woundedness', the basis for aggressive individual and collective affirmation of identity. Present-day Europe is struggling with and currently failing to find coherent solutions to the many disparate definitions, feelings, aspirations and expectations that clamour for expression, both within a context of EU unity and opposed to it.

The Integration of Nations in the European Union

Though it is well recognized that the establishment of the European Union was, at its core, a peace project, unity is today also troubled to the east as any moves towards expansion of its membership are viewed by Russia as acts of aggression. It matters little that the EU was founded only on visions of peace as a continent wounded from two world wars and reeling from the horrors of the Holocaust sought to create a new foundation on which all could unite around a common European identity. Alliances of any sort are of concern to those not within them and Russia, naturally sensitive to any transfer of allegiance on its borders, is not alone in wariness of the European bloc. In a world of endless competition, it also matters little that, in the words of Walter Hallstein, the first president of the European Commission:

> This community is not due to military power or political pressure, but owes its existence to a creative act. It is based on sound legal standards and its institutions are subject to legal control. For the first time, the rule of law takes the place of power and its manipulation of the equilibrium of forces, of hegemonic aspiration and

7 As noted in Charles Kupchan (1995), when the state neglects to perform the basic functions expected by its citizens, they may turn to other forms of political and social organization.

of the game of alliances […] In the relations between Member States, violence and political pressure will be replaced by the preeminence of the law. (Quoted in Danwitz 2018: 4)

It was hoped that as the strategic importance of the supranational context increased in political, social and economic terms, the significance of ethnic, cultural and national differences would diminish, with minority identities finding accommodation in sub-state arrangements.

This hope has begun to look increasingly forlorn as in the twenty-first century these differences – far from being subsumed within an overarching 'European' identity – are gaining a new intensity in parts of the continent as unities (including some not owed to the European Union but rather forged over centuries) begin to fracture under the weight of localized perceptions of identity. Europe sees itself at ever-greater risk of splitting apart as in the analysis of some sub-state nationalist parties the prospect of European Union membership reduces the economic and political risks that secession would otherwise bring them.

To the internal conflicts of Europe we may add an enforced participation in other threats that are sweeping the world. As Francis Fukuyama has argued: 'Identity politics has become a master concept that explains much of what is going on in global affairs' (2018b: 92) and '[d]emocratic societies are fracturing into segments' (2018b: 93). This threat is focused less on national and ethnic identity alone as on gender, sexuality and social class. It is almost as though globalization, far from being an antidote to the narrow tribalism of nationalism, is itself the generator of another kind of multiculturalism, and one not envisaged by its antinationalist proponents. Where once it was possible to conceive of ethnocultural congruence as the essential core of multiculturalism, of internationalism, the rise of identity politics has added yet another component to intraculturalism.

Alongside such unity destabilizers, Jan-Werner Müller cautions against over-simplifications that equate the recent rise in populism with a straightforward resurgence of nationalism: what we are seeing is the instrumentalization of nationalism by populist leaders who 'seek out and thrive on conflict; their political business model is permanent culture war. In a way they reduce all political questions to questions of belonging. Whoever disagrees with them is labelled an "enemy of the people"' (2019: 36). Perhaps few recent world events illustrate the emotive power of Müller's innocent word 'belonging' or of the divisive potential of independence aspirations better than the British people's experience of Brexit.

If these contentions were not of themselves sufficient to erode the EU, Cézar Baena and Michael Neubert claim that mistrust of 'elites' and 'the establishment' lies at the heart of many of the societal divisions witnessed across Europe today:

> In some countries, anti-establishment movements are in power: Lega and the Five Star Movement in Italy, Law and Justice in Poland, the Freedom Party in Austria, Fidesz in Hungary. These movements share a critique of the EU bureaucracy and its attempts to regulate markets, impose rules on economic and technological development, and establish quotas for migrants. Often called populists, they seek to dismantle the EU bureaucracy and take power back to the people (i.e. the nation state or smaller units of decision-making). Brexit and the *gilets jaunes* movement in France have emerged within this context. (Baena and Neubert 2019: n.p.)

Yet all this seems to have erupted from faultlines thought to be no longer active beneath the construction project of European unity. By the 1990s, nationalism had seemed to be a spent force, overcome by policies of globalization, and with any fears of a kind of featureless multicultural identity – the sort that would make Barcelona indistinguishable from Berlin – allayed by notions of federalism. Hence the ease with which it was possible to conclude that nationalism was ultimately a dead end, merely another artefact of the creators of 'us' and 'them' animations.[8] Or, alternatively, to dismiss nationalism as little more than popular local reactions to what are perceived as distant elites. It seemed farsighted of Ernest Renan (1882) to have maintained that 'nations are not something eternal', that they 'have their

---

8   For positive aspects of nationalism see Moore (2001); De Schutter and Tinnevelt (2011); Tamir (2019).

beginnings and they will end' and that '[a] European confederation will very probably replace them'.⁹ And it did not seem wildly premature of Rousseau to have long since observed that 'these days, whatever else one may say, there are no longer any Frenchmen, Englishmen, Germans or Spaniards, there are only Europeans' (quoted in Seth and Kulessa 2017: 132).

But by the new millennium there were already signs of a growing unease over internationalist fervour and, perceptively, Smith (2009: 128–9) challenged the demise of nations, pointing to their staying power, to their ability to continually evolve as socio-cultural communities ('ethnies', from the French). Research between 2008 and 2009 showed that loyalty to Europe among EU citizens took third place after the first loyalty to the nation and the second to the region of origin; but, perhaps significantly, when asked about what contributed most to a European identity, 41 per cent selected 'democratic values', with far fewer (at 24 per cent each) opting for 'geography' and 'common history'. Overall, the strongest feelings of being European were found in the north of Europe and the weakest with Britain and Greece.¹⁰

Whether causal or correlational, perhaps the most unsettling and alarming development has been the rise of nationalism and identity politics in Hungary, Poland, Spain and Austria, a mounting populist anti-migrant feeling in Italy, Sweden and Germany, an insistent anti-European sentiment in, for example, the UK and the appearance of newly formed populist parties of the left and of the right in Austria, France, the Netherlands and Spain. Opposition to the very thought of a politically united Europe is becoming more overt, with Catalan secessionist aspirations offering a

---

9   'Qu'est-ce qu'une nation?' Lecture delivered by Renan at the Sorbonne in March 1882. Apart from the proliferation in the past decade of international conferences and symposia on nationalism and identity politics, the number of publications on the EU has also increased – see for example: Cohn-Bendit, et al. (2012); Verhofstadt (2017).

10 <https://ec.europa.eu/commfrontoffice/publicopinion/archives/eb/eb71/eb713_future_europe.pdf> accessed 25 January 2019, pp. 34–44.

recent illustration: 'Así no nos interesa esta Europa' [So we are not interested in this Europe].[11]

A factor in the gradual re-emergence of affective nationalism in Europe must be a widely perceived dichotomy between the EU as an ideal and its institutional realization, with both the European Parliament and the European Commission generally viewed unfavourably even by the strongest supporters of a united Europe. For example, Germany, currently showing some 63 per cent support for the EU, manages only 47 per cent for the Parliament and 38 per cent for the Commission; weaker supporters such as England and Greece (48 per cent and 37 per cent respectively in favour of the EU), drop to 35 per cent and 30 per cent for the Parliament, and 32 per cent and 26 per cent for the Commission (Wike et al. 2019).[12]

Both England and Greece lay particular emphasis on the 'national sovereignty' that, within its limits, the sociologist Frank Furedi today defends, supporting the common perception that EU bureaucrats are out of touch with the realities of EU citizens, and declaring the EU oligarchs as detrimental to the European ethos, as having 'pathologized' populism by 'turning it into a toxin poisoning the continent'. National sovereignty, he maintains, provides 'a far more democratic and meaningful setting for the conduct of public life than the transnational institutions favoured by

11 Carles Puigdemont, the exiled conservative ex-president of the Catalan Generalitat, angrily criticized the EU when his claim to an MEP seat was rejected: the Spanish government had not included him on the official list on the grounds that he had not gone to Madrid to collect his official card and to swear loyalty to the Spanish Constitution as required by law (*La Vanguardia*, 3 July 2019). Reflecting on the critical stance taken by Puigdemont and others among his followers, Francesc-Marc Álvaro reflected: 'Two million people who have voted in favour of [pro-independence parties] may feel justifiably let down by the EU machine but it would be dangerous for them to join the ranks of Europhobia, a lair where the company is not very pleasant nor the rhetoric very inspiring' (*The Irish Times*, 13 July 2019) <https://www.irishtimes.com/news/world/europe/catalan-leader-rails-against-eu-as-spain-rules-out-referendum-1.3946875> accessed 13 July 2019.

12 The bodies in question are major parts of the complex European bureaucracy, along with the Council of the European Union (easily confused with European Council or Council of Europe).

EU cosmopolitans do.'[13] This accords with, albeit is less extreme than, the perceptions of, for example, Pablo Iglesias (leader of the left-wing party Podemos in Spain)[14] or Nigel Farage (ex-leader of UKIP and leader of the Brexit Party in Britain) who describe the history of the EU as one of failure and deception.[15]

Furedi's stance is thus given vigour by a key challenge facing European attempts at unity: member states do not in fact share a common vision of the future EU. The Brexit vote itself as much as its divisive aftermath have clearly shown that a perceived otherness, however marginally approved or ill-prepared for, can trump any advancement towards a more integrated or quasi-federal institution. Reports of the death of 'the nation' are therefore premature as members of the EU continue to play this 'national interest' card on issues such as centralism versus regional autonomies, open interior borders and immigration from outside Europe. More pulling apart than pulling together, the EU has yet, in the first quarter of the twenty-first century, to find a consolidated European identity in accord with the ideals of its architects. Socio-political foundations once thought to be firmly established are being undermined by a seeming inability to present a co-operative, let alone a united, front.

From one perspective the start of the current wave of internal pressures on the EU may be traced to the 2007–8 economic crisis, to be followed too closely by the 2012–13 recession. And just when Europe needed most to focus on the economy it had to give attention to the ongoing migrant

---

13 Frank Furedi 'Why I wrote a radical democratic defence of populism' <https://www.spiked-online.com/2017/08/22/why-i-wrote-a-radical-democratic-defence-of-populism/> accessed 20 August 2019.

14 Mariano Calleja, 'El populismo de Iglesias y Le Pen, contra la UE'. *ABC*, 12 April 2017 <https://www.abc.es/espana/abci-populismo-iglesias-y-contra-201703152108_noticia.html> accessed 12 April 2017.

15 For example: Richard Hartley-Parkinson, 'Nigel Farage declares June 23 the UK's independence day', *Metro*, 24 June 2016 <https://metro.co.uk/2016/06/24/nigel-farage-declares-victory-for-vote-leave-5963659/> accessed 23 January 2018; Camila Domonoske, Brexiteer Nigel Farage to EU: "You're Not Laughing Now, Are You?"', *National Public Radio* (Washington, DC), 28 June 2016 <https://www.npr.org/sections/thetwo-way/2016/06/28/483857209/watch-brexiteer-nigel-farage-to-eu-youre-not-laughing-now-are-you?t=1566050298125> accessed 16 July 2018.

and refugee crisis from 2015 onwards (whose main effects were felt by Greece, Italy and Germany), to terrorist attacks in Paris, in Brussels, in Spain, Denmark, the UK and Germany, and to the unanticipated effects of the 2016 Brexit vote.

Within the EU itself national representatives confront its mandarins: in the newly elected European Parliament, MEP and committed Brexiteer, Ann Widdecombe, vigorously accused the institution of being undemocratic, a charge fuelled in part by the dissatisfaction of many MEPs with the process of top-level appointments, and by the refusal of Donald Tusk to provide any kind of satisfactory response to it. Widdecombe expostulated:

> If I needed any convincing at all that the best thing for Britain is to leave here [...] it was the way that those elections were conducted yesterday [...] there is a pattern consistent throughout the history of oppressed peoples turning on the oppressor. Slaves against their owners, the peasantry against the feudal barons. Colonies, Mr Verhofstadt, against their empires and that is why Britain is leaving [...] *Nous allons, wir gehen, we're off*.[16]

And in Britain, perhaps more than elsewhere in Europe, new internal divisions can be seen to some extent at least as re-articulations of old discontents, notwithstanding the very considerable democratic and egalitarian strides made there during the past 100 years. Where irreconcilable social discord might previously have fed into a discourse of class division, it is now, with the coupling of globalization and multiculturalism with the whole European question, able to embrace with greater fervour much broader definitions of difference. The Spanish sociologist Manuel Castells, influenced by Touraine, perceived in the upsurge of populist identity politics across the social spectrum – once solely the preserve of the left and anti-globalization groups – the consequence of a process of reassertion, of reaffirmation of identity by individuals and communities in response to globalized networks: '[I]n a world of global flow of wealth, power and images, the search for identity, collective or individual, ascribed or

---

16 James Crisp, 'Ann Widdecombe compares EU to slave owners in maiden European Parliament Speech', *The Telegraph*, 4 July 2019, <http://www.telegraph.co.uk> accessed 4 July 2019.

reconstructed, becomes the fundamental source of social meaning'. He goes on to note the dangers of disassociation between how we work and the way we feel, between a 'techno-economic-network society and identity' as originator of the need of individuals to rely on themselves and of the appearance of 'communities' (weaker individuals who come together to vindicate a cause: nationalism, environmentalism, etc.) while civil society and the state are progressively becoming less effective.[17]

Contemporary Challenges to Nationalism from Globalization and Migration

While, by the 1990s, many experts on multiculturalism believed that globalization was going to change how we interacted and lived, what was meant by globalization was not necessarily clearcut, as Natalie Sabanadze's 2010 study vigorously and meticulously (if controversially) has pointed out.[18] And whereas globalization optimists might once have believed that frontiers would become irrelevant and peoples, capital and goods would freely move – that transnational entities would weaken the nation-state, which in turn would lead to a kind of cultural and economic universalism – the economic crisis of 2007–8 was to show that socio-economic realities could swiftly confound these aspirations in what has been labelled the socialization of losses and the privatization of profits.[19]

17 Harry Kreisler. *In Conversation with History: Manuel Castells.* <https://www.youtube.com/watch?v=0GBB7U5mvow> accessed 9 December 2018. For an in-depth analysis of the impact of globalization on identity politics and nationalism see Castells (2007).
18 The controversy is less concerned with the complexities of definitions than with her claim that globalization and nationalism have become partnered, the former now promoting the latter internationally.
19 The consequences of such economic practices have also been felt in Germany, particularly in Eastern Germany, where economic exclusion has prevailed owing to the import of 'Anglo-Saxon management practices.' In 'Ceçi n'est pas un hype!', *The Economist*, 14 April 2018, pp. 7–8.

In Europe and beyond, the present upsurge of nationalism and what has come to be known as 'populism' were identified by Zygmunt Bauman (2000) in a world of constant change. Some eight years later, in discussion with Bauman, Mark Haugaard remarked: 'The so-called "unintended effect" of neoliberalism is globalization which augments fears through the constant movement of capital, which makes jobs insecure and creates the threat of the "economic migrant"' (Bauman and Haugaard, 2008: 120). In a 2016 interview Bauman was to reiterate that what lies at the root of crises of identity and feelings described as nationalist is a 'continuous uncertainty, which makes us afraid.'[20] This is highly fertile ground for populism to flourish, for representative populist parties from the right and the left across Europe to demand power for the people against the elites, that is, against liberal and democratic institutions which they consider outmoded and, above all, corrupt, and thus people power against the neoliberal technocrats of the EU, and international financial institutions. Examples of these demands abound.

Many are concerned that globalization and multiculturalism have diluted the meaning of 'European' and simultaneously hastened the decline of the unique and continuous historical and cultural narrative that allowed for an affirmation of a specific identity as, for example, French, or Polish.[21] Others attribute the rise of terrorism to the inability of traditional societies to accept the changes: in maintaining that nationalism (of a certain kind) and multiculturalism, both being social constructs, are not mutually exclusive, Asari, Halikiopoulou, and Mock (2008: 1) have remarked on 'the failure to produce a discourse that integrates various ethnic groups under the umbrella of a common British identity'.[22] This present volume illustrates that much the same could be said of other countries.

20 'Zygmunt Bauman: Behind the World's "crisis of humanity"', *Al Jazeera* (23 July 2016) <https://www.aljazeera.com/programmes/talktojazeera/2016/07/Zygmunt-bauman-world-crisis-humanity-160722085342260.html> accessed 23 November 2018. For an analysis of the nature of contemporary fear see Furedi (1997, 2005, 2018a) – he considers contemporary fear as a response to moral uncertainty, which has replaced hope, optimism and assurance. For a measured analysis of how the West must proceed to preserve its own values and the rights of minority cultures against a background of terrorist attacks and fear, see Todorov (2010).
21 See Guibernau and Rex (2010) for a comprehensive range of insights into and analyses of the ethnic dimensions of nationalism.
22 An extremely interesting discussion.

Richard Ashcroft and Mark Bevir have argued that '[c]ultural pluralism was a clear cause of Brexit. Post-war non-white immigration created a modern multiculturalism that some see as a threat to social cohesion and security' (2016: 355). In April 2018 the European Commission published a report on the integration of immigrants in the EU (*Special Eurobarometer 469*). The survey, conducted across the twenty-eight member states, revealed that in all but two (Croatia and Estonia) respondents overestimated the number of immigrants living in their country and in nineteen states the level of immigration was perceived as more than double what it really was; this is a significant indication of a less than positive response to immigration. The study is also revealing of the member state divisions that have become more pronounced in recent years, as the flow of migrants and refugees to the southern borders of the Union have increased. Citizens living in countries on the Mediterranean coast, and at the Eastern border, are much more likely to be concerned about illegal migration.[23] As the numbers of migrants seeking access to the EU shows no sign of slowing in the near future, and with migrant labour an essential requirement for many member states, it is therefore a priority concern that, according to the Eurobarometer, 40 per cent of Europeans view immigration from outside the EU as a problem while only 20 per cent see it as more of an opportunity.[24]

23   For example, Greek islands are having to cope with the constant arrival of more and more refugees fleeing military violence. For an overview report on individual islands, with numbers of immigrants from 2015/16, see <https://www.telegraph.co.uk/travel/destinations/europe/greece/articles/greek-islands-affected-by-refugee-crisis/> accessed 24 July 2019.
24   In a recent poll carried out by the EU, both pro-Europe voters and anti-Europe voters identified Islamic radicalism as the greatest threat. Only 11 per cent of the former saw immigration as a problem while 26 per cent of the latter considered it as much of a threat as Islamic radicalism: 'What Europeans really feel: the Battle for the Political System', European Council on Foreign Relations, 2018; <https://www.ecfr.eu/publications/summary/what_europeans_really_feel_the_battle _for_the_political_system_eu_election> accessed 25 June 2019. See also: <https://ec.europa.eu/commfrontoffice/publicopinion/archives/eb/eb71/eb713_future_europe.pdf> accessed 25 January 2019. See also: <https://ec.europa.eu/commfrontoffice/publicopinion/archives/eb/eb71/eb713_future_europe.pdf> accessed 25 January 2019. For a more recent comparison of statistics on attitudes to Europe see also Rachel Ormston (2015) <https://whatukthinks.org/eu/wp-content/uploads/2015/10/Analysis-paper-2-Do-we-feel-European.pdf> accessed 25 January 2019.

Multiculturalist and cosmopolitan outlooks have increasingly had to confront challenges to notions of shared spaces, of racial and cultural hybridity as well as to views of contemporary society as horizontal networks rather than territorial spaces or hierarchies.[25] In addition, they have had to heed the arguments from both right and left that the multicultural project (notably in regard to assimilation) has been branded a 'failure' and a 'tragedy'[26] while in academia the realization that there is no agreed and clear definition of the concept of multiculturalism presents difficulties in researching its failure. Some see the answer lying solely, since 2001, in the racial and religious rejection of Muslim immigrants by the majority of EU member states, citing the impact on Europe of the displacement of millions of peoples by conflicts in which the West has become embroiled,[27] fleeing 'from tyranny, from poverty, from famine, from ecological disaster' with 'the dream of a better life somewhere else' (Schlesinger 1998: 12).

Notwithstanding that, as Schlesinger put it 'the history of our planet has been in great part the history of the mixing of people' his further observation still resonates: 'Mass migrations have produced mass animosities from the beginning of time' (1998: 12). Terrorist attacks in Europe simply fuel present-day nationalist fears of overwhelming immigration. Examples of

---

[25] See Todorov (2010: 182–3) for positive aspects of cosmopolitanism. Our present concern is not with the conflicting theoretical notions of hybridity so much as with its simplest exemplifications.

[26] Right-wing and conservative groups are not alone in maintaining that multiculturalist policies have not succeeded (see, for example, 'White, Right and Pretentious', *The Economist*, 31 March 2018, pp. 25–6); between 2010 and 2012 several leaders of the EU openly declared their belief that the multiculturalist agenda had failed in their countries and expressed concerns about the blurring or weakening of their countries' collective identities. For an interesting analysis of the perceived decline of multiculturalism see Lentin and Titley (2011). An expanded re-edition of Taylor (2011) explores political controversies surrounding the concept. For a recent publication which examines differences between the more current concept of interculturalism and the 1970s concept of multiculturalism see Meer, et al. (2016); and, for transculturality's ability to better accommodate the opposing forces of the particular and the global than either multiculturality or interculturality, see Welsch (1999).

[27] Germany alone, between 2015 and 2016, took in over 1.5 million immigrants.

measures to control both the fear and the immigration are found in France where, in 2007, the Sarkozy government established the short-lived Ministry of Immigration, Integration, National Identity and Co-Development; Germany has created a *Heimat* Ministry because, as the Health Minister acknowledged: 'People have a need for comfort and Heimat'.[28] Where once such measures might have been seen as a sop to the more conservative (and generally older) elements of society, today the expansion of youth groups and organizations defending an exclusive European-continent identity has seen the 2016 and 2017 protests in Germany against immigrants include attempts to stop refugee boats.[29] Castells has noted that the use of social-media communication networks allows today's identitarian groups to be both 'glocal' and 'global' on specific issues, such as immigration or the authoritarianism of the EU,[30] and a recent article also identified these populist groups as a challenging change in politics.[31] Schlesinger put his finger on it when he said, with deceptive simplicity: 'The more the world integrates, the more people cling to their own in groups increasingly defined [...] by ethnic and religious loyalties' (1998: 12–13).[32]

Overview of the Case Studies Reported in this Volume

The discordant notes touched on so far in a European-wide context are evident as this present volume explores the limitations of a top-down

---

28   'Whose Heimat?', *The Economist*, 14 April 2018, pp. 6–7. For the rise of nationalist feelings in Eastern Germany see Hogwood (2001).
29   'Secure Borders – Secure Future.' <https://www.splcenter.org/fighting-hate/extremist-files/group/identity-evropa> accessed 20 November 2018.
30   Harry Kreisler. *In Conversation with History: Manuel Castells*. <https://www.youtube.com/watch?v=0GBB7U5mvow> accessed 9 December 2018.
31   'The Self-Preservation Society', *The Economist*, 6 July–12 July 2019, pp. 17–19 [19].
32   While outside the scope of this present volume, the current violence in so many countries of (what Europeans call) the Middle East more than bears out Schlesinger's observation.

approach to national problems of unification. The conference and this volume take as their point of departure the case of Spain, a country whose attempts at nation-building are instructive not only in a wider global context but in their more immediate impact at EU level today. The unity of the state, of loyalty by 'nations' within that state to the central authority, is a constant theme in Spanish history. While the ways in which *El Caudillo* sought to mould a nation in his image and likeness have been extensively analysed by scholars of the Franco era (1939–75), Richard Gow takes an in-depth look at what may be regarded as its precursor, the Primo de Rivera dictatorship (1923–30). The failure of its attempt to enlist the military as key allies in support of national regeneration through the eradication of corruption and the mobilization of civil society only served to reinforce mistrust of the 'political classes', a perception which has clear resonance today.

Several contributors address the response to competing national identities in the post-Franco era of the late 1970s and early 1980s when the nascent Spanish democracy sought to accommodate the hopes and aspirations of all in a new Constitution. Leyre Arrieta Alberdi considers the response of the moderate wing of Basque nationalism (the Basque Nationalist Party, PNV) to the new opportunities presented in the transition to democracy, and the risks and compromises that this entailed. The significance of the European context for minority nationalities is evident. Gorka Etxebarria Dueñas, in considering the coexistence of Basque and Spanish nationalism at political and social levels during the same period, examines how the battle for hegemony on the ground in the Basque Country was played out in emotional conflicts in the bitterly contested area of national symbols, emblems and flag displays on public buildings.

Reflecting on the failure of the constitutional compromise agreed in 1978 to abate national and regional tensions, Joan Romero et al. argue that the way in which the original vision of a State of Autonomies has been executed in political terms has been seriously flawed. The authors conclude, hopefully, that a viable framework for integration does exist, provided there is the political will to 'rebuild bridges'. Again, the European context is viewed as a critical support for the plurinational state. This is a timely contribution as federal models are currently being considered as a possible basis for conflict resolution in other contexts, notably in response to calls for a border poll on the island of Ireland.³³ Taking the Basque and Catalan Autonomous Communities as negatively impacted by the Spanish government's current model of autonomy, Iñigo Urrutia examines the legal context in which a new constitutional consensus might be developed, drawing on relevant international precedents. He highlights the dichotomy that exists between the practices of devolution and the aspirations of self-determination, a contributory factor to the 'constitutional crossroads' at which Spain now finds itself.

Jan-Werner Müller has recently referred to the way that in a representative democracy, '[r]epresentation is a dynamic process, in which citizens' self-perceptions and identities are heavily influenced by what they see, hear and read: images, words and ideas produced and circulated by politicians, the media, civil society, and even friends and family members' (2019: 40). Fukuyama places particular emphasis on the digital sphere: 'Social media and the internet have facilitated the emergence of self-contained communities, walled off not by physical barriers but by belief in shared identity' (2018a: 182). Given the critical role played by the media in identity formation, a study by Marçal Sintes et al. usefully analyses media coverage from the moment in 2012 when the constitutional controversy in Catalonia became a news story at local, national and international level, and considers the extent to which news coverage reflects, and supports, a pluralist approach to national identity.

Taking us from the Spanish case to the wider European context Xosé M. Núñez Seixas, in a wide-ranging interview with the editors, reflects on what other nations might learn from the Spanish experience, with particular reference to the current trends towards emotionally charged referenda on national identity questions. Continuing the emphasis on the powerful draw of nationalism, Robert Saunders reflects on how ethnic separatism has been a driving force in European history for over a century. His analysis rejects an east/west divide, highlighting instead the common features that characterize how the challenge of secessionist movements has been

---

33   See, for example, Burgess (2018), and Spain (2019). For an overview of the legal context for the border poll see Basset and Harvey (2019).

experienced across the continent. In the process of dividing nations and re-drawing boundaries, pragmatic choices and compromises have had to be made, sometimes with significant implications for the future of people and nations.

Decisions about minorities in the redrawing of territorial boundaries have had an acutely de-stabilizing effect throughout the course of European history, and Daniel Purcell highlights the profound impact on Ulster Protestant identity of the choices made by the Ulster Unionist community at the moment of the partition of Ireland and the establishment of the Northern Ireland State. His study exemplifies how any political decision to 'leave behind' part of an ethnic group is charged on many levels of emotion and consequence while, equally, the inclusion of minorities who identify with a nation outside the state may, as history has shown, have political, social and cultural ramifications far into the future.

Both Sorina Soare and Carles Jovaní Gil consider the powerful pull of irredentism. Soare reflects on the attitude adopted by post-communist Romania to the territory lost to the former USSR, as illustrated in outreach to its kin community in the Republic of Moldova through preferential access to Romanian citizenship. This has become a concern not only for the government of Moldova, which experienced the move as a challenge to its sovereignty, but also for the European Union, as a Romanian passport could provide access to EU citizenship for Moldovans, thereby implicating the EU as a whole in the tensions between Romania and Moldova. Jovaní Gil argues argues that the Kremlin, in its approach to the conflict in Crimea and the Donbas/Donbass, has been seeking to consolidate a Eurasian bloc as a geopolitical and cultural alternative to the West. Political developments in Ukraine presented Moscow with grounds for intervention justified as protection of Russian nationals abroad, setting a dangerous precedent that challenges the conventions established by international law in general and the EU in particular.

Katerina Garcia, writing on the cultural and linguistic heritage of the Jewish community of Salonika (Thessaloniki), reminds us that for all that national and ethnic identity can be defined in legislation, and shaped and re-shaped by pragmatic political choices, there is a deeply emotional element to it that finds perhaps its truest expression in the arts and cultural heritage of a national or ethnic group and in the traditional practices of the family and/or religious community. Such is the strength of this emotional connection and sense of belonging that people will hold fast to the identity it both creates and sustains, even at the greatest cost, as the Jewish communities of Europe bear witness.

Looking to the future, Fukuyama has suggested that the antidote to the increasing fragmentation of the nation-state could be found in 'creedal national identities' which, he explains, 'are built not around shared personal characteristics, lived experiences, historical ties or religious convictions but rather around core values and beliefs. The idea is to encourage citizens to identify with their countries' foundational ideals and use public policies to deliberately assimilate newcomers' (2018b: 106). However, several of our contributors have identified cases where a values-based analysis is employed to make a case for secession on moral and ethical grounds. Mark Friis Hau uses an approach more commonly associated with religious behaviour to explore how Catalan identity can be construed as a moral, as well as a political, choice and how this influences the sense of belonging and community that develops as a result. Erik Vanderheyden, in a similar vein, considers the example of 'ethical nationalism' in Belgium, examined comparatively alongside the case of Scottish nationalism, with reference to how social policy is articulated in the political discourse of the nationalist parties in both cases.

The response of the European Union to conflicting notions of identity is of critical importance, given the centrality of shared values to its founding vision for European citizenship. Emmanuel Dalle Mulle examines the challenges posed by the Scottish and Catalan attempts to enlarge the EU 'from within', highlighting the importance of 'Independence in Europe!' as a rallying call for both movements, and analysing the contrasting responses of the British and Spanish authorities.[34]

---

34 The then president of the European Parliament (2017–19) said that EU institutions would not recognize Catalan independence <youtube.com/watch?v=Ooq3mmp4sOI> accessed 18 February 2018.

Learning from the Past to Build for the Future?

Of course, from the British perspective, Brexit has fundamentally altered the context, in ways that have yet to be fully clarified. At the time of writing, the shock of Brexit among other EU member states has given way to a deep frustration at the lasting uncertainty arising from the failure to achieve political consensus in the UK. It may prove to be the case that the likelihood of other member states seeking to follow the British example will have been greatly reduced as the political and social consequences for the UK become even more evident.[35]

Meanwhile, EU leaders must remain confident that the present difficulties can be overcome with patient understanding on all sides. On 3 July 2019 David-Maria Sassoli, the newly elected centre-left president of the European Parliament, declared his hopes for the future of Europe and reminded MEPs that there was a need to recall the spirit of the founding members of the EU, who determinedly rejected military confrontation and nationalism in favour of peace and equality.[36] These were necessary injunctions, as leaders observe the deep fissures within the EU not only turning into major challenges to the European ideal but acting against any ability to tackle together issues of joint concern, among which Michel Barnier, in defending the preparations made by the EU for Brexit, identified: 'Climate change, migration, industrial and technological disruptions, and terrorism' all 'seismic challenges on which Member States cannot deliver alone'.[37] He did

---

35 For an overview of the regional tensions within the UK arising from Brexit, and the pending political challenges in terms of devolution see Torrance (2018).
36 'MEPs choose David-Maria Sassoli as new European Parliament President', *BBC News*, 3 July 2019.
37 In December 2016, in order to preclude separate deals by the UK with individual member states, the French politician Michel Barnier was appointed European Chief Negotiator for the United Kingdom Exiting the European Union.

not evade the reasons for disunity, but admitted grounds for division among the member states:

> There is also the feeling that Europe, its governments and institutions are not responding to legitimate concerns:
> - A Europe that does not prepare for, and protect against, the excesses of globalisation. That has for too long advocated economic freedoms without paying enough attention to the social and environmental consequences.
> - A Europe that has not been able to fully control its external borders nor stand united in the face of migration and refugee crises.
> - A Europe where we have often abandoned jobs and industries without creating the conditions for new ones.
> - And above all, the feeling that Europe does not respond to the dreams of Europeans or promise them a better future.
>
> This view is not unique to the UK. We need to listen, understand where it comes from, and respond. Acknowledge that Europe has sometimes been wrong. Rediscover a Europe that allows each nation, people, and citizen to feel protected and part of a collective ambition. (Barnier 2019)

Fukuyama states that '[i]dentity can be used to divide, but it can and has also been used to integrate. That in the end will be the remedy for the populist politics of the present' (2018a: 183). In an increasingly globalized world, European nations have greater incentive than ever to foster positive relations of trust to facilitate the kind of political, social and economic integration and collaboration that will allow them to compete collectively in the global economy. As recent developments have shown, however, economic incentives alone will not suffice to prevent the European Union and its individual member states being torn apart by conflicts centred on values and emotional understandings of belonging and identity and how these translate into concepts of sovereignty and perceptions of the legitimacy of political authority. Understanding the history of identity conflict in the European context is an essential foundation for efforts to resolve or limit such conflicts in the future. In addition, there is a need to create the space for new and emerging categories of identity that are providing alternative routes to building community, outside the traditional national/ethnic lines.

Bibliography

Anderson, B. (1983). *Imagined Communities: Reflections on the Origins and Spread of Nationalism*. London: Verso.

Asari, E.-M., Halikiopoulou, D., and Mock, S. (2008). 'British National Identity and the Dilemmas of Multiculturalism', *Nationalism and Ethnic Politics*, 14 (1), 1–28 <https://doi.org/10.1080/13537110701872444> accessed 17 August 2019.

Ashcroft, R., and Bevir, M. (2016). 'Pluralism, National Identity and Citizenship: Britain after Brexit', *The Political Quarterly*, 87 (3), 355–9.

Baena, C., and Neubert, M. (2019). 'The European State has become a Modern Leviathon', *European Politics and Policy*, 11 February <https://blogs.lse.ac.uk/europpblog/2019/02/11/the-european-state-has-become-a-modern-leviathan/> accessed 28 February 2019.

Barnier, M. (2019). Speech at the EPC Breakfast, Brussels, 1 April <https://ec.europa.eu/commission/publications/speech-michel-barnier-epc-breakfast-brussels_en> accessed 17 August 2019.

Basset, M., and Harvey, C. (2019). 'The Future of our Shared Island: A paper on the logistical and legal questions surrounding referendums on Irish Unity' (February) Research Report published by the Constitutional Conversations Group <https://.brexitlawni.org> accessed 1 March 2019.

Bauman, Z. (2000). *Liquid Modernity*. Cambridge: Polity Press.

Bauman, Z. (2016). 'Zygmunt Bauman: Behind the World's "crisis of humanity"', *Al Jazeera* (23 July) <https://www.aljazeera.com/programmes/talktojazeera/2016/07/Zygmunt-bauman-world-crisis-humanity-160722085342260.html> accessed 23 November 2018.

Bauman, Z., and Haugaard, M. (2008). 'Liquid Modernity and Power: A Dialogue with Zygmunt Bauman', *Journal of Political Power*, 1 (2), 111–30.

Berger, S., and Conrad, C. (2015). *The Past as History: National Identity and Historical Consciousness in Modern Europe*. Basingstoke: Palgrave Macmillan.

Breuilly, J. (2006). 'Introduction'. In E. Gellner, *Nations and Nationalism (New Perspectives on the Past)*, 2nd edn, pp. xiii–liii. Hoboken, NJ: Wiley-Blackwell.

Brown, W. (1995). *States of Injury: Power and Freedom in Late Modernity*. Princeton, NJ: Princeton University Press.

Brown, W. (2019). *In the Ruins of Neoliberalism. The Rise of Antidemocratic Politics in the West*. New York: Columbia University Press.

Brubaker, R. (2015). *Grounds for Difference*. Cambridge, MA: Harvard University Press.

Burgess, P. (2018). 'Has Brexit brought a United Ireland closer?', RTÉ, 12 October <https://www.rte.ie/eile/brainstorm/2018/1011/1002425-has-brexit-brought-a-united-ireland-closer/> accessed 28 February 2019.

Burgum, S., Raza, S., and Vazquez, J. (2017). 'Redoing the Demos? An Interview with Wendy Brown', *Theory, Culture & Society*, 8 June <https://www.theoryculturesociety.org/interview-wendy-brown/> accessed 8 February 2019.

Calhoun, C. J. (1997). *Nationalism*. Minneapolis: University of Minnesota Press.

Castells, M. (2007). *The Power of Identity*. Oxford: Blackwell.

Cohn-Bendit, D., Verhofstadt, G., and Quatremer, J. (2012). *For Europe! Manifesto for a Postnational Revolution in Europe*. Munich: Carl Hanser Verlag.

Danwitz, T. von (2018). 'Values and the Rule of Law: Foundations of the European Union – An Inside Perspective from the ECJ', *PER/PELJ* 21, 1–11.

De Schutter, H., and Tinnevelt, R. (eds) (2011). *Nationalism and Global Justice: David Miller and his Critics, 1st Edition*. London: Routledge.

Deutsch, K. W. (1953). *Nationalism and Social Communication: An Inquiry into the Foundations of Nationality*. Cambridge, MA: MIT Technology Press.

Fukuyama, F. (2018a). *Identity: Contemporary Identity Politics and the Struggle for Recognition*. London: Profile Books.

Fukuyama, F. (2018b). 'Against Identity Politics: The New Tribalism and the Crisis of Democracy', *Foreign Affairs*, 97 (5), 90–115.

Furedi, F. (1997). *Culture of Fear*. London: Cassell.

Furedi, F. (2005). *The Politics of Fear. Beyond Left and Right*. London: Continuum.

Furedi, F. (2018a). *How Fear Works: Culture of Fear in the 21st Century*. London: Bloomsbury.

Furedi, F. (2018b). *Populism and the European Culture Wars: The Conflict of Values between Hungary and the EU*. Abingdon, Oxon.: Routledge.

García, L. (2018). *El naufragio: la deconstrucción del sueño independentista*. Barcelona: Península.

Gellner, E. (1983). *Nations and Nationalism (New Perspectives on the Past)*. Ithaca, NY: Cornell University Press.

Guibernau, M., and Rex, J. (eds) (2010). *The Ethnicity Reader: Nationalism, Multiculturalism and Migration*. Cambridge: Polity Press.

Hayes, C. J. H. (1926). 'Nationalism as a Religion' <https://www.panarchy.org/hayes/nationalism.html> accessed 13 April 2018.

Hobsbawm, E. (2014). *Globalisation, Democracy and Terrorism*. London: Abacus.

Hogwood, P. (2001). 'Identity in the Former GDR: Expressions of "Ostalgia" and "Ossi" Pride in United Germany'. In P. Kennedy, and C. Danks (eds), *Globalization and National Identities: Crisis or Opportunity*, pp. 64–79. Basingstoke: Palgrave Macmillan.

Jensen, L. (ed.) (2016). *The Roots of Nationalism: National Identity Formation in Early Modern Europe, 1600–1815*. Amsterdam: Amsterdam University Press.

Kupchan, C. A. (ed.) (1995). *Nationalism and Nationalities in the New Europe*. Ithaca, NY: Cornell University Press.

Lentin, A., and Titley, G. (2011). *The Crises of Multiculturalism: Racism in a Neoliberal Age*. London: Zed Books.

McClements, F. (2019). 'McAliskey warns about nationalism', *The Irish Times*, 13 August, p. 7.

Malesevic, S. (2013). *Nation-States and Nationalisms: Organization, Ideology and Solidarity*. Cambridge: Polity Press.

Meer, N., Modood, T., and Zapata-Barrero, R. (eds) (2016). *Multiculturalism and Interculturalism. Debating the Dividing Lines*. Edinburgh: Edinburgh University Press.

Moore, M. (2001). *The Ethics of Nationalism*. Oxford: Oxford University Press.

Müller, J.-W. (2019). 'False Flags: The Myth of the Nationalist Resurgence', *Foreign Affairs*, March/April, 35–41.

Núñez Seixas, X.-M. (2012). 'Historiographical Approaches to Sub-national Identities in Europe: A Reappraisal and Some Suggestions'. In J. Augusteijn, and R. Storm (eds), *Region and State in Nineteenth-Century Europe: Nation-Building, Regional Identities and Separatism*, pp. 13–35. Basingstoke: Palgrave Macmillan.

Ormston, R. (2015). 'Do we feel European and does it matter?' <https://whatukthinks.org/eu/wp-content/uploads/2015/10/Analysis-paper-2-Do-we-feel-European.pdf> accessed 25 January 2019.

Renan, E. (1882). 'Qu'est-ce qu'une nation?' Lecture delivered at the Sorbonne in March <http://ucparis.fr/files/9313/6549/9943/What_is_a_Nation.pdf> accessed 18 February 2019.

Rustow, D. A. (1967). *A World of Nations: Problems of Political Modernization*. Washington, DC: Brookings Institution.

Sabanadze, N. (2010). *Globalization and Nationalism. The Cases of Georgia and the Basque Country*. Budapest: CEU Press.

Schlesinger, A. M., Jr (1998). *The Disuniting of America: Reflections on a Multicultural Society (Revised and Enlarged Edition)*. New York: Norton.

Sepúlveda Muñoz, I. (ed.) (2018). *Nación y nacionalismos en la España de las autonomías*. Madrid: Centro de Estudios Políticos y Constitucionales.

Seth, C., and Kulessa, R. von (eds) (2017). *The Idea of Europe: Enlightenment Perspectives*. Cambridge: Open Book Publishers <https://www.jstor.org/stable/j.ctt1sq5v84> accessed 7 November 2018.

Smith, A. D. (1971). *Theories of Nationalism*. New York: Harper and Row.

Smith, A. D. (1995). *Nations and Nationalism in a Global Era*. Oxford: Polity Press.

Smith, A. D. (2009). *Ethno-Symbolism and Nationalism: A Cultural Approach*. New York: Routledge.
Spain, J. (2019). 'Would a United Ireland fix Brexit? It's just not that simple', *Ireland Central*, 21 February <https://www.irishcentral.com/news/irishvoice/united-ireland-fix-brexit-britain> accessed 28 February 2019.
Special Eurobarometer 469 (2018). Brussels: European Commission. <https://ec.europa.eu/home-affairs/news/results-special-eurobarometer-integration-immigrants-european-union_en> accessed 28 February 2019.
Stalin, J. V. (1913). 'Marxism and the National Question', *Prosveshcheniye*, 3–5, March–May <https://www.marxists.org/reference/archive/stalin/works/1913/03.htm> accessed 13 April 2018.
Tamir, Y. (2019). *Why Nationalism*. Princeton, NJ: Princeton University Press.
Taylor, C. (2011). *Multiculturalism: Expanded Paperback Edition*. Princeton, NJ: Princeton University Press.
Tierney, S. (ed.) (2018). *Nationalism and Globalisation*. London: Bloomsbury.
Todorov, T. (2010). *The Fear of Barbarians: Beyond the Clash of Civilizations*. Chicago: University of Chicago Press.
Torrance, D. (2018). 'Strengthening the Union', Debate Pack No. 0186. London: House of Commons <https://researchbriefings.parliament.uk/ResearchBriefing/Summary/CDP-2018-0186#fullreport> accessed 28 February 2019.
Touraine, A. (1977). *The Self-production of Society*. Chicago: University of Chicago Press.
Verhofstadt, G. (2017). *Europe's Last Chance: Why the European States Must Form a More Perfect Union*. New York: Basic Books.
Welsch, W. (1999). 'Transculturality – the Puzzling Form of Cultures Today'. In M. Featherstone, and S. Lash (eds), *Spaces of Culture: City, Nation, World*, pp. 194–213. London: Sage.
Wike, R., Fetterolf, J., and Fagan, M. (2019). 'Europeans Credit EU with Promoting Peace and Prosperity but Say Brussels is out of Touch with its Citizens', Pew Research Center <https://www.pewresearch.org/global/2019/03/19/europeans-credit-eu-with-promoting-peace-and-prosperity-but-say-brussels-is-out-of-touch-with-its-citizens/> accessed 5 May 2019.

LEYRE ARRIETA ALBERDI

The Basque Country within Spain and Europe: Basque Nationalist Party Proposals during the Spanish Transition to Democracy (1975–1980)

ABSTRACT

This chapter examines the public discourse of the Basque Nationalist Party (the PNV) following the end of the Franco dictatorship in Spain (1975–80). It highlights an important transitional period during which the traditional ethnic and religious criteria of 'Basqueness' gave way to a wider political understanding of identity. The political demands of the PNV centred on the restoration of the historical rights of the Basque People to self-government. The party's aim was twofold: to reinforce the consciousness of a Basque identity, while simultaneously justifying its involvement in the newly emerging Spanish democracy. The wider European context had a defining influence on the party's self-understanding and the way in which it framed its political agenda. The chapter concludes with an epilogue on the development of Basque nationalist discourse and its political project over time.

As recently noted by Anwen Elias and Ludger Mees, stateless nationalist and regionalist parties 'have in common their shared demand for a reform of the territorial structure of the state in which they operate, in order to provide some kind of self-government for a distinctive territorial community' (2017: 133). This is the case today and has been in previous historical periods, particularly in times of transition to democracy. The Basque nationalist movement made this kind of demand for territorial reorganization at the end of Franco's dictatorship.[1]

The aim of this chapter is to describe the discourse produced during the process of transition to democracy in Spain (1975–80) by the Basque

---

1   This chapter is part of a research project funded by the Secretariat of State for Research, Development and Innovation (ref: HAR2015-64920-P, MINECO/FEDER) and of the research activity carried out by the Communication Team of the University of Deusto, recognized and financed by the Basque government.

Nationalist Party (known by its Spanish initials, 'PNV'), which represented the moderate wing of Basque nationalism.[2] In particular, it focuses on the place that the PNV thought the Basque Country ought to have, both within Spain and in Europe. The party endeavoured to achieve a higher degree of self-government for the Basque Country by relying on its *fueros* [historical rights].[3] The Basque Country was on good terms with the Spanish state and sought to find a 'natural' fit within the European environment. While it acknowledged the contribution that migrants had made to its welfare (and its ethos) in the past, it maintained with varying success but unwavering determination its own ethnic and cultural distinctiveness as a 'nation' within the wider nation of Spain.

This chapter discusses how that determination manifested itself after Franco's dictatorship. It highlights an important transitional period during which the historical ethnic and religious criteria of 'Basqueness' gave way to a wider political understanding of identity, an understanding which, while (re)claiming its distinctive nature, also agreed to remain within the Spanish state, with its sights set on Europe. The *fueros* were a key component of the

---

2   The PNV was founded in 1895 by Sabino Arana, who advocated the secession of the Basque territories from Spain and France and their reorganization as an independent confederation.

3   The various Basque political cultures throughout history have interpreted the *fueros* very differently. As Professor Coro Rubio affirmed, the *fueros* have been regarded as 'normas consuetudinarias garantes del modo de vida tradicional' [customary rules that guarantee the traditional way of life], 'códigos liberales' [liberal codes], 'restos del Antiguo Régimen' [remnants of the old regime], 'modelos de descentralización' [decentralization models], 'compendio de libertades democráticas y expresión del derecho de autogobierno del pueblo vasco' [a compendium of democratic freedoms and an expression of the right of self-government of the Basque people], etc. It is a polysemic concept that has undoubtedly acquired significant symbolic value over time, according to Rubio (2012). Most prominent among these meanings is that of 'símbolo de las libertades del pueblo vasco' [symbol of the freedoms of the Basque people]. Following Eider Landaberea, remembrance of the *fueros* began to take shape with their abolition in 1876 and since then 'los fueros han estado presentes en los debates políticos más relevantes de los siglos XIX y XX' [the *fueros* have been present in all the major political debates of the nineteenth and twentieth centuries] (2018: 199).

PNV's definition of 'national identity' and of its proposal for the territorial organization of a democratic Spain.

The first section briefly discusses the changes brought about by the death of Francisco Franco and the internal reorganization that the PNV underwent at the time. The second section analyses the discourse of the demands for the restitution of the historical rights of the Basque people generated by the PNV. The third section examines the party's proposals for the role that they saw the Basque Country playing within both Spain and Europe. The chapter concludes with an epilogue on the development of Basque nationalists' discourse and political project over time.

Reorganization of the PNV in the New Historical Context

The death of Franco in November 1975 opened a new political era in Spanish history, one which the PNV had long awaited and prepared for, having spent years calculating and analysing the behaviour that they should adopt in this new period, estimating their chances, their choices and every potential consequence.[4] They had adopted a moderate strategy in the previous decade. The party had made small advances through a pragmatic policy of limited co-operation with Spanish democratic forces, both in the Peninsula and in Europe. This long-term strategy was aimed at ensuring the PNV's active role during the post-Franco political era. They had planted the seeds for the future, and that future had finally arrived.

---

4   The party had moderated its demands over several decades, focusing on developing a Statute of Autonomy for the Basque Country, an objective that it achieved in 1936. After Franco prevailed in the civil war, the leaders of the PNV and many of its members had to take refuge abroad, a point which marked the start of a forty-year exile. The most exhaustive and complete study of the history of the PNV is undoubtedly that by Santiago de Pablo, Ludger Mees, and José Antonio Rodríguez Ranz (1999–2001).

In the late 1960s the PNV underwent an internal reorganization to prepare for the new political scene. Their command centre was relocated from Paris and the French Basque Country to the Spanish Basque Country. A generational handover took place, and the relations between party leaders on both sides of the border deteriorated. Disagreements arose not only from the lack of communication that geographical distance caused, but also from differing political slants: those in exile were more open to co-operation with others, whereas those in the Spanish territory were more radical and uncompromising. These two tendencies coexisted within the PNV from very early on. One was more radical and sought independence, and the other was more pragmatic in its approach. This has led experts to use the metaphor of the pendulum to explain the historical oscillation between these two positions (Pablo 1999–2001).

At the end of the 1970s, the PNV's goal was to appear as an approachable, young and attractive party, shaking off the traditional image of anachronism and exile. ETA (*Euskadi ta Askatasuna* [Basque Country and Freedom])[5] was born in 1959 and their message appealed to a large part of the PNV, particularly the young members of *Eusko Gaztedi* [Basque Youth], who were already vocal in criticizing what they perceived as their elders' modest ambitions.[6]

The key landmark in the process of restructuring and ideologically updating the PNV during the first few years of the transition to democracy was the National Assembly held in Pamplona in March 1977. There, the party reasserted Sabino Arana's founding principles, kept the motto he devised, *Jaungoikoa eta Lege Zarra* [God and Old Law] and strove to present themselves as a Basque people's party with mass appeal. As they sought

---

5   All translations are my own. ETA has been the subject of a large number of academic studies, the most noteworthy being those by Domínguez Iribarren (1998), Elorza (2006), Fernández Soldevilla and López Romo (2012), Garmendia (1996), and Jáuregui (1985).

6   The influence of historical leaders such as Juan Ajuriaguerra, Manuel Irujo, Jesús María Leizola, Jesús Solaún, etc., did not vanish overnight, but a new generation of young leaders had largely taken the helm: Mikel Isasi, Luis María Retolaza, Xabier Arzalluz, Joseba Leizaola, Pello Irujo and others, whose names would become better known, particularly after the death of Franco.

legitimacy for the new era after a record of fighting against Francoism alongside the defeated Spanish Republic they highlighted their near-century of history, in contrast to the recent hodgepodge of new political formations, stressing its democratic ethos and the continuity of its political project.

However, notwithstanding efforts to defend this ongoing political project, the connection with the founder's ideological proposals was now irreversibly damaged, as the party's identification with Christianity was set aside and the integration of migrants from within Spain was accepted.[7] In this way, the race-based, essentialist definition of the Basque people was abandoned; 'no lo constituye la sangre ni el nacimiento, sino la voluntad integradora, la impregnación cultural y la aportación a su desarrollo en cualquier orden de la vida' [they were no longer defined by blood or birth, but by the will to become a part of the community, by cultural permeation and by contributions to development in all orders of life]. Independence was not mentioned at this stage, although references to an 'Estado vasco autonómico' [autonomous Basque state]' left this open to interpretation.[8] This eclectic proposal was their way of bringing together the variety of internal schools of thought and preserving the allegiance of those who might feel tempted by other new proposals of the Basque nationalist scene.

The Discourse: Reclaiming Historical Rights

The choice of the phrase 'autonomous Basque state' was in itself a declaration of intent in which ambiguity was valued over specificity. This could be interpreted as a demand for a high degree of autonomy from Spain, but also as a call for independence. For the PNV, a potential 'Basque state' required the construction of a network of relationships with other peoples

---

7   Alfredo Crespo has stated that by doing so, 'el PNV parecía establecer una ruptura' [the PNV seemed to have established a break (with the past)]. In his view, the party's modernization process 'estuvo guiada las más de las veces por criterios pragmáticos' [was mostly guided by pragmatic concerns] (2012: 287 and 290).
8   EAJ-PNV (1977).

in the Spanish state, within the context of a 'Europe of the Peoples', where *Euskadi* [the Basque Country] would finally find its rightful place on an equal footing with the other peoples of the continent.

In the words of the nationalist leader Xabier Arzalluz, the central point of the party's discourse was the demand for 'los derechos propios de los vascos' [the rights belonging to the Basques] (*fueros*), which became the recurring theme of the PNV's discourse during the early years of the transition to democracy.[9] For the party's support base, fighting to recover such historical rights provided a legitimate reason to participate in the Spanish political transition process, for this would allow them to recover what had once been taken away from them.

The Basque people (defined as 'cuantos viven y trabajan en Euskadi' [all those living and working in the Basque Country]) were the intended subjects of those historical rights. Thereby Sabino Arana's racist and essentialist definition was explicitly set aside. There was now a Basque people who had a set of defining ethnic, historical, linguistic and cultural features of their own:

> [V]ascos que tienen sus derechos de los que no pueden apartarse si quieren vivir como tales. El vasco no olvida y reclama los suyos, y pretende, como todos aquellos pueblos que tienen conciencia de su ser, realizarse lo más ampliamente posible.
>
> [Basques who have some rights that they cannot give up if they want to live as such. Basques do not forget their rights, but instead demand them, and intend, as do all peoples with a consciousness of their own being, to find fulfilment in the widest possible sense.][10]

Recovering the sovereignty that the *fueros* once granted would therefore provide the Basques with a sense of their 'political being'. In other words, the traditional charters enabled a centuries-old definition of a very specific Basque national identity and of their communal will.

The transformation of an ancient legal code into the basis for a modern political campaign required, in the first instance, a reconstructed narrative

---

9 Xabier Arzalluz (1976). PNV's rally at Frontón de Anoeta, Donostia-San Sebastián, December 1976, *El Diario Vasco*, 7 December, p. 8.

10 Interview with Gerardo Bujanda (1977), a member of the EBB (executive committee of the PNV) (*El Diario Vasco*, 5 March, p. 10).

of the past to affirm the existence of a distinctive political identity. At a time of change, hope and opportunity (of which the party was fully aware), it was necessary to 'recover' and update the history of a people thousands of years old, as that history shaped the connection between the past (the original sovereignty), the present (the fact that they were the same people with the same rights) and the future (the advances to be made in their self-government). This narrative gave the PNV's discourse the desired continuity and legitimized their political project.[11]

In their analysis of the past, the PNV identified two historical epochs: the first witnessed the supremacy of the 'modernos reinos europeos' [modern European kingdoms], interpreted by Basque nationalists as 'formaciones políticas heterogéneas, en las que coexistían bajo una misma Corona entes políticos de estructura diferente y de desigual vinculación con esa misma Corona' [heterogeneous political formations, with political entities that had a wide range of structures coexisting under the same rule under varying degrees of relation to the Crown]. Such was the case of the Crown of Castile, under whose influence several political units coexisted: Álava, Vizcaya, Guipúzcoa, and later, also Navarre. Their coexistence rested on a pact between these units and the Crown, which saw its power diminished by the mere existence of the pact. During this period the Basque community enjoyed a high level of self-government.[12]

According to the PNV's thesis, the rise of so-called 'nation-states' produced by the application of the doctrines of the French Revolution put an end to this period of coexistence. The birth of the nation-state brought about centralized, homogenized communities which lost power in favour of central governments and stopped being subjects of law in their own

---

11   The argument about the traditional charters also played a central role in the discourse of the Basque right during the early transition to democracy. Both the PNV and UCD (Unión de Centro Democrático) used the reference to the *fueros* as 'pieza clave de sus distintas maneras de entender y definir la idea de nación y la idea de España' [a key part of their different ways of understanding and defining the idea of nation and the idea of Spain]. But while for the PNV the *fueros* justified the existence of a Basque people as a subject of political rights, for the UCD it demonstrated a specific way of being Spanish (Landaberea 2018).

12   EAJ-PNV (1977: 33–9).

right, thus becoming a mere collection of individuals. From this point on, individual citizens became the subjects of law. For the PNV, the laws passed on 25 October 1839 and 21 July 1876 epitomized this change and culminated in a reduction of their power and the suppression of Basque historical rights.[13]

However, the time had now arrived to reclaim the rights that had once been taken away. The PNV's demands and their federal project (an adaptation of the traditional charters) provided the tools to achieve self-government. This was considered a right and not a privilege, 'un derecho de nuestro pueblo que nace de su propia identidad y que ya tuvo realidad en épocas anteriores' [a right of our people which stems from its own identity and which already existed in previous times], and was therefore a legitimate claim in a democratic landscape.[14] For the *jeltzales*[15] there was nothing revolutionary or extreme about this demand, since it only involved the Basque people exercising a right that they had previously possessed and which ought to be restored by the budding democratic system.

The essential first step was the formation of an autonomous government integrated into the Spanish state, together with retention of their original goal of building a Basque state. To achieve this as swiftly as possible

13   A law issued on 25 October 1839 confirmed the application of the Basque charters, preserved the 'unidad constitucional de la monarquía' [constitutional unity of the monarchy], and opened the door to a modification by parliament to further adapt their status to the conditions of the Spanish liberal state. Since the times of Sabino Arana, this law represented the loss of Basque independence in the eyes of nationalists. For the PNV the law issued on 21 July 1876 only made the situation worse, as it partially suppressed the charters and abolished the tax and military exemptions for the Basque provinces. Although it included no explicit abrogation of the charters, it was interpreted as such by nationalists and supporters of the charters alike (Rubio 2003).

14   *El Diario Vasco*, 2 June 1977, p. 13. Similarly, 'Euzkadi es una comunidad con personalidad propia, y tiene derecho a defender esa personalidad. Dentro de ese derecho, se encuentra el de determinar su propio status jurídico' [*Euskadi* as a community has a character of its own and has the right to defend this character and to determine its own legal status]. Stated by Juan Ajuriaguerra in the electoral campaign (*Deia*, 8 June 1977, p. 6).

15   Another name for members and supporters of the PNV. It derives from the motto of the party: Jaungoikoa eta Lege Zarra (JEL) [God and Old Law].

and as a way to start addressing the historical debt owed to the Basques the PNV supported efforts to draft a democratic constitutional text. Joining forces with other parties in the Assembly that shared their charter-based discourse, the PNV reached a compromise in support of the Spanish State of the Autonomous Regions,[16] a decision which would have aroused fierce opposition just a few years earlier. Participation in Spanish politics was justified by the demand for the restitution of the traditional rights.

First, the *jeltzales* demanded a constitution which would support the legal and political structure of a democratic state, the only possible environment for their project to thrive. Second, they called for it to grant the 'ejercicio de los derechos individuales y sociales y el control del poder y de quienes lo ejercen' [exercise of social and individual rights, as well as due control of power and of those who exercised it].

The PNV's concept of individual rights was inextricably linked with the rights of the community, since the former were to be exercised by the individuals belonging to the community of the Basques and operating through that community. Third, and perhaps most important, the constitution had to guarantee autonomy 'para los pueblos de Euzkadi, Catalunya, Galicia, Andalucía y demás pueblos, para que se estructuren conforme a su propio carácter, desarrollen su propia lengua y cultura y resuelvan sus problemas con arreglo a su propia manera de ser' [for the peoples of *Euskadi*, Catalonia, Galicia, Andalusia and others, so that they may organize according to their own character, develop their own language and culture, and solve their problems while remaining true to their own selves].[17]

The campaign slogan chosen by the party for the first democratic elections ('seguiremos donde siempre hemos estado' [We will remain where

16   This was the name of the new model of Spanish State developed in the period of transition to democracy. This model granted autonomy to the nationalities and regions within the State. Between December 1979 and February 1983, seventeen autonomous regions were created, each with its respective statute of autonomy. As argued by Elias and Mees (2017), the ambiguity of the 'State of the Autonomous Regions' encouraged the PNV (and also the Catalan nationalist party CiU, Convergència i Unió) to implement and expand self-government over the 1980s and 1990s (2017: 152).
17   Extracted from the PNV's campaign for the general election held on 15 June 1977 (*El Diario Vasco*, 26 May 1977, p. 16).

we have always been]) summed up their history and discourse thus far. It was specifically based on the Basque traditional charters, and continued to advocate 'los intereses del Pueblo Vasco allá donde se nos discutan' [the interests of the Basque people wherever they are challenged].[18] By asserting their idea of the old law, the PNV shielded their concept of community, which was modernized by the incorporation of federal notions.

The past and its codes of law also formed the basis for the second essential element of the discourse for the restitution of historical rights: territory. This is one of the defining elements of any nationalist project and represents the substrate on which to develop and preserve a community.

For the PNV, the ideal was a Basque territory that contained the four historical units included in the Spanish state (Álava, Vizcaya, Guipúzcoa, Navarre) and the three included in the French state (Lapurdi, Zuberoa and Lower Navarre). Despite their different characteristics, throughout history all seven have shared a set of institutions, rights, customs and traditions, notwithstanding various attempts to take them away. In the case of *Iparralde* [French Basque Country], this happened in the late eighteenth century, and in the case of the other four provinces, in the nineteenth century.[19] These territories were the home of the Basque community. However, despite the official discourse, during the process of transition to democracy the PNV mostly focused on the three provinces currently in the Basque Autonomous Community plus Navarre, omitting the provinces beyond the French border. What was at stake at that time was the future of the Spanish State, and that set some specific geographical boundaries to action and influence.

Navarre became central to the PNV's idea of a community, and constant references were made to this territory during the development of the

18 *El Diario Vasco*, 29 May 1977, p. 9.
19 In the case of Navarre, the PNV dates the beginning of the process to 1512, 'when we were conquered by the Duke of Alba' and Navarre became part of the Crown of Castile. This was stated by Carlos Garaikoetxea, who later became *lehendakari* [president] of the Basque government (*Egin*, 4 November 1977, p. 5).

Spanish Constitution and the period that preceded the arrangement into Autonomous Regions.[20] Navarre was the touchstone of the PNV's historical chronicle and their definition of a Basque community. However, this was precisely the main obstacle in the negotiations that led to the State of the Autonomous Regions, and the cause of the frontal opposition between the *jeltzales* and the Navarran UCD (Union of the Democratic Centre).[21]

The Place of the Basque Country within both the Spanish State and Europe

In the PNV's view, the seven Basque territorial units should be articulated on a confederal and a local basis. A territorial confederation would ensure full respect for the institutions and the particularities of each Basque region, and would also allow for some shared entities and a 'national' statute of autonomy (the nation being the Basque Country). This framework would enable the 'personalidad vasca integral' [integral Basque personality] to be preserved, and would provide the mechanisms for addressing financial, political and social issues as required, while maintaining Basque culture and the Basque language throughout the territory. This pact among Basques needed to be supplemented by another pact between the Basque territories and the new Spanish democratic State. The federal idea, as an updated version of the system outlined by

20   Furthermore, when confronted by other nationalist parties, the PNV insisted that the primaeval claim for the inclusion of Navarre in the Basque Country was their doing and nobody else's: 'no olvidemos que hace ya 85 años por vez primera se oyó el grito de Nafarroa, Euzkadi da, salido precisamente de este partido' [Let us not forget that eighty-five years ago we first heard the cry of 'Nafarroa, Euzkadi da' (Navarre is the Basque Country), which came from this party and none other]. This was stated by Carlos Garaikoetxea at a press conference after the ordinary National Assembly of the EBB held in Pamplona (*Deia*, 11 March 1978, p. 11).
21   For further information on the Navarran issue, see Baraibar (2004).

the charters, protected Basque identity and at the same time enabled an agreement with the emerging Spanish State.

The Constitution was the specific means for realizing the *jeltzales'* ideas, and very early on the PNV decided to become an active agent in the constitutional process and to run in the first democratic election held after Franco's death.

Euskadi within the Spanish State

Participating in the general election turned out to be a good decision. After the vote held on 15 June 1977, the UCD had a majority in the whole of Spain, and the PNV was the majority party in the Basque Country.[22] It appeared that the discourse woven around the demand for the historical rights of the Basques had reached a wide sector of the population, and the PNV had been given the support base to initiate the path to restitution through self-government.

However, problems soon arose in the process leading to the Spanish State of the Autonomous Regions, the first of which was the Navarran question. The irreconcilable proposals of Basque and centre Navarran parliamentarians hindered the negotiations between the Basque Parliamentarians' Assembly (established in June 1977) and the Spanish government. The agreement for a preliminary structure based on Autonomous Regions was reached on 30 December 1977, and two important decrees were signed on the following day. The first decree approved the Basque preliminary autonomous arrangement and came into force in January 1978; this led to the establishment of the Basque General Council (CGV). The second decree outlined the procedure for the possible incorporation of Navarre into the Basque Country in the future. For some nationalists, the fact that this incorporation did not take place immediately was interpreted as a concession from the PNV.

---

22   The PNV obtained 290,000 votes (approximately 29 per cent), which granted them eight members of Congress and four members of the Senate.

The party justified its decision on the grounds that a pragmatic approach was required at that particular time.

The Basque Country's preliminary autonomous arrangement was not particularly fruitful as far as the PNV's aspirations were concerned. Consequently, their efforts focused on the constitutional process, to ensure that provisions to guarantee Basque self-government in the future would be included in the Constitution. In December 1977, the rapporteurs submitted the bill to the constitutional commission. The parliamentary group formed by the PNV submitted 101 amendments, most of which rejected the model of a unitary State and demanded that the Constitution recognize the sovereignty of the Basque people. Title VIII, on the Autonomous Regions, and the First Additional Provision, referred to historical rights, which were the most important issues at this stage.

The definition of the Basque community brought to the constitutional debates by the PNV was difficult to adapt to the new political, legal and institutional framework in Spain. From the start, it was apparent that it would be highly problematic to articulate concepts such as 'soberanía original' [original sovereignty] and 'teoría del pacto' [pact theory] within the wording of a Constitution focused on the indivisible sovereignty of the Spanish nation. Aware of this situation, the PNV's spokesperson, Xabier Arzalluz, submitted an additional verbal amendment in June 1978, in an attempt to reconcile recognition of the Basque historical rights with the structure that was being outlined, which was based on Autonomous Regions. This second attempt also failed. Instead, the Commission approved a different verbal amendment, with the agreement of the rest of the parliamentary groups, which was included in the First Additional Provision: 'La Constitución ampara y respeta los derechos históricos de los territorios forales. La actualización general de dicho régimen foral se llevará a cabo, en su caso, en el marco de la Constitución y de los Estatutos de Autonomía' [The Constitution protects and respects the historical rights of *fueros* territories. This *fueros*-based system may be updated within the scope of the Constitution and the Statutes of Autonomy] (Larrazabal 1997: 361). Ignoring the guidelines of the EBB, Arzalluz voted in favour of this amendment because it guaranteed that the Constitution would refer to historical rights. He also submitted and defended the PNV's original amendment as an individual vote before the full Congress.

The PNV issued a statement on 21 June 1978 expressing its disappointment with the outcome of the constitutional debates. The party again justified Arzalluz's support for the amendment on the grounds that otherwise historical rights would not even have been mentioned at all. However, the statement criticized the amendment because it made the recognition of historical rights conditional upon their falling within the scope of the Constitution and the Statutes of Autonomy.

The PNV attempted to change the wording of the Provision by negotiating with the UCD and the PSOE [Socialist Party].[23] They even agreed with the PSOE on a proposal to replace the phrase 'en el marco de la Constitución' [within the scope of the Constitution] with one that stated that the Statute would be the 'norma institucional básica' [basic institutional rule], as provided in the Constitution. The UCD approved the PSOE's wording and even seemed to be willing to support the PNV's amendment related to an increase in the jurisdictional competencies of the Autonomous Regions, provided that the *jeltzales* voted against the right to self-determination defended by Euskadiko Ezkerra (EE).

The PNV kept its word, but when the amendment was brought to a vote in the Congress of Deputies the UCD opted for the wording of the Additional Provision that had been provided and approved by the Constitutional Commission, instead of the wording proposed by the PNV. The PNV's representatives were so angry that they left the Parliament building, so that when the Constitution bill was approved they were not present.

They continued to negotiate, but to no avail. On 5 October 1978 the Senate also approved the amendment that had been agreed by the Congress (the PNV senators voted against it and the PSOE abstained).

Then the Constitution had to be ratified by a referendum. The PNV's National Assembly had mixed views: they ruled out voting 'no' because the Constitution was a break-away from the dictatorship and it established the

---

23 According to Ludger Mees, 'el PNV actuó con firmeza y supo aprovechar hábilmente su papel que también los demás partidos le otorgaban como actor clave para la solución del "problema vasco"' [the PNV acted firmly and managed to make good use of the role that the other parties gave it as a key actor in solving the 'Basque problem'] (2013, 341).

rule of law and they also appreciated some of its positive aspects, such as recognition of the various nationalities within the State and the reference to the historical rights; however, they were unwilling to support a 'yes' vote because some articles in the Constitution were difficult for the nationalists to accept, and the PNV questioned the concept of the State envisaged by the constitutional provisions. They advocated abstention.

This was also a way to put pressure on the central government to increase the Basque Country's level of autonomy and to distance themselves from the nationalist left, which voted 'no'. The campaign for abstention was full of references to historical rights. 'Defiende los fueros: abstente' [Defend our historical rights: abstain] was one of the most common slogans. The referendum on the Constitution took place on 6 December 1978. Abstention was higher in the Basque Country than the Spanish average. Very high abstention rates were recorded in Guipúzcoa and Vizcaya, and less so in Álava and Navarra.

After the disappointment with the constitutional process, the PNV devoted their efforts to the preparation and approval of the Statute of Autonomy. The drafting of the Statute of Autonomy began in November 1978. The General Basque Council entrusted production of the text to the Assembly of Basque parliamentarians, and a Commission was appointed to prepare the first bill based on the project submitted by the PNV. The Commission included members of parliament from all Basque parties, except *Herri Batasuna* (left nationalist party) which excluded itself. At the end of December the Assembly of Basque parliamentarians officially ratified the text and submitted it to the Spanish Congress. The debate on the bill for a Basque Statute in the Congress began on 2 July 1979. The PNV had previously started to negotiate with the UCD and the PSOE, but relations with the former were tense. Ultimately, negotiations succeeded largely as a result of discussions between Adolfo Suárez (UCD leader, president of the government of Spain) and Carlos Garaikoetxea (the then president of the PNV's Executive Committee). An agreement was eventually reached on 17 July 1979 and the final version of the Statute was published in the Official Gazette of the Spanish Parliament on 1 August 1979.

The Statute was approved in a referendum held on 25 October 1979, a date which thus far, for the nationalists, had symbolized the end of

Basque independence. The PNV considered it 'un buen Estatuto. El mejor que podríamos haber sacado' [a good Statute. The best we could have got].[24] Still far from their ultimate ambition, this was nevertheless a fundamental step in the process, a time when 'se abren las puertas para cohesionar institucionalmente la Nación Vasca, dotándole de un importante instrumento para su autogobierno' [a door has opened for us to strengthen the institutions of the Basque nation, now that we have an essential tool for self-government].[25] Once the Statute was approved, an election for the Autonomous Regions was held in March 1980. Results once again backed the proposals made by the PNV, the party with the highest number of votes. Its leader, Carlos Garaikoetxea, became *lehendakari* of the Basque government and initiated the process of building the Basque autonomy. Several milestones were soon achieved, such as the creation of the *Ertzaintza* [Basque police force], the official recognition of *Euskera* [the Basque language] and the establishment of public media. With no time to waste, the symbolic elements were put in place: the *ikurriña* [Basque flag] and the *Eusko Ereserkia* [Basque national anthem], both conceived by Sabino Arana, which now functioned as identifiers of the Basque community.[26]

Euskadi in Europe

Continuing on from this first step in the PNV's discourse about the restitution of historical rights, that is, finding a place for the Basque Country within the institutions of the Spanish State, it was now time to move to the second step, as described in the document produced by the Pamplona Assembly. The ill-defined 'Basque State' mentioned in the document had to fit (along with other peoples of the Spanish State) into a Europe of the

---

24 Carlos Garaikoetxea, interview with *El Diario Vasco*, 3 June 1979, p. 3.
25 Document produced by the EBB (*Deia*, 22 December 1979).
26 Whereas the *ikurriña* was unanimously accepted, the *Eusko Ereserkia* was approved only by the PNV and the CDS. Other parties such as the PSE-PSOE, EE (Euskadiko Eskerra), and AP (Alianza Popular) favoured a different anthem, *Gernikako Arbola*, written by José María Iparraguirre (Pablo et al. 2012).

Peoples, which was advocated by the PNV so that *Euskadi* could be on an equal footing with the other peoples of the continent.

The reference to Europe was nothing new in the history of the PNV. The years following the end of the Second World War had been marked by the reasonable (if perhaps excessive) optimism of Basque nationalists, who hoped the resulting Europe would be not only democratic, but nation-based instead of state-based. Between 1945 and 1950 the PNV's leaders had played an active role in important European organizations thanks to the links they had had with senior figures in the Christian Democrat parties from the days of the Second Spanish Republic. These organizations included the *Nouvelles Equipes Internationales* (NEI), the leading Christian Democrat association in Europe at that time, and the Union of European Federalists (UEF).[27]

However, 1975 Europe was no longer the Europe that had been dreamt of in 1945, a federal union of nations that was able to reconcile the diversity of its constituent elements. The Europe that Basque nationalists now faced was based on strong states, whose foundational role precluded the independent participation of sub-entities like the European peoples, and Western democracies had inclined towards Franco on several occasions.

Despite all the difficulties, the PNV acknowledged that the moral support of the European organizations of which they had been a part 'había contribuido en grado notable a sostener ante el mundo la justicia de la causa vasca' [had contributed notably to making the world see the justice of the Basque cause].[28] For this reason, the strategy remained markedly pro-European. References to Europe in the text produced by the Pamplona Assembly highlighted two principal ideas: the alleged crisis of nation-states and the party's support for a 'Europe of the peoples', both of which shaped the PNV's pro-European discourse during the years of the transition to democracy. Regarding the crisis of nation-states, the text stated:

> Los Estados europeos, anclados aún en sus estructuras de Estado-Nación, no disponen ya, sin embargo, de la capacidad de decisión soberana de la que hasta hace poco disfrutaron. La aparición de las grandes potencias y la política de bloques les han arrebatado el protagonismo político e internacional que ejercieron hasta la II Guerra

27 For the pro-European policy of the PNV see Arrieta (2007).
28 [No author] (1961). 'Europa', *Alderdi*, 3 (August), 172–3.

Mundial. Se anuncian elecciones generales para un Parlamento europeo, porque el nuevo marco económico europeo exige ineludiblemente un nuevo marco político. Si Gran Bretaña, Francia o Alemania ya no pueden sostener su autoestatalidad en la plenitud de soberanía como hasta ahora, es lógico que el pueblo vasco no debe caer en la tentación de pretender darse a sí mismo una estructura estatal caduca y superada.

[European states, still clinging to their Nation-State structures, do not have at their disposal the power of decision they enjoyed until not long ago. The rising of the great powers and their bloc politics have deprived them of the central international and political role they had until the Second World War. General elections are announced for a European Parliament because the new European economic environment demands a new political framework. If the United Kingdom, France, and Germany can no longer remain fully sovereign states as they have until now, it is only logical that the Basque people should not fall into the temptation of longing for the same obsolete and outdated state structure.]29

From this alleged crisis of nation-states, Basque nationalists deduced (as their leader José Antonio Aguirre had done many years before) that fighting to provide the Basque Country with the state structures defined thus far was unrealistic. The only reasonable alternative was a supranational European organization which was not opposed to the independence of stateless nations and was willing to recognize political autonomy within member states. The Europe envisioned by the PNV was united in all senses: politically, culturally, socially and financially. It should be

una Europa en la que cada pueblo pueda desarrollarse plenamente a partir de su propio ser y peculiaridad, laborando codo a codo con los demás en la construcción de una Europa nueva, libre, progresiva, democrática y con vocación mundial [...]. El Partido Nacionalista Vasco reitera su vocación europea [...]. Esa Europa, en cuya creación y desarrollo debe influir y participar también el Pueblo Vasco, la concibe el PNV: como una Europa de pueblos libres, con una base común de civilización y de cultura, libre en su ser político y diferencial y unidos bajo un techo estructural común político y económico, susceptible de cubrir un desarrollo comunitario, y no exclusivamente como una Unión de los Estados actuales, superados como estructura política y dominados por intereses económicos internacionales.

[a Europe in which all peoples may fully develop in their own specificity, working alongside other peoples in constructing a new, free, progressive, democratic and

---

29   EAJ-PNV (1977).

world-oriented Europe [...]. The Basque Nationalist Party reaffirms its European calling [...]. This Europe, that the Basque people must also contribute to building and developing, is envisioned by the PNV as a Europe of free peoples, with a common base of civilization and culture, free to express themselves in their politics and in their differences, united under a common political and financial structure capable of fostering the development of communities. It should not be exclusively a reunion of the currently existing states, which are obsolete as political structures and ruled by international financial interests.][30]

Without a doubt, the description most frequently used in the PNV's European proposal was a 'Europe of the peoples'. This notion implied a federal Europe which would be willing to protect small and stateless nations. It would be founded on the right of all peoples to express their will and on acknowledging the artificiality of existing states, which the PNV believed were limited and ill-adapted to the needs of the real Europe. Therefore, it was necessary to create wider political units which allowed for the expansion of markets and the financial advancement of peoples. In the words of the *jeltzale* Gerardo Bujanda, the PNV aspired to realizing 'una Europa de los Pueblos en cuya geografía política el pueblo vasco pueda desarrollar plenamente su personalidad' [a Europe of the peoples in whose political geography the Basque people may fully develop their character], a Europe that was 'suma de culturas de todos los que han de integrarla – incluida, claro está, la de Euzkadi [*sic*] – formando un todo armonioso en que Pueblos y hombres puedan cultivar su personalidad en libertad' [the sum of the cultures of all members, including, of course, that of *Euskadi*, forming a harmonious whole in which peoples and men can freely cultivate their personalities].[31] Although the phrase 'Europe of the peoples' had only occasionally been used before, it became common at the end of the 1950s, when Francisco Javier Landaburu (chief representative of the Basque government in pro-European organizations) employed it in his book *La causa del pueblo vasco* [The cause of the Basque people], and especially in the 1960s, with the emergence of European regionalism.

30 EAJ-PNV (1977).
31 Urrun (1963). 'Euzkadi-Europa', *Alderdi*, 16–17 (April–May), 204–5. Second quotation from Urrun (1968). 'La Unión Europea', *Alderdi*, 8, 244–5.

However, such PNV discourse, woven as it was around the concept of a 'Europe of the peoples' was not aligned with the party's practices. After the 1948 Hague Congress, faced with the choice of accepting the real Europe or being sidelined, they decided to participate actively in the Europe of states as a lesser evil and as a stepping stone towards a nation-based Europe. During the Spanish transition to democracy, once again, the party was halfway between theory and practice, between the desire to become a free *Euskadi* in a federal Europe of nations and acceptance of the predominant regionalist approach, which allowed the Basque Country to take part in the European project only as a region, and not as a nation.

In the years prior to Franco's death, as nationalists anticipated a transition to democracy in the foreseeable future, they started co-operating with Spain-wide democratic forces as a way of ensuring their participation in European institutions.[32] In the 1960s this approach enabled the PNV to take part in state-wide organizations such as the CFEME (the Spanish Federal Council of the European Movement, which they had contributed to establishing in 1949), the Christian Democratic Team of the Spanish State and, during the early years of the transition process, the Democratic Convergence Platform. The strategy of moderate co-operation with Spanish forces clearly eased their participation in those years. Meanwhile, in their French exile, the PNV kept alive their bonds with institutions like the European Christian Democrat International (previously NEI, *Nouvelles Equipes Internationales*), in which they were part of the Spanish Christian Democrat Team.

From the Transition to Democracy to the Present Day

In the years before Franco's death the exiled PNV had been preparing to position themselves in the new democratic Spain which it was anticipated

---

32 In previous years, the PNV's potential co-operation with Spanish forces had been the origin of many disagreements among the various factions of the party.

would soon come into being. They intended to participate in the transition process and in the articulation of the new democratic State in order to achieve the highest possible levels of self-government for the Basque Country. And the truth is that the party 'had a remarkable influence', as noted by Alfredo Crespo (2012: 285).

As in previous periods, the PNV adopted a pragmatic approach, but without ever relinquishing their aspiration to independence. They structured their discourse around the claim for the 'historical rights' of the Basques, which was sufficiently ambiguous to accommodate both the secessionist and the more pragmatic positions (Elias and Mees 2017: 136). Their long-term goal was independence, but it was supplemented by a more moderate discourse that interpreted Basque autonomy as the first step towards their ultimate aspiration. The Basque Country was articulated within the Spanish State through its status as an Autonomous Region. This duality also existed in Europe; while the PNV's discourse advocated a Europe of the Peoples in which the Basque Country would be a nation, in practice it accepted the Europe of the States of which it was a part, together with other Spanish political parties.

Over the following years, the PNV was a key actor in the establishment of a fully autonomous structure in the Basque Country. Mees noted that the party was 'el máximo protagonista de la nueva Euskadi democrática' [the major player in the new democratic *Euskadi*] (2013: 324). Following on from the PNV's 'pendular' tradition, their political strategy has continued to oscillate between the aspiration to become independent from Spain and a more moderate realpolitik, which has sought to have a greater degree of self-government and more consensus with non-nationalist Basque parties.

A clear example of the former was the declaration made by the PNV at the end of the 1990s. On 12 September 1998, the leaders of the Basque nationalist parties gathered in the Navarrese town of Lizarra (known in Spanish as Estella) and signed the 'Lizarra Pact', in which they asserted that the Basque nation was a political subject entitled to self-determination from Spain and France. The PNV sought to create a Basque nationalist bloc, which was separate from non-nationalist parties such as the PSOE, with which they had previously formed a coalition in government.

In September 2002 the *lehendakari* Juan José Ibarretxe presented a proposal for a new political status for the Basque Autonomous Region that demanded the right to self-determination and the establishment of a new bilateral relationship between Spain and the Basque Country through 'free association'. The plan was presented before the Spanish Parliament in February 2005. It was supported only by Basque, Catalan and Galician nationalists.

The failure of the Lizarra proposal placed the PNV in an extremely difficult situation. The more moderate sector of the party criticized the pro-sovereignty strategy advocated by Ibarretxe, and the PNV gradually turned towards more pragmatic positions under the presidencies of Josu Jon Imaz (2004–7) and Iñigo Urkullu (2007–12). In the first decades of the twenty-first century the strategy of building up nationalist forces has given way to agreements between parties (both nationalist and non-nationalist). The traditional duality, between radical long-term demands for an independent state within Europe and relatively more realistic short-term demands, has been reinstated.

Taking into account the tenets discussed in this chapter, it is interesting to note that the current moderate discourse of the PNV continues to include the key concepts of 'historical rights' and 'pact':

> Como nación foral que somos, nuestros derechos históricos, amparados y respetados, pueden dar de sí tanto cuanto pueda alcanzar nuestra capacidad de lograr pactos institucionales, adoptar decisiones políticas que sean refrendadas por la ciudadanía y respetadas. El futuro del Autogobierno vasco pasa por la recuperación del espíritu de pacto, el mutuo reconocimiento y la bilateralidad.
>
> [Since our nation is based on historical rights, these rights need to be protected and respected, and their scope will depend upon our capacity to reach institutional agreements and make political decisions that are respected and supported by the people. The future of a self-governing Basque nation is dependent upon the recovery of a pact-based approach, mutual recognition and bilateralism.][33]

33 Iñigo Urkullu, *lehendakari* of the Basque government, general policy debate, the Basque Parliament, 24 September 2015 <https://www.irekia.euskadi.eus/es/events/28306-pleno-politica-general?criterio_id=1032349&track=1> accessed 10 September 2018.

Bibliography

Aja, E. (2014). *Estado autonómico y reforma federal*. Madrid: Alianza Editorial.
Archilés, F., and Saz, I. (2012). *La nación de los españoles. Discursos y prácticas del nacionalismo español en la época contemporánea*. Valencia: Publicaciones de la Universidad de Valencia.
Arrieta, L. (2007). *Estación Europa. La política europeísta del PNV en el exilio (1945–1977)*. Madrid: Tecnos.
Arrieta, L. (2012). 'Por los derechos del Pueblo Vasco. El PNV en la Transición, 1975–1980', *Historia del Presente*, 19, 39–52.
Balfour, S., and Quiroga, A. (2007). *España reinventada. Nación e identidad desde la Transición*. Barcelona: Península.
Baraibar, A. (2004). *Extraño federalismo. La vía navarra a la democracia, 1973–1982*. Madrid: Centro de Estudios Políticos y Constitucionales.
Beorlegui, D. (2017). *Transición y melancolía: la experiencia del desencanto en el País Vasco (1976–1986)*. Madrid: Postmetropolis.
Castells, J. M. (1986). *Reflexiones sobre la autonomía vasca*. Oñati: IVAP.
Castells, L., Cajal, A., and Molina, F. (eds) (2007). *El País Vasco y España: identidades, nacionalismo y Estado (siglos XIX y XX)*. Bilbao: Universidad del País Vasco.
Castells, L., and Cajal, A. (eds) (2009). *La autonomía vasca en la España contemporánea (1808–2008)*. Madrid: Marcial Pons.
Corcuera, J. (1991). *Política y derecho: la construcción de la autonomía vasca*. Madrid: Centro de Estudios Constitucionales.
Crespo Alcázar, A. (2012). 'Autonomía vs. Independencia en el PNV durante la transición española'. In C. Navajas Zubeldia, and D. Iturriaga Barco (eds), *Coetánea. Actas del II Congreso Internacional de Historia de Nuestro Tiempo*, 285–90. Logroño: Universidad de la Rioja.
Domínguez Iribarren, F. (1998). *ETA: Estrategia organizativa y actuaciones, 1978–1992*. Bilbao: UPV-EHU.
EAJ-PNV. (1977). *Iruña 77: la Asamblea*. Bilbao: Geu.
Elias, A., and Mees, L. (2017). 'Between accommodation and secession: Explaining the shifting territorial goals of nationalist parties in the Basque Country and Catalonia', *Revista d'estudis autonòmics i federals*, 25, 129–65.
Elorza, A. (ed.) (2006). *La historia de ETA*. Madrid: Temas de hoy.
Fernández Soldevilla, G., and López, R. (2012). *Sangre, votos, manifestaciones: ETA y el nacionalismo vasco radical. 1958–2011*. Madrid: Tecnos.
Fernández Soldevilla, G., and Toral, M. (2015). *La calle es nuestra: la Transición en el País Vasco (1973–1982)*. Bilbao: Paradox.

Fusi, J. P., and Pérez, J. A. (eds) (2017). *Euskadi 1960–2011: dictadura, transición y democracia*. Madrid: Biblioteca Nueva.

Garaikoetxea, C. (2002). *La transición inacabada. Memorias Políticas*. Barcelona: Planeta.

Garmendia, J. M. (1996). *Historia de ETA*. San Sebastián: Haranburu.

Granja, J. L. de la (2003). *El siglo de Euskadi. El nacionalismo vasco en la España del siglo XX*. Madrid: Tecnos.

Granja, J. L. de la, Beramendi, J., and Anguera, P. (2001). *La España de los nacionalismos y las autonomías*. Madrid: Síntesis.

Granja, J. L. de la, and Pablo, S. de (2002). *Historia del País Vasco y Navarra en el siglo XX*. Madrid: Biblioteca Nueva.

Herrero de Miñón, M., and Lluch, E. (eds) (2001). *Derechos históricos y constitucionalismo útil*. Barcelona: Crítica.

Jaúregui, G. (1985). *Ideología y estrategia política de ETA. Análisis de su evolución entre 1959 y 1968*. Madrid: Siglo XXI.

Juliá, S., Pradera, J., and Prieto, J. (1996). *Memoria de la transición*. Madrid: Taurus.

Landaberea, E. (2012). '"España, lo único importante": El centro y la derecha española en el País Vasco durante la transición (1975–1980)', *Historia del Presente*, 19, 53–68.

Landaberea, E. (2016). *Los 'nosotros' en la Transición: memoria e identidad en las cuatro principales culturas políticas del País Vasco (1975–1980)*. Madrid: Tecnos.

Landaberea, E. (2018). 'Representaciones políticas de la foralidad vasca en la Transición: los casos de EAJ-PNV y UCD', *Sancho el Sabio*, Extra 2, 197–215.

Larrazabal, S. (1997). *Contribución a una teoría de los derechos históricos vascos*. Bilbao: IVAP.

Mees, L. (2013). 'El nacionalismo vasco democrático durante la Transición (1974–1981)'. In R. Quirosa-Cheyrouze (ed.), *Los partidos en la Transición. Las organizaciones políticas en la construcción de la democracia española*, pp. 323–43. Madrid: Biblioteca Nueva.

Mees, L. (2015). 'Nationalist politics at the crossroads. The Basque Nationalist Party and the challenge of sovereignty (1990–2014)'. In R. Gillespie, and C. Gray (eds), *Contesting Spain? The Dynamics of Nationalist Movements in Catalonia and the Basque Country*, pp. 41–59. New York: Routledge.

Pablo, S. de (ed.) (2012). 'La Transición en el País Vasco', *Historia del Presente*, 19, 5–68.

Pablo, S. de, Granja, J. L. de la, Mees, L., and Casquete, J. (eds) (2012). *Diccionario ilustrado de símbolos del nacionalismo vasco*. Madrid: Tecnos.

Pablo, S. de, Mees, L., and Rodríguez Ranz, J. A. (1999–2001). *El Péndulo Patriótico. Historia del Partido Nacionalista Vasco*. Barcelona: Crítica.

Pérez, J. A. (2009). 'Foralidad y autonomía durante el Franquismo (1937–1975)'. In L. Castells, and A. Cajal (eds), *La autonomía vasca en la España contemporánea (1808–2008)*, pp. 285–320. Madrid: Marcial Pons.

Pérez Nievas, S. (2002). *Modelo de partido y cambio político: el Partido Nacionalista Vasco en el proceso de transición y consolidación democrática en el País Vasco*. Madrid: Centro de Estudios Avanzados en Ciencias Sociales.

Portillo, J. M. (2018). *Entre tiros e historia: la constitución de la autonomía vasca (1976–1979)*. Barcelona: Galaxia Gutenberg.

Ramírez, J. L. (ed.) (1999). *Democratización y Amejoramiento Foral: una historia de la transición en Navarra (1975–1983)*. Pamplona: Fondo de Publicaciones del Gobierno de Navarra.

Rubio, C. (2003). 'Guerra y memoria (La "destrucción" del acta del Convenio de Vergara en 1873)', *Sancho el Sabio*, 19, 203–26.

Rubio, C. (2012). 'Fueros'. In S. de Pablo, et al. (eds), *Diccionario Ilustrado de símbolos del nacionalismo vasco*, pp. 357–72. Madrid: Tecnos.

Tamayo, V. (1994). *La autonomía vasca contemporánea, foralidad y estatutismo (1975–1979)*. Donostia-San Sebastián: IVAP.

Tusell, J., and Soto, A. (eds) (1996). *Historia de la transición, 1975–1986*. Madrid: Alianza Editorial.

Ugarte, J. (ed.) (1996). *La transición en el País Vasco y España: historia y memoria*. Bilbao: Universidad del País Vasco.

Nationalism and Identity: An Interview with Professor Xosé M. Núñez Seixas[1]

May we begin, Professor, by asking you for your own favourite description of Nationalism, given that during the past century and a half or so no world authority has been able to provide an unchallenged definition?

There are indeed as many definitions of nationalism as nationalism scholars, and I'm afraid that I shall be no exception to the rule. I'm a pragmatic modernist, and I tend to be 'parmenidean', in Anthony Smith's terms. In my view, nationalism is the political ideology and political culture that holds in the public sphere that a given territory is a nation, that is, a subject of sovereignty. Within this broader definition, many different ideologies may ascribe to a nationalist creed – yet, there are nationalists who are more visible than others, depending on the intensity and visibility that their national claim acquires within their political agenda. And there are nationalists who define the criteria of belonging to their nation – the condition to be a national, a member of the nation – in cultural terms, while others put emphasis on civic elements, and many others on a blend of civic and ethnic requisites.

What can historians bring to the twenty-first-century debate among political scientists, philosophers and sociologists on the revival of nationalist claims across the world?

In my view, as far as their definitions of nationalism and the nation are concerned, historians of nationalism are in greater agreement than are political scientists and sociologists. Yet, historians may make a substantial contribution in three respects. First, they may accurately appreciate what is new and what is not so new in the revival of nationalist claims – and perhaps question whether there is a 'revival' as such. Second,

---

[1] Conducted by Susana Bayó Belenguer and Nicola Brady.

they may better identify why national identity and national allegiance becomes so extremely important for people at very specific moments – at turning points, junctures where people experience increasing incertitude towards the near future (transition from Ancien Regime to new liberal order; break up of communist regimes; Great Depression since 2007 and decadence of Europe ...). Third, historians always have a greater sensitivity towards continuity and change, and tend not to make snapshots of a moment, or take static pictures, but rather to see mid- and long-term evolutions. This is especially important for the analysis of nationalist mobilization and discourses, since they all claim to be rooted in history and tradition and founded on past grievances and myths. Historians prefer instead to stress that nations are constructs, and that the past is always much more complex than nationalist discourses want it to be.

Further referendums are being called for in, for example, Catalonia, Scotland, the UK – how appropriate, in your opinion, is a referendum as a mechanism for dealing with contested national identity?

Wherever and whenever there is a consistent claim, sustained by a majority of people in a given territory over a certain time, to collectively decide what their future form of shared government may be, I see no better solutions. Certainly, referendums are not necessarily the perfect solution, but they are an expression of democratic will. Sooner or later, that reality will impose itself. In my view, the main question is not whether a referendum is an appropriate mechanism for dealing with contested identities in a given territory, but rather how the referendum must be implemented, what are the questions to be asked (just two questions or many options?), how binding must the result be, whether a qualified majority is required ... Obviously, no one discusses whether Norway's access to independence in 1905, based on more than 90 per cent of affirmative votes, was fully legitimate. Yet: is a 50.1 per cent majority vote enough to legitimize such an important step as secession? Doubts may arise. But this must be dealt with in democratic terms, allowing democratic deliberation to take the protagonist role.

In the aftermath of a divisive referendum, or a breakdown in political relations, what can a government do in the short term to heal a divided nation?

If you mean the state government, a first priority should be the reconstruction of political dialogue and de-escalation of written and oral confrontation. By all means, political fractures must not become social fractures. Civil society tends to be wiser than political elites, and to prefer bridges and dialogue rather than clash of identities. Yet, in many cases international mediation is the only solution left.

Would you agree with those historians who see the major achievement of the Spanish transition to democracy as the creation of the 'Estado de las Autonomías'?

It was the best solution that could be achieved in the late 1970s, within the rules that conditioned the process of the Spanish transition to democracy. Certainly, the State of the Autonomous Communities managed to channel ethno-territorial concurrence in a mostly peaceful and constructive way, and contributed to reinforcing meso-territorial identities, as well as to deepening democratization and welfare. Most Spaniards are satisfied with decentralization. Certainly, it may be debated whether the spread of political decentralization all over Spain and the creation of regions 'from above' was necessary, or whether the financial system was appropriate. Yet, political systems are subject to evolution, and to the changing demands of each new generation.

What can other nations learn from efforts to deal with competing national identities in Spain since the transition to democracy?

Basically, that cohabitation of different levels of territorial governance is good for democracy and for building pluralism and democratic consensus. Also, they may note the fact that most social and political actors during the democratic transition gave preference to the achievement of democracy over the territorial structure of the state, and hence the demos of that democracy. I would add that until the first decade of the twenty-first century, Spain was also an example of how hybrid territorial loyalties can be, and therefore of how important it is to keep tolerance towards ethnocultural and national diversity as a basic principle of democratic deliberation.

What in your view have been the major influences in converting recent Catalan nationalism from a relatively moderate force of compromise into a major threat to the Spanish nation-state?

In my view, this has been the outcome of three intertwined processes. First, a generational change within Catalanist leadership and enforced political competition among political parties: existing Catalanist elites now believed that the time for independence was come. Second, growing political and social uncertainties derived from the impact of the Great Economic Depression since 2007/8: social fears may be expressed in terms of reinforced national identity and the aim to preserve threatened welfare by building a state of its own. Third, the short-term social frustration generated by the winding evolution of the reform of the Home-Rule Statute since 2006 and the parallel reinforcement of Spanish nationalism. Among additional factors may have been the fact that the paradigm that the European Union will be a union of states has dominated EU politics since the beginning of the twenty-first century, and the dream (or the utopia) of the 'Europe of regions' is definitively dead. Catalonia may be a further, peculiar expression of a general phenomenon: the return of the nation-state in Europe.

From the three books you have very recently published on nationalism and identity, each with a different emphasis, what lessons can be drawn in distinguishing current Spanish nationalism from Francoist nationalism?

I've tried to be consistent with my own definition of nationalism, and therefore I have identified diverse currents of thought and different trends under the umbrella of Spanish nationalism, or Spanish patriotic discourses. Spanish nationalism is shared by very diverse political actors today, from Vox to Podemos, yet each of them has very divergent concepts of what the nation is, who its members are, what its limits may be and even what its symbols were in the past and are in the present. I don't see Spanish nationalism as a sheer expression of Francoism, but rather Francoist (or rather National-Catholic) nationalism as a distinctive stage in the history of right-wing Spanish nationalism, within which Fascist features coexisted with other markers inherited from Catholic-traditionalist nationalism. Yet, many Republicans-in-exile also upheld a particular view of the Spanish nation, and were convinced that they had fought in 1936–9 and beyond for the independence of the Spanish nation. Since the 1970s, there are Spanish democratic nationalists or 'patriots', as much as there are neo-Francoist or simply 'constitutional' patriots who may share some nostalgia for Francoist tenets. What is true is that the shadow of the Francoist eagle persists, and affects the political legitimacy of openly expressed Spanish nationalist tenets in the left-wing spectrum.

In light of rising nationalisms, what do you think are the prospects for maintaining a European Union in its present form?

I tend to be pessimistic, as the return to the nation-state seems to gain more and more acceptance among many European citizens, who believe that a solution for their future problems may be found in the past. The EU should have advanced more decidedly in the past towards the creation of a real European demos, empowering the European Parliament and creating a really transnational constituency. Now I'm afraid that it is too late.

To what extent do you think the rise in sub-state nationalism may be a reaction to multiculturalism and mass immigration?

I don't see sub-state nationalism as a reaction to those challenges, since most of them, from Scotland to Frisia and Galicia, existed before the advent of multiculturalism and even of non-European mass immigration. There are indeed some radical currents within these movements which developed as a reaction against mass immigration and gained currency within them, as happened in Flanders. In many other cases these tendencies do exist, but remain as marginal trends. In most cases, substate nationalisms have attempted to deal with mass immigration in an imaginative way, and this necessity has generally reinforced their embrace of civic concepts of the nation, as well as their leaning towards progressive positions. Actually, in present-day Europe, state nationalisms are far more restrictive towards mass immigration, and feel tempted to return to ethnocentric concepts of the nation.

In your view, will increasing globalization eventually completely erode the statist 'nationalities principle' of every nation having its own state and every state its own nation?

This is what many scholars (including myself) believed in the 1990s. Some even predicted the upcoming end of the nation-state and the advent of a global era, in which post-national governance will allow regions, nationalities, metropolitan areas and municipalities to gain foot, while European and/or transnational co-operation and federalism would erode the power of nation-states. Yet, the capacity of state nationalisms, and of ethnic nationalism as a driving emotional force in times of uncertainty, has been definitively underestimated. A return to the nationality principle, and to the belief in the correspondence of ethnic/linguistic borders with political borders, seems for many people to be a safe shelter in a time of globalization and uncertainties. Yet, the nations of the future will have to be transcultural, post-national, fully civic and, if one will, transgender. The extraordinary ability of the national idea to adapt to changing circumstances will make it possible, I hope.

EMMANUEL DALLE MULLE

Enlargement from Within? Secession and EU Membership

ABSTRACT
In their recent drives for full self-determination, separatist actors in Catalonia and Scotland have taken for granted their regions' continued membership of the European Union after independence. Is such an assumption warranted? This chapter tries to provide an answer by looking at the arguments put forward by the actors involved and at the relevant literature, especially the legal arguments on the status of a territory seceding from an EU member state. It highlights the highly political nature of this situation and presents alternative scenarios concerning the two cases. It concludes that, although final outcomes will depend on the characteristics of each self-determination process, it is likely that an interim solution preserving at least some core substantive elements of the rights and duties attached to EU membership over the territory of these two regions is likely to be agreed upon pending the results of negotiations on a permanent settlement.

Introduction

In recent years Catalonia and Scotland have been in the news because of the growing strength of movements calling for independence. A self-determination referendum was held in Scotland in September 2014 and, although the No side won, 45 per cent of voters indicated their preference for an independent Scottish state. In Catalonia, a long process of confrontation with the Spanish state on the organization of an independence referendum (declared illegal by the government in Madrid and legitimate by the Catalan executive) led to an unrecognized vote on the issue being held on 1 October 2017. This saw the heavy-handed intervention of the Spanish police, a 'temporarily suspended' declaration of independence on the part of the Catalan president Carles Puigdemont, and the Spanish government's subsequent application of article 155 of the Constitution aimed at taking control of the Catalan autonomous executive. Several Catalan pro-independence leaders were prosecuted and some jailed while others, among them Carles Puidgemont, fled abroad.

Separatist actors have predicated their drive for self-determination upon the slogan 'Independence in Europe'. In other words, they have presented the Union as a means of minimizing the disruption brought about by secession and of taking greater advantage of the opportunities offered by the single market. Yet, in doing so, they have taken for granted their region's continued membership of the European Union after independence. Is such an assumption warranted?

This chapter tries to provide an answer by looking, first, at the arguments put forward by the actors involved, that is, the political parties campaigning for independence, the governments of the states they belong to and the representatives of the European Union (EU), the European Commission in particular. Then, the chapter examines the relevant literature, especially the legal arguments on the status of a territory seceding from an EU member state. In that section, it focuses on both the domestic and international law regimes, aiming at establishing which state would be the rightful successor to EU membership and what procedure would then be engaged in to redefine its relationship with the EU. It highlights the highly political nature of this situation and deals with such political aspects in more detail. The chapter finally presents alternative scenarios concerning the specific cases of Catalonia and Scotland.

Currently, demands for full self-determination are still made by large swathes of the population in both Catalonia and Scotland. This chapter argues that, although final outcomes will depend on the characteristics of each self-determination process, it is likely that, regardless of the concrete legal procedure that might be followed, an interim solution preserving at least some core substantive elements of the rights and duties attached to EU membership over the territory of these two regions – notably with regard to the single market – is likely to be agreed upon pending the results of negotiations on a permanent settlement. While events may overtake some specifics within this chapter, the outline of the debates as well as the basic principles under discussion will remain valid.

The Debate over EU Membership of Scotland and Catalonia

The SNP's case for independence in Europe is an old propaganda argument. The point was first made by Jim Sillars (1989), influential SNP member, in his seminal pamphlet *Independence in Europe*, where he argued that, contrary to Tory thinking, Scotland would not be expelled from the EU as soon as it declared independence. Sillars pointed to the absence of precise rules about secession within the Community's legislation and, therefore, to the necessity to flexibly accommodate such a situation within the existing treaties. To reinforce his argument, he also referred to the case of Greenland – which left the EU after long negotiations while remaining part of Denmark – and the (then forthcoming) process of German reunification that, he suggested, 'could be accommodated without the need for serious disruption to the Community' (Sillars 1989: 33). Furthermore, quoting the 1978 Vienna Convention on the Succession of States in Respect of Treaties, Sillars argued that Scotland's independence would entail the dissolution of the UK and the rise of two new independent states, Scotland and the rump-UK, both successors to the UK membership of the EEC (Sillars 1989: 34).

The SNP's arguments have not changed much since. Almost every manifesto after 1989 took for granted Scotland's continued EU membership (SNP 1992, 1994, 1997b, 1999, 2005, 2009, 2011) and the observations made above were reiterated in the most complete publication on the subject, the 1997 pamphlet entitled *The Legal Basis of Independence in Europe* (SNP 1997a). The debate flared up again in the months preceding the 2014 independence referendum. In this context, the SNP's reasoning focused on two versions of the arguments already illustrated: as Scottish citizens have been members of the EU and the EEC for about forty years, it would be against the democratic principles of the EU to strip them of the rights so acquired; and, given the lack of any procedures to deal with issues of secession within the EU, Scotland's membership would be negotiated within the Treaties, notably through the application of art. 48 of the Treaty on the European Union (TEU) (see Maddox 2012a; Scottish Government 2013: 216–24).

The position of different UK governments has not changed much since the SNP adopted the 'Independence in Europe' slogan, that is, Scotland would cease to be a member of the Union as soon as it declared independence and would need to reapply. In the run-up to the referendum, David Cameron's government stated through the Scottish Office that it had been 'consistent and clear in its view that an independent Scotland would most likely need to seek re-entry into the EU on renegotiated terms' (quoted in Maddox 2012b). This position was later confirmed in the first of a series of UK government papers supporting the case for the Union in the run-up to the referendum (Secretary of State for Scotland 2013). Nevertheless, no UK major politician assumed a confrontational stance towards Scotland's EU membership. Furthermore, nobody implied that the UK, as an EU member state (at that time), would stand in Scotland's way, either by vetoing her entry or opposing automatic membership or a kind of fast-track application procedure.

When studying Catalan nationalism one does not find, until very recently, any full-fledged arguments about the issue of Catalonia's membership of the EU and this is because the Catalanist movement has until recently been dominated by its autonomist wing, represented by *Convergència i Unió* [Convergence and Union] (CiU), rather than its separatist offspring, *Esquerra Republicana de Catalunya* [Catalan Republican Left] (ERC). Therefore, the debate is just in its infancy and the arguments in favour of an automatic entry scenario are not as developed as in the case of Scotland. In this respect, it is quite telling that, when making the case for automatic Catalan membership of the EU in a speech held in Brussels on 7 November 2012, Catalonia's former president and leader of the CiU, Artur Mas, did not use any legal arguments in favour of such automatic membership, but rather asked the EU to take into account the democratic will of the people of Catalonia and – in his words – to 'not let us down' (Mas 2012). A more complete reasoning was delivered by Oriol Junqueras, leader of ERC, in a televised debate with the Spanish Minister of Foreign Affairs Juan Maria Margallo on 23 September 2015 (Catalan TV channel 8TV). There, Junqueras based his position in favour of Catalonia's continued EU membership on two principal arguments. First, there were no provisions in the EU Treaties for the automatic exclusion from the EU of a seceding territory of a member state. Second, after independence, and unless they explicitly rejected it, Catalan citizens would still hold Spanish citizenship and therefore EU citizenship. More than that, having enjoyed EU citizenship for about thirty years, Catalan citizens had acquired rights and duties that could not be forfeited, since EU citizenship has assumed an expansive character in the context of EU legislation and jurisprudence.[1]

Unlike the reaction of the British government to Scotland, Madrid's response to Catalonia's call for self-determination has been deliberately confrontational. Prime Minister Mariano Rajoy called the drive for independence 'madness of colossal proportion' (quoted in Moffet 2012, see also Mateo and Diez 2017), while the People's Party member and vice-president of the European Parliament, Aleix Vidal Quadras, along with two members of the military, invoked article 8 of the Constitution whereby the Army should 'guarantee the sovereignty and independence of Spain, defend her territorial integrity and constitutional order' (Diez 2012). More recently, major Spanish parties united in their opposition to an independence referendum that they considered illegal (Diez and Mateo 2017). With regard to Catalonia's EU membership, the consistent position of the Spanish authorities has been that upon independence Catalonia would immediately be excluded from the EU and would have to reapply in the same way as any other external candidate (see Torres 2016).[2]

In 2004, in answer to a question by the Welsh MEP Eluned Morgan about the consequences of independence for a secessionist region's EU membership, the then president of the European Commission Romano Prodi affirmed that

> when part of the territory of a Member State ceases to be a part of that state, e.g. because that territory becomes an independent state, the treaties will no longer apply to that territory. In other words, a newly independent region would, by the fact of its independence, become a third country with respect to the Union and the

---

1 The full video of the debate is available at: <https://www.youtube.com/watch?v=5tdyg9ffiSU> accessed 27 September 2017.
2 See also Margallo's position in the televised debate (note 1).

treaties would, from the day of its independence, not apply anymore on its territory. (European Commission 2004)

Talking to the BBC on 12 September 2012, his successor, José Manuel Durão Barroso, asserted that 'a new state, if it wants to join the European Union, has to apply to become a member like any state' (quoted in Carrell 2012). Such a scenario, later labelled by some as the 'Barroso theory', had been hinted at a day before by a Commission spokesman, Olivier Bailly, who pointed out that 'there are two different steps, there is a secession process under international law and the request for accession to EU member state under the EU treaties. In the meantime, of course, the new country is not part of the EU as he [*sic*] has to make request for accession' (quoted in Carrell 2012). Finally, the president of the European Commission, Jean-Claude Juncker stuck to this line of reasoning when quoting verbatim Prodi's citation above in a reply to a question by the liberal MEP Beatriz Becerra on 7 July 2017 (Pérez 2017).

Therefore, despite its reluctance to provide final answers and its tendency not to state its views 'on matters which, as things stand, are purely hypothetical' (European Commission 2007), the rare pronouncements of the Commission, and some other EU representatives, seem to confirm that secessionist regions will most likely have to reapply, although there probably will be room for flexibility in choosing the precise procedure to be followed. According to some EU officials, for instance, the new states could be asked to reapply, but could retain a passive membership. This means that throughout the application procedure – which might take some years – they could still enjoy the advantages of membership but without having a seat at the European Council (Fontanella-Khan, Stacey, and Buck 2012).

Legal Arguments in Favour of and against Continued Membership

In this section we will briefly review the legal arguments made by the separatist parties mentioned above and assess their validity with reference to the existing literature. The analysis is divided into three parts. The first looks at the domestic constitutional laws of Spain and the United Kingdom in order to evaluate whether the independence of Catalonia and Scotland would represent cases of secession from or rather dissolution of the parent state and which part would be considered as the rightful successor in international law. The second section focuses on the peculiar characteristics of the European Union, which is considered to have established a new constitutional order different from general international law, and on what would be the procedure followed to deal, in general terms, with the case of a territory seceding from an EU member state. The third section leaves the domain of international law and looks at the more political aspects of the issue.

Secession and Succession in Domestic and International Law

The argument that the independence of Scotland would involve a revision of the Treaty of Union and, consequently, the dissolution of the United Kingdom of Great Britain and Northern Ireland implies that the 1707 Acts of Union, establishing the United Kingdom of Great Britain as the Union of England and Scotland, enjoys the status of fundamental law and cannot be modified by an Act of Parliament, but should follow a special procedure. This, however, is not confirmed by practice. When Ireland seceded in 1922 and formed the Irish Free State, the United Kingdom of Great Britain and Northern Ireland simply succeeded to the United Kingdom of Great Britain and Ireland. After all, English constitutional law is quite clear about it: Parliament is supreme and no Parliament can bind its successor. Furthermore, even if one does not take this principle as valid and relies on the Scottish theory of popular sovereignty – whereby the Acts of Union in fact constitute fundamental law and any amendment requires a special procedure that, being unknown in British constitutional law, could only be adopted by a democratic institution representative of the Scottish people – the 1998 Scotland Act, establishing the Scottish Parliament as the representative institution of the Scottish people, provided that constitutional issues are matters reserved to Westminster. Hence, English constitutional theory prevails over Scottish and the independence of Scotland would not lead to the dissolution of the United Kingdom (Schieren 2000: 124).

The case of Catalonia is rather simpler in this respect. First, there is no equivalent of the Acts of Union in Spanish constitutional history, as Catalonia was absorbed under the Crown of Castile in 1716.[3] Although recognizing 'the right to autonomy of the nationalities and regions which make it up', article 2 of the Spanish Constitution declares 'the indissoluble unity of the Spanish nation' (Cortes Generales 1978: art. 2). Furthermore, the 2010 judgement of the Spanish Constitutional Court concerning the Statute of Autonomy voted by the Catalan Parliament in 2006 made it crystal clear that the Catalans may well call themselves a nation for political or cultural reasons, but this term has no legal value. Legally speaking, there is only one nation, Spain, while the Catalans are 'just' a nationality, and sovereignty lies with the Spanish people at large (Delledonne 2011: 8).

These considerations lead us to conclude that, from a domestic constitutional law perspective, Catalan and Scottish independence would represent cases of secession. But what about international law? Before looking at the issue in detail, there are two premises to be made. First, as confirmed by the International Court of Justice in its advisory opinion in regard to the accordance with international law of the unilateral declaration of independence of Kosovo, there is no general prohibition, in international law, of an act of declaration of independence (ICJ 2010). Most of the literature agrees that 'secession is neither legal nor illegal in international law, but a legally neutral act' (Crawford 1979: 268; see also Cassese 1995; Christakis 1999; and Higgins 1994). Second, there is no right to external

---

3   More precisely, Catalonia was under the Crown of Castile from the marriage of Ferdinand II of Aragon, of which Catalonia was part, and Queen Isabella I of Castile in 1469, but retained its autonomy until 1716. For a detailed history of Catalonia see Balcells, 1996.

self-determination either, except for former colonies and peoples subjected to foreign occupation (Buchheit 1978: 73–4).

Before looking at the practice of the UN in order to see how it dealt with similar cases, we need to examine another argument concerning the international law regime at large. The SNP has often suggested that the Vienna Convention on the Succession of States in respect of Treaties would confirm the claim that upon independence both Scotland and the rump United Kingdom would be treated equally – in this case both as successor states of the UK (UN 1978: art. 34.1). Yet, besides the fact that the SNP's reading could be questioned, the Convention, albeit in force, has been ratified only by twenty-two countries and, more fundamentally, not by the United Kingdom and most other EU member states. Therefore, it cannot be considered as being legally binding (Borgen 2010: 1027).

In 1947, confronted with the India–Pakistan split, the United Nations General Assembly's Sixth Legal Committee stated that in the case of secession the successor state automatically keeps its UN membership, while the new state has to apply (UNGA 1947). The difficulty lies in establishing who is the successor. Practice since then suggests that succession to membership occurs if the country claiming to be the successor state 'can establish sufficient legal identity with the former member' (Scharf 1995: 67). When in 1992 the Federal Republic of Yugoslavia (FRY) (made up of Serbia and Montenegro) claimed to be the rightful successor to the former Socialist Federal Republic of Yugoslavia (SFRY), the General Assembly, at the request of the Security Council, turned the claim down and asked the FRY to apply. The decision was justified on the grounds that the FRY was made up of only two out of six of the former constituent republics and represented only 40 per cent of the territory and 45 per cent of the population of the SFRY, which was therefore considered as dissolved. Earlier the same year, the UN had come to exactly the opposite conclusion when dealing with the dissolution of the Union of Socialist Soviet Republics (USSR). The Russian Federation's bid for succession to Soviet membership, involving a permanent seat on the Security Council, was secured on account of its considerable continuing coincidence with the territory, population, resources and administrative apparatus of the former Soviet Union (Scharf 1995: 43–66). The above cases thus show that in determining whether a potential successor is the continuation of a member or whether the member's international personality has been extinguished, the relevant factors include whether the potential successor has: (a) a substantial majority of the former member's territory (including the historic territorial hub), (b) a majority of its population, (c) a majority of its resources, (d) a majority of its armed forces, (e) the seat of the government and control of most central government institutions, and (f) entered into a devolution agreement on U.N. membership with the other components of the former State. (Scharf 1995: 67)

All of the above considerations seem to suggest that, in the case of Catalan and Scottish secession, the rump Spain and UK, accounting for most of the population, territory, resources and including the seat of government as well as the headquarters of the armed forces, would be considered the rightful successors to Spanish and UK membership of the EU.

Secession within the Legal Order of the EU

As many authors have pointed out, general international law is only of partial use with regard to issues of fragmentation within the EU. This is because the EU Treaties have given birth to a new legal order that has created rights and obligations for its member states as well as for the citizens inhabiting them (Tierney 2013: 383). Legal commentators have formulated two main positions concerning the EU membership of a territory seceding from a member state.

The first, probably formulated best by Happold (2000) and, more recently, by Crawford and Boyle (2013), consists in the conclusion that, upon independence, such territory will find itself automatically out of the EU and will need to reapply through the procedure set out by art. 49 TEU. In other words, the seceding territory will be treated like any other external country seeking accession, which will have to be ratified by all EU member states. The second, argued best by former judge of the European Court of Justice (ECJ) Sir David Edward (2013), outlines a different procedure whereby the secession of a territory of an EU member state will be dealt with as a case of internal enlargement by means of a modification of the Treaties in accordance with art. 48 TEU. Let us take a look at both positions in more detail.

According to Happold, international treaties – those establishing the EEC/EU included – follow the moving treaty boundaries rule, that is, they are personal and not territorial, they apply to the members of the treaties and not to their territories. Hence, if a territory leaves a member state, the treaties no longer apply there. In his opinion, this would be shown by the case of Greenland, which, curiously enough, is often cited by separatist actors to prove that political expediency tends to prevail over the moving treaty boundaries rule. Greenland's departure from the Union – Happold asserts – had to be negotiated precisely because Greenland remained part of a member state (Denmark). Had it seceded from Denmark, negotiations would not have been necessary. Happold also cites the precedent of German reunification, which required no formal consent by the other member states, but was simply treated as a case of absorption of the German Democratic Republic by the Federal Republic, whereby, according to the moving treaty boundaries principle, the Treaties automatically applied to the new territory (Happold 2000: 32–3).[4] Along similar lines, in their analysis of the Scottish case, Crawford and Boyle (2013: 100) point to the fact that 'Scotland's position within the EU will depend on the EU's own legal order. But there are no legal rules within the EU that specifically govern whether it can automatically succeed to membership'. Hence, they conclude, 'on the face of the EU treaties and other indications, it seems likely that Scotland would be required to join the EU as a new Member State'. This conclusion mainly stems from the acknowledgement that the definition of the internal territory of EU member states derives from their own domestic constitution and not from the treaties making up the EU's legal order: '[N]o treaty amendment is therefore required simply as a result of a change to the borders of a state's territory' (Crawford and Boyle 2013: 101). Being automatically excluded from the jurisdiction of the EU, the seceding

---

4   Happold also mentions the case of Algeria, arguing that when this became independent in 1962 nobody dared argue that it should be granted EEC membership (Happold 2000: 33). Yet its peculiar context suggests not considering it as a precedent (Schieren 2000: 125).

territory would have to reapply like any other third party through the procedure detailed by art. 49 TEU. Yet they also add that

> all this is not to suggest that it is *inconceivable* for Scotland automatically to be an EU member. The relevant EU organs or Member States might be willing to adjust the usual requirements for membership in the circumstances of Scotland's case. But that would be a decision for them, probably made on the basis of negotiations; it is not required as a matter of international law, nor, at least on its face, by the EU legal order. (Crawford and Boyle 2013: 103)

In other words, the EU can still act flexibly according to political expediency, but this is not a legal requirement.

A different view is defended by Sir David Edward. Starting from the ECJ's assertion in *Van Gend en Loos vs. Nederlandse Administratie der Belastingen* (ECJ 1963), that 'to ascertain whether the provisions of an international Treaty extend so far in their effects, it is necessary to consider the spirit, the general scheme and the wording of those provisions' and noting that there is no provision dealing with the secession of an EU territory in the Treaties, Edward concludes that 'we must look to the spirit and general scheme of the Treaties' (Edward 2013: 1163). Here, four articles are key, that is, 2, 4 and 50 TEU, as well as article 20 of the Treaty on the Functioning of the European Union (TFEU) – with which we will deal in more detail below. Article 2 stipulates that the Union 'is founded on the values of respect for human dignity, freedom, democracy, equality, the rule of law and respect for human rights, including the rights of persons belonging to minorities', while article 4 provides that 'pursuant to the principle of sincere co-operation, the Union and the Member States shall, in full mutual respect, assist each other in carrying out tasks which flow from the Treaties' and 'shall facilitate the achievement of the Union's tasks and refrain from any measure which could jeopardize the attainment of the Union's objectives'. Article 50, on the other hand, details the procedure that should be followed in the case of withdrawal of a member state from the EU and foresees the conclusion of a negotiated agreement between the Union and the state to disentangle the complex set of rights and obligations uniting these two entities. Given these premises, Sir David Edward dismisses the 'Barroso theory' already referred to whereby upon independence a seceding region will find itself automatically out of the Union, and argues that there would be a legal obligation to follow a negotiated procedure akin to that described in article 50 (Edward 2013: 1165–7; for a similar position on the application of art. 50 see Chamon and Van der Loo 2014). This conclusion is further grounded on the following two points. First, it would be unreasonable to believe that the drafters of the Treaty thought it necessary to hold negotiations in the case of withdrawal of a member state and not in the case of separation of one of its territories. Second, Edward questions the plausibility of the Barroso theory in relation to its concrete application:

> [I]t seems to be assumed that – at the moment of separation or on some other unspecified date – the 'separating State', its citizens and its land and sea area would find themselves in some form of legal limbo vis-à-vis the rest of the EU and its citizens, unless and until a new Accession Treaty were negotiated. Until the moment of separation, they would remain an integral part of the EU; all EU citizens living in the separating State would enjoy all the rights of citizenship and free movement; and the same would apply, correspondingly, to all other EU citizens and companies in their relations with that State. Then, at the midnight hour, all these relationships would come abruptly to an end. (Edward 2013: 1165–6)

Arguing that this is an absurd scenario, he concludes that before independence comes into force all the parties involved would have a legal duty to negotiate the new status of the seceding territory in accordance with the principle of 'sincere co-operation, full mutual respect and solidarity' enshrined in the Treaties (for a similar position see also MacCormick 2000: 735; Schieren 2000: 131–3) and this because 'maintaining the territorial and political integrity of the EU and the vested rights of its citizens is surely of greater importance than blind acceptance of the contestable doctrines of public international law' (Edward 2013: 1167).

The concept of European citizenship, introduced by art. 20 TFEU, plays a momentous role in the arguments of those scholars in favour of the internal enlargement scenario. As mentioned above, the EU legal order has established rights and duties not only for member states but also for citizens. The ECJ made clear already in 1963 that such rights and duties constitute a 'legal heritage' for EU citizens. Recent ECJ jurisprudence (see in particular *Ruiz Zambrano v Office national de l'emploi*, ECJ 2011), relying on the notion of EU citizenship, has expanded such legal heritage so as to constrain national legislation when this might jeopardize the enjoyment of rights deriving from the status of individuals as EU citizens (Douglas-Scott 2014a: 16–18). Hence, although it is certainly not the case that automatic EU membership for a seceding territory would directly descend from EU citizenship rules, O'Neill (2011) argues that in the context of Scotland's independence, 'the question to ask is whether the CJEU [Court of Justice of the European Union] would consider that the fact that Scotland became independent required that all (or any portion) of the previous UK citizenry thereby be deprived of their acquired rights as EU citizens?' He, along with other jurists (see for instance Douglas-Scott 2014a: 19), concludes that the Court would most likely intervene to defend the acquired rights of EU citizens. Such a position has been criticized by Crawford and Boyle (2013: 104–8). Pointing out that EU citizenship is additional to citizenship of a member state and, relying on public international law rules, they have argued that upon secession, the successor state will withdraw its nationality (British or Spanish in our cases) from the inhabitants of the seceding territory, who will therefore be left solely with the nationality of the new state and, as a consequence, will lose EU citizenship. Yet, as argued by Barber, this is likely to trigger challenges in court which could eventually come before the ECJ, which could then 'conclude that the removal of European citizenship from such a large number of people runs contrary to European Law' (Barber 2014). Most notably, as argued by Tierney and Boyle (2014: 21) with regard to Scotland's case, 'the CJEU could intervene to declare a duty on both the institutions of the EU and the Member States to negotiate, in a spirit of sincere co-operation, to secure Scotland's full accession and to protect the interests of European citizens in the interim period prior to this formal accession'.

An Essentially Political Question?

The two views expressed above differ in that the first foresees the immediate egression of a seceding territory from the EU and a subsequent procedure of reapplication, while the second argues that there is a legal obligation to negotiate the new status of a seceding territory with a view to minimizing disruption, both in terms of EU territorial integrity and the enjoyment of acquired rights by EU citizens. While the former envisages the application of art. 49 TEU regulating the admission of new members, the latter suggests that negotiations will follow the procedure outlined by art. 50 and art. 48 TEU, thus following an internal enlargement procedure through modification of the existing treaties.[5]

Yet the difference between these two views might not be so great in practice. Even Crawford and Boyle (2013: 98), who have otherwise expressed clear-cut and assertive opinions about a seceding territory's need to reapply for EU membership, have concluded that 'in practice, to an even greater extent than questions of state continuity or membership of the UN, the consequences of Scottish independence within the EU will depend on the attitude of other EU Member States and organs, and on negotiations'. To put it more bluntly, 'a purely legal view of the matter is of little use' (Gratius and Kai, quoted in Guirao 2016: 196).

In this connection, there is a growing consensus in the legal literature that after a pro-independence vote in a legal referendum – agreed by both the seceding entity and the central government of the successor state – the best interest of all actors would be to find a swift agreement that minimizes disruption (see Armstrong 2014: para. 39, Avery 2014, Douglas-Scott 2014b, Tierney and Boyle 2014: 11–12). Hence, even in the case in which a seceding territory would need to reapply for membership in accordance with art. 49, an interim status preserving 'core substantive aspects of the accession treaties' would most likely be agreed upon (Armstrong 2014: para. 39). Hence, regardless of the specific legal route that might be followed – either through art. 48 or art. 49 TEU – there seems to be a consensus that, while automatic EU membership of a seceding territory is likely to be ruled out, negotiations with a view to ensuring an interim status preserving key rights and duties associated with EU membership

---

[5] For a halfway view, whereby the application of art. 50 will be followed by that of art. 49, see Chamon and Van der Loo (2014).

should be pursued, pending the results of negotiations aimed at obtaining a permanent outcome.

But what are these substantive elements? Guirao (2016) convincingly distinguishes between the three areas of: membership of the single market, membership of the Eurozone and EU citizenship.

The single market is probably the most rosy area for seceding regions, meaning that it is probably the area in which, even if the Barroso view should prevail from a legal perspective, it is most likely that a political solution will be found to preserve the integrity of the common market and thus guarantee the continuation, after independence, of the rights and obligations enjoyed by the citizens of the seceding unit before separation. This is because the integrity of the single market is one of the key goals of the EU, hence its members have not only an interest in trying to preserve it, but also an obligation to do so (Douglas-Scott 2014a: 12). Furthermore, past EU and EEC practice is in line with this privileged furtherance of the single market, even in the presence of political turbulence (see Guirao 2016: 206). Concretely speaking, the integrity of the single market could also be preserved by swiftly granting the seceding territory membership of the European Economic Area (EEA), as an interim solution pending negotiations concerning its internal or external procedure for full membership (Chamon and Van der Loo 2014: 627).

Continued membership of the Eurozone might be more complicated. As a matter of fact, euro currency membership requires EU membership. Hence, if a seceding territory, where the euro is already in use, were among those still awaiting accession according to art. 49, it might also have to switch to a different currency. Yet this would not necessarily be the case. The seceding territory and the EU could come to an agreement similar to that in force between the latter and Monaco, San Marino and Vatican City (Chamon and Van der Loo 2014: 628) or it could keep using the euro unilaterally, as does Montenegro, and even get liquidity from the European Central Bank (ECB) if its banks have subsidiaries in Eurozone countries (Galì 2014: 88). In this latter case, the greatest problem would be that the ECB would not act as a lender of last resort, which might entail huge risks in moments of economic and financial distress and increase the costs of borrowing in normal times.

The final question concerns the rights and duties acquired by the citizens of the seceding territory as a consequence of their status as EU citizens. Although, as we have seen above, such status is additional to citizenship of a member state, ECJ jurisdiction has ruled that even with regard to decisions pertaining to nationality the negative consequences for EU citizens should be diminished (see *Rottmann v Freistaat Bayern*, ECJ 2010). For instance, in the case of the bilateral agreement concerning the free circulation of people between the EU and Switzerland, it is asserted that 'rights acquired by private individuals shall not be affected. The Contracting Parties shall settle by mutual agreement what action is to be taken with respect to rights in the process of being acquired' (cited in Guirao 2016: 213). This does not mean that EU citizenship will be guaranteed in full no matter what, but rather that it is likely that both political negotiators and, possibly, the ECJ, will try to limit the upheaval caused by the secession of the concerned territory by guaranteeing continuity of some rights, most probably those linked to the single market.

Yet the specific procedure that would be followed and the agreement that would be hammered out would depend very much on the concrete circumstances of each secession process, which is why we look now, in more detail, at the cases we are concerned with here, that is, Scotland and Catalonia.

Scotland and Catalonia: Some Scenarios

Scotland and Catalonia are very different cases when it comes to secession. While the former region has seen its right to self-determination recognized by the UK government and a negotiated independence referendum has already been held – which allows us to think that any future popular vote on the matter will also be the result of an agreed procedure – the latter has faced the persistent opposition of the Spanish government, which has defined any independence referendums as illegal and taken concrete measures to prosecute the organizers of any such events.

Furthermore, the outcome of the vote held in June 2016 on UK membership of the EU complicated things further by initiating the Brexit process, which was initially supposed to end in March 2019, and during which most EU rights and obligations would remain in place (Asthana and Mason 2017; BBC 2018).

After the British elections held in May 2017, the Scottish National Party, which leads the Scottish regional executive, seemed to have put on hold the possibility of organizing a second independence referendum, which had been strongly demanded immediately after the results of the Brexit referendum (*The Economist* 2017). Although it is unlikely that a new independence referendum will be organized in Scotland, that could still be an option within the 2020 deadline recently agreed by the UK and the EU. Hence, we will take here two scenarios into account: that of a Yes victory in an independence referendum held while the UK is still officially enjoying, to the extent agreed to, the equivalent of EU membership rights; and that of a Yes victory in a referendum held after that date, that is, when (without unlikely but not impossible about-turns) the UK will definitively be out of the EU.

On the face of it, the first scenario might look similar to that which would have been realized had the Yes vote won in the 2014 Scottish referendum. It would have indeed been a case of fragmentation (Chamon and Van der Loo 2014: 614). The crucial difference is that now such a fragmentation would be negotiated as part of a wider process of EU contraction, which was not the case in 2014. Hence, there would be an additional interest and, according to the considerations made above, even a legal duty, on the part of EU member states and the Commission to conduct negotiation with the Scottish government with a view to preserving the integrity of the single market. The downside of this scenario is that the parallel process of Brexit, Scottish independence and redefinition of Scotland's position towards the EU would greatly increase the complexity of these concurrent processes, delay the achievement of any final agreement and amplify uncertainties. In this connection, the specific procedure followed can make a substantial difference and even lead to what Chamon and Van der Loo (2014) have called a 'temporal paradox'. If, after the application of art. 50, the procedure outlined by art. 49 is followed, that is, Scotland would have to reapply as an external candidate, the region might find itself unable to initiate accession talks before having finalized its independence negotiations with the UK government, while in order to ensure a smooth transition to independence it would need precisely to begin such negotiations over its future status with regard to the EU. To avoid such a paradox, EU member states might decide to opt for the procedure outlined by art. 48, or internal enlargement, but this could be opposed by countries such as Spain which are having to deal with secessionist threats within their own borders (see for instance Rajoy's declarations in Torres and McTague 2017).

The argument whereby Spain or other EU countries could oppose Scotland's membership has often been made in public debates. In this context, whether the procedure described by art. 48 or art. 49 TEU is followed is not really relevant, since the final outcome would have to be agreed by all member states and thus Spain, or other countries, would be able to exercise their veto in both cases. However, a total opposition to Scottish membership is unlikely. In this connection, reference has often been made to the fact that five EU countries have not recognized Kosovo – Cyprus, Greece, Romania, Slovakia and Spain – because of their own internal minorities problems, and are therefore unlikely to accept any secession within the EU. Yet the comparison with Kosovo does not hold, since the problem with this latter case is the unilateral nature of the independence process there, rather than secession per se. Scotland's independence will be most likely agreed with the UK and therefore constitutes a very different case. Even a former Spanish Minister of Foreign Affairs (José García-Margallo y Marfil) stated that 'the constitutional arrangement in Britain is one and in Spain another, and [it] is up to them whether to separate' adding that 'no one would object to a consented independence of Scotland' (Murray 2012).[6] Hence, there is no reason why Spain should oppose Scotland's EU membership, provided that secession happens with the agreement of London (Ker-Lindsay 2012).

---

6   It is highly unlikely that the UK and/or Spain would oppose the application of their own regions if separation occurs consensually. If, on the other hand, the declaration of independence is unilateral, then opposition is almost certain.

What Spain and other countries can do, however, is to make it harder for Scotland to obtain membership. This means pushing for the procedure outlined by art. 49 instead of that engaged by art. 48, as well as hampering negotiations, notably with regard to the opt-outs currently enjoyed by Scotland as part of the UK. The result would probably come down to the sum of two opposite interests: on the one hand, that of most EU states to minimize the disruption brought about by the secession process (notably to the integrity of the common market) and to reduce, as much as possible, the contraction of the EU following Brexit; on the other, that of countries threatened by separatist movements to show these latter that independence is a risky affair and EU membership hard to win. Unfortunately for Scotland, the complexities of her application would offer Spain the opportunity to easily make the process more difficult without appearing uncooperative. As part of the United Kingdom, Scotland enjoys a number of opt-out options that would need to be renegotiated and would be hard to preserve. Furthermore, the Scottish government would face a true dilemma: the more substantive the derogations it would try to ensure, the longer the application process (Furby 2010: 5). There are six main problematic areas: the Schengen agreement, the euro, the UK budget rebate, the structural funds, fisheries and co-operation in the fields of justice and home affairs. The first seems to be the most complicated, as it threatens to force Scotland to impose customs controls at the border with England. In contrast, the euro might prove to be less troublesome than it seems at first glance, as Scotland could simply put off the adoption of the common currency indefinitely, as Sweden has done so far.[7] However, Scotland would almost certainly have to pay more for its membership and would get less back in terms of structural funds (Thorp and Thompson 2011: 10), but probably, given the importance of the fishing sector for its economy, it would be able to negotiate a better deal concerning rights in its territorial waters (Furby 2010: 5). Finally, it would likely have to agree to a full endorsement of the Union's legislation in terms of justice and home affairs, but this does not seem to be a major concern for the Scottish executive.

---

[7] We do not deal here with the difficulties entailed by the necessity of adopting its own currency, or the limitations imposed by any decision to continue using sterling.

The second Scottish scenario we mentioned above seems not to be problematic. If Scotland secedes from the UK after the Brexit process is completed, it will already be a third party, hence, there seems to be little doubt that there would not be any negotiations to redefine its position towards the EU (since this would already be redefined by the Brexit negotiations) and the region would simply have to apply as an external candidate. After more than forty years in the EU club, it would certainly have a strong case and, one might believe, the process would be quite swift. But again, countries threatened by separatist movements could exploit the many complexities normally involved in these kinds of negotiations to slow down the process.

In the Catalan case we can discern two scenarios, although these are not linked to any process of EU exit initiated by the successor state, but rather to the way in which secession could be achieved. While the Spanish state has sternly opposed any attempt by the Catalan authorities to assert the region's self-determination by means of an independence referendum, the determination of local actors to go on with the independence process despite central opposition means that the possibility of a successful unilateral secession, although still remote, cannot be ruled out entirely. Therefore, the true question in the Catalan case is whether the attempt to obtain EU membership by an independent Catalan state would follow a consensual or unilateral path.

The first Catalan scenario is certainly the easier to deal with. If the Spanish state were ever to accept Catalonia's self-determination and recognize an eventual pro-independence vote, there is no reason to believe that it would oppose the region's bid for EU membership. In this case, the wider EU's interest in minimizing disruption might prevail and either the internal enlargement procedure would be engaged or some kind of interim agreement – or alternatively, accession to the EEA pending EU accession negotiations – would be sought. Things could be a little more complicated if the Spanish government's acceptance of Catalonia's secession were to occur only after a prolonged period of institutional conflict of the kind already seen. In this case, Spain might not be the only country unco-operative at EU level – other countries threatened by secessionist movements might also prove to be so, if only to show that a hard-line secessionist policy does not pay. Once again, the result would depend on whether the EU members' interest in minimizing the disruption brought about by the secession process prevailed over the threatened countries' will to teach their own domestic separatist movements a lesson.

The scenario of Catalonia's unilateral independence is probably the less rosy in terms of avoiding disruption. Leaving aside all questions concerning the domestic consequences of such an event, there is no reason to believe that EU member states and institutions would have an interest in implicitly validating such a process by either recognizing an independent Catalan state or facilitating its accession to the EU. This is because territorial integrity is a key norm in international relations and international law, so much so that it generally prevails over self-determination, except in cases of colonization, foreign occupation or serious violations of human rights, none of which seems likely to apply to the Catalan case (see Cassese 1995: 317–23; Buccheit 1978: 73–4; Christakis 1999: 152–3; Higgins 1994: 111–28).[8] In other words, a unilateral secession does risk giving birth to a pariah state living in a juridical limbo.

Conclusion

In the last few decades, separatist movements in Catalonia and Scotland have campaigned to the sound of the slogan 'Independence in Europe', thus portraying separation as a smooth process that will not negatively affect the economic life of their regions and the welfare of their populations. The governments of the parent states and the central institutions of the EU, notably the European Commission, have generally replied by arguing that any secessionist territories will automatically be expelled from the EU upon independence, with obvious detrimental consequences for business activities and the welfare of the local populations.

8   Here, we do not take into account the scenario of a possible violent confrontation between the Spanish and Catalan governments, which might also entail such human rights violations.

This chapter has tried to assess the validity of both claims by looking at the existing international law literature as well as by examining the political aspects of this hypothetical fragmentation of the EU space. The principal conclusion is that, although nobody can foresee with a sufficient degree of certainty what would happen if and when one of these two regions declared independence, the scenario whereby all EU rights and obligations previously held by the citizens of these two territories will come abruptly to an end is unlikely at least for political, if not legal reasons. In our opinion, even if article 49 were to be preferred over article 48 as the guiding principle of the new redefinition of the relationship between the seceding territory and the EU (i.e. an external application will take precedence over an internal enlargement), an interim agreement preserving at least some substantive elements of the rights and duties currently enjoyed as EU citizens by residents of Catalonia and Scotland would be maintained, notably with regard to the integrity of the single market.

However, the process would not be at all as smooth and straightforward as depicted by separatist actors, but would rather be fraught with obstacles and uncertainties. Furthermore, it would decisively depend on the domestic peculiarities of each process of separation. On the basis of this consideration, we have proposed two scenarios for each case.

In the Scottish case, we have distinguished between two options: an independence process begun before the completion of Brexit and one initiated after it. While the latter is quite straightforward, since at that point Scotland would already be outside the EU and therefore with no reasonable alternative to an external application,[9] in the former scenario Scotland would enjoy the advantage of arguing its case at a time of 'contraction' of the EU territory, thus offering member states a possibility of reducing the disruption brought about to the integrity of the EU by Brexit. At the same time, the simultaneity of negotiations on Brexit, Scottish independence and redefinition of Scotland's status with regard to the EU would certainly increase the complexity and uncertainty of the process and might even lead to the temporal paradox highlighted by Chamon and Van der Loo (2014). Also, the

---

9   Whether this might be facilitated by Scotland's forty years of EEC/EU membership is an all too different question.

process of redefinition of Scotland's relationship with the EU might be made harder by EU countries facing domestic separatist threats, above all by Spain.

In the Catalan case, the dividing line lies in whether separation would be consensual or unilateral. If the former, the prospects of Catalonia facing a smooth accession procedure would seem to be higher, since Spain has been the most vocal country in calling for a rigid application of the external application procedure; but if the Spanish government comes to accept the independence of the region and negotiate it at the domestic level, it seems reasonable to believe that it would assume a more co-operative stance at the European level. In contrast, a unilateral declaration is likely to generate stern opposition not only on the part of Spain, but also on the part of most EU member states, since territorial integrity is a key norm in international relations and no country will have an interest in creating a precedent in this respect. One might argue that the fact that Kosovo has been recognized by most EU member states runs counter to such a conclusion. Yet one must bear in mind that the Kosovo case was accompanied by ethnic cleansing and other serious violations of human rights on the part of the Serbian government, which has not so far been the case in Spain – and hopefully it will not be for the foreseeable future. As argued by Guirao (2016: 215), 'pioneering voyages, as we all know, can end in glory or catastrophe' and as in the short term it seems highly unlikely that the Catalan government would manage to build up enough peaceful political legitimacy to get its independence claim recognized, a unilateral secession would probably lead to the latter.

Bibliography

Asthana, A., and Mason, R. (2017). 'Theresa May Asks EU for Two-Year Brexit Transition Period', *The Guardian*, 22 September <https://www.theguardian.com/politics/2017/sep/22/theresa-may-asks-eu-for-two-year-brexit-transition-period> accessed 26 September 2017.

Avery, G. (2014). 'Could an Independent Scotland Join the European Union?', European Policy Centre Policy Brief <http://www.epc.eu/documents/uploads/pub_4487_scotland_and_the_eu.pdf> accessed 28 September 2017.

Balcells, A. (1996). *Catalan Nationalism, Past and Present*. Basingstoke: Macmillan.

Barber, N. (2014). 'After the Vote: the Citizenship Question', *SCFF Blog*, 4 August <http://www.scottishconstitutionalfutures.org/OpinionandAnalysis/ViewBlogPost/tabid/1767/articleType/ArticleView/articleId/4004/Nick-Barber-After-the-Vote-the-Citizenship-Question.aspx> accessed 28 September 2017.

BBC (2018). 'The UK and EU agree terms for Brexit transition period', *BBC News*, 19 March <http://www.bbc.com/news/uk-politics-43456502> accessed 20 May 2018.

Borgen, C. J. (2010). 'From Kosovo to Catalonia: Separatism and Integration in Europe', *Goettingen Journal of International Law*, 2 (3), 997–1033.

Buchheit, L. C. (1978). *Secession, the Legitimacy of Self-Determination*. New Haven: Yale University Press.

Carrell, S. (2012). 'Barroso Casts Doubt on Independent Scotland's EU Membership Rights', *The Guardian*, 12 September <https://www.theguardian.com/politics/2012/sep/12/barroso-doubt-scotland-eu-membership> accessed 28 September 2017.

Cassese, A. (1995). *Self-Determination of Peoples. A Legal Reappraisal*, Cambridge: Cambridge University Press.

Chamon, M., and Van der Loo, G. (2014). 'The Temporal Paradox of Regions in the EU Seeking Independence: Contraction and Fragmentation versus Widening and Deepening?', *European Law Journal*, 20 (5), 613–29.

Christakis, T. (1999). *Le Droit à l'autodétermination en dehors de situations de décolonisation*. Paris: La Documentation française.

Cortes Generales. (1978). 'Spanish Constitution' <https://www.tribunalconstitucional.es/es/tribunal/normativa/Normativa/ConstitucionINGLES.pdf> accessed 28 September 2017.

Crawford, J. (1979). *The Creation of States in International Law*. Oxford: Clarendon Press.

Crawford, J., and Boyle, A. (2013). 'Annex A. Opinion: Referendum on the Independence of Scotland – International Law Aspects'. In Secretary of State for Scotland, *Scotland Analysis: Devolution and the Implications of Scottish Independence*, pp. 64–110. Norwich: The Stationery Office.

Delledonne, G. (2011). 'Speaking in Name of the Constituent Power: The Spanish Constitutional Court and the New Catalan Estatut', *Perspectives on Federalism*, 3 (1), 1–14.

Díez, A. (2012). 'CiU tacha de "provocación innecesaria" unas maniobras militares en Catalunya', *El País*, 24 October <https://politica.elpais.com/politica/2012/10/24/actualidad/1351099495_658342.html> accessed 28 September 2017.

Díez, A., and Mateo, J. J. (2017). 'Rajoy se reúne con Sánchez y Rivera para tratar la situación en Cataluña', *El País*, 20 September <https://politica.elpais.com/politica/2017/09/20/actualidad/1505902485_977250.html> accessed 27 September 2017.

Douglas-Scott, S. (2014a). *How Easily Could an Independent Scotland Join the EU?* Legal Research Paper Series no. 30. Oxford: Oxford University.

Douglas-Scott, S. (2014b). 'Why the EU Should Welcome an Independent Scotland', *Verfassungsblog on Constitutional Matters*, 8 September <http://verfassungsblog.de/eu-welcome-independent-scotland-2-2/> accessed 28 September 2017.

ECJ (European Court of Justice) (1963). *NV Algemene Transport- en Expeditie Onderneming van Gend & Loos v Netherlands Inland Revenue Administration*, Case 26–62, 5 February.

ECJ (European Court of Justice) (2010). *Janko Rottman v Freistaat Bayern*, Case C-135/08, 2 March.

ECJ (European Court of Justice) (2011). *Gerardo Ruiz Zambrano v Office national de l'emploi (ONEm)*, Case C-34/09, 8 March.

Edward, D. (2013). 'EU Law and the Separation of Member States', *Fordham International Law Journal*, 36 (5), 1151–68.

European Commission (2004). 'Answer Given by Mr Prodi on Behalf of the Commission', *Official Journal of the European Union*, C 84 E/492, 1 March.

European Commission (2007). 'Answer to Question N. 84 by Catherine Stihler', H-1086/06, <http://www.europarl.europa.eu/sides/getDoc.do?type=CRE&reference=20070215&secondRef=ANN-01&language=ET&detail=H-2006-1086&query=QUESTION> accessed 27 September 2017.

Fontanella-Kahn, J., Stacey, K., and Buck, T. (2012). 'Independent Scotland Faces EU Application', *Financial Times*, 28 October <https://www.ft.com/content/2fd7b0f6-1f8a-11e2-841c-00144feabdc0?mhq5j=e7> accessed 28 September 2017.

Furby, D. (2010). *Scottish Independence and EU Accession*. London: Business for New Europe.

Galí, J. (2014). 'An Independent State and the Euro'. In Comissiò d'Economia Catalana (ed.), *The Economy of Catalonia. Questions and Answers on the Impact of Independence*, pp. 83–92. Barcelona: Collegi d'Economistes de Catalunya.

Guirao, L. (2016). 'An Independent Catalonia as a Member State of the European Union?' In X. Cuadras-Morato (ed.), *Catalonia: A New Independent State in Europe?* London: Routledge.

Happold, M. (2000). 'Independence: In or Out of Europe? An Independent Scotland and the European Union', *International and Comparative Law Quarterly*, 49 (1), 15–34.

Higgins, R. (1994). *Problems and Process, International Law and How We Use it.* Oxford: Oxford University Press.
ICJ (International Court of Justice) (2010). 'Accordance with International Law of The Unilateral Declaration of Independence in Respect of Kosovo', Advisory Opinion of 22 July.
Ker-Lindsay, J. (2012). 'An Independent Scotland Would Face Little European Opposition to Membership of the European Union', *LSE's EUROPP Blog*, 24 March <http://blogs.lse.ac.uk/europpblog/2012/03/21/an-independent-scotland-would-face-little-european-opposition-to-membership-of-the-european-union/> accessed 28 September 2017.
MacCormick, N. (2000). 'Is there a Path to Scottish Independence?', *Parliamentary Affairs*, 53 (4), 721–36.
Maddox, D. (2012a). 'Scottish Independence: Spain "Would Not Allow Scots Automatic EU Entry"', *Scotsman.com*, 19 October <http://www.scotsman.com/news/politics/scottish-independence-spain-would-not-allow-scots-automatic-eu-entry-1-2588253> accessed 28 September 2017.
Maddox, D. (2012b). 'Scottish independence: Separate Scotland must apply to join EU, warns Brussels', *Scotsman.com*, 6 December <http://www.scotsman.com/news/scottish-independence-separate-scotland-must-apply-to-join-eu-warns-brussels-1-2677200> accessed 27 September 2017.
Mair, P. (1978). 'The Break-up of the United Kingdom: The Irish Experience of Regime Change, 1918–1949', *The Journal of Commonwealth & Comparative Politics* 16 (3), 288–302.
Mas, A. (2012). 'Destination Europe: The Future of Catalonia in The European Union', Speech delivered at the *Friends of Europe's Policy Spotlight* held in Brussels on 7 November <http://vimeo.com/53141451-at=0> accessed 27 September 2017.
Mateo, J. J., and Diez, A. (2017). 'Rajoy al Govern: "Regresan la ley y la democracia"', *El País*, 21 September <https://politica.elpais.com/politica/2017/09/20/actualidad/1505930515_079817.html#?id_externo_nwl=newsletter_diaria_manana20170921m> accessed 27 September 2017.
Moffet, M. (2012). 'Europe's Crisis Spawns Calls for a Break-Up of Spain', *The Wall Street Journal*, 28 October <https://www.wsj.com/articles/SB10000872396390443675404578060503427163808> accessed 28 September 2017.
Murray, G. (2012). 'Spain will not Veto an Independent Scotland Joining the EU', *Express.co.uk*, 26 February <http://www.express.co.uk/Posts/View/304495/Spain-Will-Not-Veto-An-Independent-Scotland-Joining-EU> accessed 28 September 2017.
O'Neill, A. (2011) 'A quarrel in a faraway country?: Scotland, independence and the EU', *eutopia law*, 14 November <https://eutopialaw.com/2011/11/14/685/> accessed 12 July 2017.

Pérez, C. (2017). 'Juncker reitera que una Cataluña independiente saldría automáticamente de la UE'. *El País*, 14 July <https://politica.elpais.com/politica/2017/07/14/actualidad/1500029756_954198.html#?id_externo_nwl=newsletter_diaria_noche20170714m> accessed 27 September 2017.

Scharf, M. P. (1995). 'Musical Chairs: The Dissolution of States and Membership in the United Nations', *Cornell International Law Journal*, 28 (1), 29–69.

Schieren, S. (2000). 'Independence in Europe: Scotland's Choice?' *Scottish Affairs*, 31 (1), 117–35.

Scottish Government (2013). *Scotland's Future. Your Guide to an Independent Scotland*. Edinburgh: The Scottish Government.

Secretary of State for Scotland (2013). *Scotland Analysis: Devolution and the Implications of Scottish Independence*. London: Her Majesty's Government.

Sillars, J. (1989). *Independence in Europe*. Edinburgh: SNP.

SNP (Scottish National Party) (1992). *Independence in Europe. Make it Happen Now*. Edinburgh: SNP.

SNP (Scottish National Party) (1994). *Power for Change: A Manifesto for the European Election, June 1994*. Edinburgh: SNP.

SNP (Scottish National Party) (1997a). *The Legal Basis of Independence in Europe*. Edinburgh: SNP.

SNP (Scottish National Party) (1997b). *Yes we can win the Best for Scotland*. Edinburgh: SNP.

SNP (Scottish National Party) (1999). *Enterprise, Compassion, Democracy*. Edinburgh: SNP.

SNP (Scottish National Party) (2005). *If Scotland Matters to you Make it Matter in May*. Edinburgh: SNP.

SNP (Scottish National Party) (2009). *We've got What it Takes*. Edinburgh: SNP.

SNP (Scottish National Party) (2011). *Re-Elect. A Scottish Government Working for Scotland*. Edinburgh: SNP.

The Economist (2017). 'Scotland's Government Focuses on Policy, not Freedom', *The Economist*, 7 September <https://www.economist.com/news/britain/21728672-first-minister-lays-out-detailed-plan-which-independence-takes-back-seat-scotlands> accessed 27 September 2017.

Thorp, A., and Thompson, G. (2011). *Scotland, Independence and the EU*. House of Commons Library, SN/IA6110.

Tierney, S. (2013). 'Legal Issues Surrounding the Referendum on Independence for Scotland', *European Constitutional Law Review*, 9 (3), 359–90.

Tierney, S., and Boyle, K. (2014). *An Independent Scotland: The Road to Membership of the European Union*. ESRC Scottish Centre on Constitutional Change Briefing Papers.

Torres, D. (2016). 'Catalan Exit Plan', *Politico*, 10 May <http://www.politico.eu/article/the-catalan-exit-plan-carles-puigdemont-generalitat-independence/> accessed 27 September 2017.

Torres, D., and McTague, T. (2017). 'Spain to Scotland: You're not Special', *Politico*, 27 March <http://www.politico.eu/article/spain-to-scotland-out-is-out-catalonia-independence-referendum/> accessed 27 September 2017.

UN (United Nations) (1978). *Vienna Convention on Succession of States in Respect of Treaties*, Vienna, 23 August.

UNGA (United Nations General Assembly) (1947). *Letter from the Chairman of the Sixth Committee Addressed to the Chairman of the First Committee.* A/C.1/212, 8 October.

GORKA ETXEBARRIA DUEÑAS

Flagging the Nation in the Basque Country: The Flag War

ABSTRACT

This chapter questions whether the concept of 'banal nationalism' can be applied to the competing national identities in the Basque Country, with reference to the controversy and confrontation that surrounded the display of the national flag in the late 1970s and early 1980s. It explores the competing narratives about sovereignty, power and legitimacy, and how these found expression in disputes over the flying of Spanish and Basque flags from the balconies of public buildings. The chapter considers how Basque and Spanish nationalism exist side by side, both in dialogue and in tension with each other, and how changes in the political balance of power can change the context in ways that extend beyond the political sphere, impacting civil society down to the level of the individual.

After an outline of its theoretical underpinnings and an overview of the socio-political background against which it is set, this chapter considers typical examples of the Basque national flag (the *ikurriña*) – officially authorized in the Autonomous Community of the Basque Country and controversial in Navarre – becoming the iconic central symbol of Basque national identity at the heart of the 'flag war' of the early 1980s and beyond.[1]

While flags are universally and very obviously associated with displays of national solidarity and identity at such public events as football matches, rock concerts, festivals, parades and so on, what is less obviously

---

1   This chapter is part of research activity developed under the aegis of the Basque government's PREDOC 2015 programme. It draws inspiration, in particular, from the concept of *banal nationalism* introduced by Michael Billig in his seminal (1995) work of the same name. I would like to express my deep gratitude to Alejandro Quiroga for his corrections and suggestions. I would also like to thank the peer reviewers for comments that have substantially improved this chapter.

apparent is the subtle effect of their presence on official buildings, an effect described as so *banal* (so reiterated and quotidian) that it goes largely unnoticed (Archilés and Quiroga 2018: x).[2] This chapter, in exploring the Basque Country, ventures into a disputatious territory where the Spanish State's definition of national identity is far from banal, where it is routinely and openly defied.[3]

Since Basque nationalism appeared as an organized political movement in the late nineteenth century, Basque citizens have been interpellated as part of both the Spanish nation and the Basque nation.[4] This chapter focuses on official display of the national flag on town hall balconies, an issue that proved to be highly controversial in the Basque Country after Franco's dictatorship (1936–75) and which in the late 1970s and the 1980s became central to Basque politics. I will exemplify the fact that, while less overtly, it remains an unresolved problem to this day.

The chapter expounds its theme in terms of the banality and basic rational logic assumed by those political parties engaged in Basque and Spanish nationalist discourses, and hence focuses on the dialogical relationship between Spanish and Basque nationalism. The politicians identified with the Spanish nation would assume Spanish national symbols to be a

---

2 Banal nationalism in Spanish history has recently been the focus of considerable academic enquiry (Archilés and Quiroga 2018). Additionally, several works have used Billig's ideas to explore sub-State nationalisms in Western Europe, including Catalonia (Crameri 2000), Scotland (Law 2001; Higgins 2004) and Wales (Jones and Desforges 2003; Jones and Merriman 2009). These authors have found the concept of banal nationalism useful in their analyses, especially when sub-State, decentralizing political institutions do exist. This chapter connects both research areas: sub-State nationalisms and recent Spanish history.

3 I use the term *Basque Country* to refer to the Autonomous Community of the Basque Country and the Chartered Community of Navarre in Spain, an area claimed as their national territory by Basque nationalists. Here the Basque language is taught in state schools and Basque nationalist parties contest elections. The French Basque Country, which Basque nationalists also claim, and where the Basque language is not taught in the State education system, is not relevant to the present discussion.

4 Distinctions made in this chapter between 'Spanish' and 'Basque' are intended to represent the positions under discussion.

normal matter and would perceive the discourse and practice of Basque nationalist parties as an attack on that normality.

Banality and Hegemony

Michael Billig's observations on symbols as a banal daily reminder of the national identity spread so rapidly to the social sciences, to cultural studies and historical research that by the beginning of the twenty-first century he had become an essential reference for researchers interested in national identities (Quiroga 2015). I wondered at the extent to which his concept of banal nationalism could be validated by the example of the Basque Country.

What caught my attention was Billig's proposal to extend the analysis of nationalism beyond the pro-independence political movements and the extreme right, and his argument that nationalism is present in every nation and reproduced on a daily basis by each state.[5] His work – which asks every researcher to be aware of the nationalism present in the state and of how the term 'nationalist' tends to be applied only to other countries, pro-independence parties or the far right – suggested the opportunity to consider nationalism from the political perspectives of both the Basque Country and the Spanish state.

Second, I inferred from Billig's view a concern about how each state's political and economic elites use nationalism as a tool to maintain their leadership and to serve their interests. That is to say, national identities reproduce social hegemonies and help to maintain the status quo, and where the national order is not socially contested, a state is able to reproduce a

---

5   The terms 'reproduce' and 'reproduction' are to be understood in the sense that Billig describes: 'The reproduction of nation-states depends upon a dialectic of collective remembering and forgetting, and of imagination and unimaginative repetition' (1995: 10). His contention is that a sense of national identity is constantly created and re-created (reproduced) by myriad 'banal' (everyday, barely noticed) reminders (conscious and unconscious).

nationalist sentiment in a banal way. The Basque case of the turbulent 1970s and 1980s can be read as a unique and stimulating example of a contrary scenario.

In considering the link between banal nationalism and social hegemony we can take account of the perceptions of Michael Skey (2011), whose work is critically based on Billig, which explain the nation as something totally interiorized in the habitual scope of the world we live in. In that sense, 'nation' should be understood as a container, rather than a thing, reflecting as such the conflicting social views of what society means and of its goals and limits.

The period we analyse in this chapter was one of substantial flux in Spanish society, with Francoism widely contested during the 1970s, a multi-party parliamentary Monarchy finally emerging in 1978 and what is called the Spanish Transition ending with the coming to power of the Socialist Party in October 1982. Abundant research has been centred on how ideas of Spain and Spanish national identity changed and developed throughout the period[6] and at this time of contested and conflictive issues of political legitimacy, power and sovereignty at a national level, Basque nationalists struggled against the very idea of Spanish national sovereignty itself. While many studies are concerned with the Basque Country[7] none fully deal with the Spanish nationalism of the same period. This chapter seeks to complement previous research by exploring the dialogical connection between Spanish nationalism on the one hand, and Basque nationalism on the other.

I take a flexible approach to the concept of banal nationalism and its application to the case of Basque nationalism, without disregarding Molina's contention that the existence of political violence in the Basque Country precludes any analysis of the national issue linked to a sort of banal nationalism (Molina 2009). I pay attention to the ways in which Spanish and Basque nationalists compete to be the hegemonic national

---

[6] See, for example, Archilés and Martí (2002); Núñez Seixas (2004); Balfour and Quiroga (2007); Taibo (2007); Muñoz (2012); Arroyo and Izquierdo (2012); Artime (2016).

[7] Examples include Fernández and López (2012); Escribano and Casanellas (2012); Leonisio, Molina and Muro (2016); Fusi and Pérez (2017); Beorlegui (2017).

identity in the three different spheres of nationalization and apply Alejandro Quiroga's proposal to analyse mass nationalization processes through those spheres: the official sphere of state, regional, provincial and municipal institutions, the non-official public sphere of political parties, trade unions, cultural associations, sports clubs and so on and the private sphere of family and friends (Quiroga 2014). For consistent reproduction a national identity has to be hegemonic in those three spheres in a certain territory, which is not the case in the Basque Country.

In Billig's analysis, the flying of the national flag on official buildings is an example of an almost unconscious shaping of national identity, and the case study which follows illustrates the dialogue between Basque and Spanish nationalism on the meaning of national identity, sovereignty and legitimacy. It does so by examining the role played by flags in the contested social space of the Basque Country in the late 1970s and the early 1980s.

Basque Autonomy and Its Flag

This first section acknowledges the fact that Basque nationalism was extremely strong in the private and the non-official sphere during the last years of the Franco dictatorship and those years in which the parliamentary monarchy was established. We look at how that situation, in forcing the government to authorize display of the Basque national flag and to accept the creation of Basque autonomous institutions with a regional administration led by Basque nationalists, prepared the ground for reproducing Basque national identity in the official sphere.

The Basque national flag, the *ikurriña*, was to play a central role in this reproduction. Created by the founder of the conservative Basque Nationalist Party (PNV), Sabino Arana and his brother Luis, in 1894, it copied the design of the Union Flag of Great Britain (the Union Jack) with a white cross over a green saltire on a red field. During the Spanish Civil War (1936–9) it became the official flag of the Basque autonomous government, led by the PNV. That government, after a brief existence, went into exile during Franco's dictatorship (de la Granja 2007). Under Franco too, the *ikurriña* functioned as an anti-Francoist symbol, linked to a powerful Basque nationalist message (Casquete and de la Granja 2012).

Basque nationalists reframed the Civil War as an attack by Spanish nationalists on Basque autonomy (Muro 2009), and their rhetoric was successful when, as strikes and workers' protests broke out during the 1960s (Domènech 2008) the violent overreaction of Franco's government made it possible for Basque nationalists to present the dictatorship as an essentially anti-Basque regime (Casanellas 2014). Notwithstanding that a large part of the population had arrived from other Spanish regions in the nineteenth century and during the industrial development of the 1950s and the 1960s, the Basque nationalist discourse influenced all the anti-Francoist opposition.

Their message acquired an extraordinary popularity, linked as it was to the armed revolutionary group Basque Country and Freedom (*Euskadi Ta Askatasuna*; ETA), whose militants became martyrs for all the anti-Francoist opposition when they were killed in clashes with Francoist police.[8] Their prestige reached its peak in 1970, when death sentences passed on some ETA leaders were finally commuted following widespread demonstrations. ETA's prestige rose again when in 1973 they assassinated Franco's right-hand man, president of the government, Carrero Blanco, in a bomb attack in Madrid (Pérez Pérez 2013).

In October 1975 (Franco was to die in November), ETA started a campaign with booby-trapped Basque *ikurriña* flags, which exploded when attempts were made to remove them, and six members of the police force were killed within a few months. The threat eroded police morale and in the aftermath of Franco's death the government could not prevent display of the *ikurriña* at local festivals and public celebrations (Egaña 1994;

---

8 The generic term 'police' cannot capture the complexities (historical and current) of the Spanish policing system(s), but neither can any adjective applied to them in English: 'military police' should be used only of members of the armed forces whose jurisdiction is limited to military personnel; 'militia' has too many interpretations; 'paramiltary' tends not to refer to legally constituted forces. 'Police' is therefore employed throughout for both those who come under military jurisdiction (principally the Guardia Civil) and those under other national or local civil administration(s).

Echevarría 2017). Surprise turned into elation among Basque nationalists when, on 5 December 1976, in the Atotxa football stadium in San Sebastian, the captains of Real Sociedad and Athletic Club took the field with an *ikurriña*. Finally, Spanish president Adolfo Suárez had no choice but to authorize its public display in January 1977. Under the social pressure of the opposition and ETA intimidation of Francoist local authorities, the *ikurriña* was raised in almost every town council building in the Basque Country during 1977.

At that time, the government was forced to organize the first multi-party election since 1936, after huge popular protests prevented all attempts to establish a very restricted democracy (Gallego 2008; Wilhelmi 2016). A few weeks before the June 1977 elections, the PNV and the Basque section of the Spanish Socialist Party (PSOE) drafted an agreement allowing for signatories to be the representatives of the Basque people after the election and elaborate an autonomy project for the Basque territories in Spain. This 'pro-autonomy pact', was supported by the Spanish Communist Party (PCE), small leftist Basque nationalist parties, a leftist branch of the former-Francoist Carlist Party and some Spanish conservatives (Tamayo 1994).

The most significant aspect of the pact was that the elected representatives of the Basque people would negotiate with the new Spanish authorities regarding political institutions for the Basque people (*Deia*, 8 June 1977). Basque and Spanish representatives were conceived as two different bodies, with a critical element of the mindset of Basque candidates contesting the 1977 Spanish general election being the concept of the Basque people as the primary source of political legitimacy. In the Basque Country, although mixed with explicit references to Spain, a perception of Basque uniqueness was present even in the government-formed Union of the Democratic Centre (UCD) and the post-Francoist Popular Alliance (AP) of the far right (Landaberea 2012). Among Basque nationalists in the late 1970s there was an almost total rejection of the Spanish nationalism of the kind that the Franco regime had tried to impose (Saz 2012; Estornés 2013).

Although in Spain the UCD of President Suarez gathered major support, the broad triumph in the Basque Country of the PNV and PSOE in June 1977 was a victory for rejection of Spanish nationalism (Miccichè

2012; Arrieta 2012). The notion of a specific body that would represent the Basque people was so widely accepted that immediately after the elections a Basque Parliamentary Assembly was formed, with membership consisting of every elected representative in the Basque provinces, including those from UCD and AP. On 21 July 1977 they issued a joint statement:

> La Asamblea de Parlamentarios [...] manifiesta su decisión de defender el derecho del pueblo vasco a recuperar sus instituciones históricas y que el primer objetivo de su acción parlamentaria es precisamente conseguir [...] libertades originarias de los vascos.[9]
>
> [The Parliamentary Assembly [...] announces its decision to defend the right of the Basque people to recover its historical institutions and its first parliamentary activity's objective will be to achieve [...] the original freedoms of the Basques.] (Cited in Tamayo 1994: 254)

Spanish government hegemony having been deeply eroded in the Basque Country, a Basque national identity became socially predominant during the first years after Franco's death (Molina and Míguez 2012) not only in the private sphere among Basque nationalist families, friends and colleagues, but also in the public sphere of political parties, trade unions, neighbourhood associations, local festival committees, literature, music and so on (Pérez-Agote 1984; Aizpuru 1998; Urrutia 2006; Larrinaga 2016; Eser 2016). The social acceptance of Basque symbols was not far from being banal at the time, and although some authors have argued the contrary, on the grounds of ETA violence (Molina 2017; Fernández 2017), others have underlined the importance of generational feelings and the link between Basque nationalism and anti-Francoism (Mata 1993; Letamendia 1994; Arriaga 1997).[10] An implicit and widespread anti-Francoist Basque nationalist feeling can be identified among the young during the period, in Basque nationalist as well as Spanish migrant families.

---

9   All translations are mine, unless otherwise stated.
10 The initial conclusions of my own ongoing research, based on personal interviews and thorough analysis of the election results, point towards the second interpretation.

Related to that Basque nationalism and the protester environment, a radical coalition, People's Unity (*Herri Batasuna*; HB), was created in 1978.[11] HB did not accept the elected government, nor the Constitution project being drafted in the Spanish Parliament, arguing that Francoist Army officers were still in power and, therefore, Spain could not be considered a democracy. They maintained that the Basque autonomy project had to be drafted following local elections and should contain the right of self-determination, no matter what the recently elected Spanish multi-party parliament decided. HB, believing that a leftist and Basque nationalist ideal was widely accepted in Basque society, felt confident about future local and regional elections, their perception implying that Spanish national identity had almost disappeared in the region. This coalition of pro-independence parties publicly supported ETA's assassination campaign against Army officers and Spanish policemen in the Basque Country and against their alleged local collaborators.

Nevertheless, the simultaneous presence of different and more or less successful Spanish nationalist discourses in the Basque Country should not be overlooked. Spanish nationalism did not disappear with Franco but continued being a crucial element in every Spanish political culture (Arroyo and Izquierdo 2012; Izquierdo 2014). The major newspapers (still those previously linked to Franco's National Movement) took a pro-democratic stand but never supported a Basque nationalist view; the Spanish Football League matches were the main event every Sunday afternoon; Spanish radio was listened to in the Basque Country and only State television was available at the time. ETA members from urban areas sang the same Spanish hit songs and saw the very same films that might be enjoyed by any young woman in Madrid (Florido et al. 2017).

Through nationwide television, newspapers and radio stations, different Spanish nationalist narratives were socialized: the central government's conservative message for national concord, the Communist Party's pursuit

---

11   HB, founded in 1978 as a Basque nationalist coalition of four far-left groups to promote a 'no' vote in the Spanish Constitution referendum of that year, became a political party in 1986. Refounded as *Batasuna* in 2001 but then proscribed by the Supreme Court as it was considered the political wing of ETA, it was dissolved that year.

of national reconciliation and the Socialist Party's identification with a modern and European Spain (Sassoon 2001; Gallego 2008; Andrade 2012; Rodríguez-Flores 2018). That is to say, following the theoretical model of the three spheres of nationalization, the Spanish national identity was being spread, though in a much weaker manner than that of the Basque identity, in the non-official public sphere. However, the official public sphere, related to State institutions such as the education system, administration, social security, the postal service, currency, road signs and so on, reproduced on a daily basis a sense of shared territory, symbols and cultural references, as it did everywhere else in Spain. Added to that, we can assume that those migrants arriving in the Basque Country as adults never lost their Spanish national identity.[12]

Moreover, the Spanish government and the principal opposition parties fostered the positive idea of a newly founded democratic Spain, allegedly achieved through the Constitution agreement of 1977–8. As previously noted, the primary source of political legitimacy in the Basque Country, for both Basque nationalists and Spanish Basques acting in opposition parties, was understood to be the Basque people themselves. Nevertheless, in 1977 the Socialists and Communists abandoned their conception of Spain as a federation of different sovereign peoples. This constituted a U-turn in their positions (Jiménez and López 1989; Quiroga 2009; Geniola 2018).

During Franco's dictatorship, sub-State nationalists and leftist parties shared a common oppositional and underground activity that homogenized their messages. After the 1977 elections, Spanish nationalism became the common ground for agreement between the government and the nationwide opposition parties. While not one Basque nationalist party supported the 1978 Constitution, Spanish national identity became the only officially recognized national identity in the Constitutional Monarchy. The Constitution established the Spanish people as its unique source of legitimacy and state power; hence, other sources of legitimacy such as the so-called nationalities that referred to Catalonia, the Basque Country and Galicia were discarded or treated as subordinated to that primary

---

12 An interesting case is that of several Spanish anarchist militants who in old age supported HB.

source (Álvarez 2005). The Constitution is legally based on the 'indisoluble unidad de la Nación española' [indissoluble unity of the Spanish nation] (Article 2), a provision which sets such a clear limit to every regional pro-independence political project that Xacobe Bastida suggests that, being drafted in such a way, the article amounted to an imposition by high-ranking Francoist military on the parliament (2007: 121–2). After approval of the Constitution, Spanish nationalism obtained a notable advantage over Basque nationalism, which did not have official State recognition. Without control of any public institution, and despite an overwhelming presence in the non-official public sphere, a banal reproduction of Basque national identity was not yet possible.

That situation was to enter a new phase when, after the first local elections in April 1979, Basque nationalist parties obtained a clear victory. A few weeks later, the Basque autonomy project, passed by the Spanish Parliament after hard negotiations between the government and the PNV leaders, established the *ikurriña* as the official flag for the newborn Autonomous Community of the Basque Country. The fact that this was not challenged by Spanish parties indicates the strength of Basque nationalism in the late 1970s. The official status acquired by its national flag and the election of the first autonomous government led by the PNV set the stage for a future banal Basque nationalism.

The Basque Flag in Navarre

However, despite the fact that the *ikurriña* was flown in the Navarrese town councils after 1977, Spanish nationalism still flourished in the Basque province. Although the Basque Autonomy Law of 1979 stated that Navarre could be part of the new Autonomous Community of the Basque Country, its incorporation was blocked. UCD obtained six out of the nine Parliament seats contested in the province, although gathering only a third of the popular vote. The specific discourse which had been developed through the pre-democratic regional institutions in Navarre claimed that although its people were Basques, it was already an autonomous region under Franco and did not need to call for a new autonomy (Baraibar 2004). Accordingly, Navarrese members of UCD, who were linked to the former Francoist regional elites (Aoiz 2005), declined to participate in the Basque Parliamentary Assembly, feeling that in this way they might put a barrier between an autonomous and an independent Basque Country. Moreover, while the Spanish Constitution of 1978 had included the possibility of a referendum in Navarre that would mean incorporation of the province into the Autonomous Community of the Basque Country, the position of the PSOE gradually moved closer to that of the Navarrese members of UCD and, when the regional Navarrese parliament was elected in 1979, UCD and PSOE voted together to postpone such a referendum *sine die*. As previously noted, Spanish nationalism functioned as a shared ground for nationwide parties during 1977 and 1978 and widened the gap between the main leftist parties and the sub-State nationalists.

From an essentially passive, albeit determined stance, Spanish nationalism moved into a higher gear after the unsuccessful reactionary *coup d'état* in Madrid on 23 February 1981 (known as 23 F). An offensive strategy was adopted to reinforce the constitutional monarchy, and the Spanish national flag became a central element. The Spanish political elite felt that Spanish symbols needed to be relegitimized and their monopolization by far right and pro-military agents averted. The massive anti-*coup* demonstrations on 27 February 1981 were marked by the number of Spanish constitutional flags. Members of the government were told that they were always to be portrayed with the flag in evidence. The patriotic-constitutional fervour of 1981 made monarchic symbols almost hegemonic in the Spanish democracy, overwhelming the residual use of republican emblems. At the PSOE Congress in 1981 the Spanish flag replaced the red flag for the first time (Moreno and Nùñez 2013).

A law passed by the Spanish Parliament in June 1981 stated that the Spanish flag 'simboliza la nación; es signo de la soberanía, independencia, unidad e integridad de la patria y representa los valores superiores expresados en la Constitución' [symbolizes the nation; it is a sign of the sovereignty, independence, unity and integrity of the fatherland and represents the superior values expressed in the Constitution] (*Boletín Oficial del Estado*,

12 November 1981). The law also made it mandatory to fly the emblem outside every public administration building, and, if displayed with other flags, it was to hold a preferential place. It seems that, much as foreseen by Michael Billig's 'hot' scenario (when, for example, people take to the streets) the 23 F attempted *coup* allowed the political elite to appropriate patriotic sentiment and double the presence of national symbols in society. This further step towards ensuring the hegemony of the young parliamentary monarchy and its social and political values paved the way for further banal reproductions of national identity. According to the PSOE spokesman Luis Solana, the Spanish flag should from then on be 'algo habitual y normal' [something habitual and normal] (*El País*, 23 June 1981), precisely, that is, as banal as Billig was to describe. But in small localities where Basque national identity was hegemonic, this injunction was systematically ignored, with City councils flying either the *ikurriña* alone or, like the Basque autonomous government in the new institutions, no flag at all.

But in Navarre in 1981 the regional parliament officially recognized only the Spanish and Navarrese flags.[13] While the new regulation did not ban the flying of the *ikurriña*, the Spanish parties were determined to leverage the new law and prevent any public presence of the Basque national flag in Navarre, understanding that its presence in the official sphere would seriously undermine a banal reproduction of the Spanish national identity. In December the PSOE started a campaign to remove the *ikurriña* from every town council in Navarre and in order to avoid Spanish nationalist rhetoric presented the issue as a simple legal adjustment. Their spokesman in Navarre argued that the law allowed for the flying of only the Spanish national flag, those of the autonomous communities and a local flag, and asserted that the flag of one autonomous community was not that of another (*Egin*, 1 December 1981).

Basque nationalists considered this issue to be an attack on their national identity, with PSOE's arguments about a mere legal fit not ringing true during a year celebrating Spanish national identity. The *ikurriña* continued to be the national symbol for Basque nationalists, who remained attached to the idea of the Basque people as the source of political legitimacy,

---

13   *Obra Legislativa del Parlamento Foral de Navarra*, 26 October 1981.

whatever the Spanish Constitution said, and who knew that if the *ikurriña* disappeared in Navarre they would lose any opportunity to reproduce the Basque national identity there in the official sphere. The Basque autonomous government was then led by the PNV member Carlos Garaikoetxea, a Navarrese himself, who asserted:

> [C]on independencia de que la ikurriña haya sido establecida como bandera oficial de esta Comunidad Autónoma, en opinión de este Gobierno, constituye un símbolo que puede considerarse patrimonio universal de la comunidad natural vasca, cualquiera que sea su localización o adscripción política.
>
> [Regardless of the establishment of the *ikurriña* as the official flag of [only] this Autonomous Community, in the opinion of this government it is a symbol that can be considered as universal patrimony of the Basque natural community, whatever its location or political ascription.] (*Egin*, 2 December 1981)

The fact that the 1981 celebration of Spanish nationalism was uncontested in most of Spain allowed promotion of the constitutional flag to set the scene for a banal reproduction of Spanish national identity linked to the new multi-party institutions.[14] However, the existence of Basque nationalism served to highlight the contrasting goals of Spanish nationalism, as was evident at a meeting of the Town Council in Pamplona on 9 December 1981 when the pro-independence HB, the second largest political force in the city, called for demonstrations 'para que la bandera de los vascos no sea quitada de Pamplona que durante siglos y siglos ha sido considerada la capital de los vascos' [to avoid Basque flags being removed from Pamplona, which has been throughout the centuries considered the capital city of the Basques]. HB councillor Zabaleta recalled that two PSOE members were responsible for the *ikurriña* flying in the Pamplona City Hall in 1977 and that the Navarrese PSOE members participated in the Basque Parliamentary Assembly (*Egin*, 10 December 1981). HB and PNV asked for a referendum but the Pamplona mayor (PSOE) rejected the idea, with the PSOE spokesman Álvarez declaring that 'mientras Navarra no se integre en Euskadi, la ikurriña no sea utilizada por las

---

14 On 6 December 1981, the anniversary of the approval by referendum of the 1978 Constitution, Spanish flags were distributed with newspapers.

entidades locales de Navarra' [as long as Navarre is not incorporated into the Autonomous Community of the Basque Country, the *ikurriña* should not be used by local institutions] (*Egin*, 11 December 1981).

Finally, with the majority PSOE, UCD and far right former UCD members voting on one side, and the PNV and HB on the other, the *ikurriña* was removed from Pamplona City Hall, with the decision instantly greeted by demonstrators throwing stones at its windows. Following these events in the Navarrese capital, and despite the opposition of Basque nationalist, communist and far left councillors (*Egin*, 24 December 1981), the *ikurriña* was also removed from a number of town halls in Navarre (*ABC*, 26 December 1981).

Far left parties denounced the PSOE as 'alineándose con la derecha más reaccionaria y centralista' [aligning itself with the most reactionary and centralist right] and asserted that 'la retirada de la ikurriña es entrar de lleno en la lógica de los sectores golpistas' [the removal of the *ikurriña* is accepting the logic of those involved in the *coup d'état*] (*Egin*, 12 December 1981). In that context, the sixteen pro-independence members of the Navarrese regional parliament (out of seventy seats in total) refused further participation, asserting that they could not support 'una reforma que se tambalea cada vez que se marca el paso en los cuarteles' [a reform that totters every time military quarters set the tone] (*Egin*, 30 December 1981). Thus, the parties opposed to the 1978 Constitution, linking removal of the *ikurriña* in Navarre with approval of the unsuccessful *coup* of 23 February, saw a 'military hand' behind the exaltation of Spanish national identity in 1981, and explained the reinforcement of Spanish symbols as the way in which that exaltation was embodied in the region.

Following the attempted *coup*, ambivalence was impossible for the PSOE, who felt that the constitutional system needed to be reinforced, with the whole Spanish people the sole source of legitimacy. When Pérez Balda, the PSOE councillor in Pamplona, was forced to resign after voting against the removal of the *ikurriña*, he declared: '[Y]o no cambio de chaqueta […] soy socialista, navarro y vasco' [I do not change sides […] I am socialist, Navarrese and Basque] (*Deia*, 20 December 1981). Other Basque PSOE leaders feared that removal of the *ikurriña* would only encourage more support for HB and ETA. But their Navarrese colleagues responded that 'la ikurriña es hoy pura y simplemente la bandera de la Comunidad Autónoma vasca [...] no puede ser utilizada con carácter oficial en las instituciones de Navarra que, obviamente no pertenece al ámbito territorial de dicha comunidad' [the *ikurriña* is nowadays solely and simply the flag of the Autonomous Community of the Basque Country [...] it cannot be used officially in the institutions of Navarre, which is obviously not part of that community] (*Deia*, 17 December 1981).

These arguments supported the policy of normalizing the Spanish national identity in Navarre, and its counterpart, removing the Basque national flag from the official landscape, a policy underpinned in 1982 by a Navarrese autonomy law passed by the regional parliament and approved by the Spanish Parliament in June. It was called 'the improvement', an alleged renewal of the previous autonomous status granted by Franco. At that point, the Navarrese PSOE members left the Basque section of the party to create their own section within the PSOE.

Whatever the differences of opinion among officials, where Basque nationalism was particularly strong in Navarre was in the non-official public sphere, an area in which attempts were also made to normalize Spanish national identity by displacing the *ikurriña*. One example occurred in the summer of 1982 when, for the first time since 1977, the San Fermin fiestas started without the *ikurriña* on the official balcony of Pamplona City Hall. The Navarrese regional parliament decided not to support traditional dance groups which used the *ikurriña* (*Deia*, 3 August 1982) and the official dance troupe of Pamplona Town Council was boycotted by the Mayor because of the use of the *ikurriña* in their performances (*El País*, 30 November 1982). Several *ikurriña*s were removed by the police, no matter whether they were flown officially or not. There were even fines for having an *ikurriña* sticker on the rear of a car, with traffic police referring to a 'distintivo de nacionalidad no reglamentario, por ser de varios colores' [non-regulated national symbol, one of several colours] (*Egin*, 2 July 1982).

In summing up these events, it must be stressed that the Spanish parliamentary monarchy was still far from being a stable regime. Hence, the swell of nationalist feeling that followed the 23 F attempted *coup* of 1981 could be seen from quite different perspectives: the principal nationwide parties agreed that popular support for the multiparty system assured the break with Franco's Spain; in contrast, the pro-independence Basque nationalists and the far left saw it as a surrender to Francoist army officers, and continued to describe the Spanish government as basically nationalist and reactionary. HB and ETA argued that no government could call itself democratic if it did not accept the legal possibility of a future independence referendum in the Basque Country. Such joint opposition to the established parliamentary monarchy made it possible for HB and the radical left to contest the following general elections together.

The landslide victory of the PSOE in the general elections of October 1982 and the formation of a socialist government under Felipe González meant that a formerly anti-Francoist opposition was in power for the first time since the dictatorship. During the previous months, the PSOE had accused president Suárez of using the threat of another military *coup* for his own advantage, and Felipe González would present himself as the only chance to achieve a real rupture with Francoism (Marín 2016). The socialist government underlined the necessity to modernize Spain, their cabinet was described as a group of 'young Spanish nationalists' (Quiroga 2013: 78) and their political project, based on a normalization of Spain according to Western European standards, was strongly and successfully presented in nationalist terms.

At the same time, the 1978 Constitution had become a shared reminder of the unity of the Spanish nation for Spanish parties, whether leftist or conservative. Concepts of unity had been linked, especially by the PSOE, to other ideas such as inter-regional solidarity and citizen equality, and every stance that differed from what was found in the Constitution, usually represented by sub-State nationalist movements, was discredited as contrary to such equality and solidarity (Muñoz 2012).

In May 1983 new town councils and regional parliaments were elected throughout Spain. While the PSOE in Navarre obtained a clear victory and Basque nationalist parties had poor results, it was a different story in the Autonomous Community of the Basque Country, where the conservative Basque nationalist PNV obtained almost 40 per cent of the votes, HB came third after the PSOE, and almost 2,000 Basque nationalist local councillors were elected against fewer than 500 for Spanish parties. The growth of Basque nationalism in the territory where an autonomous government led by Basque nationalists was created, and its decline in Navarre (renamed as the Chartered Community of Navarre), is key to understanding the importance of national identity reproduction in the official sphere.

Despite the fact that the victory of PSOE might have been thought of as the final proof of democratization in Spain, and although the government made an unsuccessful attempt at peace talks with ETA early in 1983, during that year the assassination campaign continued against army officers, Spanish policemen and alleged collaborators. In response, senior officials of that socialist government financed a corresponding campaign by a group of police officers and far right mercenaries (known as GAL) against pro-independence sympathizers and ETA members exiled in the French Basque Country.[15]

The following section will explore the still-contentious issue of flying the competing national symbols, at that time an aspect of the struggle between socialists in power and pro-independence Basque nationalists, marked not only by verbal clashes in the council chambers but by spontaneous street demonstrations.

The Flag War

The summer of 1983 was to mark the beginning of the so-called flag war, a conflict which started in Tolosa, a relatively industrialized town near San Sebastian of almost 20,000 inhabitants. At that time no flags were normally flown in town halls controlled by Basque nationalists but in Tolosa, where the Basque nationalist councillors numbered sixteen out of nineteen, it was decided that both the Tolosa flag and the *ikurriña* would fly on local celebration days in June. On the morning of 25 June 1983, after two days of celebrations, a police unit brought a Spanish flag to the

---

15 Links between far-right mercenaries, Francoist police officers and the Spanish secret service had resulted in the assassination of Basque nationalists and far left militants since the mid-1970s. But after the 23 F attempted *coup d'état* in 1981, this activity had drastically diminished (Casals 2016).

town hall. They told the PNV mayor, Mirentxu Etxebarria, that flying an *ikurriña* without the Spanish flag was 'against the Constitution'. She decided to remove the *ikurriña*.

Later that day, when Tolosa councillors were summoned, HB members and other elected leftist nationalists stated that if the *ikurriña* was removed, they would fly it again. The PNV councillors agreed and the Basque flag was flown again in the afternoon (*Egin*, 26 June 1983). At almost midnight, dozens of policemen entered the town hall and raised the Spanish flag. The *ikurriña* of the plenary room was later found full of cigarette burns. The mayor described the event as 'un espectáculo alucinante [...] improcedente y desmedido' [an extraordinary spectacle [...] improper and excessive]. She said that the police only managed to 'crear tensión' [create tension] (*Deia*, 26 June 1983).

Pro-independence nationalists were able to present the Tolosa incident as the imposition of an anti-Basque Spanish nationalist government on the Basque Country and on the sovereignty of its town councils. With the other councillors abstaining, HB members approved a proposal that the Spanish flag brought by the police should be delivered to the Madrid Home Affairs Ministry by the Tolosa town council. In the same way that PSOE had argued in Navarre two years earlier, HB members presented their decision as a logical adjustment to the established legal scenario: in the town councils where Basque nationalism was hegemonic, there was no room for the Spanish national flag. The HB members in Tolosa presented the action not as 'una postura visceral' [a visceral stance] but rather as a way of correcting a sort of administrative error, sending the Spanish national flag back to Madrid 'para que esté entre los que la aman y sienten' [so that it should be among those who love it and have a feeling for it] (*Egin*, 5 July 1983).

HB declared that the *ikurriña* should be flown accompanied by the local flag only, in every town hall where possible (*Egin*, 14 July 1983). The official presence of the *ikurriña* without the Spanish flag during local festivities would be a sign of moving towards a future banal reproduction of the Basque national identity in the official sphere. Equally, Spanish authorities were aware that this had to be prevented unless sub-State national symbols were accompanied by a reminder that the territory was in fact part of Spain. Eduardo Sotillos, the government spokesman, declared that the state would assert its 'autoridad legítima' [legitimate authority] in the event of any further acts like those in Tolosa, and the Spanish conservatives, then in opposition, described the Tolosa council's decision to send the Spanish flag back to Madrid as an 'ofensa intolerable' [intolerable offence] (*La Vanguardia*, 7 July 1983).

Another flare-up in the flag war occurred near San Sebastian, in Errenteria, a town of more than 40,000 inhabitants, suffering from industrial decline, rampant unemployment and high drug addiction rates. Although an HB stronghold, it was controlled by PSOE after the 1983 local elections, with nine PSOE councillors and the remaining twelve – who included five HB councillors – being Basque nationalists. HB asked for an extraordinary meeting of the town council to decide which flags should be flown on festival days. The mayor rejected the request for a meeting and simply directed that the Spanish national flag should be flown along with the local flag and the *ikurriña* (*Egin*, 21 July 1983).

On 21 July 1983, before the festival began, plainclothes police armed with truncheons and chains were guarding the town hall while HB sympathizers were protesting in the Main Square. In this tense atmosphere, and just minutes before the start of the celebration, violence erupted and dozens of people were injured in the clashes between police and protesters that followed. When, an hour later, with an empty Main Square and the sole presence of PSOE councillors inside the town hall, the Spanish flag was flown with the *ikurriña* and the local flag, the policemen applauded and made the 'V for victory' sign (*Deia*, *Egin* and *El País*, 22 July 1983).

Later that day the police left the town hall, taking the Spanish flag with them but leaving the *ikurriña* flying during the night. They returned the next morning and hung the Spanish flag again. That day, Basque nationalist councillors and festival organizers asked the government representative in the region to ban the flying of any flag. While demonstrators marched under a banner declaring yes for the *ikurriña* and no for the Spanish flag, the police fired live rounds into the air to discourage an attempt to burn the town hall Spanish flag. The celebrations were called off, although the mayor opposed the decision (*Deia* and *Egin*, 23 July 1983).

These events in Errenteria demonstrated the determination of HB to prevent any situation in which a normalized flying of Spanish national symbols was possible. A few weeks later, when the PNV mayor of San

Sebastian decided that during the local celebrations the Spanish flag would be flown with the local flag as well as the *ikurriña*, HB councillors entered the town hall without his permission and removed the Spanish flag (*Egin*, 16 August 1983). In contrast, the Socialist Party in Errenteria, recognizing that flying no flags during local celebrations would mean no official reminders that the Basque Country was part of Spain, reinforced its commitment to Spanish nationalism by flying the Spanish national flag, knowing that the police presence would lead to street clashes.

The determination of the PSOE government that the Spanish flag should be flown officially at least in large towns meant that even when a town council decided to avoid conflict by flying no flags the Spanish authorities intervened. That was the case in Bilbao where, although the PNV mayor tried to avoid displaying any flags, police officers entered the Town Hall and raised the Spanish flag with the local flag and the *ikurriña*. With police officers guarding the building for the festivals (*Egin*, 21 August 1983), Basque nationalist councillors declared that they would not enter the town hall until all the police and all the flags were gone.

While Basque national symbols were hegemonic in the non-official public sphere in the Autonomous Community of the Basque Country (a heritage from the 1970s and the widespread anti-Francoist opposition), and although informal display of Spanish nationalist symbols was deterred by the menace of ETA, a Spanish national identity was constantly reaffirmed by Spanish television, radio and newspapers. However, official buildings continued to be the only places where a Spanish flag could be flown as both the Spanish government and Basque nationalists understood that the future possibility of a banal and hegemonic national identity was at stake.

Conclusion

Michael Billig has stressed that the banal reproduction of national identities, far from being a matter of little importance, is in fact at the heart of preserving the established hegemony and social order. Hence, the situation in the Basque Country during the late 1970s and early 1980s cannot be explained away as being what the conservative opposition to the PSOE government, the former-Francoist Popular Alliance (Alianza Popular; AP) claimed, that is, a clash between Spanish democrats and totalitarian Basque nationalists. The AP, in calling for the pro-independence HB coalition to be banned, characterized them as hating Spain and Spaniards, and intending to impose their agenda on everybody else (*Egin*, 29 July 1983). The PSOE mayor of Errenteria had already made a similar point when he stated that 'unos pocos no deben nunca imponer al conjunto de la población sus ideas' [a few people should never impose their ideas on the whole population] (*Egin*, 23 July 1983).

On the opposite side the claim was made that 'al igual que el 14 de agosto de 1936 lo hicieron las fuerzas nacionales, colocaron por la fuerza de las armas la bandera española en el mástil del Ayuntamiento tolosarra' [just as the nationalist forces did on 14 August 1936, they placed the Spanish flag on Tolosa Town Council's flagstaff by armed force] (*Egin*, 14 July 1983). The flag war, however, was not, as HB would have it, a re-creation of the Spanish Civil War, nor did it reflect a Spanish nationalist government's intent to conquer an autonomous democratic Basque Country. With the more conservative PNV presenting itself in the flag disputes as trying to 'evitar males mayores' [avoid greater evils], the president of PNV, Xabier Arzallus, declared the flag war a chapter in HB's 'intento de agitación permanente' [attempt at permanent agitation]. He emphasized, however, that the presence of Spanish police in the town halls only served to reinforce the message of HB, creating as it did the appearance of 'una situación de país colonial donde hay que custodiar la bandera' [a colonial country situation, where the flag has to be guarded] (*Deia*, 25 August 1983). The Spanish government was aware that, however necessary to ensure the flying of the Spanish national flag during local celebrations in Basque towns, a police presence only served to undermine its democratic credentials in the region.

In the years that followed, while the flag war was never again to flare up with such intensity, a reminder of the 'hot summer' of 1983 remained during Bilbao festivals, where the town council decided to fly the Spanish flag for half an hour on the principal day of the local celebrations. The ensuing clashes between demonstrators and police were to become an annual event during the 1980s and 1990s (Perugorria 2010). However, the flag issue seemed gradually to settle down in the Autonomous Community of the Basque Country as two scenarios arose: wherever the town councils had a Basque nationalist majority, only the local flag and the *ikurriña* were present on the municipal balconies; where nationwide parties had a significance presence, the Spanish national flag was added. And in Navarre, where in 1986 and 2003 the regional parliament issued regulations prohibiting any official flying of the *ikurriña*, the ban was usually ignored by those town councils with a Basque nationalist majority.

If, after the flag 'hot war', we fast forward to 2012 and 2013, into what might be called the flag 'cold war' era, we find the Spanish government delegate in the region reporting more than 100 town councils as not flying the Spanish flag on their balconies. Some Basque nationalist mayors reacted by placing Spanish flags in the town halls and enormous *ikurriña*s in the main squares. Alongside the Spanish flag, several leftist Basque nationalist mayors, in calling for a multinational society, raised the flags of various immigrant groups (Bolivian, Ecuadorian, Moroccan, Nigerian, Romanian, etc.). Others opted to fly the rainbow flag, the Palestinian flag, the Spanish republican flag, and so on, alongside the Spanish flag.

Such responses have done little, of course, to abate the ongoing problems of sovereignty in Spain, although the flag wars in the Basque country have thrown the issue into sharp relief. As more recent events in Catalonia have amply demonstrated, whether only the whole Spanish people are the sole source of national legitimacy or whether and to what extent there could be a place for separate hegemonic identities in Spain is an issue that successive governments of the left and of the right have long struggled to resolve, and seem fated to contend with for the foreseeable future.

Bibliography

Aizpuru, M. (1998). 'El asociacionismo popular ¿reverso del modelo de organización social del franquismo? El caso de Barakaldo'. In S. Castillo, and J. M. Ortiz de Orruño (eds), *Estado, protesta y movimientos sociales. Actas del III Congreso* de *Historia Social de España*, pp. 477–92. Leioa: Servicio editorial de la Universidad del País Vasco.

Álvarez Junco, J. (2005). 'El nombre de la cosa. Debate sobre el término nación y otros conceptos relacionados'. In J. Álvarez Junco, J. Beramendi, and F. Requejo (eds), *El nombre de la cosa. Debate sobre el término nación y otros conceptos relacionados*, pp. 11–77. Madrid: Centro de estudios políticos y constitucionales.

Andrade Blanco, J. (2012). *El PCE y el PSOE en (la) transición. La evolución ideológica de la izquierda durante el proceso de cambio político*. Madrid: Siglo XXI de España.

Aoiz, F. (2005). *El jarrón roto. La transición en Navarra: una cuestión de Estado*. Tafalla: Txalaparta.

Archilés Cardona, F., and Martí, M. (2002). 'Un país tan extraño como cualquier otro. La construcción de la identidad nacional española contemporánea'. In M. C. Romeo Mateo, and I. Saz Campos (eds), *El siglo XX: historiografía e historia*, pp. 245–78. València: Universitat de València.

Archilés Cardona, F., and Quiroga Fernández de Soto, A. (eds) (2018). *Ondear la nación. Nacionalismo banal en España*. Granada: Comares.

Arriaga Landeta, M. (1997). *Y nosotros que éramos de HB: sociología de una heterodoxia abertzale*. Donostia: Haranburu.

Arrieta Alberdi, L. (2012). 'Por los derechos del Pueblo Vasco. El PNV en la Transición, 1975–1980', *Historia Del Presente*, 19 (II Épo), 39–52.

Arroyo Calderón, P., and Izquierdo Martín, J. (2012). 'Españolitud: la subjetividad de la memoria frágil en la España reciente'. In P. Arroyo, M. Casáus, C. Garavelli, and M. L. Ortega (eds), *Pensar los Estudios Culturales desde España. Reflexiones fragmentadas*, pp. 205–31. Madrid: Verbum.

Artime Omil, M. (2016). *España. En busca de un relato*. Madrid: Dykinson.

Balfour, S., and Quiroga Fernández de Soto, A. (2007). *España reinventada. Nación e identidad desde la Transición*. Barcelona: Ediciones Península.

Baraibar Etxebarria, A. (2004). *Extraño federalismo. La vía navarra a la democracia (1973–1982)*. Madrid: Centro de Estudios Políticos y Sociales.

Bastida, X. (2007). 'La senda constitucional. La nación española y la constitución'. In C. Taibo (ed.), *Nacionalismo español. Esencias, memorias e instituciones*, pp. 113–58. Madrid: Los libros de la Catarata.

Beorlegui Zarranz, D. (2017). *Transición y melancolía. La experiencia del desencanto en el País Vasco (1976–1986)*. Madrid: Postmetropolis.

Billig, M. (1995). *Banal Nationalism*. London: Sage.

Casals, X. (2016). *La Transición española. El voto ignorado de las armas*. Barcelona: Pasado & Presente.

Casanellas, P. (2014). *Morir matando. El franquismo ante la práctica armada, 1968–1977*. Madrid: Catarata.

Casquete Badallo, J. M., and Granja Sainz, J. L. de la (2012). 'Ikurriña'. In S. de Pablo, J. L. de la Granja, L. Mees, and J. Casquete (eds), *Diccionario ilustrado de símbolos del nacionalismo vasco*, pp. 508–31. Madrid: Tecnos.

Crameri, K. (2000). 'Banal Catalanism?', *National Identities*, 2 (2), 145–57.

Domènech, X. (2008). *Clase obrera, antifranquismo y cambio político. Pequeños grandes cambios, 1956–1969*. Madrid: Catarata.

Echevarría Pérez-Agua, J. J. (2017). 'La socialización foral en el País Vasco al inicio de la transición democrática'. In C. Ferrer González, and J. Sans Molas (eds), *Fronteras Contemporáneas. Identidades, pueblos, mujeres y poder. Actas del V Encuentro de Jóvenes Investigadores en Historia Contemporánea. Volumen 2* (Universita) pp. 77–95, Barcelona.

Egaña, I. (1994). *Ikurriña. Cien años*. Tafalla: Txalaparta.

Escribano, D., and Casanellas, P. (2012). 'La precipitación del cambio político (1974–1977). Una mirada desde el País Vasco', *Historia Social*, 73, 101–21.

Eser, P. (2016). 'La fiesta del Ogro. Canciones y lo carnavalesco en la cultura de la transición vaca (y española)'. In C. Collado Seidel (ed.), *Himnos y canciones. Imaginarios colectivos, símbolos e identidades fragmentadas en la España del siglo XX*, pp. 115–34. Granada: Comares.

Estornés Zubizarreta, I. (2013). *Cómo pudo pasarnos esto. Crónica de una chica de los 60*. Donostia: Erein.

Fernández Soldevilla, G. (2017). 'Terrorismo y nacionalización en Euskadi: el caso de la margen izquierda', *Sancho El Sabio. Revista de Estudios Vascos*, 40, 93–122.

Fernández Soldevilla, G., and López Romo, R. (2012). *Sangre, votos y manifestaciones: ETA y el nacionalismo vasco radical (1958–2011)*. Madrid: Tecnos.

Florido Berrocal, J., Martín-Cabrera, L., Matos-Martín, E., and Robles Valencia, R. (eds) (2015). *Fuera de la ley: asedios al fenómeno quinqui en la Transición española*. Granada: Comares.

Fusi, J. P., and Pérez, J. A. (eds) (2017). *Euskadi 1960–2011. Dictadura, transición y democracia*. Madrid: Biblioteca Nueva.

Gallego, F. (2008). *El mito de la Transición. La crisis del franquismo y los orígenes de la democracia (1973–1977)*. Barcelona: Crítica.

Geniola, A. (2018). 'El estado de la nación, las naciones del Estado. El socialismo español y la cuestión nacional/regional en la Transición', *Pasado y Memoria*, 17, 11–42. Universidad de Alicante. Departamento de Humanidades Contemporáneas <http://doi.org/https://doi.org/10.14198/PASADO2018.17.01> accessed 15 October 2018.

Granja Sainz, J. L. de la (2007). *El oasis vasco. El nacimiento de Euskadi en la República y la Guerra Civil*. Madrid: Tecnos.

Higgins, M. (2004). 'Putting the Nation in the News: the Role of Location Formulation in a Selection of Scottish Newspapers', *Discourse and Society*, 15, 633–48.

Izquierdo Martín, J. (2014). '"Que los muertos entierren a sus muertos". Narrativa redentora y subjetividad en la España postfranquista', *Pandora. Revue d'Ètudes Hispaniques*, 12, 43–63.

Jiménez de Aberásturi Corta, J. C., and López Adán, E. (1989). *Organizaciones, sindicatos y partidos políticos ante la transición: Euskadi 1976*. Donostia: Eusko Ikaskuntza-Sociedad de Estudios Vascos.

Jones, R., and Desforges, L. (2003). 'Localities and the reproduction of Welsh nationalism', *Political Geography*, 22, 271–92.

Jones, R., and Merriman, P. (2009). 'Hot, banal and everyday nationalism: Bilingual road signs in Wales', *Political Geography*, 28, 164–73.

Labrador Méndez, G. (2017). *Culpables por la literatura. Imaginación política y contracultura en la transición española (1968–1986)*. Madrid: Akal.

Landaberea Abad, E. (2012). '"España, lo único importante": el centro y la derecha española en el País Vasco durante la Transición, 1975–1980', *Historia del Presente*, 19 (II Epoca), 53–68.

Larrinaga Arza, J. (2016). *Euskal musika kosmikoak. Euskal musika popularra gizartearen isla eta aldatzailea*. Mungia: Baga-biga.

Law, A. (2001). 'Near and far: banal national identity and the press in Scotland', *Media, Culture and Society*, 23, 299–322.

Leonisio, R., Molina, F., and Muro, D. (eds) (2016). *ETA's Terrorist Campaign: from violence to politics, 1968–2015*. London: Routledge.

Letamendia Belzunce, F. (1994). *Historia del nacionalismo vasco y de ETA*. San Sebastián: R&B.

Marín Arce, J. M. (2016). 'La oposición del PSOE al tercer gobierno Suárez'. In C. Molinero, and P. Ysàs (eds), *Las izquierdas en tiempos de transición*, pp. 87–114. València: Universitat de València.

Mata López, J. M. (1993). *El nacionalismo radical vasco: discurso, organización y expresiones*. Leioa: Universidad del País Vasco.

Miccichè, A. (2012). 'Radicalismo y nueva imagen del socialismo en los años setenta: el caso vasco', *Historia del Presente*, 19, 9–22.

Molina Aparicio, F. (2009). 'Realidad y mito del nacionalismo español: bibliografía reciente y estado de la cuestión', *Historia y Política*, 21, 275–89.

Molina Aparicio, F. (2017). 'Violencia en comunidad. El terrorismo nacionalista y la política del miedo, 1976–1982'. In J. P. Fusi, and J. A. Pérez (eds), *Euskadi 1960–2011. Dictadura, transición y democracia*, pp. 129–50. Madrid: Biblioteca Nueva.

Molina Aparicio, F., and Miguez, A. (2012). 'Boinas, zuecos y política. Rerruralización ideológica e identidades española, gallega y vasca en el franquismo y la transición'.

In D. Lanero (ed.), *Por surcos y calles. Movilización social e identidades en Galicia y País Vasco (1968–1980)*, pp. 212–51. Madrid: Catarata.
Moreno Luzón. J., and Núñez Seixas, X. M. (2013). 'Rojigualda y sin letra. Los símbolos oficiales de la nación'. In J. Moreno Luzón, and X. M. Núñez Seixas (eds), *Ser españoles. Imaginarios nacionalistas en el siglo XX*. Barcelona: RBA.
Muñoz Mendoza, J. (2012). *La construcción política de la identidad española: ¿del nacionalcatolicismo al patriotismo democrático?* Madrid: Centro de Investigaciones Sociológicas.
Muro, D. (2009). 'The politics of war memory in radical Basque nationalism', *Ethnic and Racial Studies*, 32 (4), 659–78.
Núñez Seixas, X. M. (2004). 'Sobre la memoria histórica reciente y el "discurso patriótico" español del siglo XXI', *Historia del Presente*, 3, 137–56.
Pérez-Agote, A. (1984). *La reproducción del nacionalismo. El caso vasco*. Madrid: Centro de Investigaciones Sociológicas & Siglo XXI de España.
Pérez Pérez, J. A. (2013). 'Historia (y memoria) del antifranquismo en el País Vasco', *Cuadernos de Historia Contemporánea*, 35, 41–62.
Perugorría, I. (2010). 'La Aste Nagusia de Bilbao: génesis y estado actual de una tesis de doctorado', *Euskonews*, 542, 23–30.
Quiroga, A. (2009). 'Coyunturas críticas. La izquierda y la idea de España durante la Transición', *Historia del Presente*, 13, 21–40.
Quiroga, A. (2013). *Football and National Identities in Spain: The Strange Death of Don Quixote*. London: Palgrave Macmillan.
Quiroga, A. (2014). 'The three spheres. A theoretical model of mass nationalisation: the case of Spain', *Nations and Nationalism*, 20 (4), 683–700.
Quiroga, A. (2015). 'Michael Billig en España. Sobre la recepción de "Banal Nationalism"'. In P. Folguera, J. C. Pereira Castañares, C. García García, J. Izquierdo Martín, R. Pallol Trigueros, R. Sánchez García, and P. Toboso Sánchez (eds), *Pensar con la historia desde el siglo XXI: actas del XII Congreso de la Asociación de Historia Contemporánea*, pp. 4109–26. Madrid: UAM ediciones.
Rodríguez-Flores Parra, V. (2018). '¿Construyendo banalmente la nación? Comunismo e identidad en el tardofranquismo y la Transición'. In A. Quiroga, and F. Archilés (eds), *Ondear la nación: nacionalismo banal en España*, pp. 205–24. Granada: Comares.
Sassoon, D. (2001). *Cien años de socialismo*. Barcelona: Edhasa.
Saz Campos, I. (2012). 'Negativo y parasitario. El franquismo y la conmemoración de la nación española'. In R. López Facal, and M. Cabo Villaverde (eds), *De la idea a la identidad: estudios sobre nacionalismos y procesos de nacionalización*, pp. 247–59. Granada: Comares.

Skey, M. (2011). *National Belonging and Everyday Life. The significance of Nationhood in an Uncertain World.* New York: Palgrave Macmillan.

Taibo, C. (ed.) (2007). *Nacionalismo español. Esencias, memorias e instituciones.* Madrid: Los libros de la Catarata.

Tamayo Solaberría, V. (1994). *La autonomía vasca contemporánea. Foralidad y estatutismo (1975-1979).* San Sebastián: Instituto Vasco de Administración Pública.

Urrutia, T. (2006). *Alcaldes en lucha. El grupo de Bergara en la Transición. 1975-1979.* Tafalla: Txalaparta.

Wilhelmi, G. (2016). *Romper el consenso. La izquierda radical en la Transición española (1975-1982).* Madrid: Siglo XXI de España.

KATERINA GARCIA

Al tyempo del kuechko dulse: History, Language and Identity in Enrique Saporta y Beja's Account of Jewish Life in Salonika

ABSTRACT

Enrique Saporta y Beja's *En torno de la Torre blanca* [Around the White Tower] was one of the last works to be published in Judeo-Spanish. It is an homage not only to the Salonika of the author's youth, but, above all, to the traditional ways of life of his native Sephardic community. Conceived as a fictional, semi-autobiographical narrative against the backdrop of the Great War, it is fundamentally a testimony of a place and a time which no longer exist, yet which remain as a symbol of the resilience and prosperity of the Sephardim as a diasporic community. Ultimately, the novel is a monument to the Judeo-Spanish language, displayed in all its lexical and idiomatic richness; in the pages of *En torno de la Torre blanca*, language becomes an intangible dimension within which the collective memory of Salonikan Sephardim can be re-created and brought to life.

> La lingua maternal: [...] En ella vive tu pasado, en ella te sientes presente a ti mismo. Las palabras son tu verdadero lougar y tu esperanza.[1]
>
> — Marcel Cohen

Introduction

The novel *En torno de la Torre blanca*, written by Sephardi author Enrique Saporta y Beja (1982),[2] employs the Judeo-Spanish idiom *al tyempo del*

---

1 [The mother tongue: [...] There lives your past, there you feel the present within yourself. Its words are your true place and therein lies your hope] (Cohen 1997: 48). All translations are my own.
2 Saporta y Beja was born in Salonika in 1898 and died in Paris in 1984.

kuechko dulse [literally meaning 'at the time of the sweet seeds'] to convey a feeling of nostalgia for the lost times of his youth, when the Jewish community of Salonika was vibrant and prosperous; its closest English equivalent would be the 'good old times.' The expression *kuechko dulse* has its origins in the Sephardic marriage custom, whereby the bride and groom offer each other spoonfuls of nuts dipped in honey as a symbol of prosperity.[3]

En torno de la Torre blanca is one of only three major novels written in Judeo-Spanish in the second half of the twentieth century.[4] The Judeo-Spanish vernacular, also known as Judezmo, is the language of the Sephardic Jews, a distinct linguistic variety which has evolved in the areas of Sephardic settlement since their expulsion from Iberia at the end of the fifteenth century. As a diasporic language based on Hispanic Romance varieties, principally Castilian, it has absorbed a variety of linguistic influences which shape mainly its lexis and syntax. Among these influences are especially noteworthy the other linguistic varieties which form its Peninsular Romance basis, and the languages of the environment, such as, for instance, Turkish, various Slavic languages, Greek, Romance languages such as Portuguese and Italian and, particularly from the second half of the nineteenth century onwards, French. Once a commercial lingua franca spoken widely among the Sephardic population of the former Ottoman Empire, the Balkans and the North of Africa, where it is referred to as Haketiya, it is now (particularly since the Second World War) a severely endangered linguistic variety used to various degrees of competence by about 400,000 speakers, as reported by UNESCO (Moseley 2010).[5] In such a context *En torno de la Torre blanca* takes a highly significant place in studies of identity, yet, in spite of its unquestionable value in both historical and linguistic terms, it

---

3   I am indebted to Dr Evangelos Kapros for this valuable observation.
4   The remaining two notable works of fiction written in Judeo-Spanish in the post-War period are *El sekreto del mudo* by Itzhak Ben Rubi (1952), and *La Megila de Saray* by Eliezer Papo (1999). Among other works of Judeo-Spanish prose are, for instance, the novels written by Itzhak Ben Rubi and published in Israeli newspapers during the years 1954–67. See Gruss (2015).
5   According to estimates published on the web page *Ladinokomunita*, some 200,000 were in Israel (Alfassa 1999).

has received limited scholarly attention, and the purpose of the present study is therefore twofold.

First, it is intended, in outlining Enrique Saporta y Beja's work, to show that it was in fact an attempt to salvage what was left of the memory of pre-war Jewish Salonika (Thessaloniki), which at the time he wrote had been largely obliterated and 'belonged' only to those who still remained from its original pre-war Jewish population. Simultaneously, it offered the post-war generations of Salonika Sephardim an artistic recreation of the 'Mother City' in the times of her splendor. This image would in turn represent a link to their past (albeit a past re-imagined with tones of nostalgia), and as such become instrumental in the re-enactment of their identity-affirming narrative. The present study does not intend to provide a detailed literary analysis of *El torno de la Torre blanca* but rather briefly to explore its role in reconstructing the memory of pre-war Jewish Salonika and in securing its place in the collective imagination of Salonikan Sephardim.

Second, the author's linguistic strategies will be analysed, as the choice of language of composition, in this case Judeo-Spanish, is key to the authorial intent. Thus, the text of *En torno de la Torre blanca* also represents an invaluable source for the documentation of the Salonikan Judeo-Spanish variety, not merely as material for study in the area of Hispanic linguistics, but above all for its key significance as an important marker of Salonikan Jewish identity in a broader sense. In the pages of his novel, Enrique Saporta y Beja wished to preserve the richness of the Judeo-Spanish linguistic and cultural heritage, which was at the heart of his vocation as a folk collector and Judeo-Spanish activist. Salonikan Judeo-Spanish thus becomes not only a literary medium, but also a space in which the memory of a vanished past is recreated and brought to life.

Enrique Saporta y Beja

Published sources on the life of Enrique Saporta y Beja are unfortunately rather scarce and therefore the information provided here will focus principally on his work as a Judeo-Spanish folklore collector. According to Haïm-Vidal Sephiha's introduction to the edition of *En torno de la Torre blanca*, Saporta y Beja was born in 1898 in Salonika, at that time a major Ottoman port with a significant Jewish population,[6] into a Sephardic family of Spanish-Portuguese origin and Spanish nationality. His education was characteristic of middle- and upper-middle-class Sephardim: he received primary and secondary schooling in the privately run Lycée Français de la Mission Laïque Française, which was one of the many pro-European educational institutions founded in Salonika and other Ottoman cities after the 1860s, as the pro-Western reforms of the Tanzimat allowed Western European cultural and political influences to be introduced into the Oriental society of the Empire.[7] After obtaining his Baccalauréat, Saporta y Beja transferred to Paris, as did many young Sephardim from his socio-economic background, where he studied physics and chemistry, followed by a degree course in Medicine. He did not obtain his degree, however, as contracting the Spanish flu in 1919 prevented him from completing his studies, and thus pursuing a medical career. He decided not to return to Salonika, preferring rather to settle in Paris (a choice not uncommon among young educated Sephardim), where he remained until his death in 1984.

Saporta y Beja showed a keen interest in the language and traditional songs and proverbs of his native Judeo-Spanish community, and later in

---

6   At the turn of the nineteenth and twentieth centuries, Salonika's Jewish population numbered about 62,000, half of the actual population of the city. See Molho (1996: 75).

7   For a detailed analysis of the impact of the *Tanzimat* reforms on Ottoman Jewry see Levy (1992: 98–124). The principal institutions which were founded in Salonika with the aim of providing (in the views of European philanthropists a much needed) Western education to Ottoman Jewish children and youth were mainly the schools of the *Alliance Israélite Universelle*, the schools of the *Società Dante Alighieri*, and those of the *Anglo-Jewish Association* and the *Hilfsverein der Deutschen Juden*. While the majority of middle- and lower-middle-class Sephardic children attended the schools of the *Alliance*, the *Lycée Français* was, due to its high tuition fees, only accessible to children of the wealthiest Sephardic families. Very few Sephardic children attended Greek schools, even after the city became part of the Greek state in 1912. For a detailed analysis of the educational background of Salonikan Sephardim, see Lewkowicz (2006: 93–9).

his career became widely acclaimed as a prominent scholar and collector of Judeo-Spanish folklore.[8] In recognition of his tireless work as a folklorist and Judeo-Spanish activist, Saporta y Beja was elected first honorary president of the *Association Vidas Largas*, founded in Paris for the promotion of Judeo-Spanish in 1974 by Haïm Vidal Sephiha, foundational figure of Judeo-Spanish linguistics and first Chair of Judeo-Spanish at the Sorbonne (Sephiha 2001: 58). Simultaneously, its sister organization *Los Muestros* was established in Brussels. The ethos of the *Association* very clearly corresponded with Saporta y Beja's own interest in the safekeeping of the linguistic and cultural legacy of the Sephardic Diaspora: to the present day the *Association* organizes cultural events with the aim of promoting the Judeo-Spanish language and raising awareness of Sephardic culture and history. It also publishes works of Judeo-Spanish interest. Most important, however, it conducts the *Ateliers de judéo-espagnol*, regular linguistic and cultural gatherings and workshops with the participation of native Judeo-Spanish speakers, whose chief purpose is to gather and record the memory of a slowly vanishing tradition.

With the progressive displacement of traditional Sephardic communities into the areas of the so-called Second Sephardic Diaspora,[9] and particularly after the annihilation of the vast majority of European Sephardim in the *Shoah* [the Holocaust], Sephardic oral culture as well as its medium, the Judeo-Spanish language, were fast becoming relics of a rapidly vanishing past. In this context, Saporta y Beja's efforts as a folklore collector, language

---

8   Among Saporta y Beja's most noteworthy publications are: *Refranero sefardí. Compendio de refranes, dichos y locuciones típicas de los sefardes de Salónica y otros sitios de Oriente* (1957); *Refranes de los judíos sefardíes y otras locuciones típicas de los judíos sefardíes de Salónica y otros sitios de Oriente* (1978); *Selanik i sus djidyos (Salonique et ses juifs)* (1979).

9   The First Sephardic Diaspora begins with the expulsion of the Jews from the territories of Sepharad. The term Second Sephardic Diaspora denotes the transfer of Sephardic Jews from the communities of the First Diaspora to other geographical areas, mainly due to the cultural and economic transformations undergone by their primary countries of settlement at the turn of the nineteenth and twentieth centuries. The terms First and Second Sephardic Diaspora correspond to what Max Weinreich refers to as Sepharad II and Sepharad III, as opposed to Sepharad I, which denotes the Iberian Peninsula until 1492. See Weinreich (1980).

activist and ultimately literary author were not isolated: contemporary Sephardic testimonial literature,[10] which particularly from the 1960s and 1970s onwards acquires the form of autobiographical narratives (Romeu Ferré 2011), intended to record what could be salvaged of the wealth of Sephardic oral culture. Its main goal was to bridge the void in collective memory created by the *Shoah*, and to ensure the continuity of a cultural tradition which would allow for the transmission to the coming generations of fundamental aspects of Sephardic identity.

It is important to bear in mind that within the Ottoman Empire's complex demographic mosaic, the role of Judeo-Spanish as a marker of identity had historically been so central to the Sephardic diasporic experience that the language had become synonymous with its speakers' ethnicity and religious affiliation: proof of this is that among the various terms used to denote the language were *djudezmo* and *djudyó/djidyó*, Judeo-Spanish for 'Judaism' and 'Jewish', respectively. So strong was the identification of Sephardim with their language, that anecdotal accounts exist from as recently as the early twentieth century of Sephardim for whom it was startling to discover that someone might speak Spanish, and not be a Jew.[11] Similarly, the non-Jewish Ottoman population identified the Spanish language with Jewishness (Harris 1994: 217).

In more recent times, and particularly since the Second World War, Judeo-Spanish has found itself in a situation of severe linguistic

---

10   The renaissance of Judeo-Spanish literature occurred mainly in the sphere of poetry and, to a lesser extent, in prose. Among authors of testimonial literature particularly worthy of mention are the novelist and playwright Itzhak Ben Ruby and the poets Clarisse Nicoïdski, Salamon Bidjerano, Lina Albukrek, and Avner Perez, to name but a few. Noteworthy among Sephardic folklore collectors are Matilda Koen-Sarano and Jaime B. Rosa. There is also a significant body of Sephardic testimonial literature in other languages, which includes works by Annie Benveniste, Brigitte Peskine, Nelly Kafsky, and Jacques Aelion. See Sephiha and Weinstock (1997: 35–6).

11   As Tracy K. Harris (1994: 23–4) notes: 'It is true, according to various scholars such as Bunis […] that in the research literature of the nineteenth and early twentieth centuries the vast majority of Sephardim interviewed were not aware that they spoke Spanish or a Romance language. They only knew that they spoke "Jewish" or a Jewish language.'

endangerment. For numerous reasons, the language has not been inter-generationally transmitted,[12] and according to the sociolinguistic research conducted by Tracy K. Harris (2011: 51), the majority of fluent speakers are at present over the age of 70, and there are few people under the age of 60 who are capable of active language use; at the same time, the number of occasional users of the language, and of those who have acquired it through processes alternative to conscious inter-generational transmission (e.g. passive acquisition) continues to be relatively high (Varol 2000: 25),[13] and in the last several decades academic interest in the language has been consistently on the rise.[14] As well as that, Judeo-Spanish has a remarkable presence on the web and on social media, which encourages its learning and use among the internet community.[15] Nevertheless, Marie-Christine

12   Most notably the annihilation of approximately half of its speakers during the Second World War (these are total estimates and include the communities of Turkey, which were not affected; in Salonika, 96.5 per cent of the Jewish population were deported to concentration camps), and the subsequent reluctance of Holocaust survivors to transmit the language to their children. This was reportedly partly motivated by a fear that they would acquire a particular Judeo-Spanish 'accent', which was known to have revealed Jews to Nazi authorities during the German occupation. Last but not least, the imposition of the national languages of the new states which emerged in the wake of the dismantlement of the Ottoman Empire, gained new momentum after the Second World War and posed added difficulties to the maintenance of minority languages, including Judeo-Spanish.
13   Furthermore, field research undertaken by Mary Altabev (1996: 232–46) in Istanbul even revealed that within the local Sephardi community, young people take an active interest in the language and show active language competence.
14   Notwithstanding the endangered status of Judeo-Spanish as a spoken language, academic interest in Judeo-Spanish and Sephardic literature and culture in general has steadily risen since the mid-twentieth century. As Varol (op. cit.), emphasizes, Judeo-Spanish speakers generally no longer learn the language in their homes; however, they can acquire it in the classroom and in the academic sphere. For a complete account of academic institutions which currently provide Judeo-Spanish language tuition and promote academic research in the field, see Harris (2011: 53–60). Likewise, a comprehensive online review of existing initiatives focused on Sephardi language and culture can be found on the web site Sefardiweb, which is a project co-ordinated since 2006 by the Spanish Consejo Superior de Investigaciones Científicas.
15   For a fascinating analysis of Judeo-Spanish as a cyber-vernacular, see Romero (2017).

Varol mentions that Sephardic Jewish identity is nowadays rather manifested through the ability to alternate between multiple linguistic codes,[16] one of them being Judeo-Spanish: 'La mezcla lingüística es un rasgo de identidad. Los sefardíes son judíos porque hablan muchas lenguas y las pueden mezclar, siendo el judeoespañol la más mezclada e identitaria de todas' [Language mixing is a sign of identity. The Sephardim are Jews because they speak many languages and they can mix them, Judeo-Spanish being the most mixed and identity-bearing of all] (Varol 2000: 25).

This notwithstanding, Saporta y Beja's narrative is situated in a time when, despite being subject to pressure due to competition against local national and European languages, Judeo-Spanish was still the dominant spoken language of the majority of Salonika's population.

The Historical Background of the Novel

The plot of *En torno de la Torre blanca*, although essentially fictional, bears some clear resemblances with Saporta y Beja's own life.[17] The narrative follows the trajectory of Moises (Muchiko) Toledo, later known by his French name Maurice, from the day of his birth into Sephardi Salonika of the late 1890s, to the immediate aftermath of the First World War, when he returns from the French front to his native city in order to reunite with his family and marry his childhood sweetheart Esterina. Simultaneously, in the opening thirty-six pages of the novel we encounter

16   Historically, multilingualism and the ability to alternate between multiple linguistic codes was common among male Sephardim in particular. In fact, Yom Tov Assis (cited in Varol 2000: 23) argues that multilingualism was already intrinsic to the life of Jewish communities on the Iberian Peninsula, prior to their expulsion in 1492.
17   For the purposes of this chapter, the original spelling of *En torno de la Torre blanca*, which adheres to the Vidas Largas transliteration norm, has been maintained in all quoted passages: here *ch* represents the voiceless postalveolar fricative [ʃ], which corresponds to *sh* in *Aki Yerushalayim* standardized spelling (which was adopted in 1999 also by Vidas Largas in order to facilitate a unified orthography).

a parallel reconstruction of the history of the Toledo family: the author 'traces' their lineage back to the Castile of 1391, where one of their ancestors, Avram ben Moche ben Acher converts to Catholicism and adopts the surname of Toledo, which the family will bear henceforth. We then follow the vicissitudes of Maurisyo Toledo, his descendant who, 100 years later, secretly reverts back to Judaism and after years of precarious existence in fear of the Inquisition decides to leave Spain. After a painstaking journey to the Kingdom of Navarre and Bayonne beyond the Pyrenees, the Convert Maurisyo Toledo arrives and settles in Ottoman Salonika, a city which has been described to him as *Madre en Israel* – Mother City among the People of Israel.

The inclusion of this parallel historical context could be interpreted as Saporta y Beja's participation in what Bea Lewkowicz (2006: 85–6) refers to as the foundational myth of the cultural memory of Salonikan Jewry: upon the rupture of all ties with their ancestral Iberian homeland, their arrival in Salonika, a city that thanks to their industry and success would become known as the 'Pearl of the Orient', is, all the tribulations of exile notwithstanding, seen no longer as the tragic end of an era, but rather as the positive beginning of a new age of cultural brilliance and economic prosperity. Rather than the distant and, at times indeed cruel and hostile *Sepharad*, it is the welcoming Ottoman Empire and the prosperous Salonika of the late Ottoman and early Greek periods when Jews still enjoyed the privileged position of demographic majority and dominant economic power, which figures prominently in collective memory,[18] and which is re-created with nostalgia in the pages of *En torno de la Torre blanca*.

As the narrative brings us forward to modern times, we learn of the key historical events that shaped the political and demographic landscape of Northern Greece in the first half of the twentieth century: the constitution in 1903 of the *Balkan Alliance* of Greece, Bulgaria, Serbia and Montenegro, and their struggle against Ottoman Turkey for national self-determination; the subsequent Balkan wars of 1912–13 which brought the end of Turkish

18 'Collective memory' is understood here as defined by Maurice Halbwachs (1992): despite being based on individual processes of remembering, it is formed by the collective experience of a particular community, resulting in a shared memory and identity.

rule in the region; the Young Turks' revolution of 1909 (Mustafa Kemal Atatürk was born in Salonika); the capitulation of the local Turkish garrison in November 1912 and the occupation of the city by Greek forces; and, finally, the outbreak of the Great War.

The last, but by no means the least, of the historical events portrayed in the novel is the Great Fire of 1917, which had particularly disastrous consequences for the Jewish community, leaving some 70,000 of its members homeless and causing their emigration *en masse* to countries of the Second Diaspora, particularly Palestine, France and the United States (Pierron 1996: 96). This catastrophe, together with the influx of about 1–1.5 million Greek refugees as a result of the exchange of population minorities between Greece and Turkey following the Asia Minor Disaster in 1922–3 (Pentzopoulos 2002), contributed crucially to a demographic shift in the region and ultimately to reduction of the Jews to the status of a religious and ethnic minority within a predominantly Greek Orthodox society. The narrative concludes in 1918, however, shortly before these key changes take place, and thus the author leaves us with the image of 'Old Jewish Salonika', Salonika *al tyempo del kuechko dulse* [at the time of the sweet seeds], still resonant with Ottoman accents.

The Novel as Repository of Judeo-Spanish Folklore

Against this turbulent historical backdrop, and in the forefront of the narrative, we witness the unfolding of the day-to-day life of Salonikan Sephardi Jewry. We are introduced to all the significant landmarks in the life of the community (represented by the Toledo family and their friends and relations), whose daily existence is dictated, simultaneously, by the rotation of the Jewish liturgical calendar. Here Saporta y Beja's interest in Judeo-Spanish folklore is particularly well reflected: woven into the novel's narrative are a vast array of *kantigas* and *komplas* [traditional songs of diverse genres], and of course *refranes* [proverbs], aimed at illustrating in the most faithful and idiomatic manner possible the customs and life-cycle celebrations of the Sephardic community of Salonika in the first two decades of the twentieth century.

In his descriptions Saporta y Beja focused both on the public and religious spheres of Jewish life, as well as on the domestic and more intimate, offering a very detailed and vivid image of Sephardic life, in a wide range of social and cultural contexts.

The following passage, for instance, describes the customs associated with the traditional Sephardic wedding ceremony, at the same time listing several traditional songs which were performed on such occasions (1982: 42–3):

> Para eskapar la tcherimonia el haham,[19] a su torno dicho algunas palavras:
>
> [In order to conclude the ceremony, the rabbi in turn said a few words]
>
> 'Akodrate lo ke dize el Talmud: Ama a tu mujer komo a ti mizmo. Perkura de no provokar su yoro, porke el Dyo – benditcho El – yeva el kuento egzakto de sus lagrimas.'
>
> [Remember what is said in the Talmud: You shall love your wife as yourself. Make sure not to cause her to weep because God – blessed be He – keeps an exact count of all her tears.]
>
> El kiduch se eskapo. Los kombidados se mityeron a kantar en koro un ayre relijyozo. Despues, la djente vino a augurar 'besimantov'[20] i a abrasar el novyo i la novya. Esta, esmovida, estaba yorando ansi ke las kushuegras. Ma eran lagrimas de gozo.
>
> [The kiddush was ended. The guests, in unison, began to sing a religious air. Later, people started to come and congratulate and embrace the groom and the bride. The latter, moved, was crying, as were both mothers-in-law. But those were tears of joy.]
>
> El konsograje i los amigos fueron, estonses, a sientarse por grupos en todas las udas del apartamento. Las servideras pasaron, en primero, tablas de konfites[21] de almendra, kon rozolyo o kon una tira de kanella adyentro. Despues uvo grandes platos de dulse: de roza, de vijna o charope, kon agua arrefreskada kon bus del Hortyatch.

---

19 *Haham* (Heb. *hakham* [wise man]), in Muslim countries is the title given to a rabbi.
20 *Augurar besimantov* (Heb. *BeSiman Tov* [under a good sign]), to congratulate.
21 According to Claudia Roden (1996: 498), such *tavlas de konfites*, or trays of sweets, were a traditional symbol of hospitality in Sephardic communities of the Ottoman Empire. They were a particularly important gastronomical element on festive occasions such as weddings and engagements.

Los marrotchinos vinieron a su torno kon tajikos de almendra, de bimbriyo o de alhachu. Los kombidados asentados por amistades o por ofisyo platikavan a bos alta.

[The in-laws on both sides and friends were then seated in groups in all the rooms of the apartment. The maids walked around first offering trays of sweets made with almonds, with 'rozolyo' [rose liqueur] or stuffed with a piece of cinnamon. Then they brought large trays of sweets made with rose essence, 'vijna' [sour cherry jam] and sweet syrup, accompanied by water cooled with ice from Hortiach. Then the 'marroshinos' [meringue pastries] were brought in, decorated with pieces of almond, quince and 'alhashu' [almond nougat]. The guests, seated together with their friends and colleagues, were chatting aloud.]

El tchalgi se mityo a tanyer una kantiga tradisyonal de boda:

[The musician then began playing a traditional wedding song]

Eskalerika de oro, i de marfil[22]
para ke suva la novya a dar kiduchim,
venimos a ver, venimos a ver;
i gozen i logren i tengan mutcho byen.

[A little staircase of gold and ivory
for the bride to go up and take her wedding vows,
we came to see, we came to see;
may they have joy and prosper, and have great happiness.]

Ansi ke en todas las okazyones alegres de los sefarditas, se kanto romansas datando del sekolo XV.

[As on all happy occasions among the Sephardim, there was singing of songs whose origins date back to the fifteenth century.]

Avreme Galanika[23]
ke ya va amaneser
– Avrir, vos avriria
mi lindo amor,
la noche no durmo
pensando a vos.

22 This is the first verse from a well-known Sephardic wedding song entitled 'Skalerika de oro' [The Golden Staircase]. Variants of this stanza can also be found in other wedding songs in the Sephardic repertoire, such as 'Morena me yaman' [They call me the Dark One].
23 'Avreme Galanika' [Open, my beauty] is a very popular Sephardic song, found in several textual variants among the Sephardim of the former Ottoman Empire, sometimes under the title 'Avrix, mi Galanika'.

['Open, my beauty,
for dawn is near.'
'I would open,
my sweet love,
at night I cannot sleep
for thinking of you.'] (Saporta y Beja 1982: 42–3)

Transcending the public and religious aspects of life-cycle celebrations, the text at times provides the reader with fascinating details of the daily life of the community in its more intimate spheres. The following excerpt portrays a selection of nursery rhymes recited by Sephardic parents to their children:

Ma lo ke plazia mas a Muchiko era kuando su padre le tomava la mano i fazyendole koskiyas en la palma le dizia:

[But what Muchiko loved the most was when his father would take his hand and tickling his palm would say]

'Ven Muchiko, dame la manezika.
Aki mete uevo la gayinika.'

['Come here, Muchiko, give me your little hand,
Here the hen has laid her egg.']

I tomandole los dedos uno a uno kontinuava:

[And taking his fingers one by one he would continue]

Este dize kyero pan.
Este dize no ay mas.
Este dize vamos a arrovar.
Este dize: No, ke mos mata el haham.
Este dize: Por aki, por aki, por aki.

[This one says I want bread.
This one says there is none left.
This one says let's steal some.
This one says: No, the rabbi would kill us.
This one says: This way, this way, this way.]

suvyendo el dedo fista de debacho el braso i el ninyo se 'pichava' de reir. Djugava, tambyen kon el, a 'bau-tach'. Este djugo de kriaturikas konsiste a fazer taparse los ojos del bebe despues de averle mostrado una koza. Se eskonde sea en la mano o en el vestido. Se dize al bebe de abrir los ojos. Si no la topa presto, se la mostra en gritando: tach. Kuando en djugando el ninyo se mitia a sarnudar, al primer sarnudo Avram le dizia: Bivas. Al segundo: Kreskas i al tersero: 'Komo pechiko en el agua freska'.

[and he would bring his finger up to the boy's armpit and the child would start laughing with delight. He also played with him the game of 'bau-tash' [peekaboo]. This children's game consisted in covering the baby's eyes after having shown them an object. The object would then be hidden either in one's hand or among one's clothes. Then the baby would be called to open their eyes. If they didn't find the object fast, it would be shown at the cry of 'tash'. If at play the boy started sneezing, at the first sneeze Avram would say to him: 'May you live'. At the second sneezing: 'May you prosper', and at the third one: 'Like the little fish in fresh water'.] (Saporta y Beja 1982: 54–5)

In consonance with the documentary nature of the novel, the wealth of folk material collected by Saporta y Beja, of which illustrative examples have been shown here, is bestowed upon a receptive readership through the medium of Judeo-Spanish, his language of choice.

The Defining Role of Language in *En torno de la Torre blanca*

As Astrid Erll in her analysis of literature as a medium of cultural memory observes, in times of identity crisis literary authors tend to resort to traditional narrative genres (2011: 144–71). Such is the case of Saporta y Beja's novel: his *kuento romanseado*[24] is an homage to tradition – religious, folkloric, literary, and above all, linguistic. It is a monument to the linguistic and cultural memory of a people dispossessed of almost all physical landmarks reminiscent of their past. Although speakers of an endangered language may retain linguistic fragments or even diverse aspects of their culture which take on the role of foremost identity markers the reality is that with the vanishing of a language the greatest part of the oral tradition and a very significant portion of the cultural memory of a community is

---

24 [novelistic tale], as defined by the author in his own introduction to *En torno de la Torre blanca*.

lost (Grenoble and Whaley 2006: 50–68). While some traces may survive, however precariously, in translation, most of this unique material, which has been transmitted from generation to generation and which finds its most perfect and exact expression precisely through the native language, fades into oblivion. And this is exactly what Enrique Saporta y Beja attempted to prevent both through his pursuit as folk collector, and as author of *En torno de la Torre blanca*. His novelistic account appeals to readers not just as a picturesque and nostalgic image of a lifestyle and a place which no longer exist. The key function of the text is to portray and bear witness to a past whose memory is fading, through a *language* that is disappearing, in all its lexical and idiomatic richness. By describing in detail the life of Sephardi Salonika through his mother tongue, the author provides the necessary context for the language to reclaim its social and communicative role, and unfold in all its breadth of register. When all traces of the past have been eroded, when its physical territory has been altered beyond recognition, the only link existing between the author, his readership and 'sweet Ottoman Salonika' is memory and *language*. Language becomes an imagined space where memories of the past are brought to life, a space where all the rich traditions and lore of its people are recreated, a space where they can be preserved and saved from what Saporta y Beja calls *el negro olvido* (1982: 132).[25]

The link between language, memory and collective identity is particularly strongly experienced by the author's generation of Sephardi men and women who still possess the memory of a vibrant culture and its language,

---

25 [dark oblivion]. This sentiment is expressed in strikingly similar terms by Maurice Cohen (1997: 53) in his poignant *Lettre à Antonio Saura* [Letter to Antonio Saura], the bilingual letter that he wrote in Judeo-Spanish and French to the Spanish painter: 'Reyes deskaydos … Reyes deskaydos son los saloneklis. Deskaydos y, aindamas, viejizikos. En New York o en Montreal, en Paris o en Londra, los puedes ver indose komo pacharos enfermos ke se akodran del sol. "Ke jaber?", "Todo bueno" […] Ama se dan de pared en pared. No olvidar: esto es el negro puro' [Fallen kings … the Salonikans are fallen kings. Fallen, and old. In New York or Montreal, in Paris or London, you can see them wither like sickly birds remembering the sun. 'What is new?', 'All is good' […] But they are hitting against walls. They must not forget, for that would be pure blackness].

and who are painfully aware of their inevitable fall into obscurity and forgetting. Marcel Cohen describes in these terms the nostalgia of displaced Salonikan Sephardim, making an emphatic reference to the paramount role played by language in their collective historical experience:

> Se akodran del molo donde ivan a rafraganearse kon un trespil en la mano, de la Torre blanka ke los turkos yamavan Beyas koule, de las murayas komo el kal ke paresyan kaerse tanto ke se reflechyan en la mar. […] Se akodran ke, fin al siglo veynte, los exilados de Espagna no tuvieron ni el gusto de aprender realmente al grego o al turko, seguros ke stavan de avlar la mas precioza lingua del moundo, una lingua jalis sakrada, dulce komo la myel. Se akodran k'al siglo dyez y syete los merkaderes del orguyozo Louis el katorse se devyan de aprender djudyo para azer sus etchos en Grecia y Turkya, ke los primeros libros imprimidos en los Balkanes y Turkya lo fueron en ladino.
>
> [They remember the docks where they used to pass the time with a *trespil* [string of beads] in their hands, the White Tower which the Turks called *Beyas Kule*, the city walls so white they seemed to fall into the sea, so clear was their reflection in the water. […] They remember that, until the twentieth century, the exiles from Spain didn't really wish to learn Greek or Turkish, as they were certain to be speaking the most beautiful language in the world, a truly sacred tongue, as sweet as honey. They remember that in the seventeenth century the merchants of proud king Louis XIV had to learn 'Jewish' to be able to conduct their business in Greece and Turkey, that the first books printed in the Balkans and in Turkey were in Ladino.] (Cohen 1997: 54)

It is in this light that we must approach Saporta y Beja's text, for here language does not merely represent a medium of verbal expression: it becomes a statement of the intent and identity of the author.

The Edition of *En torno de la Torre blanca*

The first edition of *En torno de la Torre blanca* is an understated one, consisting of 337 pages of typewriter font, bound in soft, light green paperback. The front cover features the reproduction of a historical postcard of Salonika's most iconic landmark: the White Tower, *Torre blanka* for the Jews, *Beyaz Kule* for the Turks, and *Levkos Pyrgos* for the Greeks.

The editorial process was undertaken by Haïm-Vidal Sephiha, who wrote a brief introduction and linguistic notes, including a succinct guideline for the pronunciation of the vocalic and consonantal sounds of Judeo-Spanish. In his introduction Sephiha also emphasized the immense value of the text for future generations as a repository of the linguistic richness of Salonikan Judeo-Spanish:

> Grâce à En Torno de la Torre Blanka, nous voici en possession d'un excellent matériel d'enseignement de notre langue judéo-espagnole. Enrique y a accumulé le vocabulaire de la vie quotidienne et laissé ainsi aux futures generations de veritable pages anthologiques.
> Grâce à lui, le judéo-espagnol, sa langue maternelle, la nôtre, peut-être sauvé et perpétué.[26]
>
> [Thanks to En Torno de la Torre Blanka, we are in possession of an excellent document for the teaching of our Judeo-Spanish language. In its pages, Enrique has gathered the vocabulary of everyday life and thus leaves a true anthology for future generations.
> Thanks to him, Judeo-Spanish, his mother tongue, and ours, can be saved and maintained.]

Clearly, Saporta y Beja's work was from the outset envisaged not only as an important testimonial narrative, but crucially as a linguistic document and potentially also as a valuable didactic tool. It is therefore reasonable to presume that the author's choice of language register and selection of vocabulary also conveyed this intent to a considerable degree.

Transliteration and Orthography

Judeo-Spanish is a language which traditionally belonged to the sphere of orality and to rather informal domains, being occasionally transferred into writing mostly by means of Hebrew square script, *Rashi*

---

26 Sephiha (1982) from his introduction to *En torno de la Torre blanca*.

script or the hand-written cursive script known as *solitreo*. The use of Latin script became widespread only in the 1920s, and the transliteration of Judeo-Spanish shows a wide variety of uses which, in turn, is indicative of the fact that speakers adhered to the spelling conventions of the European languages through which they had received their 'Western' education. Given that until recently Judeo-Spanish did not receive institutional support of any kind, its spelling on the one hand generally reflects the geographical and/or institutional affiliation of the author, and on the other indicates the potential linguistic or didactic purpose of the given text.[27]

In his novel, Saporta y Beja embraces the Judeo-Spanish transliteration system promoted by the *Association Vidas Largas*. This choice seems logical, given his own French-medium education and background, and also given that it is the very system proposed by the organization that published his novel, and of which he was honorary president. However, I believe that the choice of this particular graphic format conveys added motivations: it makes the text at first glance strikingly different from contemporary standard Spanish texts as well as situating the author in a Francophone context; at the same time it emphasizes the uniquely Jewish essence of his work and its belonging to the Jewish cultural and linguistic tradition.

---

27   The adoption of a prescriptive orthographic norm, a reflection of a unified, centralized approach to language standardization, alongside the implementation of effective language policies, requires strong institutional support, as well as widespread recognition by its prospective users. Although there are institutions with the potential to achieve these goals, such as the Autoridad Nasionala del Ladino i su Kultura in Israel, this has not yet occurred with regard to Judeo-Spanish (which is defined, after all, by its diasporic character). Although the *Aki Yerushalayim* transliteration system (developed by Moshe Shaul and named after the journal published between 1979 and 2016) is the most widely accepted nowadays, there currently still exist several transliteration norms which reflect, to some degree, the orthographic conventions of the languages of the host countries in the Diaspora. Interestingly, suggestions and initiatives to apply Spanish orthographic norms to Judeo-Spanish have overall not been met with positive reactions on the part of native Judeo-Spanish speakers.

The Author's Choice of Register

Another key issue when addressing aspects of the use of language in *En torno de la Torre blanca* is the author's choice of register and the possible underlying motivations of his strategy. Just as would be expected in any other language community with a high number of speakers, Salonikan Judeo-Spanish of the first decades of the twentieth century was a socially stratified language. The language used by the Westernized and thoroughly Francophone upper and upper middle classes differed notably from the speech of the lower working classes, which was strongly infused with Turkish loanwords and turns of phrase. Avoiding both such extremes, Enrique Saporta y Beja chose to write in a register that was his own both by family background and by education, but which at the same time was sufficiently neutral to serve as a model of style for future learners of the language. It is a Judeo-Spanish devoid of any excessive Turkish influences, save the necessary lexical borrowings:

> En la vyeja sivda, 'al tchorro' (la fuente) ya avia una koda de mujeres venidas para intchir los kantaros i las kuvas. Despues atornavan a la kuzina, ke avian deslechado el dia entero, para asender el *odjak* yelado dezde vyernes la tarde. Se metian a gizar o, mas simplemente, a kayentar los restos del medyodia. Los ombres, eyos, asentados al portal de la kaye, djugando kon las *ambaras* del *trespil*, fumavan sus primer sigaro de la semana. *Avagariko*, la djente de retorno de la paseada entravan en sus kazas. En la *mehane* dezyerta a esta ora, un borratcho etchava su ultimo *mekan* komo una fletcha. Estava tinta i al salir penava para kaminar deretcho.
>
> [In the old city, at the fountain, there was already a long queue of women who had come to fill their jars and buckets. Afterwards they would return to their kitchens, which they had left unattended for the whole day, in order to light the *hearth* which had been cold since Friday evening. They would start cooking or simply heating up the leftovers from lunch. The men, sitting in their doorways and playing with the *beads* on their *strings*, smoked their first cigarette of the week. *Slowly*, people returned home from their walk. At the *inn*, which was deserted at that time, a drunkard finished up his last *glass* in a shot. He was tipsy and had a hard time walking in a straight line.] (Saporta y Beja 1982: 130–1, emphasis is mine)

The relatively small number of Turkish loanwords used by Saporta y Beja becomes evident when his text is compared, for instance, with those edited by David M. Bunis (1999) in his compilation *Voices from Jewish Salonika*, which recreate, for satirical purposes, the speech of traditional Salonikan Sephardim generally resistant to the modern ways of life *a la franka*. Alternatively, an analysis of the seminal *Dictionnaire du judéo-espagnol* by Joseph Nehama (1977/2003) reveals a large proportion of Turkish loanwords, which appear only moderately in the pages of Saporta y Beja's novel.

Saporta y Beja's style shows remarkably few Hebraisms, which were in contrast embedded in the register of more traditional, especially male, Sephardic speakers. Among the most common Hebrew loan words are the following examples, which generally occur in instances where religious practices or traditional customs are described (emphasis is mine):

> Ansina, el ninyo avia sido konsagrado djidyo. Resivyo segun la tradisyon el nombre de su nono porke era *bohor*.
>
> [And thus, the boy had been consecrated a Jew. According to the tradition, he was named after his grandfather, because he was the *first-born*.] (1982: 30)
>
> Se la dava atras a Muchiko ke la yevava kon kuidado al nono. Este despues de averse kitado los *tefilim* i ditcho su *beraha* lo asperava para salir.
>
> [He would give it back to Muchiko, who brought it carefully to his grandfather, who, after having removed his *tefillin* [phylacteries] and having said his *berakhah* [blessing] was waiting for him so they could leave.] (1982: 66)
>
> Enkolgado afuera de la ventana, el kanyel (komo una kacha fetcha de una red de tel muy fino) kontenia todos los komeres ya gizados protejyendolos de las mochkas, besbas i otras *hayekas*.
>
> [Hanging outside the window, the 'kanyel' (a type of container made with very thin wire) contained all the cooked food, protecting it from flies, wasps and other *insects*.] (1982: 62)
>
> Segun la tradisyon djudia se konsidera ke a los tredje anyos el ninyo pasa de la kondisyon de tchiko a la de ombre. Se konsidera tambyen ke le a venido el *sehel*. [...] A esta eda [...] el faze su '*bar mitzva*', esta resivido en la relijyon i puede kumplir *minyan*. Estonses puede tambyen kumplir el dezeo de todo djidyo, ke es ke el fijo diga el *kadich* a la muerte de su padre.
>
> [According to Jewish tradition it is considered that at the age of 13 a boy is no longer a boy and becomes a man. It is also believed that this is when he acquires the *use of reason*. [...] At this age [...] he undergoes his '*bar mitzvah*', he is welcomed into the

Jewish faith and he can account for a *minyan* [gathering of ten men, indispensable for the celebration of a religious service]. It is then that he can also fulfil the wish of any Jew, which is that the son will recite the *kaddish* [mourning prayer] for his father.] (1982: 114)

En buena *balabaya* ke era se okupava mutcho de su kaza, tenia syempre mutchos kombidados ke tratava a la grande.[28]

[Being a good *mistress of her house* she took very good care of her home, and she always had many guests which she treated in grand style.] (1982: 64)

Estas flores [las krizantemas] no eran, para los djidyos, flores de *bedahey* komo para los kristyanos.[29]

[For the Jews, these flowers [chrysanthemums] were not *graveyard* flowers, as they were for the Christians.] (1982: 95)

El numero de pyedrikas dava el kuento de las *berahas* ke se avian ditcho para ke la alma de la persona repozara en *ganeden*.[30]

[The number of pebbles represented the number of *blessings* that had been said so that the soul of the person would rest in *Heaven*.] (1982: 194)

The significant influence of Hebrew on the lexis of some registers of Salonikan Judeo-Spanish can be seen, for example, in the written memoirs of Sa'adi Besalel a-Levi (1820–1903), edited by Aron Rodrigue and Sarah Abrevaya Stein (2012) or, in a yet more notable manner, in Eliezer Papo's novel *La megila de Saray* (1999), which, although written in Sarajevo Judeo-Spanish, provides good examples of traditional Sephardic philosophical and religious discourse rich in Hebrew loanwords and syntactic calques.

Saporta y Beja's text shows only relatively moderate French influences, considering the general degree of Gallicization that Judeo-Spanish underwent after the establishment of the institutions of the *Alliance Israélite Universelle*,[31] and bearing in mind that the author spent most of his adult

---

28   *Balabaya* (Heb. *Ba'al ha-Bayit* [master of the house]).
29   *Bedahey* (Heb. *Beit ha-Chayim* [the house of the living]).
30   *Ganeden* (Heb. *Gan Eden* [the Garden of Eden]).
31   That the influence of French on Judeo-Spanish was otherwise generalized and reached truly overwhelming proportions was first emphasized by Sephiha (1991: 44–5) who even saw fit to coin the term *judéo-fragnol* when addressing this issue.

life in France. French loanwords are limited to contexts where the author's cultural and intellectual background manifests itself most evidently. A good example of this is a passage in which he addresses the interest and involvement of the Sephardim in issues of modern culture, politics and current affairs (emphasis is mine):

> Los *dirijentes* de la revolusyon del 1908 ke estavan afuera fueron yamados a Selanik. Maurice *vido de muevo su padre* en grandes konversasyones politikas kon sus amigos turkos i mamines. De muevo, favlavan de la limitasyon de las *libertas*, de la abolisyon de la konstitusyon i de *averse, el sultan, desbarasado* de los deputados *en aserrando* el parlamento. Los dirijentes de los 'Jeunes Turcs' seguros de *kontar sovre* las armadas de Masedonya (ke no avia segido la de Stambol) *detchidyeron de fazer* una martcha *verso la kapitala*.
>
> [The *leaders* of the revolution of 1908 who were away were called back to Salonika. *Again*, Maurice *saw his father* absorbed in heated political debates with his Turkish and Ma'min friends. Again, they discussed their limited *freedom*, the abolition of the constitution and *the fact that* the Sultan *had got rid of* all the members of the parliament *by dissolving* the institution. The leaders of the Young Turks, sure of *having the support of* the Macedonian armies (which had not followed that of Istanbul) *decided to organize* a march *on the capital*.] (1982: 205)

In brief, the style which Enrique Saporta y Beja presents through this work as representative of Salonikan Judeo-Spanish could be defined as that of an educated, middle-class, pro-Western speaker. His style is lively and rich in Judeo-Spanish vocabulary and turns of phrase, which is remarkable taking into consideration that *En torno de la Torre blanca* was written many decades after its author left his hometown and ceased to be immersed in the vernacular of his native community.

Saporta y Beja's portrait of Jewish Salonika *al tyempo del kueshko dulse* is, although set within a very concrete historical frame, in many ways atemporal. Similarly, the language through which the novel is rendered represents a self-enclosed, timeless linguistic reality, but one which is simultaneously deeply rooted in a concrete place: Salonika. So prominent is the role of language in Saporta y Beja's novel, and such is the care that has been devoted to its faithful representation, that one could even venture to argue that it is precisely Judeo-Spanish that ultimately emerges as the work's protagonist.

Guadrar sus Membrasyon kon Kavod i Onor[32]

En torno de la Torre blanca was from the outset intended to serve not only as the semi-fictional memoir of its author, but also as the repository of the collective memory of Salonikan Sephardim. Its author, *vis-à-vis* the near-disappearance of his native Jewish community feels compelled to bear witness to the vanished world of his youth: it is imperative that he, as one of the few who still remember, transmits his memories to the next generation:

> Es un kuento romanseado ke syerve de kuadro i de preteksto a una deskripsyon de los uzos, de las kostumbres i de las tradisyones de los Sefardis de Selanik (Thessaloniki). Si no es los de todos, es, al menos, de la majorita de eyos tal komo eran al empesijo de este sekolo.[33]
>
> [This is a novelistic tale which serves as a pretext to provide a description of the ways of life, the customs and the traditions of the Sephardim of Salonika (Thessaloniki). If not of all, then, at least, of the majority of them, such as they were at the beginning of this century.]

The process of remembrance of the city in pre-war times is particularly important given the fact that Salonika was, as attested by the historical context provided above, an unprecedented example of a successful and influential 'Jewish' city within the parameters of the Jewish Diaspora. The case of Salonika is also unparalleled in the manner in which its urban landscape was altered throughout the twentieth century, to the point of changing the city practically beyond recognition. After the Great Fire of 1917, a much-awaited urban reconstruction was undertaken, forever obliterating practically all traces of the city's Jewish quarters, which were the most severely affected (Fleming 2008: 77). The gradual process of Hellenization of Salonika, which had begun in 1912, was one that led, in a physical as well as intellectual sense, to the virtual obliteration of the historical and

---

32 [To keep their memory with dignity and honour.] From the author's foreword to *En torno de la Torre blanca* (Sephiha 1982).
33 From the author's foreword to *En torno* (Sephiha 1982).

cultural memory of the city. During the Second World War, some 96.5 per cent of the members of the local Jewish Community were deported to concentration camps, mainly Auschwitz.[34] In a further step which contributed to erasing any evidence of the city's pre-war Jewish prominence, the Jewish cemetery, which was once the largest in Europe and is described in detail in Saporta y Beja's novel, was expropriated under the Nazi occupation and donated to the Aristotle University of Thessaloniki, which used its grounds to build its campus, where visitors can still find scattered fragments of Jewish tombstones (Naar 2013).[35] Salonika, once renowned as the 'Jerusalem of the Balkans' and *Ir vaEm beIsrael*, 'Mother City among the people of Israel', *Saloniko* of the Jews, *Selânik* of the Turks and *Thessaloniki* of the Greeks, a city known by the polyphony of its many voices, became what historian Mark Mazower (2005) referred to as a *city of ghosts*. Although the contemporary Jewish Community of Thessaloniki strives to keep the memory of its long and illustrious past alive, their surrounding urban space has been entirely transformed, effectively turning Salonika from Pierre Nora's concept of *site of memory* into a *site of amnesia* (Nora 1997).[36]

Memory and identity are particularly tightly interwoven in the case of diasporic nations; moreover, as Baronian, Besser and Jansen (2007: 11–12) point out, 'memory – understood as the complex relation of personal experiences, the shared histories of communities and their modes of transmission – must be seen as a privileged carrier of diasporic identity'. In the pages of his novel Saporta y Beja attempted to evoke an image of Sephardic life when Salonika was still 'Mother City' to its Jewish children, recreating a landscape whose traces had been largely obliterated. In so doing, he offered the future generations of Salonikan Sephardim, both those who

---

34 Data provided by The Simon Marks Museum of the Jewish History in Thessaloniki.
35 Not until 2014 was a monument erected and unveiled on the grounds of the Aristotle University to commemorate the existence and destruction of the main Jewish cemetery of Salonika.
36 For an analysis of the official Greek discourse regarding the obliteration of Jewish memory in Salonika see, for instance, Naar (2013). For a breathtaking investigation of the city's depletion of its Jewish (and Turkish) landmarks, see Maurice Amaraggi's fascinating documentary film *Salonika, City of Silence* (2006).

remained within the original home community, as well as those in the Second Diaspora, a thread that would enable them to retrace their steps back to their past, and in so doing, to affirm and renegotiate their identity. This is key as, indeed, with the loss of collective memory, the contours of diaspora become blurred and ultimately effaced; and as Baronian, Besser and Jansen further observe, 'forgetting the trans-local diasporic connections means the ultimate disbandment of diasporic identity' (2007: 12).

Saporta y Beja's portrait of Jewish Salonika is, despite its genuine historical background, to a certain degree, mythical. Its Jewish community, as portrayed by the author, exists in a chronological contradiction of sorts, in what Carol Bardenstein (2007) terms *diasporic anachronism*. The lives of Salonikan Sephardim unfold as if 'out of time',[37] in an atemporal dimension which, as emphasized by Philip Bohlman, is a fundamental characteristic of diasporic essence (2008: 48–9). The collective time-line of Salonikan Jewry is framed by two liminal events which symbolize both its genesis and its near-destruction: *Gerush Sefarad*[38] and the *Shoah*. Within these two landmarks, Oriental Jewish Salonika figures in the collective imagination as a timeless image and powerful identity symbol.

It is important to note that the author's nostalgic evocation of the ways of life of old Jewish Salonika to which the Judeo-Spanish language is inextricably linked, is the ultimate expression of a very real sense of loss. It is the expression of a shared anguish that is experienced by Sephardim both individually and collectively and which has been caused by the drastic disruption of the way of life of their community. With the rapid decline in numbers of Judeo-Spanish speakers in Salonika as well as worldwide, it is in the realm of fiction that the memory of the 'Mother City' is brought back to life most vividly and where its language can be allowed to resonate in all its grammatical, lexical and idiomatic complexity. And it is this language, enriched with the many nuggets of popular wisdom collected in the course of his lifetime, that the author wishes the coming generations to know and cherish.

---

37 This is demonstrated by Lewkowicz (2006: 111) in her analysis of the accounts of some of her Salonikan interviewees, who referred to the arrival of their families from Spain as if it had happened only recently.
38 The Expulsion from Sepharad.

Bibliography

Alfassa, S. (1999). 'A Quick Explanation of Ladino (Judeo-Spanish)' <http://www.sephardicstudies.org/quickladino.html> accessed 30 July 2018.
Altabev, M. (1996). 'Judeo-Spanish in the Turkish Social Context: Language Death, Swan Song, Revival or New Arrival?' Unpublished PhD thesis, University of Essex.
Amaraggi, M. (2006). *Salonika, City of Silence*. Brussels: Nemo Films, WIP Wallonie Image Production.
Bardenstein, C. (2007). 'Figures of Diasporic Cultural Production: Some Entries from the Palestinian Lexicon'. In M.-A. Baronian, S. Besser, and Y. Jansen (eds), *Diaspora and Memory*, pp. 19–32. Amsterdam: Rodopi.
Baronian, M.-A., Besser, S., and Jansen, Y. (eds) (2007). 'Introduction: Diaspora and Memory', *Diaspora and Memory*. Amsterdam: Rodopi.
Ben Rubi, I. (1952; repr. 1953). *El sekreto del mudo*. Tel Aviv: Lidor.
Benbassa, E., and Rodrigue, A. (2002). *Histoire des Juifs sépharades*. Paris: Éditions du Seuil.
Bohlman, P. V. (2008). *Jewish Music and Modernity*. Oxford: Oxford University Press.
Bunis, D. M. (1999). *Voices from Jewish Salonika*. Jerusalem: Misgav Yerushalayim, Ets Ahaim Foundation.
Cohen, M. (1997). *Lettre à Antonio Saura*. Paris: L'Échoppe.
Eberhard, D. M., Simons, G. F., and Fennig, C. D. (eds) (2019). *Ethnologue: Languages of the World. Twenty-second edition*. Dallas, TX: SIL International. Online version: <http://www.ethnologue.com>.
Erll, A. (2011). *Memory in Culture*. London: Palgrave Macmillan.
Fleming, K. E. (2008). *Greece – A Jewish History*. Princeton, NJ: Princeton University Press.
Grenoble, L. A., and Whaley, L. J. (2006). *Saving Languages*. Cambridge: Cambridge University Press.
Gruss, S. (2015). 'El polifacético Itzhak Ben Rubí: un autor sefardí moderno', *Sefarad*, 75 (1), 163–79.
Halbwachs, M. (1992). *On Collective Memory*. Chicago: University of Chicago Press.
Harris, T. K. (1994). *Death of a Language – The history of Judeo-Spanish*. Newark: University of Delaware Press.
Harris, T. K. (2011). 'The state of Ladino today', *European Judaism*, 44 (1), 51–61.
Levy, A. (1992). *The Sephardim in the Ottoman Empire*. Princeton, NJ: The Darwin Press.
Lewkowicz, B. (2006). *The Jewish Community of Salonika: History, Memory, Identity*. London: Valentine Mitchell.

Mazower, M. (2005). *Salonica, City of Ghosts*. London: Harper Perennial.
Molho, R. (1996). *Les Juifs de Salonique 1856–1919: une communauté hors norme*. Strasbourg: Thèse de doctorat de l'Université des Sciences Humaines de Strasbourg.
Mosesly, C. (ed.) (2010). *Atlas of the World's Languages in Danger*, 3rd edn. Paris: UNESCO Publishing <http://www.unesco.org/culture/en/endangered languages/atlas> accessed 30 July 2018.
Naar, D. (2013). 'Jerusalem of the Balkans', *Jewish Review of Books*, 4 (1) <http://jewishreviewofbooks.com/articles/134/jerusalem-of-the-balkans/> accessed 30 July 2018.
Nehama, J. (1977; repr. 2003). *Dictionnaire du judéo-espagnol de Salonique*. 1st edn. Madrid: Instituto Arias Montano. Paris: Les Éditions de la Lettre Sépharade.
Nora, P. (1997). *Les Lieux de Mémoire*. Paris: Éditions Gallimard.
Papo, E. (1999). *La Megila de Saray*. Jerusalem: The Author.
Pentzopoulos, D. (2002). *The Balkan Exchange of Minorities and its Impact on Greece*. London: Hurst & Company.
Pierron, B. (1996). *Juifs et Chrétiens de la Grèce Moderne*, with an Introduction by Haïm Vidal Sephiha. Paris: Éditions l'Harmattan.
Roden, C. (1996). *The Book of Jewish Food: An Odyssey from Samarkand and Vilna to the Present Day*. London: Penguin.
Rodrigue, A., and Abrevaya Stein, S. (eds) (2012). *A Jewish Voice from Ottoman Salonica: The Ladino Memoir of Sa'adi Besalel a-Levi*. Stanford, CA: Stanford University Press.
Romero, R. (2017). '*En tierras virtualas*. Sociolinguistic Implications for Judeo-Spanish as a Cyber-Vernacular.' In S. Mahir, and J. I. Hualde (eds), *Sepharad as Imagined Community. Language, History and Religion from the Early Modern Period to the 21st Century*, pp. 275–90. New York: Peter Lang.
Romeu Ferré, P. (2011). 'Sefarad ¿la "patria" de los sefardíes?', *Sefarad*, 71 (1), 95–130.
Saporta y Beja, E. (1957). *Refranero sefardí. Compendio de refranes, dichos y locuciones típicas de los sefardíes de Salónica y otros sitios de Oriente*. Madrid: Instituto Arias Montano.
Saporta y Beja, E. (1978). *Refranes de los judíos sefardíes y otras locuciones típicas de los judíos sefardíes de Salónica y otros sitios de Oriente*. Barcelona: Ametller Ediciones.
Saporta y Beja, E. (1979). *Selanik i sus djidyos (Salonique et ses juifs)*. Paris: Éditions Vidas Largas.
Saporta y Beja, E. (1982). *En torno de la Torre blanca*. Paris: Éditions Vidas Largas.
Sefardiweb del CSIC: <http://sefardiweb.com> (ongoing since 2006).
Sephiha, H.-V. (1982). 'Introduction'. In E. Saporta y Beja, *En torno de la Torre blanca*. Paris: Éditions Vidas Largas.
Sephiha, H.-V. (1991). *L'agonie des judéo-espagnols*. Paris: Éditions Entente.

Sephiha, H.-V. (2001). 'The instruction of Judeo-Spanish in Europe', trans. B. Mitchell. *Shofar* 19 (4), 58–70.

Sephiha, H.-V., and Weinstock, N. (1997). *Yiddish and Judeo-Spanish: A European Heritage*. Brussels: European Bureau for Lesser Used Languages.

Varol, M.-C. (2000). 'La lengua judeoespañola, presente y porvenir'. *Ínsula* 647, 23–5.

Weinreich, M. (1980). *History of the Yiddish Language*. Chicago: University of Chicago Press.

RICHARD GOW

Patria and Citizenship: Miguel Primo de Rivera, *Caciques* and Military *Delegados*, 1923–1924

ABSTRACT

In 1923, General Miguel Primo de Rivera seized power in Spain and established a dictatorship that would last until 1930. Obsessed by a belief in Spanish decline and the threat of imminent national disintegration, Primo intended to reshape the Spanish national psyche and create a new, virtuous citizen. This chapter explores the rise and fall of the ill-fated Delegados Gubernativos [Government Delegates], members of a corps of military inspectors dispatched throughout Spain to reform local government and instil patriotism in the population. By contrasting official regime discourse on the Delegados with an original selection of letters sent to the government by ordinary Spaniards, the chapter shows that the Delegados' work proved to be unreliable and, often, damaging to the regime, a matter that rapidly put paid to Primo's messianic belief that the military could achieve his vision of national homogeneity from above.

Introduction

Shortly after seizing power in a *coup d'état*, General Miguel Primo de Rivera, the dictator who ruled Spain from 1923 to 1930, declared his intention to create a new citizenry in the towns and villages of the nation (*Gaceta de Madrid,* 21 October 1923).[1] Though not a belligerent in the First World War, Spain had been profoundly affected by the conflict and in 1917 entered a period of sustained crisis that the creaking, undemocratic institutions of the Restoration State (1874–1923) seemed unable to overcome, culminating in this six-year period of dictatorship. From its

1 La Gaceta de Madrid is the former name of the Spanish State gazette of record.

outset, the Primo de Rivera regime was motivated by an obsession with the perceived threat of imminent national disintegration and by a belief that Spain was afflicted by a backwardness brought on by the widespread political demobilization that had previously facilitated the predictable alternation of the main Restoration political parties in government, the so-called *Turno Pacífico* [Peaceful Turn].[2] In its attempts to overcome these dangers, the regime made a considerable impact on the development of right-wing thought in Spain by articulating an anti-liberal ideology that was both modernizing and nationalist, threads that had not yet been synthesized coherently by any mainstream Spanish political movement.

For Primo de Rivera, Spanish political modernity was to be realized largely through mobilization of the population and nationalism became the primary tool through which the previously apathetic masses were to be reconciled to the State in the form of citizens. This led the regime to carry out a programme of indoctrination aimed at educating the population in the values of a new, authoritarian national identity that would replace the identity promoted by the seemingly moribund liberal State, a process of 'mass nationalization'.[3] While the regime, like its many authoritarian counterparts in inter-war Europe, made use of such means as the public education system, cultural associations and the pageantry of mass rallies and ceremonies for this purpose, the nationalizing project launched in the earliest months of the Spanish dictatorship was perhaps best embodied by the curious and ill-fated figure of the *Delegado Gubernativo* [Government Delegate].

Appointed by decree in October 1923, a little over one month after Primo's *coup d'état* against the Liberal government of Manuel García-Prieto, these military functionaries were charged with assisting the army officers that Primo installed as Governors in each of Spain's forty-nine provinces in the task of inspecting and reforming municipal and provincial government, a notorious site of political corruption at this time (*Gaceta de Madrid*,

---

2   All translations are my own; however, I have transcribed the original Spanish inclusive of any orthographical errors that are present in the source material. I would like to thank both the editors of this volume and its anonymous peer reviewers for their helpful comments on earlier drafts of this chapter.

3   This is the central thesis in Quiroga (2007). On the Italian case see Gentile (1996). On the German case see Mosse (1974/2001).

21 October 1923). As the next section will outline in more detail, Primo regarded municipal reform as an important nationalist cause and, accordingly, assigned a critical role to the Delegados in this process: first, they were to root out and eliminate the patronage networks of *caciques* [local political bosses], the class of local notable that had dominated municipal life during the Restoration era and, in the eyes of the dictator, inhibited the spirit of citizenship in the population; then, once the corrupting influence of *caciquismo* [domination by caciques] had been stamped out, the Delegados were to set about catalysing the emergence of the regime's new, prototypical Spanish citizen through cultural and propagandistic means. This would require them to serve in a tutelary role to the population and curate ambitious programmes of patriotic ceremonies and events, while also promoting participation in healthy, civic-minded organizations such as gymnastics clubs, scout troops and the regime's two key institutions, the *Somatén Nacional* [National Somatén], its militia, and *Unión Patriótica* [Patriotic Union], the single party.[4]

The Delegados, as figures that came to exert a considerable influence on municipal politics in the earliest months of the dictatorship, served as a public face for the new administration and featured prominently in the everyday lives of local residents. Their near ubiquity for this short period of time is reflected in the many letters sent by ordinary Spaniards to the government on the topic of reform, one of the few channels of public expression to be tolerated openly by an otherwise highly repressive regime. This chapter examines the Delegados' inspectorial work during the first eighteen months of the dictatorship and situates it in the wider context of the regime's nationalizing programme in an exploration of a series of correspondences between the population and the authorities from this time.[5] It argues that while public enthusiasm for the Delegados was initially high, their efforts soon proved damaging to the image of the regime;

---

4   The *Somatén* was a Catalan parapolice organization of medieval origin that was co-opted by the regime and extended nationwide shortly after Primo's seizure of power in September 1923.

5   While the work of the Delegados has already featured in a number of other studies, these have tended to consider their two main roles separately. Such studies include Tusell (1977: 85–115), González Calbet (1987: 152–7) and Quiroga (2004).

indeed, as the letters clearly reveal, these officers knew very little about the nation they were supposed to be exalting, a fact that profoundly undermined Primo's belief that the army could lead the national regeneration which he proposed.

Such an approach sits well with recent developments in the historiography of contemporary Spain. Although previously neglected as a topic of inquiry, a burgeoning literature on the nationalization process in Spain has emerged in the last decade.[6] Earlier trends in the field had tended to emphasize what scholars perceived as a failure by the State to impose a cohesive national identity on the population, along with the resulting tension between the *patria* [homeland], that is, the nation or national community on a grand scale, and the *patria chica* [small homeland], the more localized realm of everyday existence.[7] However, as argued by scholars outside Spain beginning in the 1990s, national identification should, in fact, be considered something 'grounded in everydayness and mundane experience' (Eley and Grigor Suny 1996: 22). More recent Spanish scholarship has assimilated this broad view into a new generation of studies that suggest that national and locally oriented identities were not necessarily dichotomous and could co-exist quite successfully. Moreover, an expanding body of research has argued that regional identification could serve as a nationalizing channel and that individuals could move between these overlapping identities quite fluidly as it suited them. Indeed, by the time of the dictatorship, the boundaries of the *patria chica* had expanded somewhat to incorporate one's province, as well as one's village or town.[8]

The influence of the new 'history from below' on the study of Spanish nationalism is quite apparent in these developments. This movement has its origins in the work of Lucien Fevre and the French *Annales* School and

---

6   As a point of departure, see the numerous essays in Moreno Luzón (2007a; 2007b); Vega and Calle (2010); Saz Campos and Archilés Cardona (2011; 2012); Gabriel et al. (2013); Luengo Teixidor and Molina Aparicio (2016).

7   The *patria chica* might be thought of as a Spanish equivalent to Ferdinand Tönnies' concept of *Gemeinschaft*.

8   For a discussion of these developments see Molina Aparicio and Cabo Villaverde (2012). A number of studies reflect these developments: Quiroga (2013b); Archilés Cardona (2013); Molina Aparicio (2013).

in the celebrated studies in English by E.P. Thompson (Beyen and Van Ginderachter 2012: 4). In the 1970s and 1980s the German *Alltagsgeschichte* [history of everyday life] built upon this considerably and began to apply similar methodologies to the study of dictatorship, particularly the Nazi regime. The *Alltag* historians' work was rather idealistic, however, and rejected the notion that power relations have an 'unequivocal disciplining effect' on individuals, highlighting instead the means through which ordinary people resisted the discourses of power that surrounded them. The result of this was that, for all its promise, the *Alltag* trend tended to marginalize national history or avoid it altogether (Berger 2005: 659). In contrast to this, the history written after the cultural and linguistic turns in the humanities has wholeheartedly embraced both the nation and the idea that it is a discursively constructed entity. However, as Marnix Beyen and Maarten Van Ginderachter (2012) have written, while such scholarship mostly rejected that this cultural constructivism was entirely elite-driven, it tended to 'critically [engage] its modernist aspects rather than the popular impact of nationalizing policies in the nineteenth and twentieth centuries'. This has left significant gaps in the study of nationalism in Spain and elsewhere. As Beyen and Van Ginderachter (2012: 10) argue further, inquiry into the role played by low- and middle-ranking State functionaries like the Delegados in executing the nationalizing policies devised by political and administrative elites is an essential but largely unexplored element of the history of nationalism.

Insofar as Beyen's and Van Ginderachter's observations apply to this chapter, while we may debate the degree of creative input which each Delegado had into these policies, it is clear that these functionaries operated at an intermediate level between the military government's extremely narrow executive in Madrid and the people of towns and villages of Spain. The letters written by ordinary people about their daily interactions with the Delegados, therefore, offer us a privileged insight into the mechanics of this nationalizing process from the bottom up. The experiences which they narrate show us how personal, local and national identities overlapped, informed and competed with one another at this time. In this way, an examination of the work of the Delegados can help us to reconcile the history-from-below approach to nationalism with the modernist, top-down and typically State-centric perspectives of historians of nationalization processes, like Eugen Weber (1976) and George Mosse (1974/2001), and apply them fruitfully to the Primo de Rivera dictatorship.

Municipal Reform as a Nationalist Cause

There existed a long precedent to Primo de Rivera's thinking on the need for municipal reform in Spain. Acerbic critiques of the local government structures there became a trope of the *fin-de-siècle* regenerationist writing that entered the popular imaginary after the nation's traumatic capitulation to the United States of America in the Spanish–American War of 1898.[9] Writers like Miguel de Unamuno, Joaquín Costa and Ángel Ganivet espoused the centrality of Castile and its culture to the Spanish nation, while identifying the municipality as the point of departure for national regeneration (Quiroga 2007).[10] *Caciquismo*, the clientelist and often corrupt practices associated with caciques, was, as one historian has written, presented as 'the key to explaining the backwardness of Spain and the overriding obstacle to the urgent modernization of the country' (Moreno Luzón 2007b: 419).[11] Caciques themselves were important middle-men in the fraudulent elections behind the *Turno Pacífico*. In exchange for obtaining the votes required to produce contrived parliamentary majorities, caciques received preferential access, favours and shares of State resources from the government of the day, which they, in turn, distributed to their own clients as largesse. The result of this was, as Primo and others saw it, a political system which tended to favour local interests at the expense of collective and

9 A concise description of these writings can be found in Pro Ruíz (1998), pp. 191–215 particularly.
10 Key regenerationist works include Macías Picavea (1899); Morote (1900); Unamuno (1902); Costa y Martínez (1902); Ganivet (1905).
11 Javier Moreno Luzón's article provides an invaluable overview of the historiographical debates surrounding caciquismo.

national ones.[12] However, while the Turno initially proved both stable and flexible enough to incorporate most dissenting voices into its fold, an increasing sense of *fin-de-siècle* cultural pessimism and Spain's defeat in 1898 combined to attract a new scrutiny to the institutions of the Restoration State. Patronage and rule by notables was by no means a uniquely Spanish phenomenon, as scholars of Italy, France, Britain and, further afield, America, will attest, yet it was seized upon by cultural critics and reform-inclined politicians as an indication of Spain's national decadence.[13] As José Álvarez Junco (1996: 76–80) has argued, caciquismo, therefore, came to be denounced in nationalist terms by modernizing elites who wished to see State resources distributed in a manner more favourable to the aggrandizement of Spain.

The period 1907–12 saw major efforts by both leading political parties, the Conservatives and the Liberals, to carry out municipal reform. The first, which came about during the so-called *gobierno largo* [long government] of Conservative leader Antonio Maura, from 1907 to 1909, was an attempt to realize a *revolución desde arriba* [revolution from above] that would pre-empt any violent one from below by drawing *las masas neutrales* [the neutral masses] of the Spanish population into political life. A new electoral law introduced by Maura during this drive for reform ushered in obligatory (but not secret) voting and removed the task of supervising the electoral register from municipal governments, thus depriving caciques of two of the principal tools they used for vote management.[14] A second law,

12 More recent scholarship, however, has emphasized the caciques' role as largely independent gatekeepers, who used their influence to act as intermediaries in interactions between centre and periphery, rather than as the representatives of repressive or feudal agrarian interests. See Álvarez Junco (1996), particularly pp. 76–80.
13 On clientelism in Europe generally, see Piattoni (2001). For the American context, see Shefter (1994).
14 Maura's reforms revealed his general distaste for politicking. Article 29 of his reform law provided that no ballot would be required to return deputies to parliament in constituencies where there was just one candidate for election. While Maura's intention may have been to reduce the electoral system's exposure to manipulation as part of the campaigning and voting processes, the measure effectively disenfranchised vast sections of the population who were not afforded the opportunity to vote at all. In the general election of April 1923, shortly before Primo de Rivera's seizure of power, for example, 146 of the 437 deputies that were elected were returned to the Congress on this basis.

aimed at directly reforming the local administration, sought to give greater independence to municipal governments and to introduce a corporative system of voting to local elections. The project, however, faced significant resistance across both major political parties and had not yet been completed when the government collapsed in the aftermath of the Tragic Week in 1909. Maura's personal intransigence meant that he would remain out of government until 1918, although his thinking would influence Primo in the 1920s.[15] In 1911, the Liberal Prime Minister José Canalejas, who led an anti-clerical ministry from 1910 until his assassination by an anarchist gunman in 1912, reformed the manner in which personal tax contributions were calculated by the cacique-controlled local governments of Spain, thus achieving a long-standing goal held by progressive parliamentarians (Moreno Luzón 1996: 174). However, his attempt to democratize compulsory military service – potentially a key channel for mass nationalization, though in reality a notorious hotbed of corruption – was only a limited success as it retained partial monetary exemptions for those who could afford them (Balfour 1997: 206–9). The escalation of Spain's military campaigns in Morocco, followed by the outbreak of the First World War and the prolonged crisis it engendered, largely halted further efforts at reform until the advent of the dictatorship in 1923.[16]

As this was occurring, a distinct military-regenerationist discourse emerged within the Spanish officer corps, which had come to view itself as the only institution capable of leading reform of the political system.[17] Primo de Rivera was steeped in this culture as a junior and middle-ranking officer, and shared many of its sentiments, as he explained in the prologue of a textbook on military education published some years before his seizure of power (Primo de Rivera 1916: xi–xv). On the third anniversary of the

---

15   A concise treatment of Maura's character and political reforms can be found in González Hernández (1997).

16   Attempts made by Santiago Alba in 1913 and Manuel Burgos y Mazo in 1919, respectively, to combat the over-representation of cacique-dominated rural areas in parliament by modifying electoral boundaries and by introducing proportional representation were not passed by parliament (Moreno Luzón 1996: 182–3).

17   See Espadas Burgos (1984); (1996). For a study of a number of the thinkers behind this see Jensen (2002).

dictatorship, he summarized the vision that drove his efforts to regenerate Spain: 'Célula principal de la nación ha de ser el Municipio,' [The main cell of the nation must be the municipality] he stated in the typical biological metaphor of the regenerationists, 'y de él, la familia, con sus rancias virtudes y su moderno concepto ciudadano. Núcleo la provincia, y vértebra principal que dirija y riegue todo el sistema, el Estado' [and of this the family, with its traditional virtues and its modern civic ideas. The nucleus will be the province, and the State will be the main vertebra, which directs and regulates the whole system] (Primo de Rivera 1930: 99). On this basis, caciquismo, the corruptor of municipal life, was presented by the regime as one of the chief ills of the Spanish nation, the eradication of which was to be one of the dictator's priorities and considered foundational to establishing a new national, as opposed to local, identity.

It was in this light that Primo followed his *coup d'état* in 1923 with a series of purges aimed at both the political class in Madrid and the municipal administrations in the towns and villages of the country. Article Four of the decree which established the Military Directorate on 15 September 1923 suppressed the Council of Ministers and all posts of Minister of the Crown, except for Primo's own. The following day the combined *Cortes* (the Congress of Deputies and the Senate) were dissolved and a number of constitutional guarantees suspended nationwide. The same decree dismissed the Civil Governors (roughly equivalent to France's *Préfets*) of Spain's 49 provinces and replaced them with their equivalents from the military hierarchy, the Military Governors (Romero-Maura 1977: 54). On 30 September, Primo proceeded to dissolve the nation's 9,254 *Ayuntamientos* [municipal councils] *en masse* and summarily dismissed their councillors, mayors and secretaries in what was the most far-reaching purge of all. The same law provided that the deposed councillors should be replaced in the first instance by each Ayuntamiento's cohort of *Vocales asociados* [Associate Members], a secondary group of representatives who had a more limited role in local affairs and were elected on a corporate basis.[18] The immediate task of these Vocales asociados was to select a new mayor for their municipality from

---

18   The role of the Vocales asociados was set out in the Municipal Law of 1877. Their main function prior to the dictatorship was to approve municipal budgets.

amongst their members.[19] Some three and a half months after the dissolution of the Ayuntamientos, Primo de Rivera also dismissed the nation's *Diputaciones* [provincial assemblies], although the extent of reform at this level was much more limited than in municipal government (*Gaceta de Madrid*, 13 January 1924).

On 9 October, the newly appointed Military-Civil Governors received orders from Madrid to begin a general inspection of the Ayuntamientos in each province with the expressed aim of purging any public administrators they suspected of caciquismo (González Calbet 1987: 221). There was considerable public anticipation of the inspections which Primo promised but by the end of 1923 only 815 had been carried out, a figure that represented less than 10 per cent of the Ayuntamientos in Spain.[20] Public frustration at the pace of reform often translated into a fear of being forgotten by the regime, a theme that recurred in many of the letters sent to the government. As one resident of the village of Potes (Santander) complained in December 1923, 'Aquí en este rincón apenas hemos sentido la influencia benéfica del Directorio. No ha habido inspección en ningún ayuntamiento, aunque algunos bien lo necesitan, y se dice que ni la habrá' [Here in these parts we have barely felt the beneficial influence of the Directorate. There has not been an inspection in any of the Ayuntamientos, even though some really need it, and they are saying that neither will there be]. He wondered what the effect of this would be on the morale of the population, before concluding rather forlornly that there was 'un poquito de desconfianza, de que aquí todo quedara igual' [a little bit of suspicion, that everything will remain the same here].[21]

The reach of government inspections may have been limited at this time but the regime had at its disposal another important tool in its efforts to reform local government in the manner it envisaged. In his initial manifesto

---

19 For the laws suppressing the Cabinet, suspending the Cortes and collectively dissolving the Ayuntamientos, respectively, see *Gaceta de Madrid* (16 and 17 September, and 1 October 1923).

20 The figures cited are drawn from a *nota oficiosa* [informal note] written by Primo in December 1923 and reproduced in Soldevilla (1923: 453–4).

21 Archivo Histórico Nacional (henceforth AHN), Primo, Bundle 56, File 2071, 11 December 1923.

to the Spanish people, 'Al País y al Ejército' [To the Country and the Army], Primo de Rivera encouraged a wave of popular denunciation against caciques and corrupt officials by promising to punish 'implacablemente a los que delinquieron contra la Patria' [relentlessly those who have committed crimes against the *Patria*], while guaranteeing 'la más absoluta reserva para los denunciantes' [the most absolute discretion to accusers] (Primo de Rivera 1929: 22). The population responded enthusiastically to the invitation, delivering large numbers of accusations to the government by mail over the first four months of the dictatorship. Alarmingly, however, these letters soon began to denounce the corruption present in the new municipal councils that had just been installed by the military government in the same language that they used to condemn the caciques who had controlled the municipal councils of old. This convinced Primo de Rivera of the need for significant modifications to the new councils although, in the absence of a popular movement from which to draw loyal cadres, he was forced to turn to the military to provide a temporary solution, creating the post of Delegado Gubernativo on 20 October 1923.

The dictator envisaged the Delegados' work as both a continuation of the inspections that were being carried out in the Ayuntamientos and a means of laying the social and political foundations of the future local administration upon which a regenerated sense of nationhood would be built. In the preamble to the decree which created the role, Primo stated that these figures were to give Spanish villages 'la sensación de una nueva vida, impulsándolos y ayudándolos a emprenderla' [the feeling of a new life, to drive them on and help them to set out on it] (*Gaceta de Madrid*, 21 October 1923). As the immediate delegates of the Madrid-controlled Military-Civil Governors in each province, the Delegados were each assigned to a provincial district or capital and given near limitless powers to intervene in municipal politics, making them the final piece in the full, though temporary, militarization of the public administration in Spain. Despite the faith Primo placed in them to rescue the nation from the grip of the caciques, however, he maintained a tight grip over the Delegados and controlled them in a short and vertical chain of command that led from each officer to their provincial Governor and on to the regime's *de facto* number-two, General Severiano Martínez Anido, the Subsecretary of the

Ministry of the Interior.[22] After a series of delays which led to the original decree being referred to in the press mockingly as 'el decreto fantasma' [the ghost decree], 523 Delegados were finally appointed in December 1923, of whom 434 served in judicial districts (provincial subdivisions) and eighty-nine at provincial level. With these provisions at last in place, a new sense of nationhood, of Patria as envisioned by Primo de Rivera, might have been thought to be set on the road to success.

The Perils of the *Patria Chica*

Instructions describing in detail the mission of the Delegados as inspectors were issued by General Martínez Anido on 7 December 1923. They were as far-reaching as the plans for a new social identity were ambitious: upon their arrival in each town and village, they were to seize control of the municipal coffers and scrutinize the account books for evidence of financial malpractice. The Delegados were also to strive to improve the health and wellbeing of the village residents by discouraging unproductive pastimes like drinking and gambling, the latter of which was banned outright, and by carrying out inspections of the local market, abattoir, hospital and other public utilities to ensure they met official standards. This applied equally to schools, where the Delegados were to report on the quality of the teachers' work and speak to the children of the importance of the Army and of national symbols like the flag. The children were also to be encouraged to take part in gymnastics, rhythmic marching and weight-lifting in order to improve their fitness in preparation for conscription or for motherhood.[23] Parents, meanwhile,

---

22   It is no coincidence that Primo assigned his most trusted colleague, Martínez Anido, to this role in the Ministry of the Interior (*Gobernación*), as, historically, this Ministry was the principal channel through which vote management was co-ordinated during elections.

23   In 1925, the regime would expand upon this by creating a body dedicated to pre-military youth education, the *Servicio Nacional de Educación Física Ciudadana y Premilitar* [National Service for Civic and Pre-Military Physical Education].

were to be instructed on the duties of citizenship and, most importantly, the need to carry out compulsory military service. The Delegados, for their part, were ordered to endeavour to learn about local customs and traditions, and to attend the *fiestas* [local festivities] of each village in order to gain insight into their new surroundings. All of this would make the Delegado, as Martínez Anido stated with characteristic equanimity, 'un misionero de la Patria, de la moralidad y de la cultura' [a missionary of the Patria, morality and culture] who would be responsible for encouraging 'el valor ciudadano para no consentir caciques' [civic courage to not allow caciques].[24]

On 1 January 1924, Martínez Anido issued new instructions to the Delegados, which committed them to a further round of purges at municipal level, this time targeted at the temporary town councils formed by the regime after the mass dissolution of Ayuntamientos on 30 September 1923.[25] This required the Delegados to replace deficient local administrations with 'personas de alto prestigio social, de solvencia acreditada y a ser posible con título profesional' [people of high social prestige, of accredited solvency and, if possible, those in possession of professional titles]. In the absence of candidates with any of these qualities, the rather vague category of adult ratepayers would suffice. Those that were thought to have been too close to the previous regime, or had been councillors before, were also to be excluded from the new administrations, although in reality none of this proved to be a major obstacle to the caciques of old, who continued to meddle in municipal politics across Spain throughout the dictatorship. That such seemingly arbitrary criteria were still used to determine a candidate's suitability for the role of councillor or mayor is a clear indication of the regime's ideological poverty at this time. In truth, Primo de Rivera struggled to match his populist-nationalist iconoclasm with viable new ideas. Moreover, it highlights the difficulty that the regime faced in

---

24 'Prevenciones que para el mejor desempeño de sus cargos deben tener presentes los Delegados Gubernativos', AHN, Gob. (A), Bundle 17A, File 12, 7 December 1923.
25 'Instrucciones reservadas que los Sres. Gobernadores civiles y Delegados Gubernativos deberán tener presentes en sus misiones inspectoras de los Ayuntamientos', AHN, Gob. (A), Bundle 17A, File 12, 1 January 1924.

truly eradicating caciquismo, which, by its very nature, was a shifting, ill-defined concept.

The regime's futile eradication efforts were nevertheless spoken of in official discourse as a task on a historic scale. Yet, as the Delegados set about their work in exalting the Spanish Patria as the primary focus of the population's loyalty, their own attention was directed principally at the *patria chica* and the myriad of localisms that it contained. Their actions in wresting control of towns and villages from the grip of the caciques, therefore, were guided by the knowledge which they gathered of these often unfamiliar surroundings through their inspections of municipal accounts, the interviews they organized with local people and the denunciations they received from the population. The assessment of what was often mundane information about local goings-on through the short channels that led from the Delegados to Primo de Rivera in Madrid formed an essential part of this enormous bureaucratic undertaking.

The nature of this work of effectively reforming the national consciousness meant that the Delegados found themselves thrust deeply into the everyday life of the towns and villages under their supervision. The denunciations, petitions and complaints which they received from a population eager to have its voice heard by the government meant that they were frequently required to mediate in disputes amongst local residents, some of whom sought to take advantage of the repressive atmosphere of the dictatorship to settle old scores with neighbours and rivals. Undeterred, however, by growing misgivings within the administration about the viability of verifying the accusations made to them via denunciation, Primo ordered the Delegados to publish edicts in the villages under their inspection inviting the local population to highlight deficiencies and identify corruption in the municipal administration.[26] While this was to prove useful to the Delegados in the first instance, what made for a reformed national consciousness in the popular mind, as opposed to the official one, was soon to become evident from the enthusiasm the population showed in denouncing all types of transgressors, many of whom were completely innocent. Captain Enrique Tomás Luque, a Delegado who wrote a memoir

---

26 'Prevenciones', AHN, Gob. (A), Bundle 17A, File 12, 7 December 1923.

of his experience, described in vivid terms how residents varied wildly in their interpretations of what constituted legitimate cause for grievance:

> Hay quejas que parecen fundamentadas, sobre todo las que se refieren a deudas con los Ayuntamientos; en las de índole personal, se advierte en seguida, por el modo de expresarse, la envidia o el odio que las alienta, reflejo de la mísera contextura moral e intelectual de los denunciantes.
>
> [There are complaints which seem to be substantiated, especially those that refer to debts with the Ayuntamientos; for those of a personal nature, one can immediately observe, by the manner in which they are expressed, the envy or hate that motivates them, a reflection of the wretched moral and intellectual context of the complainants.] (Tomás Luque 1928: 47–8)

Many other Delegados seemed to share Tomás Luque's metropolitan disdain for his rural countrymen.[27] A homogeneous national community was still a very distant goal.

Most Delegados, nevertheless, approached the task of rooting out the supposed enemies of Spain with considerable zeal. In December 1923, the month they began their work, the Delegados summarily arrested and jailed dozens of public administrators and supposed caciques, although this was frequently on a dubious legal footing which forced the prisoners' eventual release. This prompted General Martínez Anido to issue new instructions on 1 January 1924, in which he emphasized the need for moderation in order to maintain the good public image of the regime.[28] The numerous reminders which Anido sent in the months and years after this, however, reveal that few Delegados followed his orders (Quiroga 2007: 94). It is clear that the popular mind was not alone in holding its own interpretation of national reform.

In marked contrast to the heavy-handed approach of some Delegados, there are numerous reports of cases in which they were accused of

---

27   This was echoed by Rodrigo de la Yglena, a Delegado in the province of Huelva, who reported that his progress in carrying out reform had been hindered because in the villages, 'el nivel cultural es deficientísimo y el sentido moral le hace pareja' [the cultural level is highly deficient – and equally so in the moral sense]. AHN, Primo, Bundle 77, File 13586, *c*. May 1928.
28   'Instrucciones reservadas', AHN, Gob. (A), Bundle 17A, File 12, 1 January 1924.

collaboration with caciques and other representatives of the so-called old politics. Alonso J., a resident of Ayora (Valencia), gave a damning assessment of the local Delegado's work in a letter to Primo in January 1924. While expressing his approval at the regime's efforts to stamp out 'el caciquismo asqueroso, feudal y cesarista' [disgusting, feudal and caesarist caciquismo], the letter-writer complained bitterly that the Delegado's reforms had left the town subject to the whims of a mayor who was 'sumamente político' [extremely political] and to 'una administración bastante peor de la de antes de existir el actual régimen' [an administration considerably worse than the one before the current regime existed].[29]

The residents of La Codosera (Extremadura) expressed similar reservations in a collective letter sent to Primo de Rivera in 1924. Like so many of those who wrote to the government during the dictatorship, they began their letter with a disavowal of politics and an appeal to the more universal values of the nation. Many of them, they outlined, had once belonged to the *Maurista* wing of the Conservative party but had abandoned this affiliation in the aftermath of Primo's *coup*.[30] In reality, however, their lingering rivalries and resentments spilled over into their complaint, which they framed in overtly political terms. The Delegado assigned to the district of Albuquerque had, in their eyes, been favouring former supporters of what they called 'la desastrosa concentración liberal' [the disastrous liberal concentration] of their former rivals in the municipal administration.[31] Proof of this lay in the twin facts that at least two village mayors in the district had once been members of that party and that the local Unión Patriótica branch, although formed only recently, was also dominated by its members. The Delegado, they believed, was surely behind this because he tended to go on long walks and even for

29 AHN, Primo, Bundle 58, File 3469, 24 January 1924.
30 The *Maurista* [Maurist] movement formed within the Conservative Party around the figure of Antonio Maura in the first quarter of the twentieth century and served as a particularly important ideological precursor to the Primo de Rivera regime through its innovative attempts to create public opinion and form a permanent, mass base of support.
31 This refers to a series of coalitions centred around the Liberal Party and its various wings from 1918 onwards.

dancing sessions with his favourites, who all happened to be Liberals. If this special treatment was not enough, he was 'altanero y despectivo con los demás que han profesado otras ideas' [arrogant and derogatory to those who have expressed other ideas].[32] Under the suspicious gaze of the local population such gestures could be, and very often were, interpreted as signs of favouritism regardless of whether this was truly the case or not. The villagers insisted that they were telling this to Primo not because they longed for power themselves, but because 'somos españoles y queremos gozar del mismo beneficio que la inmensa mayoría del resto de España' [we are Spaniards and we want to enjoy the same benefits as the immense majority of the rest of Spain]. But again we see that this ostensible longing for equality of opportunity masked a one-sided interpretation of reform: while they invoked the high ideal of the nation as their motivation in denouncing the corruption of the Delegado, they dispelled all claims to universality by asking Primo to send them 'un señor Delegado que sea completamente neutral y aplaste toda política, principalmente la odiosa concentración liberal' [a señor Delegado that is completely neutral and will quash all politics, principally the odious liberal concentration].[33] In this case, the nation clearly served as a mask for the particularisms that lingered on from the pre-dictatorship political landscape.

Those caciques who did not regard the advent of the dictatorship as an opportunity to reach a new accommodation with the authorities were invariably hostile towards the Delegados. Indeed, some would go to great lengths to discredit them, even by denunciation, and not only on political grounds: a letter written by José María C. of Granada to Primo at the end of January 1924 documents one such situation vividly.[34] Identifying himself ostensibly as a concerned citizen and journalist who had vehemently

32 A similar complaint about a Delegado was made by a doctor in Cebreros (Ávila), who decried, 'En su vida social solo tiene tratos con los antiguos caciques, cuyos convites acepta y frecuentemente asiste con su familia a excursiones que organizan las familias de los expresados caciques' [In his social life he only has contact with the old caciques, whose invitations he accepts, and he and his family frequently go on outings organized by the families of these caciques]. AHN, Primo, Bundle 63, File 6487, 25 June 1924.
33 AHN, Primo, Bundle 61, File 5746, 24 May 1924.
34 AHN, Primo, Bundle 58, File 3419, 23 January 1924.

defended the new regime in the press, the letter-writer complained that an unnamed Delegado in the province of Almería was failing to improve life in the local villages. Primo's bureau referred the complaint to the provincial government of Almería but the Governor expressed doubts about the identity of the letter-writer. A lengthy investigation carried out by a senior officer later revealed that the complaint had been made falsely by the former secretary of the village of Beninar in revenge at the Delegado's discovery of multiple cases of forgery in the municipal records. In his report to the Governor, the officer who investigated the case complained that 'sería una lástima no poder meter en la cárcel a tanto sin vergüenza que anda por ahí tratando de desprestigiar la actual situación' [it would be a pity not to be able to imprison a wretch like this, who goes about trying to discredit the present situation], adding that he had managed to have a former councillor jailed for fifteen days elsewhere for speaking ill of the Military Directorate. While the file gives no indication of the letter-writer's eventual fate, the vengeful hoax consumed considerable resources and contributed to a sense of alienation between the military and the population.[35]

It is clear from many of our examples that Primo's vision of a renewed national identity was not easily to be achieved by the means adopted at the level of local caciques, with attempts at changing the attitudes and leanings of the people, hitherto informed by the liberal regime he sought to oust, all too often thwarted by the very officers appointed to implement the reforms. Although the Delegados belonged to the military and were largely trusted by Primo on this basis, their inspection work was to be targeted exclusively at the civilian elements of the State administration. As such, they sat at an often nebulous intersection between the military and civilian spheres, leading to frequent cases in which the Delegados were seen to undermine the military hierarchy.[36] In one such case from February

35   Ibid., 28 January 1924 and 3 February 1924.
36   Samuel Finer (1962/2002: 14–23) has convincingly described the difficulty that such crossovers between the separate military and civilian administrations tend to present. While the military may temporarily achieve the legitimacy it requires in order to intervene directly in the civilian sphere of politics, it is nevertheless hindered by what he calls a 'technical inability to administer any but the most primitive community'. This arises from its specialization in violent functions.

1924, the Military-Civil Governor of Granada complained to Martínez Anido that the Delegado assigned to the town of Baza, Major Fernando Claudín, had caused feelings of 'por lo menos intranquilidad y desasosiego' [at the very least disquiet and unease] during his visit to two local villages. Subsequently, when the Governor had asked him to report on the political situation there, Claudín, taking something of a free hand, included a number of accusations 'en forma sumamente incorrecta' [in a highly incorrect manner] against fellow officers in his own garrison, including the provincial Chief of Staff, members of the Guardia Civil, the secretary of the provincial government and the Governor himself. However, that the army, like the other institutions of the Spanish State, could harbour corrupt officials was something that the regime was unwilling to consider. The Governor, therefore, felt that he had no choice but to request Claudín's dismissal for insubordination, something which Primo rubber-stamped in early February.[37] This kind of in-fighting between those appointed to clear away the patronage system of caciquismo did not bode well for the dictator's regenerated Patria. Nor was it the only source of concern for the regime: not all the Delegados were skilled in the politics of the regions to which they were assigned, nor were they capable manipulators of the situations they found within them.

The Governor of Guipúzcoa, likewise, wrote to Primo de Rivera in September 1924 to complain about the conduct of the Delegado assigned to the district of Azpeitia.[38] The town in question, he noted, was well known for its support of the political right and, as such, on the advent of the regime, 'se mostró ardiente y decidido partidario de su tendencia depuradora' [showed itself to be passionate and resolute in its support of its inclination towards purging]. The Delegado, though, had altered this favourable situation so profoundly that 'hoy el distrito en masa es hostil a nuestra representación y mira con recelo y desconfianza cuanto al Directorio se refiere' [today, the district as a whole is hostile to our representatives and regards anything to do with the Directorate with mistrust and suspicion]. The Governor reported that the Delegado had repeatedly flouted his instructions in order to wage a

---

37   AHN, Primo, Bundle 59, File 4409, 26 February 1924.
38   AHN, Primo, Bundle 64, File 7330, 9 September 1924.

personal war against the *integrista* [integrist traditionalist] party, which was then the main political group there and had deep roots in the local community. The Delegado's decision to do so revealed a clear lack of understanding of the politics of the region. The dispute started in the first of the inspections which he carried out in the surrounding villages, during which he began 'sembrando el terror y dirigiendo amenazas' [sowing terror and directing threats] at the local population, much to the detriment of the regime. The Governor thought it unsurprising, therefore, 'que la animosidad, que en un principio se concretaba en su persona, se haya extendido al Directorio' [that the hostility, which was at first fixed on his person, has spread to the Directorate]. This public animosity towards the government was encouraged by the Delegado's bizarre and often violent behaviour, exemplified by one incident in which he gathered together the mayor of Azpeitia and various other local dignitaries in the town hall to burn a Basque flag in front of them, which he then ordered be torn into rags to be used to clean the building.[39] This Delegado was also dismissed for these excesses.

The overzealousness of these Delegados, like those who continued to imprison public administrators with impunity, highlighted the unwieldy aspects of the arrangement. While the archives contain many glowing reports written by happy mayors and town councillors about the services provided to their municipalities by the Delegados, many other letters showed their work to be seriously damaging to the regime.[40] These range from cases of officers resigning in frustration at the ill-defined nature of their work, to others who were convicted of crimes while in the role.[41] Many ultimately seemed unable to meet the exalted character standards of the new national citizen which Primo envisaged.

On a more symbolic level, at the head of the national community, the military nationalism that became so influential in the Restoration period in Spain, and, ultimately, established the cultural foundations for the dictatorship, typically equated the Spanish State with the nation, in

---

39   Ibid., 20 September 1924.
40   Hundreds of these can be seen in AHN, Primo, Bundle 331 (1 & 2).
41   AHN, Primo, Bundle 64, File 7845, 15 November 1924 & Bundle 58, File 3519, 31 December 1923.

place of the people. The army, as the armed wing of the State and one of its foremost institutions, therefore, was central to this vision. It is unsurprising then that by the time of the *coup d'état* of September 1923, Primo de Rivera, like a number of other prominent generals, was a popular figure in Spain, having served notably as Captain General both of Valencia and of Catalonia in the volatile post-war period. The regime's efforts to legitimize the continuation of the dictatorship into the medium-to-long term saw it attempt to build upon this popularity through the charismatic construction of the dictator and his persona in mass propaganda. This has been shown by Alejandro Quiroga to be a process that was characterized by heavy doses of paternalism and references to divine Providence.[42] The letters that were sent to Primo during this time reflected this carefully cultivated image in the way that they frequently represented him as a benevolent father to the nation, very often in the absence of any significant references to the King, Alfonso XIII. In the case of those letters that referred directly to the Delegados, their authors frequently made use of the traditional peasant letter-writing schema which pitted the good leader of the people against ruthless State bureaucrats who abused their power.[43] This was a tension that ultimately served to challenge not only the seamless integration of Nation–State–Army which the regime promoted in its official discourse but also the new ideals of citizenship which that integration rested upon.

The residents of the district of Cúllar and Baza (Granada) wrote an exemplar letter of this type to Primo in April 1924 to denounce the actions of their interim Delegado, Major Juan Luque Fuentes. Shortly after his arrival in the district, Luque, who was a replacement for the popular Delegado Fernando Claudín (the same Delegado mentioned earlier in this chapter), had unilaterally decided to dismiss several members of the town council, which had been elected unanimously earlier in the month. In solidarity with their dismissed colleagues, however, the remaining councillors had resigned in protest shortly afterwards. The writers of the letter wondered if Claudín,

---

42 That so many ordinary people chose to write directly to the dictator between 1923 and 1930 is surely a sign that this charismatization process was at least partially successful. This process is treated in some detail in Quiroga (2013a).

43 I have borrowed this idea from Kozlov (1996: 869).

the original Delegado, knew about this, for they feared that 'en este asunto mangonea un elemento del antiguo régimen caciquil de Baza' [an element of the old caciquil regime in Baza is meddling in this matter]. In a typical concluding appeal, they asked Primo to intervene against Luque, who was surely acting without his knowledge, and to restore the previous council, stating that 'es lástima que ocurra esto a espaldas de VE que es la garantía de la Ley, y más que todo es VE la garantía de la tranquilidad de España' [it is a shame that this is occurring behind the back of Your Excellency, who is the guarantor of the Law, and, more than anything, Your Excellency is the guarantor of Spain's peace].[44] Many other letters sent to Primo de Rivera at this time framed their contents as acts of informing the dictator in the most literal, factual sense, without making any explicit requests, in the hope that his natural benevolence would inspire him to take action in their defence. On this basis it is clear that while the Delegados were styled as the servants and saviours of the nation by the regime, in the eyes of many ordinary people at this time, Primo remained its ultimate guarantor.[45] But neither the official promotion of the Delegados' role, nor the image of their leader as prototype was to prove sufficient to create the new citizen.

The Municipal Statute and the Decline of the Delegados

As these few samples of the widespread correspondence have indicated, it was becoming clear to Primo that no short-term solutions to reforming

---

44   AHN, Primo, Bundle 61, File 5609, 26 April 1924.
45   It is worth noting here that in these letters the King, Alfonso XIII, typically featured only as a secondary figure, who was occasionally invoked as the symbol of the nation and as an object of personal loyalty, rather than as a direct actor. General Francisco Franco, however, was treated in much the same way as Primo de Rivera in the period after the Civil War, as Antonio Cazorla Sánchez's work on the topic shows. See the illustrative case in which a letter-writer urged Franco to take action against 'pillos, ladrones, ambiciosos, y chaqueteros vengativos' [rascals, thieves, the power-hungry, and vindictive brownnosers] so that he would not fail as Primo de Rivera had before him (Cazorla Sánchez 2014: 306).

civic attitudes were likely to succeed and that if his changes were to have any lasting effect on perceptions of nationhood, it would be necessary to rethink the overall strategy. The months of March and April 1924 marked the first major change of course over the lifetime of the dictatorship, between a destructive phase that was characterized by the regime's efforts to purge the State administration of corruption and the beginnings of a medium- to long-term reconstruction. By this point, the first ninety days of military rule, which King Alfonso XIII had initially handed Primo de Rivera in September 1923, had long since elapsed and, consequently, the general began to take steps to stabilize and perpetuate his regime beyond the *quirúrgica* [surgical] intervention that he had first proposed in his manifesto. With the approval of the King, Primo set about institutionalizing the dictatorship by carrying out a far-reaching legislative reform to local government, adopting a single party, Unión Patriótica, and commencing the progressive recivilianization of half of the provincial Governorships.[46]

The regime's definitive reform to local government was implemented through a new Municipal Statute, a landmark piece of legislation that was overseen by the young Maurista lawyer, José Calvo Sotelo, whom the dictator appointed to a senior role in the Ministry of the Interior as Director General of the Administration and, subsequently, Minister for Finance. In a bid to end the electoral manipulation that had characterized the earlier Restoration era, the Statute firmly established the municipality as the basic administrative unit of the Spanish State and limited the scope for direct government interference in this realm.[47] It was evident that only by some such concessions to local diversity would the grander aims of revitalized national homogeneity be achievable.

---

46   For the Municipal Statute see *Gaceta de Madrid* (9 March 1924). Its main provisions were implemented in the first week of April 1924. See Noguera y Yanguas and Campos y Arjona (1926): for the instructions issued to the Governors and Delegados on the formation of Unión Patriótica, pp. 546–9; for the decree regarding the return of the Civil Governors, p. 531.
47   In this he was assisted by José María Gil-Robles, the future leader of the CEDA, and the Count of Vallellano, Fernando Suárez de Tangil, who later became Mayor of Madrid.

New instructions issued to the Delegados by the government at the end of March 1924 to coincide with the implementation of the Statute bound them to respect municipal autonomy and restricted their freedom to intervene in municipal affairs without the prior authorization of the corresponding provincial Governor (*Gaceta de Madrid,* 21 October 1923). The move was timely, as by now the Delegados were becoming unpopular figures, both among the population, as the petitions examined earlier in this chapter show, and within the administration itself. In the months following the introduction of the Municipal Statute, Martínez Anido was moved to write to the provincial Governors to complain that some Delegados were still involved in the smallest details of municipal life, contrary to their new instructions. Within the army, the future organizer of the July 1936 *coup d'état*, General Emilio Mola, stated his belief that the work of the Delegados was 'no pocas veces desafortunada y hasta inmoral [...] y siempre antipática al elemento civil' [frequently misguided and even immoral [...] and always unpleasant for civilian elements], and had served only to create public animosity towards the Armed Forces in Spain (Mola 1940: 1028 cited in Quiroga 2004: 259). Similar criticisms were also made by the senior generals Pardo González and García Benítez.[48] José Calvo Sotelo, for his part, worried that the Delegados were undermining the authority of the restored Civil Governors and contributing to states of 'incertidumbre, despego o desasosiego' [doubt, disregard or unease] across government. In October 1924, around the anniversary of the creation of the Delegados, in a move that anticipated the creation by Primo of a largely civilian cabinet (the Civil Directorate) in December 1925, he wrote to the general to suggest that it would be prudent to abolish the role altogether, thereby loosening the erstwhile militarization of the State administration (Calvo Sotelo 1931/1974: 27–9). Although Primo hesitated at doing so entirely, between late 1924 and the end of 1927 he would go on to reduce progressively the number of Delegados from a peak of 523 to just seventy-nine, all of whom were reassigned to administrative roles in provincial capitals.[49]

48   For Pardo González and García Benítez see Navajas Zubeldía (1992: 99–100).
49   For the laws ordering the reduction of the Delegados see Noguera y Yanguas and Campos y Arjona (1926: 692) and *Gaceta de Madrid* (21 March 1926 and 29 December 1927). One of the first decisions taken by the administration formed by General Dámaso Berenguer in 1930 upon Primo's resignation was to abolish the office of the Delegados Gubernativos altogether. See *Gaceta de Madrid* (22 January 1930).

Conclusion

When Primo de Rivera created the Delegados Gubernativos in October 1923, he was still entertaining the idea of relinquishing power in the short to medium term, even if he had no intention of doing so within ninety days of his *coup d'état* as he initially suggested. At a point marked by ideological poverty, during which caciquismo was presented by the regime as one of the overriding threats to the Spanish nation, the Delegados were introduced to the population as the tools with which the regeneration of Spain would finally be achieved. Very rapidly, however, their relationship with the population soured due both to their lack of preparation and to the impossibility of their task in fully eradicating caciquismo. At the root of the mission which Primo originally assigned to the Delegados was his messianic belief that civil society could be awoken and reformed by the State alone. However, as this chapter has shown, the regime encountered a population that was much less malleable and open to its top-down nationalizing efforts than it had expected. Any incorporation of the masses into national life would be a multi-layered process, in which the eradication of caciquismo would merely represent a single step. As Enrique Tomás y Luque, the memoir-writing Delegado, concluded in his own assessment of their work, the task was far more complex than Primo de Rivera could have foreseen in September 1923, for, '[e]l convertir los hombres de hoy en ciudadanos, cuando tan lejos de esto estaban, es labor muy lenta, de varias generaciones, aun siguiendo la obra regeneradora, tan intensa y enérgicamente iniciada' [Turning the men of today into citizens, when they were so far removed from this, is slow work, over several generations, even if we continue the work of regeneration that we have started so intensely and energetically] (Tomás Luque 1928: 246). Indeed, the question that dominated Spanish politics for much of what remained of the twentieth century was whether the State would base itself on civic-republican ideals that emphasized active participation in political life, or whether that State would attempt to bend its citizenry to its image and, ultimately, its will from above. The experience of the Delegados rapidly put paid to the notion that the military could achieve the latter on its own.

With hindsight, and assuming that a bankrupt State had not put a decisive end to his reforms upon the regime's collapse, one can only speculate whether Primo's vision of a new unified citizenry was ever really achievable, with or without military government. As the events leading up to the brutal civil war – and the present calls for independence – give sufficient evidence, his efforts to create a homogeneous sense of nationhood were, at the very least, premature.

Bibliography

Álvarez Junco, J. (1996). 'Redes locales, lealtades tradicionales y nuevas identidades colectivas en la España del siglo XIX'. In A. Robles Egea, and J. Álvarez Junco (eds), *Política en penumbra. Patronazgo y clientelismo políticos en la España contemporánea*, pp. 71–94. Madrid: Siglo XXI.

Archilés Cardona, F. (2013). 'Lenguajes de nación. Las "experiencias de nación" y los procesos de nacionalización: propuestas para un debate', *Ayer*, 90 (2), 91–114.

Balfour, S. (1997). *The End of the Spanish Empire, 1898–1923*. Oxford: Clarendon Press.

Berger, S. (2005). 'A Return to the National Paradigm? National History Writing in Germany, Italy, France, and Britain from 1945 to the Present', *The Journal of Modern History*, 77 (3), 629–78.

Beyen, M., and Van Ginderachter, M. (2012). 'Writing the Mass into a Mass Phenomenon'. In M. Beyen, and M. Van Ginderachter (eds), *Nationhood from below: Europe in the Long Nineteenth Century*, pp. 3–22. Basingstoke: Palgrave Macmillan.

Calvo Sotelo, J. (1931; repr. 1974). *Mis servicios al Estado*. Madrid: Instituto de Estudios de Administración Local.

Cazorla Sánchez, A. (2014). *Cartas a Franco de los españoles de a pie*. Madrid: Marcial Pons.

Costa y Martínez, J. (1902). *Oligarquía y caciquismo: como la forma actual de gobierno en España, urgencia y modo de cambiarla*. Madrid: Imprenta de los Hijos M. G. y Fernández.

Eley, G., and Grigor Suny, R. (eds) (1996). *Becoming National: A Reader*. Oxford: Oxford University Press.

Espadas Burgos, M. (1984). 'Orden social en la mentalidad militar española a comienzos del siglo XX'. In J. L. García Delgado (ed.), *España, 1898–1936: Estructuras y cambio*, pp. 345–59. Madrid: Editorial de la Universidad Complutense de Madrid.

Espadas Burgos, M. (1996). 'Ejército y "cuestión social" en la España de fin de siglo', *Torre de los Lujanes: Boletín de la Real Sociedad Económica Matritense de Amigos del País*, 31, 57–64.

Finer, S. E. (1962; repr. 2002). *The Man on Horseback: The Role of the Military in Politics*. New Brunswick, NJ: Transaction.

Gabriel, P., Pomés, J., and Fernández Gómez, F. (eds) (2013). *España Res Publica. Nacionalización española e identidades en conflicto (siglos XIX y XX)*. Granada: Comares.

Ganivet, A. (1905). *Idearium español*. Granada: V. Suárez.

Gentile, E. (1996). *The Sacralization of Politics in Fascist Italy*. Cambridge, MA: Harvard University Press.

González Calbet, M. T. (1987). *La Dictadura de Primo de Rivera. El Directorio Militar*. Madrid: Ediciones el Arquero.

González Hernández, M. J. (1997). 'Regeneracionismo, reformismo y democracia en Antonio Maura'. In J. Tusell, F. Montero, and J. M. Marín (eds), *Las derechas en la España contemporánea*, pp. 91–113. Madrid: Anthropos.

Jensen, G. (2002). *Irrational Triumph: Cultural Despair, Military Nationalism and the Ideological Origins of Franco's Spain*. Reno, NV: University of Nevada Press.

Kozlov, V. A. (1996). 'Denunciation and Its Functions in Soviet Governance: A Study of Denunciations and Their Bureaucratic Handling from Society Police Archives, 1944–1953', *The Journal of Modern History*, 68 (4), 867–98.

Luengo Teixidor, F., and Molina Aparicio, F. (eds) (2016). *Los caminos de la nación. Factores de nacionalización en la España contemporánea*. Granada: Comares.

Macías Picavea, R. (1899). *El problema nacional: hechos, causas, remedios*. Madrid: Librería General de Victoriano Suárez.

Mola, E. (1940). *Obras Completas*. Valladolid: Librería Santaren.

Molina Aparicio, F. (2013). 'La nación desde abajo. Nacionalización, individuo e identidad nacional', *Ayer*, 90 (2), 39–63.

Molina Aparicio, F., and Cabo Villaverde, M. (2012). 'An Inconvenient Nation: Nation-Building and National Identity in Modern Spain. The Historiographical Debate'. In M. Van Ginderachter, and M. Beyen (eds), *Nationhood from below: Europe in the Long Nineteenth Century*, pp. 47–72. Basingstoke: Palgrave Macmillan.

Moreno Luzón, J. (2007a). *Construir España. Nacionalismo español y procesos de nacionalización*. Madrid: Centro de Estudios Políticos y Constitucionales.

Moreno Luzón, J. (2007b). 'Political Clientelism, Elites, and Caciquismo in Restoration Spain (1875–1923)', *European History Quarterly*, 37 (3), 417–41.

Moreno Luzón, J. (ed.) (1996). '"El poder público hecho cisco". Clientelismo e instituciones políticas en la España de la Restauración'. In A. Robles Egea, and J. Álvarez Junco (eds), *Política en penumbra. Patronazgo y clientelismo políticos en la España contemporánea*, pp. 169–90. Madrid: Siglo Veintiuno.

Morote, L. (1900). *La moral de la derrota*. Madrid: Estab. Tip. de G. Juste.

Mosse, G. L. (1974; repr. 2001). *The Nationalization of the Masses: Political Symbolism and Mass Movements in Germany from the Napoleonic Wars through the Third Reich*. New York: Howard Fertig.

Navajas Zubeldía, C. (1992). *Ejército, estado y sociedad en España (1923–1930)*. Logroño: Instituto de Estudios Riojanos.

Noguera y Yanguas, J., and Campos y Arjona, A. (1926). *Dos años de directorio militar: manifiestos, disposiciones oficiales, cartas, discursos, órdenes generales al ejército* ... Madrid: Renacimiento.

Pérez, D. (1930). *La dictadura a través de sus notas oficiosas*. Madrid: Ed. Compañía Ibero-Americana de Publicaciones.

Piattoni, S. (ed.) (2001). *Clientelism, Interests, and Democratic Representation: The European Experience in Historical and Comparative Perspective*. Cambridge: Cambridge University Press.

Primo de Rivera, M. (1916). 'Prólogo'. In T. García Figueras, and J. de la Matta, *Elementos de educación moral del soldado*, pp. xi–xv. Sevilla: F. Díaz.

Primo de Rivera, M. (1929). *El pensamiento de Primo de Rivera: sus notas, artículos y discursos*. Madrid: La Junta de Propaganda Patriótica y Ciudadana.

Primo de Rivera, M. (1930). *La Dictadura a través de sus notas oficiosas*, ed. Dionisio Pérez. Madrid: Compañía Ibero-Americana de Publicaciones.

Pro Ruíz, J. (1998). 'La política en tiempos del Desastre'. In J. Pan-Montojo, and J. Álvarez Junco (eds), *Más se perdió en Cuba. España, 1898 y la crisis de fin de siglo*, pp. 151–260. Madrid: Alianza.

Quiroga, A. (2004). '"Los apóstoles de la patria". El ejército como instrumento de nacionalización de masas durante la Dictadura de Primo de Rivera', *Mélanges de la Casa de Velázquez. Nouvelle série* 34 (1), 243–72.

Quiroga, A. (2007). *Making Spaniards: Primo de Rivera and the Nationalization of the Masses, 1923–1930*. Basingstoke: Palgrave Macmillan.

Quiroga, A. (2013a). 'Cirujano de Hierro. La construcción carismática del General Primo de Rivera', *Ayer*, 91 (3), 147–68.

Quiroga, A. (2013b). 'La nacionalización en España. Una propuesta teórica', *Ayer*, 90 (2), 17–38.

Romero-Maura, J. (1977). 'Caciquismo as a Political System'. In E. Gellner, and J. Waterbury (eds), *Patrons and Clients in Mediterranean Societies*, pp. 53–62. London: Duckworth.

Saz Campos, I., and Archilés Cardona, F. (eds) (2011). *Estudios sobre nacionalismo y nación en la España contemporánea*. Zaragoza: Prensas de la Universidad de Zaragoza.

Saz Campos, I., and Archilés Cardona, F. (eds) (2012). *La nación de los españoles: discursos y práctica del nacionalismo en la época contemporánea*. Valencia: Universitat de València.

Shefter, M. (1994). *Political Parties and the State: The American Historical Experience*. Princeton, NJ: Princeton University Press.

Soldevilla, F. (1923). *El Año Político*. Madrid: Imprenta de Julio Cosano.

Tomás Luque, E. (1928). *En la dictadura. Por pueblos y aldeas: de las memorias de un delegado gubernativo*. Toledo: Editorial Católica Toledana.

Tusell, J. (1977). *La crisis del caciquismo andaluz (1923–1931)*. Madrid: Cupsa.

Unamuno, M. de. (1902). *En torno al casticismo*. Barcelona: A. Calderón & S. Valentí Camp.

Vega, M. E. de, and Calle, M. D. de la (eds) (2010). *Procesos de nacionalización en la España contemporánea*. Salamanca: Universidad de Salamanca.

Weber, E. (1976). *Peasants into Frenchmen: The Modernization of Rural France, 1870–1914*. Stanford, CA: Stanford University Press.

MARK FRIIS HAU

Becoming Catalan: Narrative Cultivation of Self among Catalan Nationalists

ABSTRACT
This chapter offers novel perspectives on how Catalan national identity, rather than being a predetermined, passively assigned ethnic category, is socially constructed through active choices and technologies of the self. Drawing on ethnographic data gathered among activists of the pro-independence, left-wing party Esquerra Republicana de Catalunya, and employing ethical self-transformation terminology previously used primarily in the study of religious behaviour, it explores the construction of contemporary Catalan national identity, cultivated and embodied through daily communicative practice and shared narratives. As national senses of belonging become inextricably linked with realpolitik, political constructions of 'the good life' increasingly take Catalan independence and Catalan national identity as the starting point, linking the political and the moral. Catalan nationalist activists attempt to align personal and communal narratives by discursively equating a Catalan ideal-self with morally correct behaviour, contrasting Catalan virtues with Spanish vices.

Introduction

> He après dels meus pares i de l'escola que som una nació. Però si creues l'Ebre allí ensenyen tot el contrari. Hi ha un conflicte de realitats, hi ha un conflicte de reconeixement. Però jo ja em reconeix, no necessito que Espanya ho faci.
>
> [I have learned from my parents and in school that we're a nation. But you cross the river Ebro and there they're taught the complete opposite. There is a conflict

of realities, there is a conflict of recognition. But I already recognize myself, I don't need Spain to do so.]¹ (Eduard, 17 June 2015)

There exists a traumatic freedom in being a Catalan nationalist. You cannot be formally born Catalan, although you are born in Catalonia, and you cannot hold a Catalan passport. On the other hand, you can call yourself Catalan without speaking Catalan or having Catalan ancestry. The choice to be Catalan appears at first to be 'free', but it can never be externally validated, and must be continuously maintained through one's own actions, speech, and values. As Montserrat Guibernau argues, the Catalan pro-independence movement specifically demands the right of Catalans to be considered a *demos*, or a people (2014: 5). Recognition as a Catalan both individually and as belonging to a specific people is essentially the central issue for Catalan nationalists; they lack such recognition within the current framework of Spain. In the Spanish Constitution Catalonia is not recognized as sovereign or even as a nation but simply as a 'nationality', a clever neologism that has no agreed-upon meaning (2014: 13). The legal definition of a 'Catalan' according to the Statute of Autonomy of 1932, reinstated in the Statute of Autonomy of 1979 (Desfor Edles 1999: 329) and continued in the Statute of Autonomy of 2005, is completely inclusive and counts anyone with administrative residence as a Catalan (Article 7). Not only are Catalan national identities not supported by institutional means, or conferred upon birth, they are actively contested by the (Spanish) state, which does not recognize Catalan as being a national identity distinct from Spanish nationality.

Explaining Catalan identity to me, my informant Enric, an ERC member since the 1980s and a retired schoolmaster, quoted the famous

1   The fieldwork on which this chapter is based took place between autumn 2011 and spring 2012 among activists from a local chapter of the Catalanist, left wing party *Esquerra Republicana de Catalunya* (ERC) in the Barcelona neighborhood of Sant Andreu. Follow-up interviews were conducted in the summer of 2015. The fieldwork was sponsored by the University of Copenhagen as part of a Research Master's degree program. All translations in this chapter are my own and I alone am responsible for any errors or faults. All interviewees appear under their original first names, in accordance with their own explicit requests.

words of former Catalan president Jordi Pujol: you only have to live in Catalonia and want to be Catalan to be so. 'El voler és la clau' [The will is the key],[2] Enric emphasized. If ever one could talk of open ethnic boundaries, it would seem to be in Catalonia. As Catalan is different from other ethnic identities supported by a state apparatus and internal political and linguistic recognition, the lack of institutionalization has the consequence that being Catalan is essentially a political choice; it is an identity one has to stick with and make work through practice and discipline. In this chapter, I argue that through a continuous process of cultivating Catalanist[3] selves through value-laden narratives, members of the party *Esquerra Republicana de Catalunya* were able to constitute themselves as true and virtuous Catalan subjects. They achieved their goal of being recognized as a nation from within through their own narratives about themselves. As they recognized themselves as Catalan and constituted themselves as Catalan subjects through practice, they sought to make irrelevant the lack of recognition they received from Spain or the international community. They were able to become Catalan through speech and force of will.

National Identity in Catalonia

National identity is, and has been for many years, a central issue on the Catalan political agenda and in the lives of many Catalans (Villaroya 2012: 31). During my time in Catalonia I principally worked with local activists from the left-wing, pro-independence party *Esquerra Republicana de Catalunya*. Although often referred to in the literature as a 'nationalist' party, with the exception of the right-wing parties PP and *Ciutadans*, [Citizens] as Ivan Serrano points out, 'Catalan parties share a broad

---

2   Enric used the Catalan word 'voler', which means 'to want', or 'will'.
3   'Catalanism' and 'Catalanist' are the preferred terms for Catalan nationalism in Catalonia, and I follow this emic usage.

conception of Catalan national identity that includes elements such as a common history, a community with its own traditions and language, and a collective will for self-government based on an inclusive conception of "Catalanness"' (Serrano 2013: 531). The people I encountered in my fieldwork necessarily understood their national identity as Catalan and thought of Catalonia as a nation distinct from that of Spain. Since such an understanding is widespread in Catalonia, it remains an open question whether or not ERC members in particular should be termed 'nationalists'. I do so in this chapter primarily because considerations of space limit a larger discussion of the word 'nationalism'. Although all national identities are necessarily socially constructed, being Catalan is generally perceived by Catalans themselves as something open, fluid and subject to choice. Writing on this open understanding of Catalan national identity, anthropologist Stanley Brandes has noted: '[T]he Catalan people have long maintained an implicit belief in something that anthropologists have long known, that is, that race and culture are wholly separable. Biological ancestry does not make a person Catalan. Catalan identity [...] can be acquired through learning, and then internalized to the point of thorough identification' (1990: 34).

The question that arises is what a Catalan nationalist can do to overcome his or her lack of institutional (and international) recognition. As my informant Eduard stated in the opening quotation: one can recognize oneself. This type of 'cultural resistance' is common among Catalan nationalists, using national symbols, language, and moral narratives to resist, contest, and upend Spanish identity (Guibernau 2014: 11). Beginning with a mass demonstration in 1977 on the Catalan national day, 11 September, such resistance actions enlisting mass support in favour of autonomy or outright independence have continually returned to Catalan politics, perhaps most notably in the 2012 demonstrations that regalvanized the independence movement. Several surveys from 2012 and 2013 showed a majority in favour of independence ranging from 52 to 55 per cent (2014: 18–19). It is clear that support for independence is experiencing unprecedented momentum, with Catalans voting in greater numbers than before and more deeply divided (Burg 2015: 289). Even more significant, the proportion of respondents self-identifying as exclusively Catalan has been increasing since 2010

(2015: 293). Although the presence of distinctive, non-Spanish, *Catalan* national identities has long been a powerful political force in Catalonia (2015: 293), in the last few years a great number of Catalans appear to feel more exclusively Catalan than before. It would seem that more and more Catalans are 'recognizing themselves' as Catalans.

Nations without states such as Catalonia are complex sites for the study of national identifications. Two main sets of identities are at play, Spanish and Catalan, and both lay claim to the same territory. Majority state nationalism 'seeks to promote a shared national identity for all the citizens of the state, while the nation without state nationalism seeks recognition as a demos, claiming a right to self-government and self-determination' (Serrano 2013: 527). People in Catalonia can feel attachment towards either Spanish or Catalan national identity with varying intensities, or both as in the case of 'nested' identities. There are competing nation-building policies at play, and national identities cannot be taken for granted at an institutional or personal level. When the state is considered by its citizens to be concomitant with the nation, Billig's seminal concept of banal nationalism (1995) is immensely illuminating. The routine, or banal, limp flag hanging by the post office is a more powerful vehicle of national 'flagging' than the confident battle-flag hoisted high (1995: 6). Billig's central thesis that ideological habits become routine and nationalist imagery permeate daily events without calling attention to themselves is a powerful analytic tool. In Catalonia, this is necessarily somewhat different as has already been explored in the literature on Catalonia (Crameri 2000; Hau 2016). Guibernau has argued that the particular constellation in Catalonia where a majority state has historically not assimilated its national minorities, causes minority nationalists to perceive the state as 'alien' (Guibernau 2013: 371). This leads to feelings of 'estrangement' and emotional detachment, which is exactly how I would characterize my ERC informants' relationship to the Spanish state and the central government in Madrid. In Catalonia, national identity becomes increasingly politicized, as neither Catalan nor Spanish national symbols can be considered truly routine and inconspicuous. When one has to choose which flag to hoist, the banality of the action decreases and it becomes subject to evaluation, debate – and choice.

Telling Stories

Stories were a recurring theme throughout my ethnographic interviews with ERC activists in Sant Andreu. Sometimes they would be abstract, ideological and semi-historical explanations, and sometimes very practical, concrete and political. I quickly took an interest in such narratives, as my interlocutors relied heavily on them when making their case and arguments. The stories were often repeated. The same political situation or similar stories were told by several interlocutors independently. During our later talks, my interlocutors would also sometimes make reference to their earlier narratives to make a new point. Sometimes such stories would have clear-cut protagonists and antagonists, and a coherent plot, but regardless of form they would be normative with clear moral implications and political consequences. They were stories of how the world was perceived by my interlocutors, but also about how the world ought to be. I analyse them as ways in which my informants reflected on who they wanted to be, and used them to tell the stories of themselves that they wanted told.

These stories could be labelled a form of presentation of self in the style of Erving Goffman: a semi-conscious performance of how someone wants to be perceived (Goffman 1959: 15). For example, my interlocutors' preference for speaking almost solely in Catalan in the otherwise linguistically plural environment of Barcelona could be seen as a personal front designed to convey impressions of their great convictions or for keeping up appearances as Catalan nationalists (1959: 24). In this light, the lack of institutional backing for their national identities leads them to almost compulsive ethnic posturing and identity performance.

However, in this chapter I take a different view: my interlocutors were not only giving a performance to convince me of their Catalanhood, but to convince themselves, using narratives and ethical evaluations to form and affirm an identity and idea of self that was more in line with the values outlined in Catalanist discourse. Ethnicity, being an aspect of a relation, is both self-articulated and subject to validation by others. It is simultaneously ascribed and achieved (Eriksen 2002: 56). If others, for example the Spanish state and international community, are unwilling to recognize one's Catalan identity, it follows that one must work even harder to convince oneself and internalize the recognition lacking from the outside.

However, this process should be understood as less of a show and more of an exercise, or a technique of the self. In Goffmanesque terms this would be an outside mask held in place from within by social discipline (Goffman 1959: 57), but I find the process to be more similar to growing a beard than wearing a mask, as the politicized identity of Catalanism is subject to nurture and active cultivation. The performance does not stop when the audience has left, but when the performer has convinced himself to such a degree that he has effected change within himself.

Benedict Anderson has famously argued that nations are imagined communities (1991), and here I take this as a starting point to investigate *how* a nation might be imagined by the people who consider themselves to belong to it. I see that my interlocutors' social narratives, drawing upon nationalist discourse, moral claims and virtues, were ways of engaging with and propagating a political Catalanist life. Drawing on Sartre, Goffman has stated that we play with our current condition in order to realize it, in the literal sense of making it real (1959: 76). Following this, I analyse how my informants' moral and ethical narratives and accounts of self are ways to formulate their identities, 'realizing' them in the process. In order to perform this analysis, I enter into a dialogue with the recent poststructuralist analyses of religious self-cultivation led by Charles Hirschkind and Saba Mahmood, and lean on Foucault's techniques of the self. Through narratives about ethics, justice, and Catalan values, members of Esquerra are able to reimagine their lives and to affirm their 'Catalanhood', cultivating and disciplining a Catalan self more in line with Catalanist discourse. To highlight the process of nationalist cultivation among ERC activists, I first relate how a feeling of injustice was a central theme in many of my interlocutors' stories and how this can be seen in a moral light. Secondly, I attempt to sketch some of the 'core', archetypical values perceived by my interlocutors as deeply Catalan, namely democracy, tolerance and pacifism.

The Cultivation of Self[4]

It is an oft-repeated trope that nationalism is religion for the modern era. The purpose of this chapter, however, is not to follow such a comparison. I use the analytical framework of cultivation, borrowed primarily from Saba Mahmood and Charles Hirschkind's poststructuralist studies of religious practices in order to illuminate how nationalist, Catalan political activists seek to consciously shape and strengthen their national identities. This enables a view of national identity as something continuously maintained, nurtured or cultivated into a distinct ideology of selfhood through narratives and social actions rather than as a given and unproblematic trait.

A key writer on the theme of cultivation, Saba Mahmood centres her work on how female Muslims in the Egyptian Mosque Movement exercise great agency in attempting to discipline themselves into more pious, moral selves. Mahmood equates the bodily practices of her interlocutors with 'spiritual exercises'. This term refers to practices both physical, as in a dietary regime, intuitive, as in contemplation, or discursive, as in dialogue. Common among them is their intention to effect modifications and transformations in the practising subject (Mahmood 2004: 122). Mahmood places great emphasis on the social actor's desire and willingness to change him or herself in accordance with a larger ideology through social discipline.

By her own admission, Mahmood's framework, which we might term an active formation of self, self-discipline or cultivation, is greatly inspired by poststructuralist thought. The transformation of self is not necessarily voluntaristic and autonomous, but formed within historically specific sets of formative practices and moral injunctions. This involves the Foucauldian paradoxical term subjectivation, referring to how the same processes and conditions that subordinate a subject are also the means by which they can become a self-conscious agent. That is, there is no undominated self

---

4   In this chapter, I use the terms identity, self and subject interchangeably, as limitations of space restrict a full-fledged discussion. My use of the term 'self' should not be seen as an ontological argument or implying the psychological solidity of 'the self', but highlights how narratives of selfhood were abundant in my field and had social consequences for the way in which my informants perceived themselves and others.

pre-existing the operations of power or a subject formed 'freely' from discursive regimes. Even our abilities and capacities for agency are the product of power operations (2004: 28). Even though the subject constitutes itself actively through practices of the self, such practices are not invented by the individuals, but culturally appropriate models (Martin et al. 1988: 121).

In my analysis this insight can be translated to mean that there cannot exist a nationalist subject outside nationalist discourse and further, there cannot exist a Catalanist unless he or she is actively being subjectivated by and subjectivating him or herself to such a Catalan, nationalist discourse. A Catalanist subject in my analysis is a subject who willingly, even if not 'freely', strives towards inhabiting the tenets of nationalist discourse, while solely existing as a social body through the subjectivation of this same discourse.

Of central importance is Michel Foucault's analysis of the Greco-Roman concept *epimelesthai sautou*, the care of the self, realized as a set of practices or techniques exercised by the self on the self by which one seeks to 'develop and transform oneself, and to attain to a certain mode of being' (Fornet-Betancourt et al. 1987: 113). Taking care of oneself constituted not only a principle but also a constant practice (Martin et al. 1988: 148). The care of the self was an active form of leisure in the Greco-Roman era, and there was a gradual shift from oral to written practices such as diary-writing and keeping notebooks (1988: 153). Gradually, the self became a theme and an object (or subject) to write about, intensifying the experience of self. Among my informants, written quotes by famous Catalanists were praised as encapsulating Catalan virtues and appreciated for their emotional quality and political salience. However, it was oral narratives and voiced expressions of values and selfhood that I encountered and have chosen to focus my attention on.

The Case for Catalanism as Cultivation

In many ways, the project of nationalism is not so far from that of Mahmood's pious interlocutors in the Mosque Movement. Nationalism relies on specific discourses and assumptions to make its claims and involve social actors' current actions working towards the completion of future goals and aspirations and, with the declared aim of independence for their nation, my interlocutors attempted to cultivate Catalan lives, surrounding themselves with other Catalan speakers, choosing not to switch over to Castilian (even though they spoke it perfectly) and repeating certain common narratives, all in the process of becoming Catalanist subjects and being recognized as Catalan.

Following in the footsteps of Talal Asad, Hirschkind (2011) has made the case for studying secular practices as part of the cultivation of a secular body. He asks if we can talk of a 'body', understood in a social constructivist way of embodied dispositions and learned sensibilities specific to secular subjects. Hirschkind argues that we must distinguish between spaces that are merely secular, and those where there is a process of secular cultivation (2011: 634). Similarly in my field, simply being Catalan is not the same as being a Catalanist subject. Just as practices we define as secular are not so because they are nonreligious, but because they are discursively identified and valorized through the discourse of secularism (2011: 639), a practice can only be termed Catalanist when it relies upon and engages with a Catalanist discourse and when it plays a part in the project of that discourse. A certain discourse must be at work for us to begin talking about the cultivation of a certain subject.

I then regard a practice or narrative as part of a Catalanist cultivation of self if social actors are able to successfully inscribe it within the wider discourse of Catalan nationalism. However banal or routine the practice, if it relies on Catalanist discourse to make sense as a social act, it has become a Catalanist act. To paraphrase from Billig, a Catalanist cannot claim patriotic feelings for Catalonia unless the assumptions about what a nation is and what values patriotism involves are already discursively in place (Billig 1995: 61). National sentiments do not appear *ex nihilo* in a vacuum.

Cultivating Ideals

The discursive 'field' of Catalan nationalism did not emerge as a unified phenomenon in the nineteenth century, as different political and cultural influences informed different types of nationalism, ranging from conservative to Marxist (Guibernau 2014: 10). Catalanism has always been a political terrain, and this is no different today, although it is generally a phenomenon of the political left. My informants sought to uphold and affirm certain moral claims and virtues implicit in their understanding of Catalan nationalist ideology, cultivating specific dispositions in a parallel to religious subjects seeking to become more pious. The tales told to me during my fieldwork were ways in which my informants could reflect on the moral values important for them as political Catalanist activists of the centre-left. I saw that their idealism was the virtue most often praised, as their political activism was seen in moral, almost spiritual terms.

When I asked Mireia how she first became involved with *Esquerra,* she told me about 'awakening' as a Catalanist in ideological, moral terms, focusing on the values of justice, equality and liberty, without any mention of the party itself: 'Arriba un moment que tu dius, ostres, justícia, no? Igualtat. I tu comences a veure que tu … ets nascut, crescut i viscut en un territori que la llibertat no la tens plenament' [There comes a time where you say 'well, what about justice', right? Equality. And you start to see that you … You're born, raised and living in a place where liberty is simply not something you have] (Mireia, 24 April 2012).

Carles told me a somewhat similar story of being 'awakened' as a Catalanist. When he was 6 years old, he had been to a holiday celebration in Plaça Sant Jaume, the square in central Barcelona in front of the Catalan *Generalitat* [Parliament]. Here he had seen a Spanish flag flowing and asked his parents what it was doing in their country (Carles, 30 March 2012). He emphasized that he was not aware of politics at that age, only later forming his political views over the following years and getting involved with political issues in his early teens. However, he still saw this experience as being the first time it dawned on him that his country was not free. The narrative of this experience greatly emphasizes the preconscious, affect-filled aspects of Carles's awakening as a Catalanist.

In speaking of their political formation, both Mireia and Carles, rather than telling me about how they became active in the party, emphasized an ideological, moral awakening. This speaks to how being an idealist was a key factor in being a Catalanist, an affective, moral understanding of the world that had to be nursed and cultivated. My interlocutors demonstrated an understanding of national identity as processual and subject to evolution over time, as when one of them, Jaume, told me that he did not just look at the scenic Catalan mountains one day and decide he wanted independence, but that the realization came with a knowledge of Catalan culture, customs and history (Jaume, 27 February 2012). This finding parallels Ivan Serrano's claim that national identities in Catalonia are not static, but currently subject to a shift from the 'non-conflictive, dual, or nested identities' (Serrano 2013: 528). Catalans seem to be becoming more Catalan, as those identifying as exclusively Catalan increased from 24 per cent in 1979 to more than 40 per cent in the 2010s; claims of exclusively Spanish identity have halved during that same period (2013: 527).

This fluid view of Catalan national identity also means that at some level it is a consequence of choice, a matter of subjecting oneself to certain Catalan dispositions. The disciplined nature of these preferences can be seen in Dolors' insistence on setting her cell phone language to French. Catalan had not been available and she was adamant about refusing to use Spanish. Similarly when I asked Cristian about speaking Castilian in his daily life, he shrugged and said: 'Intento no fer-ho. Per raons sentimentals' [I try not to. For sentimental reasons] (Cristian, 7 June 2012).

Catalan identity has long been seen as intrinsically connected with the Catalan language and since the contentious 1983 Catalonian Linguistic Normalization Law (which gave Catalan and Spanish equal official status in the region) actors have campaigned ardently to make sure Catalan is the main vehicle of social communication in Catalonia (Villarroya 2012: 38). This has not yet been accomplished, especially in the multi-ethnic and heterogeneous Barcelona, where both language-choice and spatial strategies can become instruments of national identity politics (Hau 2016) and where exposure to Castilian is constant – radio commercials are often in Spanish, and while some programs and service announcements are in Catalan, others are made for a Spanish-speaking audience and music brings in a mix of American, Spanish and Catalan artists. My interlocutors, however, as convinced nationalists, would never switch to Spanish when out to eat or at a café, even if the waiter did not speak Catalan. I witnessed this once when we went to pay for our coffee and the South American waiter received us in Castilian – in accordance with their usual practice they simply replied in Catalan. Speaking to me of a recent vacation in the Basque Country, Carles told me he had been very surprised at how good his Spanish was, as he never used it in Catalonia. To live in Barcelona while avoiding contact with Spanish requires great effort, an extreme preference which can be seen as a technology of the self, or a discipline of preference: a constant insistence on Catalan, abilities notwithstanding, was part of how my interlocutors sought to affirm their national identities and form a more virtuous Catalan subject.

They saw nothing 'natural' or inherent about being Catalanist. Their nationality was not written in their passports, and it was not bestowed upon birth. Several of my informants came from mixed family backgrounds, or outright Spanish-speaking families. Being Catalan was a quality that could be awakened or nursed into being, and the more awareness there was of history, the stronger the Catalanist convictions and desire for independence. My interlocutors saw their national sentiment as something that was being continually produced and could be lost if it ceased to be practised. Equating the nation and the language, Carles explained the situation to me: 'Tota la vida haurem d'estar atents a la salut de la nostra llengua. Els únics que no es preocupen són els espanyols amb el castellà, i els anglesos i els mandarins' [We always have to pay attention to the health of our language. The only ones that don't worry are the Spanish with their Castilian, the English and the Mandarin-speakers]. Not even independence would allow Catalonia to relax fully: 'No podrem deixar mai les armes' [We can never lay down our arms] (Carles, 30 March 2012).

Carles did not see Catalan nationhood as an unproblematic given, but rather as something one had to work towards and fight for. Billig reminds us that identity should not be seen as a reified thing, but rather a shorthand description for ways of talking about the self within a community (Billig 1995: 60). Similarly, I see a Catalanist identity as shorthand for a cultivated self. That is, not as a natural *tabula rasa*, but as a certain type of social person acting within a specific symbolic community (cf. Cohen 1985). While a Catalan individual is already a specific type of disciplined person, belonging to a certain nationality, a Catalan nationalist takes this a step further, engaging with nationalist discourse, attempting to realize it, and to become a Catalanist subject. From this viewpoint, my informants were actively practising 'Catalanhood' through their narratives and linguistic practices.

The Catalanist subject, to be understood as a person submitting to Catalan nationalist discourse, was not free from evaluation among my informants. Charles Hirschkind has argued that listening to sermon-cassettes in Egypt is a complex of social actions, a technology of the self which is designed to fashion a moral, Muslim self (2006: 89). Similarly, my informants would examine themselves and others for the 'right' Catalanist virtues, comparing, contrasting and ranking. They sought to identify and affirm the idealism that is seen as constitutive of a righteous Catalanist, distancing themselves from other, less virtuous political players on the Catalan nationalist political scene. By engaging in their discursive cultivation, my informants necessarily entered into a struggle about what 'Catalanism' even means. There was a certain 'Esquerran way' of being a Catalan nationalist, which was seen as the 'right one', and the most virtuous. Distinctions could be made between the ways in which one could be Catalanist, which itself was stratified according to certain values and virtues. This was obvious when the ERC activists talked about another Catalanist party, the centre-right CiU,[5] traditionally the largest party in Catalonia and the one most often in government. Writing on Catalan nationalism, John Hargreaves has identified *pactisme*, translatable as contractualism or the will to negotiate, as a Catalan core value, and one often highlighted as part of the Catalan national character (Hargreaves 2000: 20). Interestingly, this was decidedly not a virtue for my interlocutors. CiU was looked down upon and ridiculed for their indecisiveness and political manoeuvering. On one occasion, Ricard emphasized pragmatic, scheming politics as classical traits of CiU politics, saying derogatively: 'Sempre busquen el consens!' [They always seek consensus!]. Emphatically waving his hand back and forth, Carles joined in, stating that it was the same with CiU's stance on independence: 'És com un joc. Sí – no, sí – no, sí – no' [It's like a game. Yes – no, yes – no, yes – no]. Enric, the group's nestor, told me how CiU were always scheming, trying to gain influence by supporting whatever

---

5 A semi-permanent coalition of the two parties Convergència and Unió.

party stood to win the Spanish elections, first keeping PSOE in power during their term and now supporting the PP. They only cared for their own interests. ERC, on the other hand, was seen as a party that stood by their beliefs. My interlocutors praised their idealism as a virtue, differentiating themselves from other, less zealous Catalanists, as when Carles termed himself an 'independentista ideològic' [ideological independentist] (Carles, 30 March 2012). For most Catalans, he said, the struggle for independence was about pragmatic, political issues and most of all, money.

But a select few Catalanists were idealists. Another activist, Xavi told me he did not care much about the potential economic benefits of independence. An independent Catalonia would not necessarily be wealthier, but it would be more social, more equal: 'No més riquesa però menys pobresa. (El catalanisme és menys com Lega Nord i més com Chiapes)' [Not with more wealth but less poverty. (Catalanism is less like Lega Nord and more like Chiapas)] (Xavi, 26 March 2012). He contrasted the purely economic right-wing separatism of the Italian Lega Nord with the poor, indigenous-rights Marxist movement ELZN in Chiapas, Mexico. Esquerra was more a movement than a party: he compared it to Nelson Mandela's anti-apartheid ANC. Such a discursive equation of left-wing policies with Catalanism and independence is not rare in Catalonia. Indeed, recent statistical data shows us that left-wing ideologies correlate positively with support for independence, while conservative ideologies have a negative relation to it (Serrano 2013: 538). Xavi's claim represented an understanding of Catalan independence as an inherently left-wing project and related to politically progressive, redistributive policy objectives.

Injustice

In my fieldwork, I was initially surprised by the widespread use of the word 'injustice' in what I had otherwise considered rather mundane and practical political arguments. At an ERC debate meeting, a young man named Hugo came up to me and passionately started explaining to me that Catalonia receives 9 per cent less than what they pay in taxes to the Spanish government, what he called a 'dèficit fiscal' [tax deficit], emphasizing multiple times that this was extremely unfair.

Xavi also spoke of this deficit. Referencing Marx's theory of surplus value, he equated the relationship between Catalonia and Spain with that of worker and a capitalist intermediary, somebody making a profit although having no part in the production (Xavi, 1 June 2012). At other times, Carles, Robert, Oriol, Cristian and Mireia all repeated similar statements on unfair taxation. There is a potential political paradox in these statements. The ERC considers itself a left-wing party and supports internal policies of redistribution in Catalonia. The very principle of redistribution is that some receive less than what they pay in taxes, but this was considered a prime example of the unjust policies of Spain towards Catalonia.

As Serrano has remarked, this perception of 'unfair treatment by the state in political but also fiscal terms' (2013: 524) has greatly aided social mobilization in favour of independence in Catalonia. It is something not only visible in the political debate but talked about and felt deeply in the daily lives of independence supporters. I would argue that this view of Spanish taxation as unfair should not be seen as solely a question of the economy but rather as a moral evaluation of the (ideal) relationship between the two nations. The problem for my informants did not lie in paying taxes as a citizen to the state, but about paying taxes as a Catalan to an illegitimate Spanish government. Their moral claim was that the 'good' Catalan life, or the way Catalans ought to live, was a life independent of Spain. It was morally right for interlocutors to fight for less taxation in spite of their leftist views, because the fight was not really about money and sharing their wealth but about ensuring 'que podem començar a treballar per nosaltres mateixos. Els nostres diners pels nostres interesos' [that we can start working for ourselves. Our money for our interests] (Christian, 7 June 2012). In other words, being free from taxation is linked to a moral demand for national self-determination. As an ideology, nationalism ironically transcends national borders. It is the underlying assumption that all nations should recognize the morality of nationhood as universal (Billig 1995: 9). By engaging with this discourse and drawing upon it, my interlocutors could shift the discussion upwards, making the paying of taxes a moral rather than a fiscal issue. It discursively transformed the struggle for tax benefits to the wealthiest region in Spain into a just fight for freedom and autonomy.

The matter of unfair treatment also came up when I spoke to Carles about the mutual animosity between Castilians and Catalans. He explained what would happen if you spoke Catalan in regions of Spain outside Catalonia:

> Si vas a Saragossa avui per exemple, i hi ha un cambrer, això m'ho han explicat, no m'ha passat a mi, 'habláis catalán? No os atiendo'. Sí! Això passa. Digueu les coses pel seu nom. Això és racisme. Això es racisme! No es diu mai d'aquesta manera que és molt fort, però és un acte de racisme. Si algú hauria dit: no os atiendo porque habláis catalan sino no entiendo porque soís negros? Aquest és racisme això. És el mateix. Aqui, afortunadament, no passa. Jo no conec ningú que digui 'ah, parleu castellà? No us atenc'. Això no ha passat mai.

> [If you go to Saragossa today for example, and there's a waiter, well, I've been told this, I haven't seen it myself, but the waiter goes: 'Are you guys speaking in Catalan? Then I'm not going to take your order.' Yes! That happens. Call the things by their right name, that's racism. It's racism! Nobody ever says it in this way because it's a very strong word, but that's an act of racism. What if someone had said, 'I won't take your order because you're black'? That's racism. It's the same thing. Here, fortunately, that doesn't happen. I don't know anybody who'd say, 'Oh, you speak Castilian? I won't tend to you'. That has never happened.] (Carles, 30 March 2012)

Carles' statement that this unfair treatment of Catalans is racism showcases the clear moral values embedded in the story. First, that Castilians discriminate and Catalans do not. A 'good' Catalan is to be respectful and speak both Catalan and Castilian, but is not met with the same recognition from Spaniards.[6] The Catalan lives the life of a victim, just like the black man in a racist environment. In drawing this comparison to what is generally considered a universal value, the equal treatment of all skin colours, Carles attempts to draw a parallel between his political views of Catalan autonomy and moral claims of equal treatment of all ethnicities. By referring to other, larger ethical givens, he lends credit to his telling of

---

6   This perspective might be set alongside the (previously referred to) refusal of Catalan nationalists in Barcelona to respond to a waiter in Castilian: 'My interlocutors, however, as convinced nationalists, would never switch to Spanish when out to eat or at a café, even if the waiter did not speak Catalan'.

the victimized Catalan. Through drawing upon universalist moral claims, Carles actively positions himself on the moral high ground, making his political views unassailable, righteous and just. He is also able to construct a moral schism between Castilian and Catalan behavior in how they supposedly react to difference and diversity and he can point to a separation, to independence, as the logical outcome of such differences in moral national character. At the same time, my informants had contradictory attitudes towards linguistic plurality. Jaume expressed great annoyance at Spanish 'immigrants' not learning what he considered a minimum of Catalan after several months in Catalonia: 'No em diguis que no saps les paraules bàsiques. Despres de 4 mesos, pots dir un "tallat"!' [Don't tell me you don't know the most basic words. After four months here, you can say a 'tallat!' [a type of espresso known as *cortado* in Castilian]]. This was especially true for those working in the service industry, as Jaume wanted to order in Catalan, his 'llengua pròpia' [own language] (Jaume 27 February 2012).

Here, Jaume's statements belie the otherwise highly praised ideals of inclusiveness and tolerance. Catalonia becomes recast as an intrinsically national territory with a language and, by extension, a culture one has to submit to and accept as one's own. The way Jaume draws a line between his Catalan culture and that of the immigrants essentially constructs a narrative of who rightly belongs and who does not.

Democracy

In highlighting positive aspects of the national character, or *tarannà*, my interlocutors were in a sense talking to me about the morally good Catalan, the ideal self according to the discourse of Catalanism. Along with the concept of *seny* [rationalism, level-headedness], a democratic bent has traditionally been highlighted as a typically Catalan value (Hargreaves 2000: 22; Desfor Edles 1999: 321). For my informants as well, democracy was seen as the prime national virtue, being mentioned first and foremost in any discussion of what being Catalan 'really meant'. Democracy as a virtue was primarily praised by my interlocutors in relation to the archetypical example of poor democratic institutions in Spain. Catalonia had historically had democratic institutions, Carles explained, stating that the first parliament in Continental Europe was the medieval Catalan institution *Les Corts*, a council of feudal lords who could vote on the king's policies:

> I aquest és un fet diferencial bàsic, que ens diferencia dels castellans. Perquè els castellans, històricament, no ho han tingut això. Han tingut el poder absolut. Han tingut un rei que regnava amb poder absolut a Castella. I després el rei borbònic. El rei borbònic [*who came from*] França que tenia una reina també absolutista, jacobina. Per tant, això, d'alguna manera, això passa de generació en generació, de segle en segle. Fixa't per exemple actualment en el parlament de Catalunya i el parlament d'Espanya. La democràcia espanyola és molt pobra. És molt pobra!
>
> [This is a basic difference, that differentiates us from the Castilians. Because the Castilians haven't had this, historically. They had an absolute sovereign. They had a king who reigned with absolute power in Castile. And after that, the Bourbons. The Bourbon king, [who came from] France, also had an absolutist reign, Jacobite. And in some way, this passes from generation to generation, from century to century. Look at the current parliament of Catalonia and the parliament of Spain. The Spanish democracy is very poor – it's very poor!] (Carles, 30 March 2012)

Several of my other informants also expressed the view that Catalonia's current multi-party system showcased a more democratic character than the Spanish.[7] The obvious ethnic implications of a virtue 'passing from generation to generation' were completely glossed over. I see these narratives as attempts to internalize the ideal of a democratic national character. For example, Carles was highlighting a morally upright value of being Catalan and in doing so, presenting the ideal in order to realize it and affirm it. Later, he made the link between history, democratic virtues and the national, Catalan identity more explicit:

---

7   The prime variable seemed to be the number of parties, though Xavi, Cristian, and Oriol all told me on other occasions that the UK was so much more democratic than Spain, and the UK also has a de facto two-party system. Oriol explained this away by saying that the UK had a better democratic tradition than Spain (Oriol, 24 April 2012).

> Un tarannà és un, és el nostre caràcter. La nostra manera de fer. I el nostre tarannà és històricament molt més democràtic que els castellans. Però qui governa Espanya, qui ha governat històricament Espanya? Els castellans. De manera que ells han pensat tota Espanya, han pensat en una Espanya uniforme. I homogènia culturalment. I clar, què passa? Que han intentat homogeneïtzar-nos culturalment i lingüísticament. Però no han pogut.
>
> [Our *tarannà*, it's our character. How we do things. Our way of being, doing things. And our *tarannà* is much more democratic than the Castilian. But who has historically governed Spain? The Castilians. They've thought of all of Spain as a uniform Spain. And culturally homogeneous. And of course, what happens? That they've tried to homogenize us culturally and linguistically. But they haven't been able to do it!] (Carles, 30 March 2012)

Carles was making a case for the moral justification for Catalan independence: A people as democratic as the Catalans should not live under the yoke of the despotic Spanish. For him, it was quite simply unfair and morally wrong that a nondemocratic people such as the Castilians had governed Spain, conquered the Catalans and waged a cultural war against them over centuries. This again raises his argument from the political to the ethical and just, carrying notions of a moral obligation for supporting Catalan independence.

My informants regarded the national, Catalan character as especially democratic, and their party Esquerra was seen as the apex embodiment of this virtue. All political parties have hierarchies, as Mireia told me, but *Esquerra* was the most democratic, because they truly made use of assemblies. She went on to state: 'El meu vot exerceix realment l'exercici democràtic amb tota la força. Jo formo part d'aquest grup i puc canviar les coses' [My vote actually performs the exercise of democracy in full force. I'm part of this group and I can change things] (Mireia, 24 April 2012). This is connected to the self-image my interlocutors had of being idealist and Xavi's earlier statements that ERC was akin to the South African anti-apartheid movement and the Zapatistas of Chiapas, being a just movement with a focus on a long-term goal rather than specific, current political issues (Xavi, 26 March 2012). If the Catalan national character embodied democracy for my interlocutors, then *Esquerra* was the embodiment of these democratic morals as a party. Through talking about *Esquerra* and their part in it, they were able to themselves appropriate these attractive virtues, internalizing them. That this virtue was constantly praised served to continually remind my interlocutors of it, essentially helping them cultivate themselves as Catalanist subjects. When positioning themselves as the heirs to the virtues of the Catalan national character, my informants sought to internalize the recognition as a virtuous people that they lacked at an official, Spanish, level.

Tolerance and Pacifism

Tolerance, openness and pacifism were another set of related values seen as distinctly Catalan, which I have chosen to conflate into one analytical category. These virtues appeared most explicitly when my interlocutors spoke of openness and tolerance in regard to ethnic and political issues such as immigration and respect for minorities in Catalonia. My interlocutors saw themselves as open to cultural and societal differences and naturally peaceful by virtue of being Catalans. Jaume, himself a historian, summed up his views on the tolerant nature of the Catalans by saying: 'Catalunya és terra de pas. Sempre ha estat així, des dels romans' [Catalonia is a marchland. It has always been so, since Roman times] (Jaume 27 March 2012). Similarly, ERC members spoke of immigration as something positive for Catalonia and highlighted the multicultural nature of Barcelona, praising how people from all over the world came to Catalonia to 'become Catalans'. They saw newcomers as adding to the Catalan nation, rather than taking away from it.

For my interlocutors, the virtue of pacifist tolerance was at once inherent in the Catalan character, but also, or perhaps precisely because of this, a virtue to strive towards. One of the most salient examples of Catalanist tolerance was the stance towards the small Aranese-speaking community of Vall d'Aran, or the Aran Valley. This *comarca* of around 8,000 inhabitants in the Pyrenees speak a language related to Gascon and Occitan, which is recognized as official in Catalonia. Robert was explicit that in the event of Catalan independence, the Aranese would be free to join – or not to: 'Si un dia volen fer l'altre pas, pues [*sic*] sí' [If one day they want to take it a step further, well then they're welcome]. Robert also told me they had indeed had discussions within the party about Vall d'Aran, but they concluded in agreement: 'Si volem que Espanya ens respecti a nosaltres, hem de respectar la Vall d'Aran' [If we want Spain to respect us, we have to respect the Aran Valley] (Robert 27 April 2012).

The virtue of auto-determination was thus seen as important to my interlocutors and something they would uphold in their own state towards their own minorities. This implies following the aforementioned universalist claim of nationalism without hypocrisy; what Catalonia morally demands for itself, it recognizes as Vall d'Aran's equally moral claim. For my interlocutors, it was seen as only natural, a necessary link between the attributed virtues of the national character and Esquerra's actual politics. They equated their own views and lives with the perceived virtues of the national character, presenting it in order to inhabit it, to realize it. It was also another way of marking the struggle for independence as ethical, because it furthered the universality of the nationalist claim, with *Esquerra*'s recognition of Vall d'Aran making Spain's lack of recognition of Catalonia seem an even greater ethical deficit. My informants' attitudes to the Vall d'Aran can thus also be seen as a vital component in creating distance between them and Spain, as an independent Catalonia would not force anybody into sharing a state with them as Spain had done. The tolerance of Vall d'Aran's right, or that of others, to decide for themselves was a concrete expression of the virtue of tolerance, as the ideals of the national Catalan character were made into actual policy. For my informants, their stance towards Vall d'Aran was determined by the tolerance naturally inherent in the national character, but this posturing was of course also a gesture of 'othering' towards Spain. Elaborating on this theme, Carles said to me: 'Mai hem votat si volem ser espanyols o no. Mai! Per tant considero que la llibertat és el valor més alt de qualsevol col.lectiu humà' [We've never voted on whether we wanted to be Spaniards or not. Never! That's why I consider freedom the highest value of any human collective] (Empirical log, 27 March 2012).

In the narratives of my interlocutors, then, Catalans had been denied the right to decide for themselves – but they in turn were willing to extend this right to others, because that was a key part of being virtuous Catalans. In the same vein, Oriol explained how an independent Catalonia would treat their large minority of Spanish speakers: 'Una Catalunya republicana no seria contra res. La independència és per a ser més lliures' [The Catalan republic wouldn't be anti-anything. Independence has to do with being more free] (Oriol, 14 June 2012). The virtuous combined trait of tolerance and openness was inherent for the Catalans, and in fighting for this politically they were striving to affirm their practices as reflecting the perceived ideal national Catalan character, with ERC policies following naturally from the national ethics of Catalonia.

Since the aggressive police actions during the unofficial Catalan referendum on independence (1 October 2017), which left over 1,000 people injured, the issue of violence and pacifism is now at the forefront of pro-independence politics in Catalonia. Although this ongoing development still lacks rigorous research, the repressive actions of Spain's central government have propelled ERC members to highlight the non-violent nature of their protests. The virtue of tolerant pacifism and the rhetoric surrounding it is becoming increasingly important as Catalanist political activists seek to emphasize differences between Spain and Catalonia, and to distance ERC and the pro-independence struggle from violence and conflict. The Spanish police response to the referendum has made it not only important for ERC members to highlight such differences, but also much easier.

Conclusion

In this chapter, I have attempted to show how political activists from the Catalan nationalist party ERC cultivate certain virtues and values as part of a national discipline. Through this discipline Catalan nationalism is internalized as an inner psychological state and an individual understanding of a virtuous, valuable self. ERC activists seek to 'live out' their Catalan nationality through a dialogue with themselves about their selves as political activists, as Catalans, and as Catalan nationalists. Ricoeur has argued that through telling a certain story we also tell a story of ourselves, that we construct an identity through narration: 'It is the identity of the story which makes the identity of the character' (Ricoeur 1995: 147). For my interlocutors, their narratives were essential to building Catalan selves and affirming the virtues important for a political Catalanist activist. The presentation of ideal characteristics becomes a way of constituting a Catalan subject, taking care of oneself and embodying the recognition one otherwise lacks. This embodiment is an important part of the construction of self, as our dispositions are formed through an identification with and internalization of certain values, norms, and ideals (Schofer 2005: 276).

This continuous cultivation of Catalanist subjects among ERC activists can only be understood in the light of their current political circumstances. My informants felt deeply Catalan, spoke only Catalan, moved in circles with people sharing their pro-independence views, and referred to Catalonia as a country. The Spanish passport my informants held did not correspond to their views of themselves as Catalans, and they felt deeply disenfranchised and alienated from the state of Spain. Through cultivating Catalanist dispositions, they were able to become the type of person they wanted to be, and secure internal recognition of their nationality, even if external recognition was unattainable.

Bibliography

Anderson, B. (1991). *Imagined Communities: Reflections on the Origin and Spread of Nationalism*. London: Verso.

Billig, M. (1995). *Banal Nationalism*. London: Sage.

Brandes, S. (1990). 'The Sardana: Catalan Dance and Catalan National Identity', *The Journal of American Folklore*, 103 (407), 24–41.

Burg, S. L. (2015). 'Identity, Grievances, and Popular Mobilization for Independence in Catalonia', *Nationalism and Ethnic Politics*, 21 (3), 289–312.

Cohen, A. P. (1985). *The Symbolic Construction of Community*. London: Routledge.

Crameri, K. (2000). 'Banal Catalanism?', *National Identities*, 2 (2), 145–57.

Desfor Edles, L. (1999). 'A Culturalist Approach to Ethnic Nationalist Movements: Symbolization and Basque and Catalan Nationalism in Spain', *Social Science History*, 23 (3), 311–55.

Eriksen, T. H. (2002). *Ethnicity and Nationalism: Anthropological Perspectives*. London: Pluto Press.

Fornet-Betancourt, R., Becker, H., Gomez-Müller, A., and Gauthier, J. D. (1987). 'The Ethics of the Concern of the Self as a Practice of Freedom: An Interview with Michel Foucault on January 20, 1984', *Philosophy Social Criticism*, 12 (2–3), 112–31.

Goffman, E. (1959). *The Presentation of Self in Everyday Life*. New York: Anchor Press.

Guibernau, M. (2013). 'Secessionism in Catalonia: After Democracy', *Ethnopolitics*, 12 (4), 368–93.

Guibernau, M. (2014). 'Prospects for an Independent Catalonia', *International Journal of Politics, Culture, and Society*, 27 (1), 5–23.

Hargreaves, J. (2000). *Freedom for Catalonia?: Catalan Nationalism, Spanish Identity and the Barcelona Olympic Games*. Cambridge: Cambridge University Press.

Hau, M. F. (2016). 'Nation Space, and Identity in the City: Marking Space and Making Place in Barcelona', *Etnofoor*, 28 (2), 77–98.

Hirschkind, C. (2006). *The Ethical Soundscape: Cassette Sermons And Islamic Counterpublics*. Columbia: Columbia University Press.

Hirschkind, C. (2011). 'Is There a Secular Body?', *Cultural Anthropology*, 26 (4), 633–47.

Mahmood, S. (2004). *Politics of Piety: The Islamic Revival and the Feminist Subject*. Princeton, NJ: Princeton University Press.

Martin, L. H., Gutman, H., and Hutton, P. H. (eds) (1988). *Technologies of the Self: A Seminar with Michel Foucault*. Amherst: University of Massachusetts Press.

Ricoeur, P. (1995). *Oneself as Another*. Chicago: University of Chicago Press.

Schofer, J. W. (2005). 'Self, Subject, and Chosen Subjection: Rabbinic Ethics and Comparative Possibilities', *The Journal of Religious Ethics*, 33 (2), 255–91.

Serrano, I. (2013). 'Just a Matter of Identity? Support for Independence in Catalonia', *Regional & Federal Studies*, 23 (2), 523–45.

Villarroya, A. (2012.) 'Cultural policies and national identity in Catalonia', *International Journal of Cultural Policy*, 18 (1), 31–45.

CARLES JOVANÍ GIL

Russian Geopolitical Thinking and the Ukrainian Crisis: Neo-Imperialist Aspirations or Merely a Survival Strategy?

ABSTRACT

The Ukrainian crisis marked the end of a post-Cold War order based on restraint and respect for the territorial sovereignty of the republics that emerged from the ashes of the Soviet Union. It represented a qualitative leap in Russia's approach to its 'near abroad' as Moscow articulated a discourse combining elements of nationalist rhetoric with a strong geopolitical rationale which set a dangerous precedent for external interference that has tested the responsiveness of the international community. The chapter explores the origins of Russian nationalism, its influence on foreign policy and the strategy underpinning its approach to the conflict in Crimea and the Donbas. It concludes that the Kremlin implemented a non-arbitrary policy of expansionism rooted in a feeling of 'geographical insecurity'. The intervention in Ukraine has opened a Pandora's Box that leads the region to a future fraught with uncertainty, not least in terms of nationality and identity politics.

The Ukrainian Republic offers intriguing, and in many ways unique, opportunities to explore how political pragmatism both moulds and emerges from evolving concepts of nationhood and national identity. Within the very uncertain bounds of almost unparalleled multi-ethnic population shifts throughout history, as well as ancestral and pre-Soviet and post-Soviet Russian hegemony, Ukraine has once again been a victim of its own singularities: these include a strategic geographical location, conflicting historical narratives, weak state structures and socio-political contradictions (Riu 2014). The difficulty of defining, let alone establishing, the kind of coherent sense of nationhood required by any state is amply illustrated by the considerations explored in this account.

The episodes of instability that have affected part of the Ukrainian territory since the end of 2013 follow a similar script to events that occurred in other areas of the former Soviet Union such as Transnistria, Abkhazia or South Ossetia. In all of them, Moscow fanned ethnic tensions and then applied force at a moment of political uncertainty. By doing so, it was able to achieve territorial changes and retain considerable power in its geopolitical *glacis*. However, the uniqueness of the Ukrainian case obliges us to avoid making simplifications or seeing events as little more than a repetition of such instances. The annexation of Crimea exceeded the traditional approach of Russia to its 'near abroad', representing an unprecedented event in the post-Cold War order. Additionally, it can be argued that Moscow consciously articulated a discourse combining a geopolitical rationale with elements of the nationalist rhetoric.

The Origins of Russian Nationalism and Its Influence on the Formulation of Foreign Policy

The Russian nationalist creed has evolved over time and now holds a central position in current Russian geopolitical thought. Since its origins in the mid-nineteenth century, this ideology has gradually permeated all layers of society and is at present a virtually all-embracing presence in post-Soviet official rhetoric. The most successful of the many expressions of this concept is neo-Eurasianism, which lacks a unified programme but encompasses the old territorial aspirations of the Russian people on the Eurasian continent, an ethereal space whose central area is homologous to Mackinder's (1919) *Heartland*. Neo-Eurasianists aim to regain regional leadership in order to restore lost great-power status. They represent an amalgam of geopolitical ideas ranging from the restoration of the Soviet Union or the establishment of a continental empire, to the strengthening of economic ties inside the former Soviet space or the use of political coercion within that area.

The years that followed the demise of the Soviet Union saw the emergence of various schools of thought that attempted to define Eurasia and determine the main regional objectives of Moscow. Contrary to what was predicted by some politicians and academics, Russia wanted to maintain its political, economic and cultural presence in this space, and most of its elites were convinced that the newly created state would be unable to cope with its most pressing internal challenges without first responding to those emanating from its traditional area of influence. In the light of the post-Cold War, no political party with parliamentary representation fully embraces the more aggressive neo-Eurasian approaches, although such thinking has permeated – to a greater or lesser extent – all the political groups represented in the *Duma*. This 'ideological entryism' extends beyond state bodies and the political sphere in its narrow sense, and touches intellectuals, academia, the world of culture as well as an important part of the Russian society. The diversity and polymorphism of this doctrine led Tsygankov (2003) to divide its many manifestations into four groups: geoeconomists; civilizationists; expansionists; stabilizers.

Geoeconomists give prominence to geoeconomic over geopolitical factors, and state that the main security objective must be economic prosperity and the social development of the state. Achieving this scenario of stability would require implementing economic macro-projects fostered by enormous public and private partnerships comprising Western and Asian players. For their part, civilizationists are associated with neo-Soviets or Eurasian communists, and look back nostalgically to a glorious past in which a proud Russian people enjoyed international respect. Meanwhile, revolutionary expansionists call for a conservative revolution and territorial expansion to guarantee state security. Finally, stabilizers or democratic statists combine democratic Western liberalism with a Russian autocratic neo-nationalist substratum. In this latter worldview, Russia is conceived as a Eurasian civilization that is not necessarily anti-Western. They advocate a model of state based on strong institutions and the maintenance of internal social and political order (Tsygankov and Tsygankov 2010: 669), as well as a pragmatic foreign policy to deal with the multipolar reality of the post-Cold War order. Stabilizers accept that Russia no longer has the superpower status that the Soviet Union once held, but they advocate occasional intervention in the ex-Soviet space to protect national interests; this has led some authors to speak of a new 'Monroesky Doctrine'. This current of thought was dominant for most of Boris Yeltsin's mandate and during the first two terms of his successor, Vladimir Putin (Tsygankov 2003: 117–20). However, Putin's return to the presidency on 4 March 2012 meant a gradual abandonment of the previous pragmatism in favour of a more vivid desire to consolidate Russia as a hegemon in the former Soviet space. The events in Ukraine led many observers to conclude that Russia's foreign policy had undergone a 'paradigm shift' driven by ethno-nationalist ideas. Nevertheless, as Tsygankov (2015: 279) has pointed out, Moscow's actions 'constituted a major escalation' encompassing 'both change and continuity in Russia's foreign policy'. Thus, it would be more appropriate to characterize the present-day attitude of the Kremlin towards its traditional sphere of influence as that of an 'assertive stabilizer' rather than simply of an ultra-nationalist expansionist.

Events in Ukraine offer a clear example of this approach to its traditional sphere of influence. In Russian nationalist imagery, Ukraine is known as 'Little Russia' and represents the cultural and ancestral heart of an ancient Slavic culture. Indeed, the ethnic group that founded the Duchy of Moscow and the Russian Empire traces its origins to a political community founded in the Kievan Rus. Leaving aside the question of identity, the geostrategic value of Ukraine was highlighted by Halford Mackinder (1919: 194) when he included the country in the western foothills of his *Heartland*. After the Soviet disintegration, the American political scientist Zbigniew Brzezinski (1997: 41) described Ukraine as a 'geopolitical pivot', that is, one of those states 'whose importance is derived not from their power and motivation but rather from their sensitive location and from the consequences of their potentially vulnerable condition for the behaviour of geostrategic players'. For his part, Wilson (2000: 292) has certified the pre-eminence of Ukraine on the Eurasian geopolitical chessboard, as its choice between integration in Europe or a rapprochement towards Russia could be crucial for the continental balance of power.

The Outbreak and Handling of the Conflict in Crimea and the Donbas

The Presidium of the Supreme Soviet decreed the transfer of Crimea from the Russian SFSR to the Ukrainian SSR on 19 February 1954, a decision which then had little significance from an administrative point of view. The authorities justified the measure as a commemoration of the 300th anniversary of the signing of the Treaty of Pereyaslav, although the text of that document did not refer to the status of the peninsula, which did not fall under the power of the Tsar until 130 years later. The real motive of the Soviet *nomenklatura* was probably to fortify its control of Ukraine by adding 860,000 ethnic Russians to its population. In addition, by transferring the Crimea, Nikita Khrushchev won the support needed to make the party Secretariat the leading position within the Soviet hierarchy (Kramer 2014).

The anomaly of Ukrainian control of the Crimean Peninsula would become evident in the final days of the USSR, when minorities such as the Tatars showed an obstinate opposition to Ukrainian secession because they believed that the old Soviet structure protected their rights against the assimilationist policies of Kiev. Although the majority of the Crimean population voted in favour of independence in the referendum held in December 1991, the level of support at 54 per cent was significantly lower than in most continental regions of Ukraine (Mankoff 2014). In another much-disputed plebiscite in January 1991, which was boycotted by pro-Ukrainian groups, the vast majority of Crimeans supported the creation of an autonomous republic within the future Ukrainian state. This demand was eventually granted by the authorities in Kiev and then recognized in Chapter 10 of the new Ukrainian Constitution (Hansen 2015: 143). However, aspirations for sovereignty in the newly created autonomous republic remained unsatisfied. In May 1992, the Crimean Parliament passed a declaration of sovereignty that forced the Ukrainian government to ease tensions by agreeing a formal division of powers between the governments of Ukraine and the Republic of Crimea (Karagiannis 2014: 407). The treaties creating the Commonwealth of Independent States (CIS) as well as the Treaty of Friendship and the Treaty of Partition[1] in 1997 finally guaranteed Ukrainian sovereignty over the peninsula by

---

[1] The treaty stipulated that Moscow would receive 81.7 per cent of the Soviet fleet and could continue to base it in the peninsula until 2017.

recognizing the territorial integrity of the state and the inviolability of its borders.

As the Russian political crisis grew worse in 2013, Vladimir Putin intensified efforts to establish an area of influence that went beyond politics and economics and included legislation and symbolism. The Russian president urged his neighbours to choose integration centred either on Brussels or on Moscow (Allison 2014: 1256). Viktor Yanukovych responded to Putin's request on 21 November 2013 by announcing the suspension of negotiations for an Association Agreement with the European Union. In the same vein, an intention to strengthen relations with the Russian Federation and its Customs Union was also announced (Karagiannis 2014: 407). With regard to other multilateral initiatives sponsored by the Kremlin in the former Soviet space, most of them have had modest results due to the loss of ideological attractiveness, progressive incompatibility of interests, chronic underinvestment and, ultimately, the lack of political will of new national elites who have devoted their main efforts to consolidating their own niches of power. The entry into force of the Eurasian Economic Union in early 2015 raises doubts about its actual political scope and capacities (Jovaní 2015), given the manifest failure of initiatives such as the CIS.

The suspension of negotiations for the Association Agreement triggered in November 2013 a wave of protests in Kiev's Independence Square which soon grew into a popular outcry against corruption, misgovernment, economic stagnation and authoritarian practices. Unlike the Orange Revolution, which was better planned, the *Euromaidan* movement was a spontaneous manifestation of a subculture of European values and showed a high level of support among broad sectors of Ukrainian society (Saryusz-Wolski 2014: 13). A harsh government crackdown by the paramilitary police (known as the *berkut*) on a few hundred students who initially gathered in downtown Kiev prompted millions of Ukrainians to take to the streets in major cities. This fact represented a qualitative and quantitative change, since the eminently liberal and pro-European nature of the initial protesters was partially displaced by a clearer nationalist discourse and the increasing prominence of extremist parties such as Svoboda or Right Sector. Such an opportunity would be seized by the Russian media to portray the alleged non-democratic nature of the new authorities and its subordination to fascism (Goode 2014).

The protests peaked between 18 and 20 February 2014, when dozens of protesters were killed and hundreds more wounded. An agreement was signed by the Ukrainian president on 21 February to form a national unity government, hold new elections and restore the 2004 constitution. Nevertheless, his subsequent disappearance led Parliament to depose him without fulfilling all the constitutional requirements (Mearsheimer 2014b: 176). Meanwhile, thousands of pro-Russian citizens were demonstrating in Donetsk, Kharkov, Odessa and other Ukrainian cities, shaping 'a unique theatre for Russian nationalism' that amalgamated neo-Soviet, Orthodox and fascist narratives. In Crimea, dozens of armed men took control of key government buildings (Laruelle 2016: 70). Although the Kremlin initially denied that these 'little green men' (as they became known) were Russian soldiers, there was speculation by such specialists in military affairs as Igor Sutyagin about the involvement of units of the 3rd Guards Spetsnaz Brigade, the Black Sea Fleet and the Rapid Reaction Force, as well as about private security companies and units from the Caucasus (Karagiannis 2014: 408–9).

In response to a call from Putin (2014a), the Council of the Russian Federation agreed on 1 March 2014 to authorize sending troops to Ukraine 'to contribute to the normalisation of the social and political situation in the country'. After the unanimous support of the upper chamber, the federal army officially took control of critical infrastructure on the peninsula (Hansen 2015: 141). On 4 March, the Russian president gave initial explanations about the supposed legitimacy of the intervention in Crimea. His argument was based on four points: the unconstitutional overthrow of Yanukovich; a distress call received from deposed Ukrainian authorities; the vulnerability of Russian 'compatriots' (*sootechestvenniki*); and the potential threat to the naval base at Sevastopol. This series of – mostly weak – arguments was intended to mobilize domestic public opinion around a presidential figure and limit any punitive response from the West.

On 11 March 2014 the Crimean Parliament finally approved a declaration of independence. Five days later, and in flagrant violation of the 1994 Budapest Memorandum on Security Assurances and many other fundamental provisions of international law,[2] a plebiscite was held without independent international observers and exclusively supervised by members of the Russian security forces (Gedmin 2014: 8–9). The outcome of the vote, which was boycotted by Tatars and Ukrainian nationalists, gave an overwhelming victory to supporters of reintegration in the Russian Federation. On 17 March the Russian president finally signed a decree recognizing Crimea as a sovereign state, its annexation being formalized the following day. Putin declared after signing the treaty: 'They are constantly trying to sweep us into a corner because we maintain an independent position, because we call things by their names, and do not engage in hypocrisy. But there is a limit to everything' (2014c). After approval from the Constitutional Court and ratification by the Federation Council, Crimea was incorporated on 21 March 2014. Shortly afterwards, on 12 May 2014, pro-Russian activists held two referendums, plagued by irregularities, on the eastern flank of Ukraine and proclaimed Donetsk and Lugansk People's Republics. Both entities should ultimately unite into *Novorossiya*, a proposed confederation that 'rests on its dual meaning in announcing the birth of a New Russia geographically and metaphorically', and that would result in being 'an anticipation of Russia's own transformation' (Laruelle 2014).

The Geopolitical Substratum of Nationalist Rhetoric

In Ukraine the Kremlin used a combination of hard and soft power intended to deflect criticism by international institutions such as NATO or

2   From a legal point of view, and at a minimum, the annexation of Crimea breached: Article 2.4 (Chapter 1) of the UN Charter; UN Resolution 2625 (XXV, 24 October 1970), which regulates the legal principles regarding friendly relations and co-operation between states; UN Resolution 3314 (XXIX, 14 December 1973), which defines the concept of 'aggression'; the Helsinki Final Act; Council of Europe Resolutions 1990 (2014) and 2034 (2014); the Treaty of Friendship and Cooperation between Russia and Ukraine (1997); the military agreement between Russia and Ukraine (1997); the bilateral agreement on frontiers (2003); the Agreement on the Status and Conditions of the Black Sea Fleet; the constitutions of Ukraine and Crimea. See Torreblanca (2015).

the European Union (*The Economist*, 2015). The first and most obvious tactical novelty in this 'hybrid intervention' was the use of covert operations. Although there was no declaration of war, unidentified gunmen took control of key parts of the peninsula and Ukrainian critical facilities. In the first weeks the emphasis was on the use of military intelligence, the distribution of arms and the infiltration of small groups of men from Russia. Moscow gradually transferred power to its marines, airborne troops and special forces. The level of violence was carefully controlled so as to blame Ukraine for a hypothetical escalation of hostilities. Although military power was crucial,[3] Russia also used an intense campaign of diplomatic, economic and media pressure aimed at legitimizing its action, isolating Kiev, and empowering local insurgents (Allison 2014: 1258).

Moscow took advantage of the collapse of the 21 February agreement, which it had not signed, to accuse the United States and other countries of being behind the overthrow of the Ukrainian president. In addition to failing to provide evidence of human rights violations against its nationals or Russian-speakers in Ukraine, the Kremlin made no real effort to demonstrate that its actions were necessary or proportional. Putin argued that Russian forces in Crimea, as well as the Black Sea Fleet, were under threat and this justified self-defence on the basis of Article 51 of the UN Charter. Moscow also argued that it faced a potential wave of refugees like that which occurred following the Balkan and Libya crises, and that Article 61 (2) of the federal constitution obliged Russia to assist its citizens living abroad. While it is true that deposed Ukrainian president Viktor Yanukovych and the prime minister of the Republic of Crimea requested military help from Moscow, the Ukrainian constitution states that only the *Rada* can approve the presence of foreign forces (Allison 2014: 1261–4). Therefore, it can be argued that although the majority of the population of the peninsula probably approved of Russia's actions, the regional institutions lacked the sovereign authority to accept foreign intervention.

---

3   Ukrainian intelligence estimated that by mid-2015 some 9,000 Russian soldiers were deployed in the *oblasts* of Lugansk and Donetsk, and another 50,000 were on the other side of the frontier. The Kremlin and various anti-Western media groups, business corporations and think-tanks also provided aid to 'anti-establishment' political parties.

Even though self-determination is not prohibited by international law, there is a presumption against its application without agreement in the absence of exceptional circumstances (Wilson 2015). The so-called 'saving clause' of the UN Declaration on Principles of International Law Concerning Friendly Relations[4] provides that '[n]othing in the foregoing paragraphs shall be construed as authorizing or encouraging any action which would dismember or impair, totally or in part, the territorial integrity or political unity of sovereign and independent States' (United Nations General Assembly 1970). Nevertheless, the statement itself provides for the right to secede for national groups not under the authority of 'a government representing the whole people belonging to the territory without distinction as to race, creed or colour' (ibid.), and this is a situation that might apply in Crimea. Be that as it may, the International Court of Justice stated in its judgement in the case of Kosovo (22 July 2010) that the right to self-determination does not apply when declarations of independence are accompanied by threats or the use of force, which would seem proven in this case.

The annexation of Crimea and seizure of its assets had an undeniable symbolic value for the Kremlin. Putin (2014c) claimed that the action was a 'restoration of historical justice' following 'a clear violation of constitutional norms' during the Soviet era. The Russian leader even resorted to identity rhetoric to describe Russians as 'one of the largest, if not the largest, divided nation in the world' (Putin 2014c), depicting Ukraine as a nationalizing state trying to assimilate their compatriots. However, the fact that support for ethnic Russian communities in other parts of the former Soviet Union has been rather low-key shows that these descriptions were used to justify purely geopolitical objectives. While patriotism has been ubiquitous in Putin's discourse, he has also warned repeatedly of the dangers of ethnic-based nationalism both for social cohesion and for Russia's statehood. Moreover, the relationship of the Kremlin with the leaders of the self-proclaimed republics in Eastern Ukraine has not always been easy,

---

4   Full title: The Declaration on Principles of International Law concerning Friendly Relations and Co-operation among States in accordance with the Charter of the United Nations.

and his reputed leniency has been questioned by numerous factions of the Russian far right (Chaisty and Whitefield 2015).

The collapse of the 21 February agreement was interpreted by Moscow as irrefutable proof that Western powers had backed the establishment of a puppet government in Kiev that would push for NATO membership. During a press conference in early March, Putin said that Western powers 'supported an unconstitutional seizure of power, declared the government legitimate and are supporting that government' (Saryusz-Wolski 2014: 15). This belief was not entirely unfounded, because American diplomacy supported opposition to Yanukovych and helped fund support through the National Endowment for Democracy. Personalities such as the former US presidential candidate John McCain took part in anti-government demonstrations, and the then US ambassador to Ukraine, Geoffrey Pyatt, even called the fall of the Ukrainian president 'an event for history' (Mearsheimer 2014a). The interim government led by Oleksandr Turchynov also presented to the *Rada* secretariat on 5 March a draft bill reiterating the objective of joining NATO, and the latter had repeatedly expressed its willingness to extend membership to Georgia and Ukraine after the Bucharest summit in April 2008.

The new Ukrainian president, Petro Poroshenko, ended the non-alignment policy proposed by Viktor Yanukovych when he stated in August 2014 his intention to continue advancing towards NATO membership. The speed of the Russian response was not a surprise. A revision of military doctrine in December 2014 identified the strengthening of offensive NATO capabilities on Russia's borders as a major threat (Putin 2014b). In June 2014 Poroshenko had signed the controversial Association Agreement with the European Union, a text that in addition to commercial agreements, proposed 'gradual convergence on foreign and security matters with the aim of Ukraine's ever-deeper involvement in the European security area' and called for 'taking full and timely advantage of all diplomatic and military channels between the parties' (Mearsheimer 2014b: 175). The Ukrainian president also stated that 'in five years [they] will have applied the Association Agreement and achieved all the conditions for applying to join the EU' (Abellán 2015).

At the national level, Russia has pushed from the beginning for a decentralization of the Ukrainian state that would give the eastern and southern regions a greater degree of self-government. This would in practice mean the formation of small protectorates linked to Moscow that would guarantee Russian influence on the Petro Poroshenko administration. Among the main demands of the Kremlin government was a commitment to respect the international neutrality of the country, as well as for equal rights for all citizens regardless of ethnic affiliation (Wade 2015). Achieving the first goal would mean limiting the eastward expansion of NATO and increasing the chances of success for the Eurasian Economic Union. After all, Ukraine has an economy that is more powerful and dynamic than other partners such as small and weak Belarus. However, the Ukrainian industrial sector suffers serious problems and requires considerable investment after years of crisis (Yann 2014: 9). For that reason, a hypothetical incorporation into the Russian Federation of the *oblasts* of Donetsk and Lugansk would also be unprofitable from a cost-benefit logic and could ultimately prove a major source of political tension.

Interventionism as a Survival Strategy?

By initiating an episode of unrest in Ukraine, the Kremlin intended to consolidate the Eurasian bloc as both a geopolitical and a cultural alternative to the West (Mankoff 2014), and its attitude in the management of the crisis can be seen from two diverging theoretical approaches.

The first proposes a sinister scenario in which Moscow embraced the most aggressive thesis of neo-Eurasianism in order to push the borders of the Russian Federation further west. The event that supposedly justified this action was the entry into the Ukrainian interim government of right-wing factions which called for the abolition of linguistic rights enjoyed by the Russian-speaking minority.[5] Bermejo reminds us that 'the protection

---

5   It is worthwhile pointing out that although the Supreme Rada voted to abolish the State Linguistic Policy Act of 2012 (which authorized the use of languages other than Ukrainian in regions where more than 10 per cent of the inhabitants spoke another language), President Oleksandr Turchinov refused to ratify the abolition.

of nationals abroad is an internationally recognized practice under certain circumstances' and so Russia could be expected to take action if these circumstances were to arise (Bermejo 2014: 310). However, unlike other cases such as the Georgian aggression against South Ossetia in 2008, Ukraine did not undertake actions against the physical integrity of civilians in Crimea and other regions with Russian-speaking majorities. Moreover, votes from these territories were crucial for the victory of the pro-Russian Viktor Yanukovych in the 2010 presidential election. With a Russian-speaking community of around 30 per cent of the population, Moscow was assured of the co-operation of Kiev on economic and security issues. Therefore, under this logic, winning Crimea by losing Ukraine would not seem a rational decision (Charap and Darden 2014: 10).

The second approach, shared in this study, sees the strategic move of Russia as a reactive effort to avoid what the Kremlin leadership views as a direct threat to the national interests of the Federation (Charap and Darden 2014: 10). To understand this position, it is necessary to analyse the root causes of the conflict, which means going back long before the events of November 2013 and focusing on relations between Russia and the United States. The events that led to the 2014 annexation of Crimea by the Russian Federation predated the *Euromaidan* protests and the debates about the Ukrainian rapprochement to the European Union, and preceded participation in the Eurasian Economic Union or even the schism between Yulia Tymoshenko and Viktor Yanukovich. The root causes stem from the early 1990s, when President George Bush and Secretary of State James Baker promised Gorbachev that NATO would not expand eastward (Kotkin 2014).

Supporters of a pro-Western orientation for Kiev, such as the American diplomat George Kennan and liberal sectors of the political class in Moscow, warned at the time that an anti-Russian stance would generate hostility in Moscow and be counterproductive to the shared interest of stability. However, successive American administrations ignored this premise and chose to implement a policy of *faits accomplis* to gradually win ground in regions traditionally influenced by Russia. The United States sponsored the eastward expansion of the European Union and NATO, approved the deployment of Western troops in former Soviet republics, launched controversial military campaigns against traditional Russian allies such as Serbia, Iraq and Libya, and supported the so-called 'colour revolutions'. Similarly, Washington was indifferent to the marginalization of Russian-speaking minorities in the Baltic countries, supported the unilateral declaration of independence of Kosovo, deplored Russia's recognition of Abkhazia and South Ossetia and did not condemn involvement by pro-fascist groups in the overthrow of the Ukrainian government in February 2014 (Lukin 2014).

The attitude of the West gave rise to the empowerment of those in Moscow who openly rejected assimilation and advocated a return to a great power status in a multipolar world. As a result, events may lead us to think that Russia wanted to recover its former area of influence in a new 'zero-sum' ideological war in which Ukraine would be a domino that followed Georgia. However, a more balanced evaluation of the facts tells us that Moscow implemented a policy of 'defensive expansionism' rather than arbitrary expansionism (Kotkin 2014). This stance, rooted in a declining imperial idea marked by a sense of inferiority and 'geographical insecurity', has been instrumental in justifying the Kremlin's action in Ukraine (Kaplan 2014), a red line because of its location as a geopolitical 'bridgehead' (Brzezinski 1997: 57) on the European side of the *Heartland*, its sentimental value along the dividing line between Western and Orthodox civilizations (Huntington 1993) and the threat it could represent to the internal stability of Russia.

Final Remarks: The Return of Greater Russia or Putin's Flight to Nowhere?

The Ukrainian crisis has marked the end of a post-Cold War order based on restraint and respect for the territorial sovereignty of the republics that emerged from the ashes of the former Soviet Union. It has also set a dangerous precedent for external interference that will test the responsiveness of the international community. According to Shevtsova, the annexation of Crimea and the division of Ukraine are not ends in themselves, but the means of a doctrine based on reasserting Russia's geopolitical interests and civilizational mission both in its neighbourhood and internationally (Shevtsova 2014: 96). This series of events marks the end of a period of relatively stable relations between Moscow and the West, and signals Putin's determination to overcome American unilateralism. This was evident in the annual address to the Duma in December 2014, when the Russian president presented a medium-term external strategy aimed at challenging the West and diversifying ties with other government actors in Asia (Putin 2014d). In other words, the illusion of a 'Greater Europe' from Dublin to Vladivostok was buried in favour of a 'Greater Asia' from Shanghai to Saint Petersburg. This made it even more difficult for Washington and Brussels to reconcile efficient sanctions against Moscow with its inescapable interests in energy, trade, anti-terrorism and strategical and nuclear security issues (Nye 2014a).

The Russian authorities also used the campaign in Ukraine to discourage internal displays of social solidarity and avoid direct threats to the hyper-presidential national regime. As a result of the management of hostilities by the Kremlin, Putin's popularity climbed to 87 per cent in August 2014. Although this would seem to indicate a strengthening of his internal position, Nye points out that his victory may not be so apparent in the long-term (Nye 2014b). Moscow may have achieved the most urgent objective of stopping the advance of Western political structures on its western borders, but its actions have helped create a more pro-Western identity among Ukrainians. In addition, the crisis weakened the Russian economy, undermined its international reputation and ended any possibility of including Ukraine in projects such as the Eurasian Economic Union (McFaul 2014: 170).

Tensions can be seen in Russian society as a consequence of economic policies designed for an exterior agenda and increasingly distant from the real needs of the people. Moscow's main weaknesses include both its inability to reform a state-controlled economy that is uncompetitive and too dependent on the energy sector, and an excessive tendency to isolationism and non-participation in the global economy (Trenin 2009: 64). The GDP of Russia is barely one-twelfth of the GDP of the United States; oil and gas account for two-thirds of national income; and the rouble has experienced high volatility in the past few years. Fluctuations in oil prices combined with political and economic sanctions have damaged state finances, but the structural weaknesses of Russia exceed any single event (Claudín and de Pedro 2014). To the difficulties associated with its relatively modest economic potential, one must add a dependency on raw materials, technological backwardness, lack of investment in basic social services, a demographic crisis, underlying ethnic tensions, widespread corruption, political scandals and grossly megalomaniac projects such as the 2014 Olympic Winter Games or the 2018 Football World Cup (Nye 2014a). Putin's regime still has the resources for survival, but attempts to tackle new challenges by resorting to old methods will prove inefficient in the long run. It remains to be seen whether a new generation of Russians which demands higher standards of living and greater respect for basic freedoms will be willing to repeat the sacrifices of the past.

Implementation of most of the points included in the Minsk-II agreement, signed in the Belarusian capital in February 2015, has proved impossible in the short term. Putin achieved his minimum objective of preventing the removal of pro-Russian rebels from the Donbas basin, and it cannot be excluded that the model of neighbouring Transnistria may be repeated. Although the Russian president has reaffirmed a commitment to maintaining Ukrainian sovereignty in the disputed area, this should not be interpreted as a curtailment of ambitions, but rather as an affirmation of the will to continue weakening Kiev diplomatically. Indeed, Moscow's proposed constitutional reform for Ukraine along federal lines would simply certify by legal means the division of the country (Trenin 2015).

Despite the relative return to normality in most areas of the country after the presidential elections of May 2014, the situation in eastern Ukraine remains highly volatile and could become worse. On 1 July 2018, the latest 'comprehensive and indefinite ceasefire regime' since the start of the conflict went into effect, although once again it did not hold. With the active armed conflict entering its fifth year, the civilian death toll already stood at about 3,000 people in May 2018, while over 9,000 were injured and more than 2 million had had to leave their homes in the same period (Office of the United Nations High Commissioner 2016). The deadlock reflects a lack of will by the contenders to reach an agreement, and everything points to the probability that it will be years before complete stability returns to the region. In any case, Kiev is unlikely to regain full control of the Donbas basin (Trenin 2014: 15).

For its part, the Crimean Peninsula is now integrated into the Russian Federation and everything seems to indicate a continuous strengthening of political ties. Donald Trump's arrival at the White House in January 2017 opened a chapter of relations with Moscow vitiated by inconsistency. On the one hand, they have been affected by, among other factors, the divergent positions on Syria's civil war, the exchange of diplomatic sanctions and the deployment of US troops in Poland. On the other hand, the US president has been systematically accused of being a tool for the Russians. In June 2018, he called for Russia to be readmitted to the G–7. One month later, on 16 July 2018, Trump's public statements during his first formal meeting with Putin in Helsinki caused a huge stir. In addition, he has been deliberately ambiguous about the annexation of Crimea by the Russian Federation. In regard to the position of the European Union, despite the application of a visa-free travel regime for Ukrainian citizens since 11 June 2017 and the entry into force of the EU–Ukrainian Association Agreement on 1 September 2017, the crisis in which it finds itself does not seem to point to a greater commitment to let Kiev off the hook. Quite the contrary, the shock wave sent by 'Brexit' has served to dash hopes for a future EU membership.

Meanwhile, since Vladimir Putin's re-election in 2018, all the signs are that Russia will continue to pursue an assertive policy in its 'near abroad' aimed at taking advantage of any opportunity that may arise. However, since a model based on 'growth without development, capitalism without democracy and great-power policies without international appeal [...] cannot last forever' (Trenin 2009: 64), a marked weakening in Moscow's capacity for action abroad must not be excluded in the medium term. Regardless of the speed of developments, Putin has already become 'a hostage to his own logic' (Shevtsova 2014: 102), with his intervention in Ukraine opening a Pandora's box that leads the region to a future fraught with uncertainty.

Bibliography

Abellán, L. (2015). 'La UE elude prometer la integración de Ucrania en el club comunitario', *El País*, 27 April.
Allison, R. (2014). 'Russian "Deniable" Intervention in Ukraine: How and Why Russia Broke the Rules', *International Affairs*, 90 (6), 1255–97.
Bermejo, R. (2014). 'De Kosovo a Crimea: La revancha rusa', *Revista Española de Derecho Internacional*, 66 (2), 307–12.
Brzezinski, Z. (1997). *The Grand Chessboard. American Primacy and its Geostrategic Imperatives*. New York: Basic Books.
Chaisty, P., and Whitefield, S. (2015). 'Putin's Nationalism Problem', *E-International Relations*, April <http://www.e-ir.info/2015/04/20/putins-nationalism-problem> accessed 20 January 2017.
Charap, S., and Darden, K. (2014). 'Russia and Ukraine', *Survival: Global Politics and Strategy*, 56 (2), 7–14.
Claudín, C., and Pedro, N. de (2014). 'El Kremlin avanza, el país retrocede', *El País*, 18 December.
The Economist (2015). 'What Russia Wants: From Cold War to Hot War', *The Economist*, 414, 14 February, 19–22.
Gedmin, J. (2014). 'Beyond Crimea. What Vladimir Putin Really Wants', *World Affairs*, July–August, 8–16.
Goode, P. (2014). 'How Russian Nationalism Explains – and Does Not Explain – the Crimean Crisis', *The Washington Post*, 3 March <https://www.washingtonpost.com/news/monkey-cage/wp/2014/03/03/how-russian-nationalism-explains-and-does-not-explain-the-crimean-crisis/?utm_term=.9f0fe4efc988> accessed 20 January 2017.
Hansen, F. (2015). 'Framing Yourself into a Corner: Russia, Crimea, and the Minimal Action Space', *European Security*, 24 (1), 141–58.
Huntington, S. P. (1993). 'The Clash of Civilizations', *Foreign Affairs*, 72 (3), 22–49.
Jovaní, C. (2015). 'La política exterior rusa hacia su frontera meridional (1991–2012). Una revisión de la teoría de los complejos de seguridad regional'. PhD thesis, University of Valencia.
Kaplan, R. D. (2014). 'Crimea: The Revenge of Geography?', *Forbes*, 14 March <http://www.forbes.com/sites/stratfor/2014/03/14/crimeathe-revenge-of-geography> accessed 4 May 2015.
Karagiannis, E. (2014). 'The Russian Interventions in South Ossetia and Crimea Compared: Military Performance, Legitimacy and Goals', *Contemporary Security Policy*, 35 (3), 400–20.

Kotkin, J. (2014). 'Crimea: Russia is Harvesting the Seeds Sown in the 1990s', *The Barefoot Strategist*, 2 March <https://medium.com/the-bridge/crimea-russia-is-harvesting-the-seeds-sown-in-the-1990s-54892d22ccbb> accessed 16 April 2015.

Kramer, M. (2014). 'Why Did Russia Give Away Crimea Sixty Years Ago?', *Wilson Center*, 19 March <https://www.wilsoncenter.org/publication/why-did-russia-give-away-crimea-sixty-years-ago> accessed 14 September 2015.

Laruelle, M. (2014). 'Novorossiya: A Launching Pad for Russian Nationalists', *PONARS Eurasia*, Policy Memo No. 357.

Laruelle, M. (2016). 'The Three Colors of Novorossiya, or the Russian Nationalist Mythmaking of the Ukrainian Crisis', *Post-Soviet Affairs*, 23 (1), 55–74.

Lukin, A. (2014). 'What the Kremlin is Thinking', *Foreign Affairs*, 93 (4), 85–93.

McFaul, M. (2014). 'Moscow's Choice', *Foreign Affairs*, 93 (6), 167–71.

Mackinder, H. J. (1919). *Democratic Ideals and Reality: A Study in the Politics of Reconstruction*. London: Constable.

Mankoff, J. (2014). 'Russia's Latest Land Grab: How Putin Won Crimea and Lost Ukraine', *Foreign Affairs*, 93 (3), 60–8.

Mearsheimer, J. J. (2014a). 'Why the Ukraine Crisis is the West's Fault', *Foreign Affairs*, 93 (5), 77–89.

Mearsheimer, J. J. (2014b). 'Mearsheimer Replies', *Foreign Affairs*, 93 (6), 175–8.

Nye, J. (2014a). 'A Western Strategy for a Declining Russia', *Project Syndicate*, 10 April <http://www.project18syndicate.org/commentary/joseph-s--nye-wants-to-deter-russia-without-isolating-it> accessed 25 February 2015.

Nye, J. (2014b). 'Putin's Calculus', *Project Syndicate* (10 April 2014) <http://www.project-syndicate.org/commentary/joseph-s--nye-asks-whetherrussia-s-short-term-gains-in-ukraine-will-be-worth-the-long-term-loss-of-softpower> accessed 25 February 2015.

Office of the United Nations High Commissioner. (2016). 'Report on the Human Rights Situation in Ukraine 16 August to 15 November 2016', OHCHR.org <http://www.ohchr.org/Documents/Countries/UA/UAReport16th_EN.pdf> accessed 16 January 2017.

Putin, V. (2014a). 'Владимир Путин внёс обращение в Совет Федерации', Kremlin.ru, 1 March <http://www.kremlin.ru/events/president/news/20353> accessed 7 May 2015.

Putin, V. (2014b). 'Военная доктрина Российской Федерации', Kremlin.ru <http://news.kremlin.ru/media/events/files/41d527556bec8deb3530.pdf> accessed 25 February 2015.

Putin, V. (2014c). 'Presidential Address to the Federal Assembly', Kremlin.ru, 18 March <http://en.kremlin.ru/events/president/news/20603> accessed 10 January 2017.

Putin, V. (2014d) 'Presidential Address to the Federal Assembly', kremlin.ru, 4 December <http://en.kremlin.ru/events/president/news/47173> accessed 11 January 2017.

Riu, A. (2014). 'Ucrania: Fotografía de un vuelco histórico', *Eldiario.es*, 14 September <http://www.eldiario.es/agendapublica/proyecto-europeo/Ucrania-fotografia-vuelco-historico_0_302370542.html> accessed 12 April 2015.

Saryusz-Wolski, J. (2014). 'Euromaidan: Time to Draw Conclusions', *European View* 13, 11–20.

Shevtsova, L. (2014). *Interregnum. Russia between Past and Future*. Washington, DC: Carnegie Endowment for International Peace.

Torreblanca, J. I. (2015). 'Las diez violaciones del derecho internacional que Rusia perpetra en Ucrania', *El País*, 18 February.

Trenin, D. (2009). 'Russia Reborn: Reimagining Moscow's Foreign Policy', *Foreign Affairs*, 66 (6), 64–78.

Trenin, D. (2014). *The Ukraine Crisis and the Resumption of Great-power Rivalry*. Moscow: Carnegie Moscow Center.

Trenin, D. (2015). *Ukraine Points towards the Start of a Tumultuous New Era in World Politics*. Moscow: Carnegie Moscow Center.

Tsygankov, A. (2003). 'Mastering Space in Eurasia: Russia's Geopolitical Thinking after the Soviet Break-up', *Communist and Post-Communist Studies*, 36 (1), 101–27.

Tsygankov, A. (2015). 'Vladimir Putin's Last Stand: The Sources of Russia's Ukraine Policy', *Post-Soviet Affairs*, 31 (4), 279–303.

Tsygankov, A. and Tsygankov, P. (2010). 'National Ideology and IR Theory: Three Incarnations of the "Russian idea"', *European Journal of International Relations*, 16 (4), 663–86.

United Nations General Assembly (1970). Declaration on Principles of International Law Concerning Friendly Relations and Co-Operation among States in Accordance with the Charter of the United Nations, A/RES/25/2625.

Wade, R. (2015). 'Rethinking the Ukraine Crisis', *Economic & Political Weekly* 21, 1–4.

Wilson, A. (2000). *The Ukrainians: Unexpected Nation*. New Haven, CT: Yale University Press.

Wilson, G. (2015). 'Crimea: Some Observations on Secession and Intervention in Partial Response to Müllerson and Tolstykh', *Chinese Journal of International Law*, 14, 217–23.

Yann, R. (2014). 'La crise de Crimée (mars 2014): Comment en est-on arrivé là?', *EchoGéo*, March, 2–15.

DANIEL PURCELL

Contested Unionism along the Irish Border at the Time of Partition

ABSTRACT

Histories of Irish partition and discussions of the Irish border portray the six-county settlement as the most 'natural' division of the island, creating a false impression of a cohesive Ulster Protestant national group with clearly defined territorial claims. This chapter focuses on two peripheral Protestant Unionist communities for whom the partition of Ireland represented a time of particular crisis: those outside the Northern state in Cavan and Monaghan, who felt a keen sense of betrayal at the partition settlement, and the Unionists of Fermanagh, who were intensely aware of the precariousness of their situation, being in the most Catholic county in Northern Ireland. These two communities, bordering one another and with strong social connections, developed strikingly different articulations of what it meant to be an Ulster Protestant. Their experiences illustrate the ambiguities of the Irish partition settlement and the way in which national identities were fundamentally altered by it.

Brexit has drawn the focus of EU member states to the Irish border and exposed a lack of awareness of this reality in the rest of the UK, including at senior ministerial level. In order to understand the true significance of the border this chapter returns to the origins of the divide as viewed through the experience of the Unionist community. While the history of Irish nationalism is comparatively well known internationally, the Unionist community considers itself to be marginalized, overlooked and misunderstood. Drawing on important archival sources, this chapter aims to shed light on the self-understanding of the Unionist population and the challenges it faced at the time of partition.

Ulster Unionism is, at its core, an Ulster nationalism. While this contention has been rendered problematic by the specific connotations associated with the term in Ireland, and in Ulster particularly, the fact remains that the fundamental goal of the establishment of Northern Ireland was to demarcate an area of Ulster Unionist dominance in accordance with the Ulster identity put forward by the Unionist community. The establishment of a six-county Northern Ireland, moving away from older definitions of a nine-county Ulster, therefore required a reconceptualization not only of where Ulster lay but also what it meant to belong to it.[1]

In May 1920, following years of tension between the two dominant and opposing groups in Ireland – the mainly Catholic Nationalists and the mostly Protestant Unionists – the Ulster Unionist Council (UUC) voted to accept the principles of Irish partition as set out in the Government of Ireland Bill (later Act) of 1920. The point of tension was the political future of Ireland: Nationalists who had initially favoured devolved government (Home Rule) declared, after the Easter Rising of 1916, for full independence. Unionists meanwhile wished to remain within the United Kingdom. It is ironic then that the first Home Rule government established in Ireland was the Unionist Northern Ireland. This change in tone was the final separation in a series of 'national moments' experienced by Ulster Unionists, who held a strong majority in the northern province of Ulster. First, they had asserted a distinct Ulster identity within Protestant Unionism, then they had formally sundered themselves from southern Irish Unionism, with its disadvantage of a small, dispersed population. Finally, they accepted the principle of partition and established an administration devolved from the very entity (the United Kingdom) to which they sought to remain attached.

If this seems inconsistent with the principles of Unionism it can be understood as an act of Ulster Protestant nationalism, the culmination of a growing sense of their own distinctiveness and confidence in their own strength. However, this nationalism was not uncontested. While many Catholic Nationalists argued for one Irish nation, the role of Northern Ireland as a nation-state for Ulster Unionism was contested even within Ulster. The new parliament in Belfast governed a state comprising six of the nine counties of Ulster, with Cavan, Monaghan and Donegal, despite

---

1   With the introduction of the 1921 border, the three counties of Cavan, Donegal, and Monaghan, while still part of Ulster ('the North of Ireland') remained within the 'Free State' (later called the Republic) while the other six counties of Ulster (Antrim, Armagh, (London)Derry, Down, Fermanagh and Tyrone) became known as 'Northern Ireland'.

having organized on a common front with six-county Unionists, being excluded from the settlement. The agreed boundaries for the new Northern Ireland state contained a significant Protestant majority and the three counties had been rejected on the grounds of their significant Catholic populations. In this regard, the establishment of Northern Ireland represented not only a reformulation of Unionism as a national movement but a reformulation of the very nation to which it referred.

Groups positioned unhappily along the edge of a political division demonstrate how permeable and negotiable their national identities can be at times of change and crisis. The two groups of Unionists on opposite sides of the partition settlement had opposing goals. The Unionists of Cavan and Monaghan were forever in a battle to prove their own Ulster Unionism and to assert their right to belong within Northern Ireland. Conversely, Fermanagh Unionists attempted to secure their own future by undermining the claims of Cavan and Monaghan.

Ulster Unionist Identity in Cavan and Monaghan

Unlike its sister variants of Ulster Unionism, Cavan and Monaghan Unionism never developed beyond the crisis of its birth. Pinned to other pan-Ulster Unionist institutions – such as the Ulster Unionist party, the Ulster Covenant and the Ulster Volunteer Force – it was ultimately sundered from its heartland by the six-county reformulation of an Ulster state. Without support from elsewhere in the province, it persisted in a cultural half-life for a number of decades, becoming broadly submerged into a southern Irish identity.

Cavan and Monaghan Unionism was a border identity in a number of ways. Within Ulster Unionism it was peripheral to the point of externality. Following partition, it became the new frontier for the southern Irish state. Cavan and Monaghan negotiated their uneasy position both before and after partition with a constant defence of their rights as Unionists. Partition, their definitive, and indeed final, crisis, represented not just a gross betrayal but an undermining of the very appeal of the Ulster Unionist identity.

Representations of Ulster Unionist identity in Cavan and Monaghan are complicated by the clear political utility that the idea held. While the Ulster Unionism expressed in the counties both before and after partition may have been deeply held, it also represented a clear avenue of escape from an increasingly inevitable southern Catholic-dominated state. As such, there was an element of pragmatism to the enthusiasm with which Protestants in Cavan and Monaghan (and to a different degree Donegal) bought into the cause of Ulster, and, as also happened with Fermanagh, an unusually self-conscious process of identity formation.

Counting Loyalism: Key Measures of Ulster Unionism in Cavan and Monaghan

With these complications in mind it is instructive to employ a numerical survey of key markers of Unionist identity to see how Cavan and Monaghan compare. The comparison will allow us to determine whether the counties contributed proportionally as much to the Ulster movement as areas such as Antrim and Down which were more clearly in the Ulster heartland. Differences between the two counties are also significant, as they emphasize that Unionist identity in both, while sharing common circumstances, was still influenced by local factors.

Signed primarily on 'Ulster Day', 28 September 1912, Ulster's Solemn League and Covenant (and the associated Women's Declaration) had marked a hugely significant moment in the development of Ulster Unionism, being an oath binding its signatories to oppose any attempt to coerce Ulster into Home Rule. The particular depth of fervour implied by signing the Covenant is problematic. The Royal Irish Constabulary (RIC) County Inspector for Cavan noted that, for some, the Covenant was a statement of political preference, while for others it was a commitment to military resistance.[2]

---

2 Royal Irish Constabulary County Inspector's Returns Cavan, September 1912 (TNA: CO 904/88).

A clearer commitment to take up arms in the name of Ulster came from membership of the Ulster Volunteer Force (UVF) a Unionist militia established in January 1913 to oppose Home Rule.[3] While the UVF suffered from a terminal lack of training and organization, membership still implied a strong commitment to fight against both the nationalist Irish Volunteers and British forces in the name of Ulster (Bowman 2002). Before the outbreak of the First World War in 1914, a civil war between the two Volunteer forces seemed increasingly likely and the UVF successfully landed 24,600 German rifles in April 1914 (Jackson 1992).

If membership of the UVF represented a commitment to military resistance then a more general political commitment can be seen in membership of the Unionist Clubs. Initially established in the 1890s as a social hub, Unionist Clubs were reconstituted in 1913 at about the same time as the formation of the UVF and in response to the same threat of Home Rule. They were intended to carry out local campaigning and propaganda work – in this they were an attempt to lay out a cohesive Ulster identity – while also serving as the social and organizational hub within the Protestant and Unionist community (Bowman 2013: 28–31). For many Unionists, unable or unwilling to commit to military resistance (and the associated frequent drilling and possession of a weapon), membership of the local Unionist Club still indicated a significant level of political dedication to the defence of an Ulster Unionist identity.

War enlistment among the non-Catholic community is a useful measure of 'Ulsterism'. The rate of recruitment in Ulster roughly matched that in Britain and was far ahead of recruitment in any other Irish province (Townsend 2005: 65). The sacrifice of the Ulster soldiers in the war and the losses at the battle of the Somme in particular became central to Ulster Unionist identity and rhetoric, a process Thomas Hennessey described as 'symbolising the psychological partition of Ireland' (Hennessey 1998: 198–200). In Table 8.4 we express enlistment rates from 15 December 1914 to 15 December 1915 as the ratio of enlistments by Protestants and Catholics

---

[3] In 1966 another UVF formed in opposition to the IRA (Irish Republican Army), claiming direct descent from the 1913 UVF although no organizational links existed between them.

Table 8.1: Signatories of the Ulster Covenant and Women's Declaration as a percentage of the adult non-Catholic population in 1911 census. Source: Fitzpatrick (2014: 243).

Counties	Men	Non-Catholic %	Women	Non-Catholic %
Cavan	4,423	71.3	3,722	65.4
Monaghan	5,397	83.2	5,082	80.0
Donegal	9,007	73.7	8,347	68.7
Three Counties average		*75.6*		*70.9*
Down	32,379	72.6	35,495	69.7
Antrim	33,185	68.4	39,395	71.9
Armagh	18,754	88.6	20,331	86.6
Belfast	67,316	76.2	61,648	58.9
Tyrone	19,653	87.9	18,532	82.9
London-derry	20,282	81.4	20,403	74.3
Fermanagh	8,219	84.6	6,884	73.8
Ulster average		*76.9*		*69.3*

Note. To establish an estimated adult non-Roman Catholic population in Ulster, Fitzpatrick took the recorded percentage of non-Catholics in the population aged 9 years or more (the only age-related breakdown of religion by area) and multiplied it by the total population aged over 16 years.

to the number of non-agricultural males of each religion in the county; agricultural workers were excluded as they were categorized as performing critical war work and thus exempted from enlistment.[4]

As tabulated figures demonstrate, while the contribution of Cavan and Monaghan to some aspects of Ulsterism lagged behind, in others it was particularly distinguished. Even where less distinguished, their proportional contribution was well within reasonable bounds. While Cavan (Table 8.1) may have had the second lowest percentage of non-Catholic men signing the Covenant, the worst contributor was the Ulster heartland of Antrim. While the rate of Protestant enlistment was poor in Monaghan (Table 8.4), it was underperformed further by County Down.

---

4   For further information see Fitzpatrick (1995: 1017–30).

Conversely, in the areas where the counties perform strongly, they are often notably ahead of the rest of Ulster. In spite of Monaghan's larger Protestant population, the Cavan UVF (Table 8.2) boasted a membership of 3,451, while Monaghan could only muster 2,188 (Mac Giolla Choille 1966: 37; Fitzpatrick 2014: 244). For Cavan, this came to over half of all eligible men joining. This was over 10 per cent more than in any other county. Cavan's enlistment ratio was only outperformed by Antrim and Belfast and was the fourth highest in the country. Monaghan had one of the highest rates of signatories to the Ulster Covenant, while both counties are among the strongest supporters of the Ulster Clubs. In November 1912 Cavan had twelve Unionist Clubs in the county with 1,425 members or 23 per cent of the adult male population. By May 1913 this had become sixteen clubs with 1,949 members. Expressed as a percentage of the non-Catholic

Table 8.2: Membership of the UVF and Ulster Clubs as a percentage of estimated adult non-Catholic population. Source: Fitzpatrick (2014: 244).

County	Ulster Clubs 1912 %	UVF 1914 %
Cavan	23.0	55.8
Monaghan	20.2	33.7
Donegal	3.0	26.1
Three Counties average	*12.5*	*35.5*
Armagh	21.7	36.0
Tyrone	34.3	45.9
Fermanagh	14.6	30.9
Derry	14.2	37.5
Belfast	17.7	25.4
Down	22.5	25.3
Antrim	19.7	24.9
Ulster average	*19.5*	*29.8*

Note. The adult non-Roman Catholic population in Ulster was estimated as indicated in the Note to Table 8.1. Membership figures for the Ulster Clubs refer to November 1912 and for the UVF refer to 31 May 1914. All data calculated by David Fitzpatrick and originally taken from Mac Giolla Choille (1966: 16, 37).

population this increase came to 3 per cent, compared to an average increase across Ulster of 0.6 per cent (Mac Giolla Choille 1966: 19–20).

Some of this strength perhaps came from their peripherality and their likely role as a front in any conflict between North and South. This is reflected in the quantity of arms the counties held for the UVF. By March 1914, Cavan (Table 8.3) boasted 2,676 weapons, including a quarter of all Martini-Enfield rifles held in Ulster. Overall Cavan held roughly 10 per cent of all arms in Ulster in the period just before the Larne gunrunning. By contrast, the county held just 2 per cent of all Protestants in Ulster. This peripherality also led to reformulation of Cavan's commitment to the Ulster Volunteers. Aware of their isolation and to diminish their association with the actions of the more bellicose Belfast Volunteers, Colonel Oliver Nugent, the Commanding Officer of the UVF in Cavan, renamed the organization the Cavan Volunteer Force and downplayed any military associations.[5]

Table 8.3: Arms held by the UVF in each county. Source: Mac Giolla Choille (1966: 34).

County	Arms Held	Non-Catholics per arm (rounded figures)
Cavan	2,676	6
Monaghan	561	32
Donegal	1,299	27
Three Counties	*4,536*	*16*
Antrim (incl. Belfast)	10,268	44
Armagh	3,010	22
Down	4,120	34
Fermanagh	183	148
Londonderry	655	116
Tyrone	2,107	30
Ulster	*24,879*	*36*

Note. Total non-Catholic population per county identified in Census of Ireland (1911), county and provincial reports.

5   Booklet entitled 'C.V.F. Scheme, Copy No. VI' (PRONI, Farren Connell papers, MIC/57119).

Table 8.4: First World War enlistments per 1,000 non-agricultural males and percentage of non-agricultural males listed as non-Catholic in the 1911 census. Source: Unpublished figures provided by David Fitzpatrick.

County	Catholics per 1,000	Protestants per 1,000	1911 Census Non-Catholic %
Monaghan	50	63	72
Cavan	58	105	80
Donegal	47	70	74
Antrim (incl. Belfast)	135	110	23
Armagh	45	67	42
Down	56	59	29
Fermanagh	116	94	55
Londonderry	72	76	45
Tyrone	56	79	56

The Ulster Identity and Partition

The Ulster identity put forward in Cavan and Monaghan was relatively uncomplicated, seeking as it did both before and after partition to strengthen the nine-county interpretation of Ulster identity and in doing so to undermine an intra-Ulster partition. The community had been aware of the possibility of a six-county partition settlement since at least March 1914, when Herbert Henry Asquith, the British Prime Minister, proposed that exclusion from partition should be decided in county plebiscites – a process which would leave Unionists in Cavan, Monaghan and Donegal with no hope of escape from a southern state. By relying on pre-established political geographies – in this case the province of Ulster as traditionally defined – Unionism in Cavan and Monaghan saw less handwringing over the national identity of specific areas than was seen in Fermanagh. Rather, they were faced with questions of how best to publicly demonstrate the depth of their Unionist fervour without by doing so conceding the precariousness of their situation.

Public rhetoric in Cavan and Monaghan aimed to underline a 'natural' Ulster connection. The 1918 Election saw Michael Knight campaigning in

North Monaghan as a self-professed 'Ulster Unionist' and he was careful to pitch his speeches as such. Despite running against the odds, his speeches aimed to give the impression that North Monaghan especially was a thriving Ulster Unionist outpost: 'Unionists in this part of Ulster have a fine opportunity [...] of being represented for the first time truly in the Imperial Parliament.'[6] In a private communication following partition, prominent Cavan Unionist Arthur Maxwell Lord Farnham sadly noted that 'we in Cavan were prouder of being Ulstermen than anyone in the whole Province.'[7]

Cavan and Monaghan Unionists expressed pride in the achievements of the province as a whole. During the War of Independence, the *Northern Standard* noted with satisfaction the 'almost complete immunity of the greater part of Ulster from the dreadful crimes that blackened the rest of Ireland.'[8] Belfast in particular was a source of admiration. In speeches such as that of Major McClean to the Monaghan Unionist Club in 1918, the virtues of the city's industry and infrastructure were taken as matters of great pride.[9] The cultural ties connecting Protestants in these counties to the city led many of them to attempt to break the general Belfast Boycott.[10] For example, Newbliss Protestants in August 1920 organized a convoy of fifty Ulster Volunteers to escort bread vans from Belfast to the town. The same escorts were planned in Clones and Drum, although they were foiled by the attack on the bread vans taking place before they could reach the escort.[11]

Following partition, attempts to reverse the settlement were implemented swiftly and with great intensity but met with little success. Resistance was articulated through the traditional Ulster Unionist identity the county had bought into – with no concession made to the uniqueness

---

6   *Northern Standard*, 14 December 1918.
7   Letter from Lord Farnham to Hugh de Fellenberg Montgomery, 13 March 1920 (PRONI, Hugh de Fellenberg Montgomery Papers, D627/435/10).
8   *Northern Standard*, 10 April 1920.
9   *Irish Times*, 13 March 1921.
10 The Belfast Boycott was a general campaign by Irish nationalists to boycott goods coming from blacklisted Unionist traders in Belfast. This extended to a social and economic boycott of merchants who continued to trade with blacklisted traders (Dooley 1994: 91–2).
11 *Northern Standard*, 28 August 1920.

of their circumstances. Rhetoric focused on the oath of the Covenant, employing a stricter and stricter definition of what the Covenant stood for.[12] Even in the preceding years something of the anxiety of the three-county community could be seen in the growing importance of 'Covenant Day', the anniversary of the signing of the Covenant. This was marked in Cavan and Monaghan by religious services around the counties. The *Northern Standard* covered these events quite heavily to counterbalance the otherwise quiet media focus on Cavan and Monaghan: '[V]ery little has been said about "the three counties" during the past week, but it is enough for us to know that the Ulster Unionists stand where they did five or six years ago – a thoroughly united party.'[13]

In the aftermath of partition, a pamphlet was produced by the delegates to the UUC from the three counties. It opened with a copy of the direct text of the Covenant as a combination of reminder and guilt-trip to sway other delegates' minds. The only edit made to the original text of the Covenant was to capitalize the word 'nine' in the title. It now read 'the Solemn Covenant entered into between the Unionists of the NINE Counties of Ulster'.[14] The pamphlet argued, fairly reasonably, that the same demographic and political facts were just as true of the three counties in 1920 as they had been in 1911. Abandoning the counties now in face of such little change was to invalidate the word of Ulster Unionism. Resolutions passed by the Unionist Associations of all three counties explicitly characterized the decision as a 'breach of the Covenant' and it was described as such in Westminster by a Liberal Member of Parliament, T. P. O'Connor.[15]

Cavan and Monaghan Unionists emphasized the common cultural ties between the three counties and the rest of Ulster which had been sundered. In a statement, the delegates from Cavan, Monaghan and Donegal appealed to the Unionists of Ulster to show solidarity with them in strongly traditional terms, declaring that 'the Ulster people have stood together for

---

12 Correspondence with the UUC secretary including letters of resignation, April 1920 (PRONI, UUC files, D1327/18/28).
13 *Northern Standard*, 4 October 1918.
14 'Ulster and Home Rule: No partition of Ulster'. Unionist pamphlet (Clones, 1920).
15 *Irish Post and Weekly Telegraph*, 13 March 1920; House of Commons Debates, 5th series, vol. 127, 29 March 1920, col. 968.

many generations and that confidence and reliance in each other has been the chief cause of their success and prosperity' (Buckland 1973: 120–21).[16] In line with this, they primarily portrayed themselves in editorials and speeches post-partition as a wronged periphery. They had been selfishly abandoned for an unnecessarily large Protestant majority in the new state. The three-county media were swift to criticize the dishonesty of the six-county delegates, maintaining that 'it is clearly obvious that to attain the full measure of selfish safety for themselves they are prepared to jeopardize the safety of their Southern friends'.[17]

The willingness of the six counties to abandon them brought about something of a reversal in Unionist ideology in the county: arguments to invalidate the Covenant (such as that the Covenant had only applied to the previous Home Rule crisis) were disparaged as 'idiotic' and 'childish'. A six-county state was dismissed as impractically small, impractically bordered and pointlessly politically uniform. In attacking the idea that the three counties should be excluded because of their Nationalist majority the key argument touched on the impracticalities of settling on a nationally sound border:

> [Cavan and Monaghan have a Catholic majority] That is true. But so does Derry City, Fermanagh County, Tyrone County, South Armagh, South Down and the Falls Division of Belfast. Yet no one proposes to exclude them. The truth is that it is impossible to fix upon any exclusively Unionist area. There are more Unionists in the Southern area than there are Nationalists in the three Counties and no provision whatever is made for them. In their case we are told minorities must suffer, but that doctrine seems to be ignored when the minority is a Nationalist one.[18]

Perhaps because of this sense of betrayal, as R. B. McDowell has described, most Unionists in Cavan and Monaghan adapted surprisingly rapidly to their new circumstances (McDowell 1997: 109–10). For some this manifested itself as expressing a willingness to co-operate with the Irish Free State, once established, as it was to become the legitimate state to which they owed allegiance. Others invested some hope in the ability of the

16 *Northern Standard*, 24 April 1920.
17 *Northern Standard*, 19 June 1920; *Irish Post and Weekly Telegraph*, 20 July 1918.
18 'Ulster and Home Rule: No partition of Ulster'. Unionist pamphlet (Clones, 1920).

Boundary Commission to rescue them from Southern domination.[19] The Unionist judge Samuel Browne KC, to general surprise, opened the Clones Quarter Sessions of February 1922 by pledging his allegiance to the new Irish government.[20] By the 1922 general election the *Northern Standard* was urging its voters to take an active role, saying that

> the votes of the Unionists, or ex-Unionists, will play an important part in deciding the contest in this country [...] the fate of Ireland is in the balance [...] we are concerned solely and absolutely for the fate of the plain people [...] the ex-Unionist voters therefore must decide which candidates are more likely to bring peace and prosperity.[21]

From 1921, Thomas Toal, chairperson of Monaghan County Council, formed a profitable alliance with Unionist councillors, whom he referred to as 'exunionists'. These 'exunionists' were still indulged when they put forward 'Unionist' motions (such as a resolution of loyalty to Edward VIII on his coronation) even if such motions always failed. That 'exunionist' members justified such proposals in Free State Ireland through Ireland's dominion status demonstrated the ambiguous meaning Irish independence had taken on for the community.[22] Unionists in both Cavan and Monaghan were also successful in electing to the Dáil one of their own – Alexander Haslett – for Monaghan in both elections in 1927 and John James Cole for Cavan in September 1927. Both men ran under the banner 'Independent Unionist' and presented themselves in very traditional Ulster Unionist terms. Both were avowed Orangemen and were elected on the last ballot, having collected either no transfers or very few from any other party, an indication of their singular appeal (Weeks 2017: 36).

Cavan and Monaghan Unionists were perhaps typical examples of a post-war secession minority, isolated politically from their old nation in Northern Ireland and socially from their new nation in the Irish Free State. Where they distinguished themselves, however, is in how they articulated and pre-empted their abandonment. Despite their obvious demographic

---

19 *Northern Standard*, 11 February 1922.
20 *Northern Standard*, 3 February 1922.
21 *Northern Standard*, 9 June 1922.
22 Thomas Toal diary (Monaghan County Museum).

differences from the rest of Ulster and their strong cultural associations with southern Ireland, Cavan and Monaghan participated in Ulster Unionism with great gusto. For Cavan in particular, it is arguable that they constructed an Ulster identity from the ground up after coming within the technical, historical definition of Ulster. In this they provided a contrast to Fermanagh Unionists who used the Ulster Unionist identity to fight for the very settlement which abandoned Cavan and Monaghan.

Ulster Unionist Identity in Fermanagh

If the vision of Ulster Unionism put forward in Cavan, Monaghan and Donegal sought to undermine the legitimacy of the Northern Irish state, then its counterpart across the border in county Fermanagh aimed to ringfence the six-county settlement. In Fermanagh, as in Cavan and Monaghan, the cultural geography of Ulster Unionism was seen as fundamental in determining the political geography of Northern Ireland (Rankin 2009: 29).

Fermanagh Unionism existed in an awkward position at the time of partition. Although Fermanagh was markedly more Protestant than its three-county neighbours, it still harboured 34,740 Catholics compared to 27,096 Protestants.[23] If national determination was to be applied on a county by county basis then Fermanagh was at serious risk of failing to qualify. In 1914, a prominent member of the Ulster Unionist Party, Major Frederick Crawford, wrote to party leader Edward Carson that any potential settlement of Ulster would probably represent the cumulative abandonment of 'the Protestants of Cavan, Donegal, Fermanagh and Monaghan'.[24] Additionally, Protestant control of local bodies in the face of an opposing popular majority was most evident in Fermanagh

---

23   National Archives of Ireland, *Census of Ireland 1901/1911* <http://www.census.nationalarchives.ie> accessed 18 July 2018.
24   Letter of Major Frederick Crawford to Carson, 13 March 1914 (PRONI, Carson Papers, D1700/5/17/1/11).

and required some justification (Phoenix 1994: 85). The Earl of Belmore, testifying to the Boundary Commission in 1925 conflated electoral success in the county with control over its identity: 'The County Councils have been very equally divided. Sometimes one side has the majority and sometimes, the other. Fermanagh is sometimes one side and sometimes the other.'[25]

Anxiety over the shape of any Irish border had always been particularly acute in Fermanagh Unionist society. Before the passage of the Government of Ireland Act in 1920, these fears had focused on either a greatly reduced partition settlement which would leave behind Fermanagh or a greatly expanded one which would dilute the Protestant majority and threaten the stability of a northern state. For most Fermanagh Unionists, the Northern Ireland that came into being represented an ideal resolution of the partition crisis. A six-county state had the largest possible Protestant majority while still incorporating Fermanagh. However, this did not lead to the alleviation of these local anxieties. Rather, they shifted to ensuring the permanence of this desirable settlement. In particular, they were concerned with defending Fermanagh's rightful place in an Ulster state. They sought to pre-empt the looming threat of the Irish Boundary Commission and the growing criticism of the unrepresentativeness of a partition drawn along ancient county lines.

These anxieties in Fermanagh Unionism resulted in a unique, bordered, articulation of Unionist identity which, instead of retreating into areas of local majority, sought to contest the nature of the county and project a Unionist identity even onto strongly Catholic areas. This was an identity at once brashly self-confident and insecure. In Fermanagh, unlike in Cavan and Monaghan, there was a strong belief that only an active and assertive Unionism would secure the county's future. Fermanagh Unionists propounded a theory of their identity that tied them very explicitly with the county itself. This was unlike three-county efforts to downplay the uniqueness of their situation (and their minority) and tie themselves into a broader nation. Fermanagh Unionism went to great lengths to add a distinct, local, element to their identity.

25   Earl of Belmore evidence (TNA, Boundary Commission files, CAB 61/30).

This identity theory was articulated most clearly by William Copeland Trimble, a prominent local Unionist, and an important figure in the development of Fermanagh Unionism. As founder of one of the first UVF regiments, the Enniskillen Horse, in 1912, he gained great prestige in the Unionist community (Bowman 2013: 29).[26] Having inherited the Enniskillen-based *Impartial Reporter* from his father, William Trimble Sr, in 1883, he became an important local journalist during his editorship, publishing between 1919 and 1922 a well-received multi-volume history of Enniskillen and also serving as chairman of the Irish Newspaper Owners Association (Newmann 1993).[27]

However, his most enduring and most popular contribution to Fermanagh public life was his clear articulation of the reasons for Fermanagh's inherent Protestantism, which he laid out in an editorial published in December 1920, after the passage of the Government of Ireland Act and just before the establishment of Northern Ireland. This article was titled 'Fermanagh, a Protestant County: Notwithstanding the Population'. In this article Trimble described two fundamental elements of the Fermanagh Unionist claim to belong in Northern Ireland, arguing that Fermanagh's Unionism and Protestantism was inherent to it and independent of whatever might appear in the census, and going on to say that the Catholic majority in the county was both unrepresentative and non-local.

Demography and Economy: The Non-cultural Argument for Fermanagh

As the title of the article suggests, Trimble's primary goal in this editorial was to downplay the significance of Fermanagh's Catholic majority. His contention was that 'in a matter of this sort heads do not count.' In his

---

26 Also: Papers relating to the Enniskillen Horse, TNA CO 904/27/1.
27 Also: *Irish* Examiner, 8 January 1919.

mind, the bulk of the Catholic population in the county was composed of landless servants and labourers. These people were less representative of the nature of the county as they were landless – they were 'not of the soil'. By contrast, the most significant communities in the county were majority Protestant – 'the landowning, land-occupying, professional, commercial, farming and industrial communities.'[28] Unionists paid more local property taxes (rates) and thus were more involved in the upkeep of the county. They were entitled to a larger part of it.

The placing of emphasis on certain communities as 'definitive' was not a rhetorical tactic unique to Trimble. A 1925 representation of Fermanagh Unionists to the Boundary Commission also sought to undermine the county's religious demography (based on a census they decried as nearly fifteen years out of date) by demonstrating Unionist dominance of all key professions in the county as well as their prominence on the lists of jurors and ratepayers.[29]

Allusions to these ideas were commonly employed in local politics. In an Enniskillen Board of Guardians debate on the payment of workhouse officials, a frustrated Unionist, William Elliott, exclaimed: '[W]e are the ratepayers. These are the men who pay the rates. I am a heavy ratepayer and you [Edmund Corrigan, Sinn Féin] are not.'[30] Many of the testimonies given by Fermanagh Protestants to the Boundary Commission, such as that by Rev. W. B. Naylor of Belcoo, also reference the preponderance of Protestants on the ratebooks as a reason for their vote to be given greater weight.[31] Major Charles Falls, Fermanagh County Council's solicitor, contested the Free State's claim to control of Lough Erne on the basis that Fermanagh County Council had financed the drainage of the lake and

28   *Impartial Reporter*, 9 December 1920.
29   Bundle of correspondence regarding the boundary of Fermanagh County Council. (PRONI, UUC Files, D1327/24/1).
30   Boards of Guardians were local bodies whose elected members represented electoral areas; their responsibilities included such things as poor relief and fixing of the rates to support it. Minutes of Enniskillen Guardians, July 1919 (PRONI, Board of Guardians Records, BG/14/A/128); *Impartial Reporter*, 4 July 1919.
31   Statement of W. B. Naylor, Fermanagh County Council Evidence (TNA, Boundary Commission files, CAB/61/65).

that, while the Council was itself evenly split at the time, the project had been funded by the ratepayers and that therefore the Fermanagh Unionist claim to the lake was strongest.[32] This argument is striking. Falls first conflated Unionist 'investment' in Fermanagh with the county's identity and then translated that into explicit territorial claims.

The 'investment' argument was merely one way in which Fermanagh Unionists aimed to undermine the Catholic majority in the county. Equally prominent was the theory that the Catholic population in Fermanagh was artificially inflated by itinerant Catholic workers from outside Ulster. A meeting of Fermanagh County Council in November 1921 degenerated into a shouting match between the two sides following a jibe made by Unionist councillor Robinson over a supposed Catholic majority of 8,000 in the county: 'Mr Healy's majority was merely made up of servant boys and hands from other counties who came up to work on the farm of Unionists. They were not Fermanagh men but came from Donegal and Leitrim. They could not speak for Fermanagh.'[33]

The appeal of this argument was obvious, allowing for an unrevealed true Fermanagh to exist, hidden behind misleading official information and polling tallies. This argument allowed the *Fermanagh Times,* for example, to argue that Catholic dominance of the County Council since 1914 did not say anything about the political persuasion of the county.[34] Any violent or dramatic expressions of a Fermanagh nationalism could similarly be discounted as an imported nuisance and not a worrying sign of future unrest. For example, the campaign of boycotting in the county from 1920 onwards was frequently blamed on servant boys from Cavan and Leitrim, as exemplified by the pseudonymous 'Fermanagh Radical' in a letter to the *Fermanagh Times* of 15 November 1921.[35] In the same month, 'South Tyrone Radical' wrote that these servant boys were betraying their employers to the IRA by providing information to the raiding parties. It was suggested that

32   Charles Falls Statement, Fermanagh County Council Evidence (TNA, Boundary Commission files, CAB/61/65).
33   Minutes of Fermanagh County Council, November 1921 (PRONI, Local Authority Records, LA/4/2/GA/3). *Impartial Reporter*, 24 November 1921.
34   *Fermanagh* Times, 22 December 1922.
35   *Impartial Reporter*, 17 November 1921.

all 'foreign' labourers be turned over the border 'and serve Roman Catholic masters, where their pay will be lighter and their diet too'.³⁶

The assertion that native-born Fermanagh people were majority Protestant and that the county's Catholic majority was an importation had little to do with demographic reality and certainly ignores Protestant 'imports' from elsewhere in Ulster and Britain. In the 1911 census, 85 per cent of the total population were Fermanagh-born and of this population 57 per cent were Catholic, which mirrors closely the overall rate of Catholicism in the county of 56 per cent.³⁷ When Major Charles Falls made a similar claim to the Boundary Commission, he was greeted with scepticism as Eóin MacNeill noted that the county was not sufficiently agricultural for there to be a large market for itinerant labourers.³⁸

That this idea should have had such cachet in Fermanagh is unsurprising. It formed part of a larger process of a growing conceptualization of southern Ireland as a malevolent and violent entity, thoroughly distinct from Ulster. Any solution other than partition was to mean the subjugation of Ulstermen. In a speech of November 1922, William Coote, MP for Tyrone, declared the willingness of Ulstermen and the Orange Order to 'make Ulster safe' before noting that the road to Dublin was 'strewn with the bodies of Loyalists'.³⁹

This contrast became much more marked during the violence of the revolutionary years. It underlined Fermanagh's difference from the Catholic south. An anonymous article published in *Blackwood's Magazine* described the crossing of the border into the six counties as the transition into Ulster, and its Protestant inhabitants as 'quite a different race'.⁴⁰ A Trimble editorial referred to Fermanagh's peaceful revolution as being akin to the experiences

---

36 *Impartial Reporter*, 10 November 1921.
37 All data from National Archives of Ireland, *Census of Ireland 1901/1911* <http://www.census.nationalarchives.ie> accessed 18 July 2018.
38 Interview with Major Charles Falls, Fermanagh County Council Evidence (TNA, Boundary Commission files, CAB/61/66).
39 Royal Irish Constabulary County Inspectors Report for Fermanagh, September 1922 (PRONI, Home Office files, HA/32/1/129).
40 'Ulster in 1921.' *Blackwood's Magazine* No. MCClXXIV Vol. CCXII (October 1922), 431.

of Down and Antrim – shorthand for traditional Ulster Unionism. By contrast, Trimble referred to southern counties 'deluged with blood'.[41] If Fermanagh were so Catholic, his argument went, why was its record so much closer to Antrim than to Cork? Trimble's rivals in the *Fermanagh Times* could not help but agree: 'Southern Ireland is a fitting commentary on the Southern Irish: they have made it what it is: and Ulstermen have made the North what it is.'[42]

This perception was heightened by reporting which focused not only on the violence of the south but also on its alleged sectarianism. Donegal was experiencing a 'reign of terror', in Cavan there was a 'War on Protestants', while the Monaghan Twelfths[43] were cancelled because of a 'vendetta against Protestants.'[44] Individual Protestant victims of revolutionary violence, such as Johnston Hewitt of Cloverhill in Cavan, were put to political use as evidence of the inherent sectarianism of the south and of the dangers facing Fermanagh Unionists in case of a shift of the frontier.[45] David Fitzpatrick has also suggested that such events were used to further alienate Ulster Unionist opinion and justify a hardline official policy being taken in negotiations with the Free State (Fitzpatrick 1998: 121). These reports became particularly pronounced following partition and the establishment of the border, which was portrayed as a bulwark against the chaos immediately beyond it. The *Fermanagh Times* constantly expressed fears that the southern border of the county, particularly south of Lough Erne was being 'surrendered' and the whole area 'subject to Free State rule'.[46]

41   *Impartial Reporter*, 14 December 1922.
42   *Fermanagh* Times, 2 December 1920.
43   The Twelfth (July) is the principal day of the (Protestant) Orange Order (founded 1795) parade season, which commemorates the 1690 victory of William of Orange over James II at the Battle of the Boyne, near Dublin. The parades remain highly contentious to the present, with certain routes subject to violent protests.
44   *Impartial Reporter*, 26 May 1921; *Impartial Reporter*, 29 June 1922; *Impartial Reporter*, 4 January 1923; for examples in the *Fermanagh Times* see *Fermanagh Times*, 16 February 1923 and *Fermanagh Times*, 29 June 1922.
45   *Impartial Reporter*, 6 July 1922.
46   *Fermanagh Times*, 20 April 1922; *Fermanagh Times*, 4 May 1922.

In 1925, the Boundary Commission received a lengthy submission from Fermanagh County Council with statements of loyalists who claimed to have been driven out of the south and who were unable to return. James Johnston, formerly of Bawnboy, went so far as to claim that half of all Protestants in his district had been terrorized and driven from the district.[47] While the pictures of a lawless, sectarian South were drawn crudely, they touched upon a genuine fear held by Fermanagh Protestants of what their position would be in the Free State. James Cooper, Enniskillen solicitor and member of Fermanagh County Council, went so far as to commission an extensive private census of Protestant migrants into Fermanagh from the Free State in hopes it would demonstrate a vast movement of population. Ultimately it captured some 2,047 individuals, although not all of them were Protestant.[48]

The Limits of Ulster: The Cultural Argument for Fermanagh

Despite the esoteric nature of the claim, a common argument for Fermanagh's presence in Northern Ireland was that the county had an inalterable, undefinable Protestantism. For Trimble this was rooted in history. Fermanagh, before the Ulster plantation, did not exist, but was rather a loose collection of farms and tribes subject to constant raids. It was only the arrival of Protestant rule and Protestant law which had brought peace and allowed the emergence of the modern county.[49] This was an argument echoed by the *Fermanagh Times* in a letter by 'Descendant of a Planter' who made the case for a chaotic pre-Protestant Fermanagh even more forcefully: 'The followers of these less or more warlike chiefs lived

---

47 James Johnston Statement, Fermanagh County Council Evidence (TNA, Boundary Commission files, CAB 61/64).
48 Interview with James Cooper, Fermanagh County Council Evidence (TNA, Boundary Commission files, CAB/61/66).
49 *Impartial Reporter*, 9 December 1920.

in wattle and mud huts much like what modern travellers find in Central Africa.'[50]

As a result of the centrality of Protestantism and Unionism to the emergence of the modern county, Trimble was able to attribute certain 'fundamental' features to it. These were, naturally, the sort of qualities an Ulster Unionist would value and added a certain recursive infallibility to his logic:

> Its record of peace and order, the maintenance of the law, its sentiments of loyalty and attachment to the constitution, its administration of public business, its ideas of public morality, its code of ethics, its views of honour, its methods of advance, its enforcement of sanitation and cleanliness, its manners traditions and customs.[51]

Such sentiments were not unique to Trimble. The evidence provided by Fermanagh County Council to the Boundary Commission provides a series of short, consistent statements making various arguments for Fermanagh to remain in Northern Ireland. Unusually for evidence provided to the Commission, these statements were frequently based on questions of preference and national identity, as opposed to economic and trade considerations. These statements characterized Fermanagh in very similar ways, particularly emphasizing its efficient administration and record of law and order.[52]

The abstract, symbolic way in which a 'Protestant' identity was conferred on a county can also be seen in a 1925 report by Fermanagh Unionists to the Ulster Unionist Council (UUC, predecessor to the Ulster Unionist Party). The report characterized certain families as being definitive to the county's identity. Naturally, these families were uniformly Protestant (examples included the Earls of Belmore and Enniskillen, the Trimbles of Enniskillen, the Brookes of Brookeborough).[53] In a similar claim, James Cooper, future Northern Irish MP and Enniskillen solicitor, claimed that

50 *Fermanagh Times*, 8 September 1921.
51 *Impartial Reporter*, 9 December 1920.
52 See for example George Lester Statement, Fermanagh County Council Evidence (TNA, Boundary Commission files, CAB/61/65).
53 Bundle of correspondence regarding the boundary of Fermanagh County Council. (PRONI, UUC Files, D1327/24/1).

the southern, heavily Catholic, half of Fermanagh could never be rightly abandoned because southern border towns such as Belcoo were important sites of Protestant history and irrevocably Protestant in their character, despite their overwhelmingly Catholic population.[54]

The association of place with a specific community instead of geography allowed Fermanagh Unionists to place their own political identity central to the exclusion of their opponent. The Ulsterman was an ethnic rather than geographic construction, and Ulster was simply where they congregated. It was inherently non-inclusive of Catholics. As Trimble asserted: 'In Ireland there are two races [...] races divergent in national traits and characters [...] The Ulsterman (two-thirds Scotch and one-third of him English) is altogether a different man from the Irish Celt.'[55]

The community's victories were celebrated along traditional religious lines – the Unionist victory in Fermanagh North in the 1918 general election was celebrated by the ringing of the Anglican Church's bells in Enniskillen, to the chagrin of the local reverend, Canon Webb. Regarding his complaints that those who rang the bells were Presbyterian, the *Fermanagh Times* jocularly asserted that it was an Ulster Protestant victory and should be celebrated as such.[56]

In his testimony to the Boundary Commission, the Earl of Belmore argued that although the county was Catholic, the central and most important part of it (around Enniskillen) was strongly Protestant.[57] Major Charles Falls also argued that as Enniskillen was the most important town in the county and that it had been constructed by 'Unionist ratepayers', that the county was indivisible and non-transferable. For Falls, some of the strongest Unionist areas such as Florencecourt, Letterbreen and Crum were south of Lough Erne and were so crucial to the identity of the county that they could not be abandoned.[58]

---

54 Interview with James Cooper, Fermanagh County Council Evidence (TNA, Boundary Commission files, CAB/61/66).
55 *Impartial Reporter*, 8 March 1917; See also *Impartial Reporter*, 20 July 1922.
56 *Fermanagh* Times, 9 January 1919.
57 Earl of Belmore evidence (TNA, Boundary Commission files, CAB 61/30).
58 Charles Falls Statement, Fermanagh County Council Evidence (TNA, Boundary Commission files, CAB/61/65).

Not all of the county was seen as equally inviolable, and political concerns influenced such discussions. Particularly in relation to smaller, border areas, partition presented an opportunity to create a 'homogeneous Ulster'. Trimble and the *Reporter* entertained some discussion about the abandoning of disturbed Catholic border areas such as Belleek and Roslea.[59] James Cooper openly floated the idea of trading the majority of the Catholic Belleek region of the county for the Protestant areas around Pettigo.[60]

However, this was not as simple as trading the green areas of the map for orange ones. It was a process that demonstrated that certain areas had stronger cultural value and religious associations than others. Much as in Cavan and Monaghan, it became of paramount importance to define the limits of the cultural Ulster which would in turn define the limits of Northern Ireland. Trimble, when discussing the electoral map of Fermanagh, claimed that South Fermanagh would have returned a Unionist MP in all previous elections were it not for the western shores of Upper Lough Erne; such an area was unnatural as it 'formerly belonged to the province of Connaught'.[61] For Trimble, the Catholic majority in this area and its supposed non-Ulster status were linked. After a major IRA raid in the area in 1921, the Fermanagh town of Roslea was declared to belong 'more to Monaghan than Fermanagh'.[62]

This cultural Ulster did not extend to the same borders as its Covenant or its Volunteer Force. At the very least, belonging to Ulster was a negotiable identity and not one simply bought into. The three 'southern' counties, and Cavan especially, were described as being only passingly within Ulster. As Trimble said dismissively, 'County Cavan was not in the ancient Ulster, it was in Connaught.'[63] The *Fermanagh Times* began to refer to the nine-counties as 'geographical Ulster' while Northern Ireland was 'true Ulster'.[64] Only northern areas of Monaghan around Clones and Glaslough

---

59 *Impartial Reporter*, 19 February 1920.
60 *Impartial Reporter*, 17 August 1922.
61 *Impartial Reporter*, 9 December 1920.
62 *Impartial Reporter*, 27 July 1922.
63 *Impartial Reporter*, 9 December 1920.
64 *Fermanagh Times*, 22 April 1922.

seemed to be regarded as truly in Ulster and these were the portions of the Free State suggested as likely to be incorporated into Northern Ireland.[65]

Going against previous definitions of Ulster and opening up the term to more shades of interpretation was ideologically problematic. That the Ulster of the Covenant and the Unionist Clubs could be broken up at all was also ideologically problematic. This unease was motivated less by any sense of cross-border solidarity with Cavan, Monaghan and Donegal and more by inward-looking anxieties about the future fate of Fermanagh. The *Fermanagh Times* republished a letter written to the *Irish Times* by T. F. Stack, the rector of Langfield in Tyrone, expressing misgivings that once the concept of Ulster was undermined in this way then Derry City, Fermanagh and Tyrone all lost their best justification for belonging to Northern Ireland – namely that they were in geographical Ulster. Once this fact was no longer the key national determinant for a county, then areas with Catholic majorities had a much stronger argument to defect southwards.[66] Stack repeated his argument years later to the Boundary Commission.[67] This was similar to the argument taken outside Ulster by the *Daily Mail*, which felt such a settlement 'stereotyped partition and renounced the spirit of Union.'[68]

Fermanagh and the Three Counties

The plight of the three counties following partition was greeted with occasional rhetorical sympathy in Fermanagh, but little organized support. Trimble, writing for the *Reporter*, said that the cause of the three counties 'excited great sympathy' but he repeated the Unionist position on why six counties were preferable to nine.[69] The *Reporter*, by 1922, was reporting

---

65 *Impartial Reporter*, 3 August 1922.
66 *Fermanagh Times*, 29 April 1920.
67 Evidence of T. F. Stack (TNA, Boundary Commission files, CAB 61/135).
68 *Fermanagh Times*, 29 April 1920.
69 *Impartial Reporter*, 18 March 1920.

on events in Cavan and Monaghan as part of its broader 'South and West' news section.[70]

Fermanagh delegates to the Ulster Unionist Council did sign a petition to the Council requesting a meeting to reconsider exclusion, motivated by the potential resignation of the three county delegates. However, while eighty-six delegates from the six counties signed the document, only six of them were from Fermanagh – only half of the total delegates sent by the county to the Council.[71] Northern signatories to a representation on behalf of the three counties included no Fermanagh voices and only two from Tyrone. The majority of such signatories came from Down and Antrim, areas with Protestant majorities large enough to diminish any fear of inclusion of the three Catholic-heavy counties.[72] Nor did any Fermanagh delegates resign in protest at the decision. Fermanagh Unionism was roused to a far greater extent only a year later when the county's Unionist Association unanimously passed a bill opposing any change in the boundaries of a six-county Ulster.[73]

The *Fermanagh Times* was less enthusiastic about the settlement and reported in April 1920 that 'some of the strongest Unionists in County Fermanagh are altogether in sympathy with the loyalist population of Cavan, Monaghan and Donegal.'[74] In a speech to the Enniskillen Guardians in February 1923, W. J. Brown, a Unionist Guardian, stated that the Northern Parliament should have included Cavan, Monaghan and Donegal.[75] In a letter of April 1920, Colonel Robert Doran, head of Brookeborough Unionist Club, told Richard Dawson Bates that he could not go against 'the three excluded counties in whom without a doubt there are true hearted loyalists.'[76]

70 *Impartial Reporter*, 26 October 1922.
71 Delegates extracted from UUC Annual Reports (PRONI, J. Milne Barbour files, D972/17).
72 Representation on behalf of the three counties, April 1920 (PRONI, U.U.C. files, D1327/18/28).
73 *Fermanagh Times*, 10 November 1921.
74 *Fermanagh Times*, 22 April 1920.
75 Minutes of Enniskillen Guardians, February 1923 (PRONI, Board of Guardians Records, BG/14/A/134); *Fermanagh Herald*, 10 February 1923.
76 Letter from Robert Doran to Richard Dawson Bates, April 1920 (PRONI, UUC files, D1327/18/28).

Even when such expressions did exist, they were not normally focused on the problematic Ulster of Cavan or Monaghan but rather on either Donegal or the Covenant itself. In August 1920, at the traditional Unionist celebrations of the Relief of Derry, a speech was made by the Rev. Thomas Walmsley regretting the loss of his cross-border friends. However, this speech referred solely to Donegal men.[77] Hugh de Fellenberg Montgomery expressed hope that Donegal, because of its unique geographical position, might ultimately be included in Northern Ireland.[78] When pressed on why he had signed the petition against partition in May 1920, James Cooper, member of Enniskillen Council and future Northern MP, reported that he and all the Fermanagh delegates to the Ulster Unionist Council had done so because of the position of Donegal and the Protestants of Pettigo, not Cavan or Monaghan.[79]

Ulster Unionism on the Irish border represented a putative national movement that was granted a state of its own before it had matured sufficiently to formulate clear territorial demands. The use of the ambiguous term 'Ulster' as its point of identity led to significant struggles over which definition of the term to use, or whether to abandon the term altogether. As late as 1935, Rowley Elliott, MP for South Tyrone, was arguing against renaming the state Ulster as 'further humiliation for our friends in Cavan, Monaghan and Donegal'.[80] Thus a very fluid national identity gave rise to competing interpretations not only of an Ulster nationality but of how these nationalities were even constructed.

The focus of this examination has meant that certain factors of no less importance have not been emphasized. One such important factor is that the presence of large swathes of unwilling Catholics in Northern Ireland further challenged its legitimacy as a nation-state while at the same time it could be argued that the acceptance of the territorial boundaries of the new Northern Ireland State by a majority within Ulster Unionism undermined

---

77 *Impartial Reporter*, 19 August 1920.
78 Letter from John Scott to Hugh de Fellenberg Montgomery, 8 April 1920 (PRONI, Hugh de Fellenberg Montgomery Papers, D627/435/24).
79 *Impartial Reporter*, 17 August 1922.
80 *Belfast Newsletter*, 24 April 1935.

its self-understanding as the political expression of the national identity of Ulster Protestantism.

Accepting this political compromise meant that Unionism neither sought to encompass the entire Ulster Protestant national group, nor limit itself to those areas with a definitive Protestant majority. If Cavan, Monaghan and Donegal were to be left behind on the basis of their Catholic majority but Tyrone, Fermanagh and parts of Derry and Armagh were not, then six-county partition was intended not so much to express the national self-assertion of Ulster Protestantism as to ensure inclusion of those territories which would achieve the most secure voting majority. In this interpretation, Ulster Unionism was not so exclusively an expression of genuine national identification as an instrument of mass political mobilization in the interests of Protestant groups in the Ulster heartlands.

Bibliography

Bowman, T. (2002). 'The Ulster Volunteers 1913–1914: Force or Farce?', *History Ireland*, 10 (1/Spring), 43–7.

Bowman, T. (2013). '"The North Began" … But when? The Formation of the Ulster Volunteer Force', *History Ireland*, 21 (2/March/April) [n. p.].

Buckland, P. J. (1973). *Irish Unionism 2: Ulster Unionism and the Origins of Northern Ireland 1886–1922*. New York: Barnes and Noble.

Dooley, T. (1994). 'From the Belfast Boycott to the Boundary Commission: Fears and Hopes in County Monaghan, 1920–26', *Clogher Record*, 15 (1), 90–106.

Dooley, T. (2000). *The Plight of Monaghan Protestants, 1912–1926* (Maynooth Studies in Irish Local History, 31). Dublin: Irish Academic Press.

Fitzpatrick, D. (1995). 'The logic of collective sacrifice: Ireland and the British army, 1914–1918', *Historical Journal*, 38 (4), 1017–30.

Fitzpatrick, D. (1998). *The Two Irelands: 1912–1939*. Oxford: Oxford University Press.

Fitzpatrick, D. (2014). *Descendancy, Irish Protestant Histories Since 1795*. Cambridge: Cambridge University Press.

Hennessey, T. (1998). *Dividing Ireland: World War I and Partition*. London: Routledge.

Jackson, A. (1992). 'Unionist Myths 1912–1985', *Past & Present*, 136 (1/August), 164–85.
Livingstone, P. (1969). *The Fermanagh Story*. Enniskillen: Cumann Seanchais Chlochair.
Livingstone, P. (1979). *The Monaghan Story*. Enniskillen: Clogher Historical Society.
Mac Giolla Choille, B. (1966). *Chief Secretary's Office Dublin Castle Intelligence Notes 1913–1916*.
McDowell, R. B. (1997). *Crisis and Decline: The Fate of the Southern Unionists*. Dublin: Lilliput Press.
Newmann, K. (ed.) (1993). *Dictionary of Ulster Biography*. 'William Copeland Trimble (1851–1941)' (entry by R. Froggatt). Belfast: Institute of Irish Studies, The Queen's University.
Phoenix, E. (1994). *Northern Nationalism: Nationalist Politics, Partition and the Catholic Minority in Northern Ireland, 1890–1940*. Belfast: Ulster Historical Foundation.
Rankin, K. J. (2009). 'The Search for Statutory Ulster', *History Ireland*, 17 (3), 28–32.
Townsend, C. (2005). *Easter 1916: The Irish Rebellion*. London: Allen Lane.
Weeks, L. (2017). *Independents in Irish Party Democracy*. Manchester: Manchester University Press.

JUAN ROMERO, JOAQUÍN MARTÍN CUBAS, MARGARITA
SOLER SÁNCHEZ, JOSÉ MARÍA VIDAL BELTRÁN, AND
CARLES JOVANÍ GIL

Rebuilding Bridges: Nations and State in Present-Day Spain

ABSTRACT
One of the greatest challenges to integration in Spain stems from the plurality of national feelings within its territory. Spain is a state built on the union of various kingdoms that, over the centuries, gave rise to specific senses of identity. Monarchical absolutism in the eighteenth century, centralist liberalism in the nineteenth century and the Franco dictatorship in the twentieth century were unable to create a unified national identity within the Spanish territory. Acknowledging this, the Constitution of 1978 provided for the coexistence of diverse national realities within the new State of Autonomies. Nevertheless, the problem of national and regional tensions has resurfaced in the last decade. This chapter traces the origins of the problem and analyses failed attempts at political resolution, before outlining a possible solution based on dialogue and consensus in order to rebuild bridges of integration in a common project of a European and plurinational Spanish State.

No discussion of nation and identity can overlook the central importance of Spain: the peninsula has throughout history presented almost a paradigmatic environment in which to explore the tangled complex of myth, aspiration, and pride that makes up any definition of either, and the situation arising after the death of Franco offers fertile ground for that exploration.[1]

---

1   This study has been developed within the framework of the research project Estructura social, encuestas y elecciones (CSO2013-43054-R) funded by the call 2013-Proyectos I+D+I-Programa Estatal de Investigación, Desarrollo e Innovación Orientada a los Retos de la Sociedad, sponsored by the Ministry of Economy and Competitiveness.

The Ways of Federalism

The ways of federalism are, as is generally the case in modern states, plural and noted for their complex character. This has tended to be true when the State has been built by superimposing, with varying degrees of success, different cultural and identity realities. The prevailing strategies for the construction of the State vary greatly, despite efforts to reduce such rich pluralities through political science or constitutional law to a few idealized models that have become the legitimizing standards for what is considered possible. Nothing could be further from reality. In practice, each State has had to seek out its own way. These ways have led key figures to use violence, pacts, and consensus in many forms and degrees, to achieve situations of equilibrium which, although presumed to be stable, in actual practice remain susceptible to further change. The recurrence of identity and territorial crises in such states, such as the one most recently unfolding in Spain, attest to this notion.

In regard to federal solutions to problems of coexistence within a State, there is much literature covering a range from normative approaches to empirical analyses. In addition, classic authors such as James Madison and Johanes Altusius have been revisited in search of new ideas (among others: Taylor 1992; Kymlicka 1995; Maiz 2000; Gagnon 2001; Guibernau 2002; Tierney 2004; Requejo 2005). Furthermore, multitudes of empirical studies have not only endeavoured to describe the reality of federal states, but also to analyse their performance and institutional efficiency in great detail (among others: Weingast 1995; Rodden and Rose-Ackerman 1997; Treissman 2000; Rodden 2004; Wibbels 2005). Most of these studies have traditionally been included as part of the debate on the relative merits (or lack thereof) of modern states' unitary or federal constitutions, without taking their normative components into consideration when formulating questions and hypotheses about the actual functioning of these states (Maiz 2006: 46).

The results of these studies and the changes appearing around the turn of the century – including globalization, the digitization of society and the economy, new transnational realities, the repoliticization of local issues, major social changes, migratory flows, among others – force us to rethink the epistemological foundations of our approaches to the study of the issue. In particular, in recent decades the division between both models of the State – the federal state (e.g. the United States) and the unitary state (e.g. France) – has been increasingly blurred as federal systems began to develop characteristics of unitary states, and unitary states have progressively become less unitary (Loughlin 2017: 23). There is a growing consensus regarding the plurality of federal solutions (among others: Elazar 1987; Watts 1996; Burgess 2013) and their evolutionary nature in terms of the constant negotiations between the actors involved in their practical formulation (Bauböck 2000; Tully 2001). Indeed, it is understood that federal states are constitutively unstable by design (Bednar 1999) and thus need reinforcement institutions to incentivize politicians at different levels of government (Figuereido and Weingast 1998; Filippov et al. 2004; Maiz 2006: 51).

This factual or, perhaps one could say, positive observation is coupled with the assertion that the old classical models of territorial power distribution and identity recognition are incapable of meeting the challenges presently facing our societies (Bou 2005: 169; Loughlin 2017: 29). We need new normative models that open new paths of understanding by means of a permanent dialogue with empirical and comparative types of studies (Maiz 2006). As the authors of this chapter, we believe that normative considerations are inseparable from the factual realities of a specific society (the case of Spain) that is the product of a history which, for better or worse, has left its mark and plays a significant role in resolving societal problems (historical neo-institutionalism). In addition, we adhere to the basic assumption that the only thing that is needed is to build bridges that will facilitate the processes of coexistence between individuals. We also hold the conviction that federal normative approaches would be better suited to achieving them (Bauböck 2000; Requejo 2001). In this regard, we understand that Spain – like other unitary states in recent decades (the United Kingdom, France, Italy, etc.) – has gone down the same path, although with evident deficiencies, particularly in matters of the functional expression of territorial powers and political identity culture that force us to rethink and correct some of the agreements or points of equilibrium achieved thus far.

The 1978 transition to democracy in Spain is considered an unprecedented success. The body of agreements arrived at over the course of the following years makes up the country's foundation for stability, institutional development and socio-economic progress. But there is one aspect that has defied closure for some four decades, that of recognition of the multinational state of affairs, that was believed to be resolved and overcome after the establishment of the Autonomic State. Today, this old problem, still unsolved, has reappeared as Spain's foremost challenge: the mistaken or deliberate confusion between State and nation has not hidden the real existence of plural national feelings. The 2010 ruling of the Constitutional Court on the Statute of Autonomy of Catalonia was a turning point, and the subsequent secessionist drift of Catalan nationalism highlights the split of important links in the integration process of diverse national feelings in the project of a constitutional State. We maintain that it has not been the model of composite state, designed by the Constitution of 1978, but the political practice of insisting on the Orteguian idea of structuring a national State, which has blocked the path to a more affectively appealing way of understanding a multinational Spain. We consider that politics, agreements and consensus must again be employed in order to restore bridges of integration in a common project, that of a Spanish, European and multinational State.

The Spanish Problem

The construction process of the Autonomic State has been a success for the Spanish constitutional State, despite obvious faults in its operation. Having said this, one must also admit that the process of recognition of the different national identities and feelings, known as nationalities or nations has been a historical failure. It is not necessary to be a 'nationalist historian' to hold this position, but merely to approach Spanish history without preconceptions and prejudice. The causes that explain the relative failure in the construction of a nation-state in Spain and the persistence of the 'problem of the Spains', which Bosch-Gimpera (1996) talked about in the 1950s, are long-standing (Romero and Furió 2015). Elorza, for example, speaks of 'secular disruption' (2012). There is nothing to be said regarding State and nation (or to put it differently, 'state-building' and 'nation-building') that has not been said before.

In a seminal text by Juan J. Linz, written in 1973, which is as important as it is little known, a phenomenon is already summarized that in our opinion has hardly changed since then:

> [P]ara la mayoría de los españoles, España es un Estado-nación que suscita en ellos un sentimiento de solidaridad que no produce ninguna otra afiliación grupal; que para importantes minorías ha sido, y seguramente seguirá siendo, sólo un Estado cuya autoridad reconocen en su comportamiento, atribuyéndole más o menos legitimidad [...] Para estas minorías, España es su Estado pero no su nación y, por lo tanto, no es un Estado-nación. Puede que esas minorías que se identifican con una nación catalana o, especialmente vasca, sean pequeñas, pero demuestran el fracaso de España y sus elites a la hora de construir una nación, sea cual sea el grado de éxito en la construcción del Estado.
>
> [For a majority of Spaniards, Spain is a nation-state that gives rise to feelings of solidarity that are not produced by any other group affiliation; it has also been, and will probably continue to be, considered by important minorities to simply be a State whose authority is recognized through its daily behaviour, with a variable conferral of legitimacy [...] For these minorities, Spain is their State but not their nation, and, therefore, it is not a nation-state. It could be argued that those minorities that identify as a Catalan or, particularly, a Basque nation, are small, but they show the failure of Spain and its elites when it comes to building a nation, no matter the degree of success in their state-building.]² (Linz 2008a: 6–7)

For Linz, the most passable way that Spain might still thrive would be 'un Estado español unificador de una sociedad multilingüe y, en cierta medida, también multinacional, sobre criterios diferentes a los del pasado, en una democracia nacida con buena estrella' [a Spanish State, capable of unifying a multilingual and, to some extent, also a multinational society, under different criteria to those of the past, in a democracy born under an auspicious star] (2008a: 71–3).

2   All translations are by the authors.

In 1975, another important study by the same author (2008b) included a section with a revealing epigraph: '*un Estado, tres naciones, cuatro lenguas*' [one State, three nations, four languages]. He insisted again on the need to make a distinction between nation and State, included a peremptory distinction between nations and regions, and introduced a remark that was very much to the point on the singularity of a Spanish nationalism that probably lacked 'trasfondo romántico del nacionalismo decimonónico que creó Estados-nación como Italia y Alemania' [the nineteenth-century romantic background that gave rise to nation-states such as Italy and Germany], coming closer instead to 'lo que los sociólogos han denominado *patriotismo*' [what sociologists have designated as *patriotism*] (2008b: 78–9).

Some years later, in 1980, with the Constitution already approved, he understood that the young democratic State was facing two major challenges:

[U]no, el paso de un régimen autoritario a la democracia, el otro, de un Estado centralizado que no reconocía la diversidad de sus pueblos a uno multilingüe y multinacional, además de descentralizado. El paso a la democracia ya había tenido una larga y accidentada historia y los españoles tienen una idea más o menos clara de lo que significa. El otro cambio es mucho más difícil de entender, está mucho más lejos de la conciencia de los españoles, fuera de las regiones periféricas, y en el fondo representa una ruptura mucho mayor con el pasado, no solo del franquismo.

[The first one, the transition from an authoritarian regime to democracy, and the other, from a centralized State that did not recognize the diversity of its peoples to a multilingual and multinational one, with a decentralized administration. The move towards democracy had already had a long and eventful history, and Spaniards have a more or less clear idea of what that means. The second change is much harder to understand, is much further from the Spanish consciousness, referring as it does to Spain's peripheral regions, and could be said to entail a much more intense break with the past, and not only with *Franquismo*.] (Linz 2008c: 121)

He concludes with another assessment that is still in force: 'España [...] es probablemente el caso más difícil entre las democracias occidentales a la hora de encontrar soluciones satisfactorias permanentes' [Spain [...] is probably the most difficult case among the western democracies when it comes to finding permanent satisfactory solutions] (2008c: 158).

In practice, political actors would end up partially facing these challenges – consolidation of democracy, decentralization, political autonomy and recognition of official languages different from Spanish – but the second revolutionary change set out by Linz was postponed and must still be dealt with (Romero and Alcaraz 2015).

The Constitutional Solution

At the time of setting in motion the process of Transition, there were many very different views of Spain. The majority of political forces, however, agreed to focus their attention on the State organization, leaving undetermined and subject to very different interpretations the debate on the Nation and the nations.

The right-wing parties (AP and UCD), with their internal contradictions, oscillated between the traditional essentialist discourse, exclusive nationalism and a programme of regional decentralization. The parties of the parliamentary left (PSOE and PCE), with their different traditions, had already carried out their particular programmatic internal 'transition', leaving behind any reference to the right of self-determination of the peoples of Spain or even to federalism (Juliá 2013; Blas 2013: 938–9; Archilés 2014; Rodriguez-Flores 2014). The democratic peripheral nationalists (CiU and PNV, fundamentally), had also faced these debates with their own divisions and different blueprints. Nevertheless, the explicit acceptance by Catalan nationalist parties and the calculated ambiguity of the PNV towards the final text of the Constitutional Draft was very clear.

Almost all had to reconcile past and future in a context that was far from stable and without clear and well-defined outcomes. It was unclear what result they intended to achieve, but there was common ground: they knew what they wanted to escape from (Caminal 2009). It was an exercise in pragmatism, not without improvisation and mutual concessions. Much has been written on this issue and the interpretations are many, but the fact is that the conflict of incompatible views of Spain occupied most of the time spent in debate. Two Articles summarize the evolution of this pact-based process.

On the one hand, Article 1.2 of the constitutional draft, inspired by the Constitution of the Second Republic, stated that 'los poderes de todos los órganos del Estado emanan del pueblo español, en el que reside la soberanía' [the powers of every organ of the State are derived from the Spanish people, in which sovereignty resides], but, in the same Proposal, AP and UCD agreed to introduce the concept of 'national sovereignty', giving rise to a text essentially identical to the one that was finally approved: 'La soberanía nacional reside en el pueblo español del que emanan los poderes del Estado' [National sovereignty resides in the Spanish people, from whom the powers of the State are derived].

On the other hand, the initial version of Article 2 said: 'La Constitución se fundamenta en la unidad de España y la solidaridad entre sus pueblos y reconoce el derecho a la autonomía de las nacionalidades y regiones que la integran' [The Constitution is based on the unity of Spain and solidarity amongst its peoples, and recognizes the right to self-government of the nationalities and regions of which it is comprised]. Discussions focused on the inclusion or not of the term *nationalities*, but the dispute was settled with the presentation of an amendment *in voce*, probably imposed from the military stratum and accepted by a large majority of the parliamentary groups, including the well-known declaration:

> La Constitución se fundamenta en la indisoluble unidad de la Nación española, Patria común e indivisible de todos los españoles, y reconoce el derecho a la autonomía de las nacionalidades y regiones que la integran y la solidaridad entre todas ellas.
>
> [The Constitution is based on the indissoluble unity of the Spanish Nation, the common and indivisible homeland of all Spaniards; it recognizes and guarantees the right to self-government of the nationalities and regions of which it is comprised and the solidarity amongst them all.] (*Diario de Sesiones*, 1978: 2314)

That was the agreement, with the sole and relevant abstention of Basque nationalists. Later, different interpretations appeared, along with criticisms from rightists and leftists, who believed themselves to have been betrayed, or to have surrendered or yielded too early to the wishes of their opponents. For some authors, such as Álvarez Junco:

> [M]ás que una fórmula de compromiso que resolviera el problema con concesiones de ambas partes, la redacción constitucional fue *un híbrido que intentó dar cabida a dos exigencias nacionalistas, inconciliables si se llevan a un extremo*. No resolvió, pues, el problema con conceptos claros y delimitaciones tajantes, sino que lo aplazó.
>
> [More than a compromise that would resolve the problem by way of reciprocal concessions, the constitutional text was *a hybrid that intended to include two nationalistic demands, irreconcilable if they are taken to extremes*. It did not solve the problem, therefore, with clear concepts and categorical demarcations, but simply put it off to a later date.] (Álvarez Junco 2013: 814)

However, as we see it, the vagueness of the adopted expression may be regarded as a good decision when it comes to the rebuilding of bridges of integration: it allows one to interpret the text as saying more than it originally intended. It becomes evident that the achieved 'national pact' involves accepting, on the one hand, the ideological and legal supremacy of the Spanish nation, and on the other, what has been known as a 'pact of differences', which becomes apparent in some particular points (our emphases) of the Constitution, notably:

- The Preamble, when the Spanish Nation proclaims its will to 'proteger a todos los españoles y *pueblos* de España en el ejercicio de los derechos humanos, sus *culturas y tradiciones, lenguas e instituciones*' [protect all Spaniards and *peoples* of Spain in the exercise of their human rights, *cultures and traditions, languages and institutions*].
- Article 2, in recognizing the right to self-government of the regions and nationalities, bearing in mind that the *recognition* of a right necessarily implies a previous reality.
- The inclusion in Article 2 of the co-officiality of *languages* different from Spanish.
- The reference in the Second Transitory Provision to *the territories that in the past* had decided to approve a Statute of Autonomy by plebiscite project – the Basque Country, Catalonia and Galicia – to whom a *first-class autonomy* was guaranteed, becoming known as *historical nationalities*, irrespective of the body of the Constitution.
- The reference in the Fourth Transitory Provision to Navarre as an autonomous reality and its possible 'incorporation' into the Basque General Council – pre-autonomous – or into the future Basque autonomous community.

- The legal protection that the First Additional Provision bestows on '*los derechos históricos de los territorios forales*' [the historical rights of the territories with chartered regimes], that should be updated in the eventual constitutional framework and in the Statutes of Autonomy.

Irrespective of the purpose of the fathers of the Constitution, these foundations allow for an interpretation of this text from a multi-national point of view that does not have to be pitted against either the national sovereignty of the Spanish people or the indissoluble unity of the Spanish nation, as stated in articles 1.2 and 2 of the Constitution.

Post-Constitutional Drift

The agreement, in any case, was useful in laying the groundwork for a new territorial organization of the State, but subject to a particular development. The general idea planned initially by the UCD government would end up undergoing substantial modifications. As early as 1979, after the approval of the Basque and Catalan Statutes, the government presided over by Adolfo Suárez adopted the clear intention of 'rationalization' of the process of development of the Autonomic State. Some relevant steps are well known: the Report issued by a commission created ad hoc by UCD and presided over by Martín Villa; the communication addressed to the Congress of Deputies by President Suárez in May 1980; the so-called Enterría Report that gave way to the Autonomic Agreements UCD-PSOE of 1981; the Organic Law on Harmonization of the Autonomic Process (LOAPA); the appeal to the Constitutional Court by the governments of the Basque Country and Catalonia; and the Ruling of the Constitutional Court declaring the text to a large extent unconstitutional. This process continued to be settled in a second major political agreement in 1992 – with subsequent enlargements and specifications – between the PSOE and the PP, that essentially opened up the possibility of generalizing full faculties in favour of the other autonomous communities.

The regional autonomic generalization provided a measure of stability to the system, at least for a time. For this purpose, the clarifying work of the Constitutional Court played a major role, particularly through the development of the concept of Constitutional Bloc, that allowed for an integration of the constitutional text and the respective Statutes in its analysis (Pérez Royo 1988). Nevertheless, other realities emerged, increasing the complexity of the situation and giving rise to new contradictions; and it must be noted that the interventionism of the Constitutional Court did not satisfy everybody. Interpretation in favour of the positions generally held by the State regarding extension of the basic or cross-cutting subjects to be regulated by the State, among other matters, would end up highlighting the intrinsic limitation of this mechanism: a rekindling of tensions between the growing dissatisfaction of the sub-state national identities and the project of rebuilding the Spanish national identity on a renewed basis. Both processes were already obvious in the early 1990s. A return to open debate on the (identitarian) constitutional pact would emerge in full force when the economic and social crisis underscored the inadequacies and weaknesses of the territorial agreement that was finally reached.

Re-emergence of the Problem

The gaps and shortfalls in this process of construction of the Autonomic State, as well as the strongly identitarian and differential demands from peripheral nationalisms, became clearly visible from the beginning of the twenty-first century. It is true that during Term VI (1996–2000) the lack of a qualified majority by the PP government, presided over by José María Aznar, had favoured a better understanding with the nationalist parties ruling Catalonia and the Basque Country. Nevertheless, during Term VII (2000–4), with the PP now having an absolute majority, disputes began to increase in regard to two major points: the reform proposal of the Basque Statute – the Ibarretxe Plan – and the reform proposal of the Catalan Statute. Intense political and social debate led to increasingly radical positions being adopted and fostered from both peripheral and central nationalist perspectives.

The reform of the Statutes of Autonomy promoted by the government of Rodríguez Zapatero during Term VIII (2004–8) attempted to embed these changes in the constitutional framework while at the same time intending to make a qualitative leap in improved co-operation and co-ordination between the Autonomous Communities and the State. It could not, however, avoid the redirection of a good many of these conflicts towards the Constitutional Court, whose rulings, rather than contributing to a solution to the essential problem, seemed rather to be giving rise to a deadlock.

The Basque process of reform concluded in 2005: first, with a vote in the Congress of Deputies that ruled out processing the Organic Law fostered by the Ibarretxe Plan and, afterwards, with Ruling 103/2008 of the Constitutional Court, issued on 11 September, that vetoed the possibility of citizen consultation on the 'right to decide of the Basque people'. The reform of the Statute of Catalonia, despite approval by the citizens of Catalonia, concluded with Ruling 31/2010, issued on 28 June, whereby a part was corrected or re-interpreted. This ruling sparked off a negative public perception by Catalan society with regard to integration with Spanish institutions, and the relationship seriously deteriorated further when the economic crisis worsened the negative consequences for Catalonia of the budget and state investment deficit, and generated a broadly accepted opinion within Catalan society that many of its problems are a product of an unfair and damaging funding mechanism decided by the Spanish State.

On the other hand, the same economic crisis served to reveal more clearly the serious functional problems of the Autonomic State. With some exceptions, mechanisms of multilateral co-ordination and co-operation are ignored, avoided or minimally implemented, thus further undermining a system where dysfunctions, co-ordination problems, a weak culture of co-operation and more than a few institutional pathologies come to the surface (Romero 2008; Sevilla, Vidal and Elias 2009). In this state of affairs, however, a reasonable amount of consensus on the diagnosis and proposal for improvement exists (see Aja 2004; Rubio and Álvarez 2006; Martín, Pérez, Romero, Soler and Vidal 2013).

But, paradoxically, the strategy followed by the government of Mariano Rajoy during Term X (2011–15) was not to foster the many long-standing demands for reform, but rather to promote the attempts at political recentralization which were supported by the academic, political, judicial and media spheres. With the Law on Rationalization and Sustainability of the Local Administrations of 2013, within the framework of economic recession and in the name of efficiency and a more rational State, Spaniards were truly witnessing an unprecedented political offensive by the right and a part of the left against the Autonomic State. A process of recentralization affecting the Autonomous Communities was championed, with measures including suppression of regional organs and institutions as well as a reduction in the number of regional deputies and elimination of their salaries (which also affected local governments). All this was based on the false notion that the public deficit, even in recession, has its source in the hypertrophic and untidy Autonomic State.

Spaniards were witnessing a delegitimizing discourse that had been gaining ground within broad sectors of public opinion, with 23.1 per cent willing to support 'only a central government without Autonomies' and 13.9 per cent in favour of a State where the Autonomous Communities 'would have a lesser degree of political autonomy than at the present time' (Centro de Investigaciones Sociológicas 2013). This is a centripetal trend that has become more pronounced in many autonomous communities with the same intensity as the centrifugal forces making progress in Catalonia and the Basque Country (Mira, Pérez and Romero 2013). It is precisely in these communities that almost half of the population is sympathetic to the separatist cause: opinion polls between 2013 and 2018 showed Catalan support for independence at close to 50 per cent, having peaked at 48.5 per cent in November 2013 and at 47.7 per cent in June 2016 (Centre d'Estudis d'Opinió 2013–18).

Nationalist political parties in the Basque Country championed this cause in the late twentieth century (whether through violence via ETA or peacefully through the Ibarretxe plan), but it was in Catalonia where, at the start of this century, the State was challenged by 'El procés independentista' [The independence process]. In 2013, and following its failure to secure a taxation agreement with the State, CiU – the then governing and principal nationalist political party in Catalonia – decided to focus its efforts on the independence movement. CiU joined forces with ERC, the other major Catalan nationalist party, to found an alliance known as 'Junts pel sí' [Together for Yes]. This alliance received the support of the anti-capitalist nationalist party CUP, the Catalan Parliament's third most represented nationalist party. The overall objective of these parties was to hold a referendum for Catalans to vote on the nature of Catalonia's relationship with Spain. Faced with repeated refusals by Spain's Prime Minister – the only person able to authorize such a referendum (backed in his position by PP, PSOE and Ciudadanos) – on 6 September 2017 Catalan nationalist leaders (from ERC, CUP and the former CiU, who together held a majority in the Catalan Parliament) in defiance of the Spanish Constitution and Catalonia's Statute of Autonomy, passed a law authorizing a referendum in Catalonia, which was duly held in Catalonia on 1 October 2017. If passed, the referendum would give the Catalan Parliament (with a nationalist majority) an excuse to unilaterally declare independence. In response, the Spanish government enforced article 155 of the Constitution, which allows the State to intervene in an autonomous community when its authorities seriously contravene their constitutional obligations. A number of key nationalist leaders of the independence Procés, led by the president of the Catalan government, fled Spain to avoid arrest. The train wreck that had been expected thus happened.

The Ideological Dispute

The crisis of the Autonomic State, nevertheless, has been years in the making. At the beginning of the 1990s, those who played a leading role during the Transition assessed the process.

Speeches in the Carlos III University of Madrid in 1991 and 1992 by the presidents Pujol and Ardanza are a good illustration of the appraisal made by both actors. Pujol regretted that perhaps he had not set out 'el problema de Cataluña con suficiente rotundidad' [the problem of Catalonia categorically enough] between 1975 and 1977 and, admitting that Spain is a unit, he wondered '¿qué temor cabe abrigar frente a una estructura que responda mejor a la personalidad diferenciada y muy particular de Cataluña?' [what kind of fear can be harboured regarding a structure that better responds to the different and very particular personality of Catalonia?] (Pujol 1994: 63–6). For his part, the *Lehendakari,* Ardanza, argued:

> Si el Estado, por el mero hecho de serlo, se proclama a sí mismo también *nación* y sobrecarga con ello su naturaleza jurídica y política, añadiéndole otras connotaciones históricas, culturales, sociales y hasta emocionales [...] nadie podrá extrañarse de que cualquier colectividad, por el mero hecho de creerse *nación*, oponga a esa pretensión, a su juicio extralimitada, la suya propia de proclamarse a sí misma también Estado y niegue su adhesión [...] Una cosa ha quedado clara y ésta es que una Nación puede encontrar cabida y encaje en otro Estado, pero no cabe, desde luego, en otra Nación. Y nosotros, los nacionalistas vascos, creemos que Euskadi es una Nación.
>
> [If the State, by the mere fact of existing, is self-proclaimed a *nation* and subsequently overreaches its legal and political nature, adding other historical, cultural, social and even emotional connotations [...] nobody should be surprised that any community, by the mere fact of considering itself a *nation*, counters that pretension, in its opinion overreaching, with its own intention of being a self-proclaimed State [...] One thing is clear, and that is that a Nation can be accommodated within another State, but it definitely cannot be contained within another Nation. And we, the Basque nationalists, think that the Basque Country is a Nation.] (Ardanza 1994: 27–8)

During 1992, the PP and the PSOE supported several versions of 'Spanish nationalism lite'. Spanish socialism, without abandoning its principally Jacobin soul, defending the well-known discourse of a plural Spain and on the basis of a positive assessment of the work achieved, attributed to the Agreements of 1991 the 'objetivo de culminar el proceso constituyente y enriquecer el funcionamiento del sistema autonómico' [objective of achieving the culmination of the constitutional process and enriching the operability of the autonomic system] (Eguiagaray 1993: 100). Not a single reference, therefore, to the *nationalities*. The right, for its part, clung to the defence, though still cautious, of the first part of Article 2 of the Spanish Constitution, that is, to the idea of a Nation within a State. But it also took preventive measures against possible claims by some nationalities in putting forward what would be a robust strategy of recomposition of Spanish nationalism several years later: '[D]ebemos asumir nuestras responsabilidades y defender en todos los foros, universitarios y académicos, en los medios de comunicación, y allá donde proceda la existencia de una nación que se llama España, la necesidad de un proyecto nacional' [We must assume our own responsibilities and defend in every forum, whether university or academic, in the mass media, and wherever else, the existence of a nation called Spain and the need for a national project] (Rajoy 1993: 46).

It was when the PP came to power in 1996 that Spanish nationalism undertook the major task of implementing a political redefinition of identity on a new ideological basis, cloaked in apparent modernity. The identification between nation and Franquism, as explained by Jordi Muñoz, had generated a kind of 'self-limitation'. During the first years of democracy, Spanish nationalism lacked 'democratic credentials'. This limitation of Spanish nationalism would be to a significant extent overcome through the assumption by the right of a kind of peculiar and 'traditional' version of Habermasian 'constitutional patriotism' (Bastida 2007: 132–55). This was a new discourse, a kind of *Spanish constitutional nationalism*, with the failed pretension of becoming an equivalent version of civic or political nationalism, that would initially turn the Constitution into a '*mito nacional* o *lugar de memoria*' [national myth or place of memory] (Muñoz 2012: 56) and later, into a metaphorical '*fortaleza*' [fortress] in order to oppose any proposal of constitutional reform or recognition of the multi-national reality.

Over time, the situation has become even more polarized. The right frequently stresses well-known expressions from exclusionary Spanish nationalism that, in several cases, seem to be moving towards some sort of 'authoritarian nationalism'. They speak of 'closing' a State model. A process of recentralization was put forward in the name of efficiency and a more rational State, and on the basis that the recession was caused by the development of the Autonomic State. Two examples will suffice: the book by Julio Gómez, Mario Garcés and Gabriel Elorriaga, *Por un Estado Autonómico racional y viable* [For a rational and viable State of Autonomies] (2010) and the publication of the article 'La España de las Autonomías: un Estado débil devorado por diecisiete estaditos' [Spain of the Autonomies: a Weak State Devoured by Seventeen Statelets] by Professor Tomás-Ramón Fernández in 2013, both under the auspices of FAES. A full consensus in their diagnosis can be noted: the Autonomic State is non-viable and a comprehensive revision and recentralization must be implemented.

Between this nationalist version, advocated by the Spanish right, and that defended by those who hold secessionist positions from Catalan and Basque nationalist perspectives, Spanish socialism tried to find a middle road. In accordance with its traditional position, it advocated the (third) way of territorial federalism, but without ever putting forth the option of plurinational federalism. The PSOE defended its stance in the document *Hacia una estructura federal del Estado* [Towards a Federal State Structure], ratified by its Federal Committee in July 2013.[3] It was a renewed version of territorial federalism (a constitutional reform in a federal direction, where greater emphasis is put on a certain recognition of the peculiarities and differential aspects of some nationalities, such as those to be found in Catalonia and the Basque Country).

In our opinion, despite the conciliatory intentions of the socialist proposal, the territorial federalist model cannot by itself contribute to solving either the political blockade or the real underlying problem. For this reason, we support a new political pact in favour of a plurinational federalism, capable of dealing with these issues with clarity and normality. This would be a project that would make possible both constitutional recognition of minority nations in a collective project, following the thesis of Gagnon, and an understanding of the Spaniards' overlapping identities, where a majority of those who feel Catalan also feel Spanish (2012). Plurinational federalism allows, from a position of freedom and equality, for the building of an integrative political realm for all Spaniards with regional identities, precisely by expressly including them.

The New Bridges of the Spanish Territorial Model

It is the responsibility of politicians to correct their mistakes and improve the existing situation, which, with all its problems and deep

---

3   See: <http://web.psoe.es/source-media/000000571000/000000571056.pdf>.

social divides, has produced the greatest political crisis in Spain since the ratification of the 1978 Constitution. This crisis has entailed: Catalonia's chief executive calling an independence referendum in 2017; the subsequent enforcement of the Spanish Constitution's article 155 in order to bring Catalonia back in line with constitutional provisions and other Spanish laws; the flight and imprisonment of some of Catalonia's executive branch officials and others who played key roles in the referendum.

In light of these events, we once again stress that, in our view, efforts should be made to emphasize the fact that respect for the rules of the constitutional system is one of Spain's greatest assets as a plurinational political community, and it should be one of our better legacies as well. Spain needs to convince the majority of the people that preservation of any national identity does not have to involve taking the perilous path of secession, but rather that being part of a plurinational State is better than being forced to decide, even if it were possible, between nationalisms or between one of the possible identities; it needs, in addition, to defend the positive values of a multinational, multicultural and multilingual political community. In accordance with the present Constitution, significant steps by public powers can and must be demanded in the area of the recognition of identitarian diversity. An interpretation of the present Constitution in plurinational terms is possible, among other things because Constitutions, far from becoming static, can and must adapt to new realities. The principal mission of any constitution is to promote coexistence and social cohesion.

It seems that certain key political leaders have recognized this reality. First, Pedro Sánchez, prior to becoming Spanish prime minister, came out in support of 'el reconocimiento en la Constitución del carácter plurinacional del Estado, aun manteniendo que la soberanía reside en el conjunto del pueblo español' [the Constitution's recognition of the State's plurinational character, even though its sovereignty resides in the whole of Spain's population] (Sánchez 2017). Second, resolutions along similar lines were approved at PSOE's 39th Congress, held on 16–18 June 2017 (PSOE 2017: 41). Last, on 20 September 2018 Basque president (*lehendakari*) Iñigo Urkullu asked his parliament to establish a 'plurinational democracy' within the

Spanish State (albeit while hoping for this initiative to be interpreted in federalist terms).[4]

It is obvious, therefore, that Spain must improve the Autonomic State in order to accommodate in a correct fashion the different *nationalisms* (in constitutional terminology) or *internal nations* (in academic terminology) that, as Ortega would say, we must *bear*. And, at the same time, it must be underscored that, as Juan José Solozábal aptly noted in 2010: '[E]l orden autonómico es un orden complejo, pero no puede ser un orden confuso' [The autonomic order is a complex order, but it cannot be a confused order] (quoted in Azagra and Romero 2012: 225), which means that it is also necessary to undertake important reforms regarding the essence of and most efficient running of a composite State.

Such a series of reforms must be undertaken within a federal perspective and coming from a position of respect for a deep diversity, that we can summarize as: recognition of the plurinationality of the Spanish State, the adoption of a new, fair and efficient funding system, and the establishment of a federal dimension in territorial relations and the functioning of the State in order to provide it with greater efficiency and political legitimacy (Martín, Pérez, Romero, Soler and Vidal 2013).

Recognition of the Plurinational Nature of the Spanish State or of the 'Nationalities' that Make It Up

The Spanish Constitution already recognizes, explicitly, that the Spanish Nation is made up of 'nationalities and regions' in its Article 2, so the recognition of this plurinational reality should be clearly and expressly assumed and the Constitution should be reinterpreted to accommodate this reality. Apart from the already adduced reasons, the Constitution Preamble encourages us to strengthen the pacific and co-operative

4   Available <https://www.eitb.eus/es/noticias/politica/detalle/5864507/debate-politica-general-parlamento-vasco-20-septiembre-2018/> accessed 23 September 2018.

relations amongst the peoples of the Earth after making an express reference to 'the peoples' of Spain. It is obvious that this interpretation requires broad consensus in order to guarantee its durability and stability over time. Perhaps, in order to underpin this interpretation, a reform of Title VIII of the Constitution could be implemented, this being a reform which would not require the special ('aggravated') procedures demanded by Articles 1.2 and 2 of the Constitution.

If no consensus were reached, the reform of both articles could also be considered. A number of possibilities exist that can be summarized in the following fashion: to break the connection between nation and sovereignty, thereby making the people, or, if preferred, the citizenry directly sovereign; explicit recognition of the multinational nature of the Spanish State; and (the most problematic solution) explicit recognition of the different internal nations.

The Adoption of a New, Fair and Efficient System of Funding

Another of the bones of contention in the organization of the Spanish territorial model is the funding system. The marked inequalities between autonomous communities in terms of per capita (i.e. 'adjusted population') funding are widely known. This inequality is up to 25 per cent amongst communities with a common regime and close to 40 per cent with regard to communities 'de régimen foral' [with a chartered regime]. At first glance, these differences (which could be justified on the grounds of dispersion of population or insularity) do not seem reasonable and, for many people, are not justified or, at least, are not justified in these proportions.

It is essential therefore, to reorganize the funding distribution of the communities in a more reasonable way. It is not our place to offer a categorical solution, but we consider that, among those proposed, the most reasonable (Martín, Pérez, Romero, Soler and Vidal 2013) is the one adopted by the Valencian socialists (PSOE-PSPV 2013), and also, at least nominally, by the federal PSOE; this would involve the creation of a kind of Guarantee Fund for the Welfare State and Solidarity, based on the minimal dimension of the functions of public expense, in proportion to the state GDP, for the following attributions: security, justice, healthcare, education and social protection, both autonomic and central. Such a Fund, whose distribution should follow population criteria, must develop along with the GDP, and not with tax collection, and in order to be maintained in times of crisis, it would be necessary to establish safeguards and contingency mechanisms similar to those of the pension system.

These Welfare State faculties having been assured, the system would guarantee sufficient financial support for the remaining autonomic sphere of competence through the collection of taxes transferred to the autonomous communities and their participation in state taxes. The distribution of this tranche among the autonomous communities, on this occasion, would take place according to the agreed necessity indicators: population, GDP, territorial extent, population density, dispersion of people in the territory, and so on. Otherwise, autonomy would be guaranteed by those additional resources that could be obtained by the Autonomous Communities when exercising their normative capacity in the tax sphere, establishing their own taxes or surcharges on top of those of the state, as well as through their participation in the collection results derived from a fiscal effort above the average of the Autonomous Communities.

It would be, therefore, a system that would guarantee to all citizens, regardless of their territory of residence and their per capita income, the same level of welfare or, at least, fair treatment in terms of education, healthcare and social services.

A New Structural and Functional Organization of the Autonomic State

For the establishment of these new bridges upon which Spain's territorial model must be built, in order to provide it with greater efficiency and political legitimacy it is also necessary to have at its disposal what we could call a federal character in the structural and functional articulation of the State.

Many paths in this process can exist, but it seems indispensable to at least implement a constitutional reform, both with regard to the configuration of a new model of the Senate, and to reform of Title VIII of the Constitution in order to define with clarity and consistency the rules that must govern the new composite State, without renouncing the achievements of the last thirty years of autonomic experience, but amending the evident dysfunctions and shortfalls detected. In conclusion, we outline for discussion a selection of guidelines for the proposed reforms.

Constitutional Recognition of the Territorial Structure of the State

The architects of the 1978 Constitution were not able to precisely specify the structure of the future Autonomic State. Nevertheless, over forty years later, the development and consolidation of these territorial entities has defined Spain's Autonomic State quite clearly. It seems, therefore, to be the moment to recognize this fact and incorporate the autonomic map within the constitutional text. Likewise, it also seems evident that local government is a State power and its autonomy must be recognized and guaranteed as appropriate. In this context, it seems to make little sense, within a state organized in autonomous communities, to maintain the provincial structure of government in the constitutional sphere.

Reformulation and Clarification of the Distribution of Competences

Autonomy, not only of the autonomous communities, but of the three government levels, must be guaranteed by a clear and evident distribution of competences which can remove strain on the system and enhance its operability. In our opinion, the problems of lack of definition in certain spheres of competence will always persist, but we have enough models, as well as cumulative and comparative experience, to be able to tackle, with full guarantees, a new formulation of the distribution of competences that can contribute to the improvement of the performance of the model. It is obvious that the 'hechos diferenciales' [asymmetries] among communities must be taken into consideration as long as they do not affect citizenship or welfare rights.

Constitutional Recognition of the Principles and Basic Rules of Functional Articulation of the State

The Constitution must establish the principles and rules that must govern the functional articulation of relations among the different levels of government. On a general basis, a common agreement exists in legal doctrine regarding the need to reinforce horizontal co-operation. Possibilities here are also diverse and not mutually exclusive.

Thereby, the constitutional reform of the Senate is a cornerstone of the proper functioning of a composite Spanish State. Although it needs further discussion, it seems reasonable to conceive of a reform involving a new composition that can better reflect the autonomic intention and reinforce the attributions of the Senate in territorial terms. We also consider it necessary to turn the Senate into a permanent forum for the other multilateral co-operation bodies.

It is particularly with regard to this last point that the new constitutional text should include the principles and rules that must govern the life of the most prominent multilateral co-operation bodies along with the Senate, that is, the Conferences of Presidents and the Sectorial Conferences. Their institutionalization should no longer be dependent on the ever-changing will of the governments in office, but should become common practice in the functioning of our model of composite State.

In the same vein, the Constitution should regulate the principles that must govern the structure of the National State Administration and its relational activity with the territorial entities, on the basis of federal models and in accordance with the distribution of competences established in the constitutional text. We cannot allow ourselves to maintain a state administrative structure with our backs turned to the functional reality of the autonomous communities or any other level of government, which means that its configuration must be adjusted to the needs of a multi-level state.

We must also find a constitutionally suitable place for the autonomies in the sphere of the European Union and, in general, their role in the international sphere. It is essential to reinforce the participation of the

Autonomous Communities in the sphere of the European Union, particularly with regard to issues that are strictly within the latter's faculties, and in those decisions that could affect the management of its faculties. In addition, the territorial governments must take part in and be acquainted with the State's external action, which requires their empowerment, but always on the basis of respect for State faculties.

For the aforementioned reasons, and for many other issues that go beyond the scope of this study, it will be possible to advance the quest for a solution to the most serious political crisis currently facing Spain's constitutional system, rooted in the poorly named 'problema territorial de las Españas' [territorial problem of the Spains] (Vidal 2013), which has been characterized by a long history of disagreements (Romero 2006) and, even today, requires solid bridges both in Catalonia and in the Basque Country between the opposing parties, this being a problem that is not confined to Spain. Other democracies – including Belgium, the United Kingdom and Canada – have faced or are currently facing similar situations and they have been tackled with courageous political decisions that have enabled progress towards new scenarios, both in the present and for the future. The direction of the solution was already pointed out by Juan Linz in the 1990s: '[Q]uienes se identifican con una nación no necesitan construir Estados nacionales si sus Estados multinacionales pueden ofrecer un *techo* a su cultura e identidad' [Those who identify themselves with a nation do not need to build national States if their multinational States can provide a *shelter* for their culture and identity] (Linz 2008c: 567).

Bibliography

Aja, E. (2004). 'La consolidación del Estado autonómico', *Corts* 15, 393–410.
Álvarez Junco, J. (2013). 'La idea de España en el sistema autonómico'. In A. Morales, J. P. Fusi, and A. de Blas (eds), *Historia de la nación y del nacionalismo español*, pp. 47–75. Barcelona: Galaxia de Gutenberg.
Aranguren, J. L. (1991). 'Naciones, Estados, nacionalismos, inter-nacionalidad', *Revista de Occidente* 122–3, 15–24.

Archilés, F. (2014). 'Una improvisada pervivencia: la Constitución de 1978 y la idea de nación española'. In F. Archilés, and I. Saz (eds), *Naciones y Estado. La cuestión española*, pp. 15–49. Valencia: Universitat de València.

Ardanza, J. A. (1994). 'A propósito del Pacto Autonómico'. In A. de las Heras (ed.), *Nacionalidades y Estado en España*. Madrid: Universidad Carlos III/Boletín Oficial del Estado.

Azagra, J., and Romero, J. (2012). *Desde la margen izquierda*. Valencia: Universitat de València

Bastida, X. (2007). 'La senda constitucional. La nación española y la Constitución'. In C. Taibo (ed.), *Nacionalismo español. Esencias, memoria e instituciones*, pp. 113–58. Madrid: Libros de la Catarata.

Bauböck, R. (2000). 'Why stay together? A pluralist Approach to Secession and Federation'. In W. Kymlicka, and W. Norman (eds), *Citizenship in Diverse Societies*, pp. 366–94. Oxford: Oxford University Press.

Bednar, J. (1999). 'Federalism: Unstable by Design'. Paper presented at APSA Meeting, Atlanta, GA.

Blas, A. de (2013). 'Cuestión nacional, transición política y Estado de las Autonomías'. In A. Morales, J. P. Fusi, and A. de Blas (eds), *Historia de la nación y del nacionalismo español*, pp. 934–50. Barcelona: Galaxia de Gutenberg.

Bosch-Gimpera, P. (1996). *El problema de las Españas*. Málaga: Algazara.

Bou i Novensà, M. (2005). 'Naciones sin Estado: ¿Acomodación en democracias plurinacionales o secesión', *Revista de Investigaciones Políticas y Sociológicas RIPS*, 4 (2), 167–81.

Burgess, M. (2013). 'The penumbra of federalism'. In J. Loughlin, J. Kincaid, and W. Swendem (eds), *Routledge Handbook of Regionalism and Federalism*, pp. 45–60. London: Routledge.

Caminal, M. (2009). 'L'Estat autonòmic espanyol: entre la resistència nacionalista i l'horitzó federal'. In M. Caminal, and F. Requejo (eds), *Federalisme i plurinacionalitat*, pp. 475–540. Barcelona: Institut d'Estudis Autonòmics.

Centro de Investigaciones Sociológicas (1996). *Barómetro Autonómico 1996*. Madrid: Centro de Investigaciones Sociológicas.

Centro de Investigaciones Sociológicas (2005). *Barómetro Autonómico 2005*. Madrid: Centro de Investigaciones Sociológicas.

Centro de Investigaciones Sociológicas (2011). *Barómetro Autonómico 2011*. Madrid: Centro de Investigaciones Sociológicas.

Centro de Investigaciones Sociológicas (2013). *Barómetro Autonómico 2013*. Madrid: Centro de Investigaciones Sociológicas.

Centro d'Estudis d'Opinió (2013–2018). *Barómentros y estudios de opinión*. Barcelona <http://ceo.gencat.cat/es/inici/> accessed 23 September 2018.

Colominas, J. (2010). 'L'intent fracassat del catalanisme polític de convertir Espanya en un Estat plurinacional'. In F. Requejo, and A.-G. Gagnon (eds), *Nacions a la recerca de reconeixement*, pp. 139–62. Barcelona: Institut d'Estudis Autonòmics.

Comisión de Expertos sobre Autonomías (1981). *Informe de la Comisión de Expertos sobre Autonomías*. Madrid: Centro de Estudios Constitucionales.

Eguiagaray, J. M. (1993). 'El Pacto Autonómico'. In VVAA, *Organización territorial del Estado*. Salamanca: Universidad de Salamanca.

Elazar, D. J. (1987). *Exploring Federalism*. Tuscaloosa: University of Alabama Press.

Elorza, A. (2012). 'Delenda est Hispania', *El País*, 1 November.

Fernández, J. J. (2009). 'La progresiva equiparación al Estado como modelo autonómico', *Teoría y Realidad Constitucional*, 24, 323–55.

Fernández, T.-R. (2013). 'La España de las Autonomías: un Estado débil devorado por diecisiete estaditos', *Revista Española de Derecho Administrativo*, 158, 25–52.

Figueireido, R. J. P., and Weingast, B. (1998). 'Self-Enforcing Federalism: Solving the two Fundamental Dilemmas', *Journal of Law, Economics, and Organization*, 21 (1), 103–5.

Filippov, M., Ordeshook, P. C., and Shvetsova, O. (2004). *Designing Federalism: A Theory of Self-Sustainable Federal Institutions*. Cambridge: Cambridge University Press.

Gagnon, A.-G. (2001). 'The Moral Foundations of Asymmetrical Federalism: a Normative Exploration of the Case of Quebec and Canada'. In A.-G. Gagnon, and J. Tully (eds), *Multinational Democracies*. Cambridge: Cambridge University Press.

Gagnon, A.-G. (2012). *Temps d'incertituds. Assajos sobre el federalisme i la diversitat nacional*. Valencia: Universitat de València /Afers.

Gómez, J., Garcés, M., and Elorriaga, G. (2010). *Por un Estado Autonómico racional y viable*. Madrid: FAES.

Guibernau, M. (2002). 'Between Autonomy and Secession: the Accommodation of Catalonia within the new Democratic Spain' <http://www.one-europe.ac.uk/pdf/w48guibernau.pdf> accessed 23 September 2018.

Juliá, S. (2013). 'Nación, nacionalidades y regiones en la transición política a la democracia'. In A. Morales, J. P. Fusi, and A. de Blas (eds), *Historia de la nación y del nacionalismo español*, pp. 886–902. Barcelona: Galaxia de Gutenberg.

Kymlicka, W. (1995). *Multicultural Citizenship. A liberal Theory of Minority Rights*. Oxford: Clarendon Press.

Linz, J. J. (2008a). 'Construcción temprana del Estado y nacionalismos periféricos tardíos frente al estado: el caso de España'. In J. J. Linz, *Nación, Estado y lengua*, vol. 2, pp. 3–73. Madrid: Centro de Estudios Políticos y Constitucionales.

Linz, J. J. (2008b). 'La política en una sociedad multilingüe con una lengua mundial dominante: el caso de España'. In J. J. Linz, *Nación, Estado y Lengua*, vol. 2, pp. 75–120. Madrid: Centro de Estudios Políticos y Constitucionales.

Linz, J. J. (2008c). 'La política en sociedades multilingües y multinacionales'. In J. J. Linz, *Nación, Estado y Lengua*, vol. 2, pp. 121–59. Madrid: Centro de Estudios Políticos y Constitucionales.

Loughlin, J. (2017). 'Federalisme, federacions i confederaciones: cap a la hibridació', *Debats Revista de cultura, poder i societat*, 131, 19–30.

Maiz, R. (2000). 'Democracy, Federalism and Nationalism in Multinational States'. In W. Safran, and R. Maiz, *Identity and Territorial Autonomy in Plural Societies*. London: Frank Cass.

Maiz, R. (2006). 'Federalismo plurinacional: una teoría política normativa', *Revista d'Estudis Autonòmics i Federals*, 3, 43–85.

Martín, J., Pérez, J. A., Romero, J., Soler, M., and Vidal, J. M. (2013). *El federalismo plurinacional ¿Fin de viaje para el estado Autonómico?* Madrid: Díaz & Pons.

Mira, A., Pérez, J. A., and Romero, J. (2013). 'Deslegitimación política y descrédito fiscal de las Comunidades Autónomas', *Pasajes de pensamiento contemporáneo* 41, 96–113.

Moreno, L. (2008). *La federalización de España. Poder político y territorio*. Madrid: Siglo XXI.

Muñoz Mendoza, J. (2012). *La construcción política de la identidad española: ¿del nacionalcatolicismo al patriotismo democrático?* Madrid: Centro de Investigaciones Sociológicas.

Ortega Álvarez, L. I. (2010). '¿Estado federal, integral o autonómico?' In J. Tutela, and F. Knüpling (eds), *España y modelos de federalismo*, pp. 91–8. Madrid: Centro de Estudios Políticos y Constitucionales.

Pérez Royo, J. (1988). 'Tribunal Constitucional y Estado autonómico'. In VVAA, *I Simposium Internacional Autonómico*. Valencia: Generalitat Valenciana.

PSOE (2017). *Resoluciones del 39 Congreso Federal del PSOE*. <https://www.psoe.es/media-content/2016/04/Resolucion-Politica-39-Congreso.pdf> accessed 23 September 2018.

Pujol, J. (1994). 'La personalidad diferenciada de Cataluña'. In A. de Heras (ed.), *Nacionalidades y Estado en España*. Madrid: Universidad Carlos III de Madrid/ Boletín Oficial del Estado.

Rajoy, M. (1999). 'El problema de la organización territorial del Estado después de los Acuerdos Autonómicos'. In VVAA, *Organización territorial del Estado*. Salamanca: Universidad de Salamanca.

Requejo, F. (2001). 'Political Liberalism in Multinational States: the Legitimacy of plural and asymmetrical Federalism'. In A.-G. Gagnon, and J. Tully (eds), *Multinational Democracies*. Cambridge: Cambridge University Press.

Requejo, F. (2005). *Multinational Federalism and Value Pluralism*. London: Routledge.

Requejo, F. (2007). 'Federalisme, descentralització i pluralisme nacional. Teoria política y anàlisi comparada', *Revista d'Estudis Autonòmics i Federals*, 4, 35–67.

Rodden, J. (2004). 'Comparative Federalism and Descentralization. On Meaning and Measurement', *Comparative Politics*, July, 481–500.
Rodden, J., and Rose-Ackerman, S. (1997). 'Does Federalism Preserve Markets?', *Virginia Law Review*, 83, 1521–72.
Rodríguez-Flores, V. (2014). 'El Estado federal en el PSOE: de Suresnes a los Pactos Autonómicos'. In F. Archiles, and I. Saz (eds), *Naciones y Estado. La cuestión española*, pp. 245–68. Valencia: Universitat de València.
Romero, J. (2006). *España inacabada*. Valencia: Universitat de València.
Romero, J. (2008). 'Autonomía política y nacionalismos', *Pasajes de pensamiento contemporáneo* 26, 13–24.
Romero, J., and Alcaraz, M. (2015). 'Estado, naciones y regiones en la España contemporánea'. In J. Romero, and A. Furió (eds), *Historia de las Españas. Una aproximación crítica*, pp. 371–429. Valencia: Tirant Lo Blanch.
Romero, J., and Furió, A. (eds) (2015). *Historia de las Españas. Una aproximación crítica*. Valencia: Tirant Lo Blanch.
Rubio Llorente, F., and Álvarez Junco, J. (eds) (2006). *El informe del Consejo de Estado sobre la reforma constitucional*. Madrid: Consejo de Estado/Centro de Estudios Políticos y Constitucionales.
Sánchez, P. (2017). *Sí es sí. Programa por una nueva socialdemocracia* <https://www.ecestaticos.com/file/ae79792ece6c055d82479339cc80bb23/1494516985-docdefinitivops_11may2017.pdf> accessed 23 September 2018.
Sevilla, J., Vidal, J. M., and Elías, C. (2009). *Vertebrando España*. Madrid: Fundación Ortega y Gasset.
Solozábal, J. J. (1999). 'El Estado social como estado autonómico', *Teoría y Realidad Constitucional* 3, 61–78.
Solozábal, J. J. (2013). 'Las naciones de España'. In A. Morales, J. P. Fusi, and A. de Blas (eds), *Historia de la nación y del nacionalismo español*. Barcelona: Galaxia de Gutenberg.
Taylor, C. (1992). 'The politics of Recognition'. In C. Taylor, *Multiculturalism and the Politics of Recognition*. Princeton, NJ: Princeton University Press.
Tierney, S. (2004). *Constitutional Law and National Pluralism*. Oxford: Oxford University Press.
Treissman, D. (2000). 'The Theory of Two Level States: Exploitation, Redistribution and Democracy Stability'. Paper presented at APSA Annual Meeting, Washington, D.C.
Tudela, J. (2009). 'El Estado autonómico treinta años después', *Teoría y Realidad Constitucional* 24, 191–242.
Tully, J. (2001) 'Introduction'. In A.-G. Gagnon, and J. Tully (eds), *Multinational Democracies*. Cambridge: Cambridge University Press.

Vidal, J. M. (2013). 'La cuestión territorial en la Constitución de Cádiz de 1812', *Revista Española de la Función Consultiva* 19, 632–45.
Vidal, J. M., and García, M. Á. (eds) (2005). *El Estado autonómico: integración, solidaridad, diversidad*. Madrid: Colex-INAP.
Watts, R. L. (1996). *Comparing Federal Systems in the 1990s*. Ontario: Institute of Intergovernmental Relations, Queen's University.
Watts, R. L. (2010). '¿Una federación multinacional encubierta?' In J. Tudela, and F. Knüpling (eds), *España y modelos de federalismo*, pp. 55–82. Madrid: Centro de Estudios Políticos y Constitucionales.
Watts, R. L. (2013). 'Typologies of Federalism'. In J. Loughlin, J. Kincaid, and W. Swendem (eds), *Routledge Handbook of Regionalism and Federalism*. London: Routledge.
Weingast, B. R. (1995). 'The Economic Role of Political Institutions: Market-Preserving Federalism and Economic Development?', *Journal of Law, Economics, and Organization*, 11 (1), 1–31.
Wibbels, E. (2005). *Federalism and the Market*. Cambridge: Cambridge University Press.

ROBERT A. SAUNDERS

Separatism in the New Millennium: Looking Back to See Forward

ABSTRACT
From Gavrilo Princip's assassination of Archduke Franz Ferdinand to the current crisis in the Donbas region of Ukraine, separatism – in both its violent and democratic forms – has shaped geopolitics across the continent of Europe. Operating from the principle that ethnic separatism has been a driving force in European history for the past 100 years, this chapter explores the vicissitudes of minority nationalism and the challenges it has posed to European states and societies. Focusing on commonalities across western, central and eastern Europe in its wide-ranging account of every national liberation struggle since 1914, this chapter contextualizes such movements as a transcontinental phenomenon, thus critiquing the 'east-west' divide which has long characterized the literature of European separatist movements.

A little more than one century ago, a South Slav nationalist named Gavrilo Princip plunged Europe into continent-wide conflict when he assassinated the heir-apparent of the Habsburg Empire with the goal of achieving complete self-rule for his fellow Serbs living under Austro-Hungarian domination. Over the past 100 years, the European continent has seen hundreds of other acts of political violence in the name of the nation, and more specifically the stateless nation. In the nineteenth century, national elites among minority populations generally saw their influence confined to university discussion clubs, secret societies, and other semi-private space; however, via mass education, near-universal literacy, and new forms of information and communication technologies, the advent of modernity endowed aspirant peoples across Europe with a variety of new tools to work towards the creation of their own sovereign states. In some cases, this involved direct action, often resulting in massive loss of life; in other instances, the transition from national minority status to full (or partial) independence occurred through peaceful transition. In a few examples, both bullets and ballot boxes made the dream of national liberation a reality. However, the project remains perpetually unfinished, with dozens of unrealized-but-active minority nationalism movements at play in contemporary Europe, both within the borders of the European Union and beyond.

Whether we use the terms national liberation, secessionism, separatism, or irredentism, the phenomenon of a people, calling themselves a nation, but lacking political sovereignty over the lands they inhabit, has been a major factor in shaping the course of European history since 1914 (Smith 1991; Panayi 2001; Laible 2016). Inarguably, nearly every European polity – whether democratic, authoritarian, or totalitarian – has grappled with the threat of separatism in this period, a factor which, I will argue, has had acute and far-reaching influences on the historical development of the continent and its structures of governance up until today. Consequently, I want to provide a brief overview of this often-bloody history, while also pointing to instances where the move towards independence has been democratic and non-violent. The geographical scope of my essay will cover all of Europe, including the former Soviet Union where there is an ongoing separatist-irredentist conflict, as well as a number of frozen conflicts wherein ethnic separatism lies at the root of the problem.

The actions of the aforementioned revolutionary, Princip, operating in the name of the secret Serbian society known as Union or Death (*Ujedinjenje ili Smrt*), colloquially branded the 'Black Hand', had far-reaching effects for national minorities, particularly those living in one of the four territorial empires (Hohenzollern, Habsburg, Romanov and Ottoman) that were dissolved in the wake of the Great War. The nationalist aspirations of Czechs, Finns, Lithuanians, and others were achieved with the breakup of Austria-Hungary and imperial Russia, whereas the Poles saw their long-dead state resurrected. Wilsonian national liberation was doled out by the victors of the First World War, both punishing the losers (i.e. Austria, Hungary, Germany and Turkey) and attempting to build a 'cordon-sanitaire' against the unpredictable Bolshevik state situated at the eastern fringe of the continent (see Johnson 1996). In the decade after the end of the First World War, a host of new states came into being – some completely sovereign like Czechoslovakia, others national homelands within a large, heavily centralized federation like the Ukrainian Soviet Socialist Republic. However, this new world order only triggered more problems with the issue of national identity, as dozens of new national minorities were now trapped inside what Rogers Brubaker (1996) has called 'nationalising states'. From Germans in the Sudetenland to Hungarians in Romania and southern Czechoslovakia, east central Europe traded a set of nationality problems stemming from the vagaries of imperial rule for another set based on decolonization, new borders, and the ethnicization of the state apparatus.[1] While the former presented a variety of dilemmas to national minorities, the latter proved much more lethal as it naturally led to what we now refer to as 'ethnic cleansing', beginning with the dramatic population transfers of Greeks and Turks between Anatolia and southeastern Europe, as well as the calamitous relocation of Armenians within Turkey.

In post-First World War Russia, a variant of the ideology that the nation and the state should be coterminous (i.e. Leninist national self-determination) ultimately resulted in a strange hybrid status for the minority nationalities of the former Romanov Empire, wherein these nations received a state within a state, from union republics to autonomous regions. With its establishment in 1922, the USSR presented a new federal model that allowed for the Soviet Union's 100-plus nationalities to establish some level of national self-determination (part of a strategy to ultimately move these populations through the Marxist dialectic towards the ultimate realization of a worker state where the concerns of so-called 'bourgeois nationalism' would be confined to the dustbin of history). At the highest level of this so-called 'affirmative action empire' (Martin 2001) were the union republics, each with a titular majority (Ukrainians, Georgians, Kazakhs, etc.); officially, these were independent states with territorial sovereignty and complete cultural autonomy (the reality was, however, much more complex). Within the Russian Soviet Federated Socialist Republic, the geopolitical

---

[1] Hungary's interwar politics were often coloured by the state's obsession with regaining its lost territories in Romania and elsewhere. Opposition to the basic tenets of the harsh peace suffused the familiar refrain: '*Nem, nem, soha!*' [No, no, never!] referring to the Treaty of Trianon, which dismembered the Hungarian half of the Dual Monarchy of Austria-Hungary.

core of the USSR, dozens of republics and autonomous regions are established with the ostensible aim of providing cultural and educational opportunities for non-Russians, including Tartarstan, Yakutia and Buryatia; the process is replicated on a much smaller scale in some of the union republics providing officially recognized 'homelands' for the Karakalpaks, Abkhaz and others. In some ways, this sea change avoided the problems inherent in the nationalizing state structure of east central Europe and the Balkans; however, as Moscow eventually learned, the federal socialist solution created problems associated with autonomist nationalism that would fester and ultimately bring down the Soviet Union less than seventy years later (see Orridge and William 1982).

Importantly, not all was quiet on the Western Front during this time frame. The Great War created conditions wherein Irish republicans who had struggled in vain against British rule gained increasing momentum, culminating in the ill-fated Easter Rising (*Éirí Amach na Cásca*) in 1916. While the rebellion was quickly crushed, forces were put into play that would devolve an ever-greater level of home rule to the people of Eire. Irish moves towards full independence continued apace even after the establishment of the Free State in 1922, ultimately resulting in a full break from the British Empire and the establishment of a republic. During the interwar period, restive populations of Basques and Catalans looked with suspicion on developments in Madrid, placing them in opposition to the more conservative forces that would soon retake control of Spain. Hoping to benefit from an alliance with the left, these minorities embraced the new freedoms granted by the establishment of the Second Republic in 1931. But with the Francoist counter-revolution in 1936, Spain took on the character of a nationalizing state as antithetical to the interests of its national minorities as any newly founded east central European country, making speaking Basque in public a crime while repressing Catalan culture and dissolving political institutions associated with the region. In time, Franco's repressive rule would germinate both forms of national liberation struggle: a terrorist insurgency among the Basques and a more peaceful and economically based movement towards independence in Catalunya.

The Second World War, like the Great War, began due to questions of irredenta, in this case, as a response to Nazi Germany's final act of 'gathering in' the 'lost' 11 million Germans (Snyder 2010). Whereas the Western Allies chose not to stand in the way of Adolf Hitler's Anschluss with Austria, which brought back in 7 million German-speakers, or when 3 million Germans 'returned' to the Third Reich through the annexation of western Czechoslovakia, Britain and France chose to act when Germany invaded western Poland to gain access to the Danzig Corridor and reintegrate a million Germans living under Warsaw's rule. This series of events provides a dark parallel to current events in Russia's so-called 'near abroad', that is, those parts of the former Soviet Union where the presence of ethnic Russians has provided Moscow with a rationale for intervention in the internal and foreign affairs of its neighbours, from economic manipulation to geopolitical bullying to outright invasion. Certainly, the active lobbying on the part of the Crimean population for a 'return' to Russia (a dual strategy of separatism followed by immediate accession) represents the most dramatic of these analogies due to its striking similarity to the actions of the Sudeten Germans in 1936–8. This is particularly relevant when one considers that the annexation only served to provide a foothold for further Russian expansionism, specifically the deployment in the Donbass of so-called 'little green men' (Russian military personnel who serve outside the normal structure of military action to avoid the bad optics of outright invasion) and massive material support to anti-Kyiv separatists in the east of the ethnically divided country.

With the end of the Second World War, the nationality question returned to the fore once again. Across the eastern half of Europe, ethnic cleansing, a major theme of the war in Nazi-occupied and allied zones, continued to reign, but with radically different geopolitical contours. While the Nazis' Final Solution had eliminated some 6 million of Europe's Jews (alongside millions of non-Jewish peoples, including Poles, eastern Slavs and Roma), the Holocaust provided a final impetus for the realization of the Zionist project with the establishment of a 'separate' Jewish state *outside of Europe*. Fearful of a second bout of genocide and facing deleterious conditions across Europe, many Jews quit the continent after 1945. A significant portion of these emigrants joined those who had already moved to Palestine over the previous decades, heeding Theodore Herzl's call to create a Jewish homeland in the Levant (a settlement trend that was significantly abetted by the 1917 Balfour Declaration) and thus rejecting other identity projects associated with minority nationalism that flourished in the interwar period (see, for instance, Lichtenstein 2016). The establishment of Israel in 1948 represented a curious sort of separatism, one which came into being through emigration from the continent and post-imperial state-building abroad. Consequently, we can consider Israel as an unintended exemplar of 'European' minority separatism.

In the zones of Europe that came under Soviet occupation, the Red Army oversaw a policy of draconian resettlement policies, combined with the remaking of borders, implementation of socialist federalism, and avocation of minority rights to prevent active secessionism/separatism (the admixture of totalitarianism also ensured that separatist/irredentist phenomena like the Sudeten German debacle would not be repeated). The preliminary stage of this scheme was the deportation of eastern Europe's 11.5 million *Volksdeutsche*, who were sent westward with little more than the clothes on their backs. East Prussia was completely emptied of its population, as were much of the Sudetenland and the former German-inhabited lands east of the Oder. The Baltic States, together with Poland, Czechoslovakia, Hungary and Yugoslavia, all sent packing the vast majority of their Germans, purportedly in an attempt to avoid a repetition of the past. Concurrently, geopolitics, nationalism and the march of socialism were fused in the eastern zones, with mass population exchanges of Ukrainians and Poles, Hungarians and Slovaks, and so forth. Tragically, these often bloody attempts at squashing separatism only plastered over the thorny issues of national identity, they did not extinguish them (a case in point being the Ruthenes of Transcarpathia, who were scattered among multiple states by post-war delimitation projects orchestrated by the Soviets, most notably the geopolitical excision of Carpatho-Ukraine in eastern Czechoslovakia, and saw their identity forcefully submerged in the new world order) (see Magocsi 2010). Yet, the death and displacement from this period serve as permanent testament to the power of separatism on the European continent, if only as a reminder of the lengths to which national governments went to negate the threat from within.

Generally unknown to the West, these forced expulsions and population exchanges were executed with blueprints established shortly before in the USSR, wherein Stalin had ordered massive transfers of 'suspect nationalities' within the borders of the Soviet Union. For real and imagined crimes against the Soviet state, eight nations were deported in their entirety from their federally recognized national homelands within the USSR. The political territories were then summarily erased from the record, though certain ones were restored following Stalin's death in the 1950s. These 'punished peoples' included the Volga Germans, the Crimean Tatars, the Chechens and Ingush, the Karachay and Balkar peoples, the Kalmyks, and the Meskhetian Turks (see Polian 2004).[2] Packed onto cattle cars and shipped to Siberia or Central Asia for these 'relocation projects', the peoples suffered mortality rates of over 30 per cent either in transit or within the first year of 'resettlement'. Generally speaking, those ethno-political territories in the North Caucasus were restored under Nikita Khrushchev, as was Kalmykia, but the Crimean Tatars, Volga Germans, and Meskhetian Turks failed to gain the legal right of return.[3] Fearing irredentism or pro-fascist sabotage, the state forced portions of other populations to join these unfortunate nations in internal captivity, including Balts, Poles, Greeks, Koreans, and Romanians (or Vlachs).[4]

Elsewhere in the socialist sphere, fears about separatism resulted in highly regimented national spaces within new federal structures. In the

[2] Unlike the other Soviet nationalities, the Meskhetian Turks did not have an ethnically delimited 'national homeland', but instead were resident in the Meskheti region of southern Georgia.

[3] The Meskhetian Turks were the victims of pogroms in the last days of the Soviet Union, leading to a secondary dispersion to Ukraine, Azerbaijan, and elsewhere, and have often sought assistance from Turkey for their plight, thus reigniting questions about pan-Turkism across Central Asia. The Crimean Tatars' right to national institutions has become a major issue of contention in post-annexation Crimea, as many Tatars fear losing the rights granted to them following Ukraine's independence in 1991. The Volga Germans tended to adapt well to their new surroundings; however, since 1991, many have employed German right of return laws, which are especially welcoming to so-called *Spätaussiedler* [late emigrants] from the former Soviet republics, to immigrate to Germany.

[4] During his early administration, Khrushchev also put an end to the Karelo-Finnish Soviet Socialist Republic, established in 1940, thereby reducing the role of ethnic Karelians in the lands which had once been part of an independent Finland.

new Yugoslavia, Josip Broz established a six-part state to ensure that all the country's major nationalities would be politically represented. The old Kingdom of Serbs, Croats and Slovenes thus established 'homelands' not only for those 'named' South Slavs, but also for the Montenegrins and Macedonians, as well as the Bosniaks (though this group shared their state with Orthodox Serbs and Catholic Croats). Within Serbia, special status was granted to Kosovo – originally known as the Autonomous Province of Kosovo and Metohija – as it was to the ethnic melting pot of Vojvodina, thus laying the groundwork for the future breakup of the country which would define European ethnic conflict in the post-Cold War era. In socialist Czechoslovakia, which had seen its Ruthenian and Ukrainian minorities mostly stripped from it by Soviet-dictated territorial changes, there was an institutionalization of the split between Czech and Slovak lands, paralleling the efforts of Tito (and similarly creating a subsequent glide path for the 1993 'Velvet Divorce' that would produce separate Czech and Slovak republics).

Following the USSR's victory in the Great Patriotic War, Moscow set about instituting totalitarian controls combined with the illusion of sovereignty both within the USSR (specifically in relation to the recently annexed nations of Estonia, Latvia, and Lithuania – as well as to the quickly forgotten independent nation of Tuva in southern Siberia)[5] and across the Eastern Bloc. For certain marginalized minorities, the imposition of socialism served them well, at least initially. The Turks of Bulgaria saw improvement in their status, as did the Lusatian Sorbs in East Germany and Romany in Yugoslavia. However, in keeping with Marxist-Leninist notions of political development, most efforts at supporting cultural development soon gave way to assimilationist schemes that sometimes did more harm than good, ultimately provoking calls for genuine autonomy. On balance, socialist countries' fears about separatism as 'bourgeois disease' led to totalitarian controls put in place to encourage assimilation or

5   The fact that ethnic Russians do not enjoy majority status in the region serves as evidence of the historical provenance of Tuva as an independent state in the twentieth century. The People's Republic of Tannu Tuva represented the third socialist state in the world, after the USSR and Mongolia, until its incorporation into the former.

remove the 'problem' altogether. Such was the case with the harsh treatment of the Hungarian/Székelys population in Romania and the 'sale' of Germans and Jews to West Germany and Israel respectively under Nicolae Ceaușescu (see Pacepa 1990). In Poland, a country that had achieved a dramatic level of heterogeneity due to Allied-dictated border changes and population transfers from 1944 to 1948, the only lingering issue was the notion of Kashubian ethnic identity in the post-war period, something that the state strenuously opposed. Similar attitudes towards expressions of Ruthene national identity were commonplace in Ukraine. Despite official policies of fostering minority cultures (*korenizatsiya*) which allowed for the promotion of national cultures and advance of 'titulars' within their republics, Russianization of the Soviet peoples through language continued apace throughout the post-Second World War period.

In the western half of Europe, post-war deprivation and recovery combined with the threat of Soviet expansion towards the Atlantic dampened the minority issue in most countries. In some cases, the issue of minority nationalism became deeply imbricated in the larger forces of history. Examples of separatism being subjugated to larger geopolitical concerns included the Danish negation of the Faeroese independence referendum in 1946, and the quashing of Vlach separatism in Greece, which became untenable after the conclusion of the Civil War in 1949.[6] Yet, the issues of separatism continued to simmer below the surface, though not yet reaching a boiling point for some two decades after 1945. While a wide variety of pro-separatist parties began to form in the 1950s and the first half of the 1960s – including the Frisian National Party in the Netherlands, the Flemish People's Movement in Belgium and the *Union Démocratique Bretonne* in France – the real groundswell came with the tectonic shift towards identity politics that characterized the late 1960s.

---

[6] We might include here separatism being impressed into service for geopolitical stratagems in the instance of Iceland. The Danish colony was occupied by British, Canadian and – somewhat later – American forces in the context of the Second World War. Using the pretence of supporting Icelandic independence, the US was able to secure a valuable near-Arctic outpost for its military forces in the North Atlantic and substituted its forces for Iceland's defence once NATO was established in 1949.

By 1968, war in Southeast Asia, a dramatic clash between left and right ideologies, the emergence of gender and sexuality as politicized identities, new questions of decolonization combining with changing attitudes to immigration and race, as well as a host of other factors, emerged and created a political nexus that would challenge the status quo in Western Europe. In many ways, both the 'East' and 'West' were linked in 1968 through the violent events in Czechoslovakia, which created a catalyst for change east of the Iron Curtain. With the brutal ending of the experiment in 'socialism with a human face', there came the realization that 'freedom', whether political or cultural, was illusory within the one-party system, and the high-minded ideals of socialism were always subject to the geopolitical whims of Moscow. So, with Eastern Bloc tanks sitting on the streets of Prague, many in the eastern part of Europe began to view themselves as 'captive nations', a discourse that opened the door for smaller nationalities to be seen likewise, from Croats and Slovaks to Estonians and Tatars.

As Western Europe erupted in protest, in generational and class conflict and militant student activism, new discourses came to the fore across the continent to deal with the nationality issue. Taking a page from the book of other practitioners of political violence, those supporting ethnic separatism began to see the value in adopting the mechanism of direct action to achieve their political goals. In France, terrorism was the result of a spill-over from its colonial war in Algeria (with *Pied-Noir* and Algerian attacks occurring on French soil) and elsewhere other countries in democratic Europe grappled with a wave of 'red' terror propagated by such groups as *Action Direct* (France), *Brigate Rosse* (Italy), *Rote Armee Fraktion* (West Germany), and Revolutionary Organization 17 November (Greece). Meanwhile there was a spillage of separatist nationalism from other parts of the world, most specifically Palestinian militant actions on European soil (most notoriously with the 1972 attacks on Israeli athletes at the Munich Olympic Games). These outbreaks of political violence provided powerful examples for a generation of separatists who had seen their plans for independence suffocated by Cold War politics and the need for 'national cohesion' during Europe's economic recovery in the 1950s and early 1960s. It was during this period that Europe witnessed the emergence of multiple terrorist organizations, which were typically guerrilla adjuncts to pre-existing political movements for independence. These included *Euskadi Ta Askatasuna* (ETA), 1968; the Provisional Irish Republican Army (PIRA), 1969; *L'Armée Revolutionnaire Bretonne* (ARB), 1974; the National Liberation Front of Corsica (FLNC), 1976; and the Catalan *Terra Lliure* (TL) in 1978. Almost overnight, identity issues associated with cultural heritage, language, and ethnicity were linked to killing in the name of the nation. Bloodshed became a tragically normal part of life in certain parts of western Europe in the coming decades, with the ethnically divided city of Belfast, Northern Ireland, coming to function as synecdoche for the darkest side of ethnic separatism.

However, violence was not the exclusive strategy in separatist circles during this transitional period which lasted from the 1960s into the 1980s. Other approaches included the emergence of the Celtic League, which sought to stimulate the integration and cultural autonomy of Ireland, Scotland, Wales, Brittany, Cornwall and the Isle of Man, of which only the counties of the Republic of Ireland could be considered truly independent.[7] Elsewhere, international rivalries between neighbouring states over their respective minorities also emerged as an issue, with co-operation and conflict seeming to manifest in equal measures. In 1972, Austria and Italy proved able to work together on the issue of Germans in South Tyrol, producing a rather innovative form of self-government that would later emerge as a paragon of success by providing a path that does not end in outright independence but one which does benefit both the state and the minority nation and effectively ended separatist tensions in the region. In the eastern Mediterranean, however, the situation turned violent as the threat of enosis between Cyprus and Greece prompted a Turkish invasion of the island in 1974, thus creating an unrecognized statelet within the territorial boundaries of Europe that still exists today, one that even the promise of EU accession could not fix.[8] At the other end of the Mediterranean Basin,

---

7   While the Isle of Man is a Crown Dependency (not subordinated to the government of the UK) for all practical purposes it is not independent and its citizens are British subjects.

8   The division of Cyprus between Turkish and Greek zones ultimately proved a doleful model for a number of other quasi-states that would come out of the USSR after 1991, notably the so-called 'TAKO nations' discussed below.

Generalissimo Francisco Franco's death and a new constitution returned much of Catalunya's lost autonomy, allowing the state to proceed forward towards ever greater levels of self-government and perhaps – if current trends continue – even independence.

As the so-called second Cold War (Halliday 1986) began in the 1980s with the advent of a belligerent anti-Communist in the US White House (i.e. Ronald Reagan), pressures on the USSR to release its 'captive nations' grew stronger. Opposition to decades of russianization across the USSR, but particularly in the Baltic States, which had enjoyed the taste of independence in the interwar period, began to grow, primarily through the organization of underground and later – under *perestroika* and *glasnost* – open and government-permitted cultural movements. In the small republics of Estonia, Latvia, and Lithuania, groups supporting distinct cultural traits (language, music, dance, etc.) were mobilized to establish the groundwork for the political parties that would ultimately emerge by the end of the decade; in fact, later these movements would be described as the 'Singing Revolutions' (Lane et al. 2013), due to the centrality of traditional music and song in fomenting national sentiment. In Ukraine and Belarus, the actual and metaphorical (political) fallout of the 1986 Chernobyl Disaster would galvanize many activists against Moscow, fuelling calls for greater levels of self-governance and eventually independence from the USSR. One of Europe's oldest nations, the Georgians, also began to move towards increasingly strident engagement in identity politics within the Soviet structure, adding to the centrifugal pressures on the already strained Soviet state. Even Kazakhstan, which had seen massive increases in standards of living, literacy, and infrastructure through Sovietization pulled at the ties that bound it to the Kremlin, with inter-ethnic riots breaking out in 1986, the first example of such tensions to be widely reported in the West in more than twenty-five years.[9] Two years later, demonstrations by Armenians in Nagorno-Karabakh would spark bloodshed and ignite a separatist-irredentist conflict that remains unsolved to this day.

9   However, it should be noted that the country was the last republic to depart the USSR, strangely leaving the borders of the USSR as coterminous with those of Kazakhstan for four days in 1991.

Elsewhere in the Eastern Bloc, the steady breakdown of the totalitarian model led to an increasing politicization of national movements. In Bulgaria, then derisively referred to as the '16th republic of the USSR', the Turkish struggle against the Bulgarian state turned violent, including bomb attacks on public transport, a bloody riposte to the acts of physical violence and intimidation exhibited by the security forces as well as to repressive measures against the practice of Islam and other forms of cultural expression (Chary 2011). In neighbouring Romania, the revolution that would ultimately unseat and then claim the life of long-time dictator Nicolae Ceaușescu was actually triggered by minority nationalism when László Tőkés, a Hungarian Calvinist pastor in Timișoara, took on the state, sparking wider uprisings against the regime in late 1989. Following the dramatic political changes across the whole of eastern Europe, a sea change occurred that would initiate what I have called elsewhere the 'Third Wave of Decolonization' (Saunders 2012), that is the breakup of the socialist federal states of the USSR, Yugoslavia, and Czechoslovakia.

Arguably, the USSR's path to dissolution began when it illegally annexed the three Baltic States in the context of the Second World War, for it was here that the loudest and most articulate voices for national liberation emerged, personified in the person of Vytautas Landsbergis, the face of Lithuania's campaign for independence in the early 1990s. From when I was a teenager, I remember his calls for assistance directed at the US and other members of the international community. Influenced by neighbouring Poland's newfound freedoms and well-versed in the language of democracy and national sovereignty, he – along with countless other activists – challenged the Kremlin to a dangerous game of chicken that ultimately took the lives of more than a dozen Lithuanians, but ultimately also triggered the dissolution of the Soviet Union. Centrifugal forces pulled the fourteen non-Russian republics away from the centre, each with its own designs on making the complete transition from union republic to independent and internationally recognized nation-state (as was happening in Estonia, Latvia and Lithuania). This occurred just as centripetal forces within the Russian core worked towards a sort of de-imperializing separatism of 'Russia for Russians' (Otto 1990), with the aim of sloughing off the economic demands of maintaining the vast array of military-industrial subsidies that kept the Baltic peoples wealthier than the average Russian and ensured that every Tajik and Turkmen had full access to education, housing, employment, and so on.

While the situation in the Baltic rim might have been contained under other circumstances, the very structure of the USSR became its greatest weakness, particularly given the almost ironic push for separatism among the imperial ethnicity, that is, the Russians. The federal system which was replete with a complex network of autonomous regions quickly became a double-edged sword for the Soviet state. The curious ethnic gerrymandering of Nagorno-Karabakh (Armenian-controlled), of Transnistria ('Slavic'-controlled), and of the Georgian regions of Abkhazia and South Ossetia all led to ethnic tensions, military conflict, and secession, ultimately producing the acronym of TAKO, a geopolitical shorthand for separatist republics which are frozen in a state of unrecognition but which possess full territorial sovereignty. Inside the Russian Federation, Chechnya tried to emulate the route to independence taken by the fourteen union republics (and Russia). Recognizing that such a path was dependent on Soviet-era federal territorial delimitations, that is, being a *union republic* rather than an *autonomous republic* within a union republic, Chechen leaders voted in favour of elevating their country's status against the wishes of Moscow. The subsequent establishment of the Chechen Republic of Ichkeria on 1 November 1991 sparked a bloody war and cascading ethnic feuds and reprisals across the northern Caucasus region (see Zürcher 2007). After a cessation of hostilities in the mid-1990s, the goal of Chechen independence simmered amongst the population but, facing almost impossible odds against the Russian state, alternative ideologies proliferated, particularly Islamist jihad which uncomfortably married itself to nationalist separatism in the Second Chechen War (1999–2009), darkly mirroring the hybridization that has characterized the Palestinian independence campaign (1948–present).

An even more violent version of the dissolution of the USSR occurred in Yugoslavia. Six months before the USSR would pass into history, Slovenia and Croatia departed the socialist federation to establish their own independent nation-states, triggering the Wars of Yugoslavian Succession (1991–2001), a series of conflicts that lasted over a decade. The

Balkans, a melting pot of ethnicities and religions under Ottoman rule, was engulfed in conflict with ethnic conflict at its root. During the 1990s, 'Bosnia' became a byword for violent separatism combined with ethnic cleansing of minority populations, rejuvenating a host of hoary prejudices about the purported 'barbarism' of the Balkans ensconced in 200 years of western travelogues about the region (Todorova 1997). Macedonia, a region so defined by national diversity that it gave a name to the mixed fruit or vegetable dish *macédoine*, gained independence but was immediately drawn into complications with the push for a 'greater Albania' linking the populations of Albania, Kosovo, and western Macedonia, further underscoring the bloody ties between separatism and irredentism. Safely ensconced within Serbia, the highly diverse Vojvodina region remained one corner that was able to preserve stability combined with intense heterogeneity (see Dragojevi 2008).

Elsewhere in post-socialist Europe, the last of the three ethno-national federations met its end, though thankfully without bloodshed or even rancour. Czechoslovakia's relatively magnanimous breakup provides us with a happy alternative, wherein a clean and peaceful break between fraternal nations might occur, in this case with both moving forward towards NATO and EU accession with exclusive control over their respective nation-states. Interestingly, however, both states now grapple with calls for more autonomy or independence from other groups, namely the Moravians in the eastern Czech Republic and the Magyars in southern Slovakia.

As Europe transitioned into the new millennium, there was a proliferation of new forms of separatism, or what might be better described as 'post-modern national movements' (Duerr 2015: 88) or what some scholars label 'separatism by other means' (Cabestan and Pavković 2013: 189). In this category, I would include the following examples from western Europe:

- the 1998 Good Friday Agreement which effectively ended large-scale separatist violence in Northern Ireland and promoted a model of increased devolution of power within the United Kingdom and evergrowing economic links between the Republic and Ulster;
- the spread of Finland's Åland and Italy's South Tyrolean models, which provide for near-complete economic and cultural autonomy within a nation-state that recognizes that diversity promotes strength;

- the Sami parliaments of Norway, Sweden, and Finland and the creation of (an imagined) Sápmi – one people and three countries without the need for a 'proper state' but instead sustainable cooperation and transborder flows;
- Belgium's government crisis (2007–11), which allowed Flanders and Wallonia to grow apart, thus representing an interesting if unintentional abandonment of many post-Westphalian principles of governance without any drastic reverberations;
- Greenland, Scotland, and Catalunya all seeking legal means towards separation from their 'imperial' states, both with and without permission, thus relying on (geo)economic considerations for the survival of the state (both parent and child) with transnational corporate/financial interests being deeply imbricated in these processes.

In post-Soviet space there have also been innovative moves towards quasi-independence, though given the long history of socialism and one-party rule, these differ greatly in nature from the previously mentioned examples from western Europe; they include:

- the Tatarstan decision to begin issuing passports, restricting (national) conscription, and conducting international trade agreements independent of Moscow (though such actions were later limited under Russian president Vladimir Putin);
- Gagauzia's push towards a post-modern separatism incorporating new forms of cultural autonomy and renewed links with Turkey and a drawing closer to the Russian Federation;[10]
- spurred by Russia's hosting of the 2014 Winter Olympics, a Pan-Circassian movement for recognition of 'Europe's first genocide' (Richmond 2013) and a 'right-of-return' for the various populations who identify as Circassian, including Adyghe, Kabardins, and Cherkess (Sochi, the site of the games, is near the site where tens of thousands of forced deportations occurred, resulting in mass casualties and dispersal across the Middle East).

10 Moldova's Gagauz are an Orthodox Christian, Turkish-speaking population which does not seek outright independence from Europe's poorest country (like Palestine, its geography is non-contiguous and non-advantageous), but are instead pursuing a variety of other methods for maintaining a separate identity after the end of Soviet-era support for such projects.

However, despite these trends towards new forms of separatism that eschew bullets and bombs, there is a disturbing continuation of political violence as a vehicle for secessionism. On the small scale, we can point to the April 2014 arrests of twenty-four people for plotting violence in support of Veneto's secession from Italy, including Franco Rocchetta, a former Lega Nord MP. On the intermediate scale, I would refer to the more recent violence between ethnic Albanians and Slavs in Macedonia, labelled 'terrorism' by the Slav-dominated government using the all-too-easy jargon of a post-9/11 world where such nomenclature is shorthand for much more complex forms of political action. On the macro-level, the situation in Crimea signals a return to the geopolitics of the interwar period, while the situation in the Donbass signals the emergence of a tragic new model of separatism-cum-irredentism involving great powers, namely the Russian Federation, the US, and the European Union.

In concluding this chapter, which has aimed at providing an historical overview of the role played by separatism in Europe's history over the past century, I will leave the reader with a series of questions about the future of separatism in Europe:

- Does EU membership provide an umbrella and/or safety net for ever greater devolution of power to national minorities, ultimately resulting in a continued fracturing of the existing nation-states of the union within a greater whole or, given the questions surrounding Brexit, do the Irish border and stirrings of Scottish independence portend simply more fracturing of the EU itself?
- Is there truly a difference between east and western Europe in terms of separatism in the new millennium? Is irredentism something that now exists or only exists east of the Oder? If so, what is predicted about the long-term effects of the Soviet experiment (1922–91) and the establishment of national homelands for all sizeable minorities?
- Does the relatively unfettered ability of wired minorities to communicate, co-ordinate, and educate via the internet create a new world order wherein separatism can be achieved in a virtual environment? With online preservation and promotion of dead and moribund languages (e.g. Cornish, Manx, Scots English) and traditionally marginalized tongues (e.g. Frisian, Breton, Sorbian, Romany), are we on the threshold of a major transformation in minority identity in highly

connected countries like the UK, France, the Netherlands, Germany, the Czech Republic and Hungary?
- Will current trends promoting hybrid, cosmopolitan and transnational identities ultimately weaken longstanding efforts for autonomy and independence or will they actually strengthen certain movements?
- With the Russian Federation now in its second decade of supporting ethnic separatism in its so-called 'near abroad' (specifically, historical support for breakaway republics in Transnistria, Ajaria, South Ossetia and Abkhazia and new heat being generated in the Donbass), can we expect to see more violent separatist movements popping up across post-Soviet space and even further afield? And if so, where are the future hotspots? Russophone populations in Latvia, Estonia, Kazakhstan? Or perhaps Ruthenes, Magyars, and Poles in western Ukraine as suggested by recent Russian propaganda efforts?

While this list of questions represents only a few of those we might ask about the future of separatism in Europe in the new millennium, these issues point to the continued salience of the politics of secession and the power of minority identity on the continent. Undoubtedly, nationalism among Europe's 'smaller peoples' (Lehti and Smith 2003) remains alive and well even as we move into the third millennium and will likely continue to influence the larger flows of European history.

Bibliography

Brubaker, R. (1996). *Nationalism Reframed: Nationhood and the National Question in the New Europe.* Cambridge: Cambridge University Press.
Cabestan, J.-P., and Pavković, A. (2013). *Secessionism and Separatism in Europe and Asia: To Have a State of One's Own.* London: Routledge.
Chary, F. B. (2011). *The History of Bulgaria.* Santa Barbara, CA: ABC-CLIO.
Dragojevi, M. (2008). 'Contesting Ethnicity: Emerging Regional Identity in Vojvodina,' *Studies in Ethnicity & Nationalism,* 8 (2), 290–316.
Duerr, G. M. E. (2015). *Secessionism and the European Union: The Future of Flanders, Scotland, and Catalonia.* Lanham, MD: Lexington Books.
Halliday, F. (1986). *The Making of the Second Cold War.* New York: Verso.

Johnson, L. (1996). *Central Europe: Enemies, Neighbours, Friends*. Oxford: Oxford University Press.
Laible, J. (2016). *Separatism and Sovereignty in the New Europe: Party Politics and the Meanings of Statehood in a Supranational Context*. New York: Springer.
Lane, T., Pabriks, A., Purs, A., and Smith, D. J. (2013). *The Baltic States: Estonia, Latvia and Lithuania*. New York: Routledge.
Lehti, M., and Smith, D. J. (2003). 'Introduction: Other Europes'. In M. Lehti, and D. J. Smith (eds), *Post-Cold War Identity Politics: Northern and Baltic Experiences*, pp. 1–10. London: Frank Cass.
Lichtenstein, T. (2016). *Zionists in Interwar Czechoslovakia: Minority Nationalism and the Politics of Belonging*. Bloomington: Indiana University Press.
Magocsi, P. R. (2010). *A History of Ukraine: The Land and Its Peoples*, 2nd edn. Toronto: University of Toronto Press.
Martin, T. (2001). *The Affirmative Action Empire: Nations and Nationalism in the Soviet Union, 1923–1939*. Ithaca, NY: Cornell University Press.
Orridge, A., and William, C. (1982). 'Autonomist Nationalism: A Theoretical Framework for Spatial Variation in Its Genesis and Development.' *Political Geography Quarterly*, 1 (1), 19–39.
Otto, R. (1990). 'Contemporary Russian Nationalism', *Problems of Communism*, 39 (6), 96–105.
Pacepa, I. M. (1990). *Red Horizons: The True Story of Nicolae and Elena Ceaușescus' Crimes, Lifestyle, and Corruption*. Washington, DC: Regnery.
Panayi, P. (2001). *An Ethnic History of Europe since 1945: Nations, States and Minorities*. Harlow: Longman.
Polian, P. M. (2004). *Against Their Will: The History and Geography of Forced Migrations in the USSR*. Budapest: Central European University Press.
Richmond, W. (2013). *The Circassian Genocide*. New Brunswick, NJ: Rutgers University Press.
Saunders, R. A. (2012). 'Brand Interrupted: The Impact of Alternative Narrators on Nation Branding in the Former Second World.' In N. Kaneva (ed.), *Branding Post-Communist Nations: Marketizing National Identities in the 'New' Europe*, pp. 49–78. New York: Routledge.
Smith, A. (1991). *National Identity*. Reno: University of Nevada Press.
Snyder, T. (2010). *Bloodlands: Europe Between Hitler and Stalin*. New York: Basic Books.
Todorova, M. (1997). *Imagining the Balkans*. Oxford: Oxford University Press.
Zürcher, C. (2007). *The Post-Soviet Wars: Rebellion, Ethnic Conflict, and Nationhood in the Caucasus*. New York: New York University Press.

MARÇAL SINTES OLIVELLA, JOSEP-LLUÍS MICÓ-SANZ, AND
FRANCESC-MARC ÁLVARO VIDAL

The Pro-Independence Movement in Catalonia: Impact on the International Agenda and Media Pluralism

ABSTRACT

This chapter analyses the media coverage of the Catalan pro-independence movement, focusing on its impact on the media agenda and on the pluralism of the coverage. Adopting both a quantitative and qualitative approach, the study evaluates just under 4,800 news items and other samples of commentary from Catalonia, Spain and the international media. The timeframe begins with the National Day of Catalonia in 2012 (11 September) and ends just after the elections to the Catalan Parliament on 25 November of the same year. This was the point at which the Catalan independence movement became a major international news story. An analysis of the articles generated reveals the increasing polarization in Spain, but also the efforts of the Catalan media to adopt a more pluralist approach to the societal divisions.

Introduction

Among the most powerful of all recent national identity claims must be that of Catalonia, part of a peninsula that has been called a mini-continent, part of the Spanish hegemony for centuries, and yet still for many of its inhabitants a place apart, a wholeness of itself. If anyone had been in any doubt about the strength of that claim, it was to be manifested most overtly in the events that followed a certain public gathering of Catalans in 2012, events that are brought out and brought up to date in this chapter.

The present study is the first carried out with the objective of analysing the impact on the international media of the movement in favour of the independence of Catalonia. In addition, it is relevant that the study covers both conventional media – print, radio, television – and digital. As far as we know, no comparable analysis has been carried out more recently, neither in respect to its international dimension nor with regard to the number of media and journalistic pieces covered.

The investigation not only robustly embraces a significant number of items – 4,795 journal pieces from more than 100 Catalan, Spanish and international media sources – but was complemented by interviews with the presidents and members of two Catalan governments. The combination of such qualitative data with quantitative and content analyses enriches the results and gives more meaning to the conclusions drawn.

Furthermore, our analysis was conducted on a key period for the pro-independence movement, from 11 September 2012 (Catalan National Day) until a few days after the elections to the Catalan Parliament on 25 November that same year.[1] It was at this time that the new and much greater scale of the civil and political independence movement, dominating Catalan and Spanish political life then as it still does today, put it firmly on the national and international public, political and media agenda.

That year, on the second Tuesday of September, hundreds of thousands of people travelled by car, motorcycle, bus and train from all over Catalonia to Barcelona city centre, coming together not to commemorate a victory, but rather in memory of a heavy defeat over 300 years ago, in 1714.[2] However, on that pleasant afternoon in 2012, no one was thinking about old defeats. On the contrary, the atmosphere was festive and peaceful and, although there was tension in the air, nobody expected, at least not to such an extent, that celebration of the Catalan National Day would become

---

1   The Catalan Parliament is called the Generalitat after its 1359 founding name.
2   Each year, on 11 September, National Day commemorates the capture of Barcelona by Castilian and French troops who supported the Borbón dynasty. Barcelona and Catalonia, which were defeated, were in favour of Archduke Carlos, of the Austrian dynasty. After the War of Succession, the people endured an extremely harsh repression, Catalan institutions and laws were suppressed and Castilian was imposed as the language of administration.

the largest demonstration ever seen in Catalonia, more massive even than the renowned 1977 rally in which the general public flooded the streets to demand, less than two years after the death of Franco, 'Llibertat, amnistia i Estatut d'Autonomia!' [Freedom, amnesty and the Statute of Autonomy].[3] Additionally, it was more numerous than the demonstration against the Iraq war in February 2003.

The 2012 demonstration (Corporació Catalana de Mitjans Audiovisuals [CCMA] 2012; *The Guardian*, 11 September 2012) rallied under a very different slogan from that in 1977: 'Catalonia, nou Estat d'Europa' [Catalonia, new European State]. The Catalan government and the Barcelona police jointly estimated the official attendance figure at 1.5 million people. For its part, the Spanish government reduced the count to 600,000. This demonstration was regarded by the international press as the great starting point of the most recent Catalan civil and political movement for self-determination and independence. According to official figures, Catalonia had a population in 2012 of around 7.5 million, or about 16 per cent of the total Spanish population, and its GDP accounted for about 19 per cent of the Spanish total.

The protesters waved Catalan flags as in 1977 – but *esteladas* (the independentist Catalan flags with a star) – were mostly to be seen.[4] Among the slogans on display at that time were several in English, such as 'Freedom for Catalonia' or 'Yes, we CAT'. The desire to present their demands to Europe and the world at large has always been foremost in the minds of the sovereigntists – in favour of Catalonia being able to decide its own future through a referendum on independence – and in the mind of the independentists – in favour of Catalonia becoming a new independent state. President Artur Mas and subsequently President Carles Puigdemont trusted

---

[3] All translations are by the authors. The Statute of Autonomy, which would set the parameters of self-government of Catalonia within the Spanish state, was approved in 1979.

[4] The *estelada* [star] flag was inspired by the Cuban and Puerto Rican flags (it is like the Catalan flag, four red stripes on a yellow background) but adds an isosceles triangle – yellow or blue – with a five-pointed star – red or white – at the centre of the triangle.

that, if the dispute between Catalonia and the central government of Spain became aggravated, the EU would intervene and even force negotiations.

The protest was organized by the Catalan National Assembly (ANC),[5] an entity that seeks Catalan independence and whose formal foundation had occurred only a few months before. After the resounding success of the 2012 event, the ANC became, along with Òmnium Cultural (an organization established in 1961 during the Franco dictatorship and dedicated to defending and promoting Catalan language and culture), one of the two largest civil drivers of the Catalan self-determination and independence movement. The 11 September 2012 demonstration was headed by representatives of the ANC and the Association of Municipalities for Independence (AMI). This partnership brought together the Catalan city councils supporting independence.

The president of the Catalan government, Artur Mas, of the centre-right autonomist coalition Convergence and Union (CiU),[6] did not consider it appropriate to attend the rally, given his institutional position. However, he did encourage others to participate. In fact, many leading coalition representatives attended: the Esquerra Republicana de Catalunya [Republican Left of Catalonia] (ERC), and the left-wing Iniciativa per Catalunya Verd-Esquera Unida i Alternativa [Initiative for Catalonia Greens-United Left and Alternative] (ICV-EUiA), as well as some members of the Catalan Socialist Party (PSC), federated to the Socialist Spanish Workers Party (PSOE).

For many, 2012 heralded the resurgence of Catalan sovereignism and separatism not only because of the massive September demonstration, but also because of the early elections called after the refusal of the Spanish Prime Minister, Mariano Rajoy, to negotiate a new funding system for Catalonia with the Artur Mas government. This demonstration and the subsequent elections would signal a change in strategy for the majority of

---

5   All acronyms that appear in the text are those that correspond to the names in Catalan, except for the Spanish parties PP and the PSOE.
6   Coalition between the Convergència Democràtica de Catalunya [Democratic Convergence of Catalonia] (CDC) and the Unió Democràtica de Catalunya [Democratic Union of Catalonia] (UDC).

Catalan nationalists, which went from asking for greater self-government, an approach based on devolution, to demanding a referendum so that the Catalans themselves could decide on independence.

Objectives

In this focus on the key year of 2012 our intent is to address two significant aspects of the independence process in Catalonia. The first objective is to analyse to what extent, at that point in time and subsequently, sovereignism managed to convert its political independence claim into a relevant issue on the international public agenda. Our second goal is to check whether, as claimed by the Spanish government of Mariano Rajoy and the political parties opposed to Catalan independence – which have repeatedly denounced the 'adoctrinamiento' [indoctrination] of the population by the Catalan media – these media were in fact in favour of self-determination and independence or not. This verification was carried out by comparing the praxis of the Catalan media with that of the Spanish media, focusing on prominent pundits and collaborators.

The Spanish State and the Independence Process

Early Elections

Just one week had elapsed after the great 2012 rally, when the then King of Spain, Juan Carlos I, in an unprecedented initiative, published a web letter defending the unity of Spain and, after referring to the harsh economic crisis ravaging Spain and Europe, added resoundingly: 'En estas circunstancias, lo peor que podemos hacer es dividir fuerzas, alentar disensiones, perseguir quimeras, ahondar heridas' [In these circumstances, the worst thing we can do is to divide forces, encourage dissension, chase after ghosts, and rub salt into wounds] (De Borbón 2012). The letter came as a surprise as, rather than maintaining a neutral stance, it constituted a clear intervention in a matter of a political nature by the monarchy.[7] Moreover, the Spanish government, headed by the leader of the Partido Popular [Popular Party] (PP), Mariano Rajoy, who had been in power for less than a year, considered that the massive response to the call for the demonstration was attributable to the unrest caused by the economic crisis.

On 20 September, two days after the king's intervention, the president of the Generalitat, Artur Mas, travelled to Madrid to meet Mariano Rajoy in an atmosphere of considerable political tension. However, the goal was clear: to demand the negotiation of a new funding agreement for the Catalan regional community.[8] At that time, the main goal of the Generalitat government was the resolution of the Catalan funding problems – a topic that we will come back to later – that is, they officially avoided demanding a referendum on self-determination or independence.

The meeting ended with Rajoy's refusal to negotiate a financing system with Catalonia that at least partially softened the fiscal deficit (the difference between the money Catalonia receives and the contribution to the State's coffers from Catalans and Catalan companies). For the period 1986–2014, the average deficit with the state calculated by the Generalitat was 8 per cent of GDP (according to the monetary flow method). If the cost-benefit method is used, this figure is 6 per cent. In 2014, the most recent year for which statistics are available, the fiscal deficit was 8.4 per

[7] Juan Carlos I, and later his eldest son and successor, Felipe VI, have spoken on some occasions about the dispute between the government of Madrid and Barcelona. In all, their position was to support the central government. The position of the Spanish monarchy is in contrast to that shown by Elizabeth II to the Scottish referendum of 2014.

[8] This is the official name given to administrations of the 'nacionalidades y regiones' [nationalities and regions] (Article 2 of the Spanish Constitution) that make up the Spanish State.

cent (monetary flow method) or 5.9 per cent (cost-benefit method) of Catalan GDP, equivalent to 16,570 and 11,590 million euro respectively.[9]

After the total failure of the Madrid meeting between Rajoy and Mas, the situation escalated. The president of the Generalitat reacted by calling early elections in Catalonia and along with CiU promised the general public that a referendum on self-determination would allow all to decide for themselves on their own future. In those regional elections held on 25 November 2012, the CiU coalition went from sixty-two seats down to fifty (the Catalan house has 135 seats), while the ERC independence party went up to twenty-one, a gain of eleven more than before. For the first time, the Candidatura d'Unitat Popular [Popular Unity Candidacy] (CUP), a separatist anti-capitalist and pro-independence radical-left formation, entered Parliament (Generalitat de Catalunya 2012). These three forces became from then on the political drivers of the independence process. In 2012, the independence movement won seventy-four seats in parliament, that is to say, surpassing the sixty-eight seats required for an absolute majority. Turnout rose to 67.7 per cent, nine points above the Catalan elections that had taken place in 2010.

In late 2012, the Centre d'Estudis d'Opinió [Centre for Opinion Studies] (CEO), offering the most reliable poll among those conducted on the political situation in Catalonia, published its monthly barometer results. The fieldwork – a sample of 2,500 interviews – was done between 22 and 31 October. According to the CEO, at that time 35 per cent of the Catalans interviewed felt themselves to be as much Spanish as Catalan. The sum of those who felt more Spanish than Catalan or only Spanish was 4.5 per cent. Conversely, those who declared themselves more Catalan than Spanish, or Catalan only, rose to 58.3 per cent. Supporters of Catalan independence represented 44.3 per cent of respondents, while supporters of a federal Spain accounted for 25.5 per cent. Supporters of Catalonia remaining an autonomous region were 19.1 per cent, and those who advocated diminished self-government, 4 per cent (Centre d'Estudis d'Opinió 2012).

In December 2012, Artur Mas and the leader of ERC, Oriol Junqueras, signed an agreement to form a government that allowed the former to be

9   Catalan Department of the Vice-Presidency, Economics and Inland Revenue, 2017.

invested as president of the Generalitat. In January, the Catalan Parliament voted the *Declaration of Sovereignty*, one of whose objectives was to pursue the referendum on self-determination. Out of the 135 possible votes, the *Declaration* received eighty-five in favour, forty-one against and two abstentions (some members of parliament did not vote). The question and the date of the future referendum were published in December. Meanwhile, Mariano Rajoy's government and the Spanish Congress of Deputies rejected allowing a referendum in Catalonia.

In 2013, what was perhaps the most spectacular demonstration so far occurred on 11 September: an estimated 1.6 million people formed a chain, holding hands along the entire length of Catalonia, from the northern border with France to the southern border with the autonomous Valencian Community, a distance of about 400 kilometres (TV3, 2013). The Catalan chain was inspired by the so-called Baltic chain, which in 1989 united the capitals of Estonia, Latvia and Lithuania. Finally, the announced referendum had to be transformed into a non-binding 'procés participatiu' [participatory process] and was held on 9 November 2014 (a few weeks after the referendum on the independence of Scotland). Almost 81 per cent of the more than 2.3 million who voted (out of an estimated 5.4 million eligible Catalans) were in favour of independence.

Background: The Failure of the Statute

Jordi Pujol (CiU), who was president of Catalonia for nearly twenty-three years, was always reluctant to reform the 1979 Statute of Autonomy. He thought it might be counter-productive, that is, he feared that it might end up harming Catalan interests.[10] In the 1995 Catalan election campaign the need to change the statute to respond to the needs and aspirations of the Catalan people had already been highlighted by the main opposition candidate, the Socialist Joaquim Nadal. This initiative was unsuccessful at

---

10 For the governments of Jordi Pujol, see volumes 1 and 2 of his memoirs (Pujol 2011; 2012) as well as the works of Antich (1994) and Álvaro (2014).

that time, as Pujol managed to form a government and continue to preside over the Generalitat. However, it was taken up again by Nadal's replacement as Socialist presidential candidate, the former mayor of Barcelona, Pasqual Maragall. In 2003, an alliance of the left (PSC, ERC, ICV-EUiA) won the elections for the first time, dethroning CiU and taking over regional power in Catalonia. During this campaign, Maragall had promised a new Statute of Autonomy, a basic pledge that, nevertheless, also contained an element of electoral tactics and a move to attract those who would ultimately be its main allies in the new cabinet: ERC.

During that election campaign in 2003, specifically on 13 November (the voting would take place three days later), the socialist José Luis Rodríguez Zapatero, the Spanish prime minister at that time, proclaimed to 16,000 people gathered at a rally in Barcelona: 'Apoyaré la reforma del Estatuto de Catalunya que apruebe el Parlamento de Catalunya' [I will support the reform of the Catalan Statute approved by the Catalan Parliament]. Maragall was exultant. Later it would turn out that Rodríguez Zapatero – who had declared himself to be in favour of what he called 'España plural' [plural Spain] – had promised something he was not going to deliver. Maragall's tripartite left-wing coalition, the result of what was known as the *Tinell Pact* among the left-wing parties, would rule for three years until its chequered career, marked by tension and rivalry between its partners, precipitated the call for a new election in 2006. During those three years, great energy was invested in the drafting of a revised Statute of Autonomy that would replace that of 1979. In 2006, the leftist coalition managed to retain the government – led by a new socialist president – José Montilla.

From the very beginning, the wording of the draft statute was subject to great difficulties, in part because of disagreements among government members (ERC being a pro-independence party and the PSC, Maragall's party, federated with the Spanish PSOE). There were also ongoing differences between leftist parties and CiU representatives. The latter, despite having won more seats in the elections, had been removed from power and did not fail to take advantage of the new statute drafting to put pressure on the members of the tripartite coalition, favouring bolder wording and, at the same time, seeking to provoke contradictions among the ruling left. CiU had a significant ace in the hole: without their acceptance of the project it would not flourish, given that the statute needed a qualified majority to pass. On 30 September 2005, the Catalan Parliament finally gave its approval to the proposal of an organic law amending the Statute: the leftists with CiU voted 120 in favour, and PP voted fifteen against. Once the proposed new statute was approved in Catalonia it needed to be sent to the Spanish Parliament for approval.

In January 2006, the president of the PP, Mariano Rajoy, then in opposition in Spain, began a campaign to promote wider public opposition to the Catalan Statute. To this end, tables were set up in different Spanish cities, including Barcelona, with the aim of collecting signatures – in all, about 4 million were obtained. The move angered the Catalan parties that supported the new Statute, with many incidents between the Catalan and Spanish representatives during the negotiations.

The process ended up being refloated in a meeting between José Luis Rodríguez Zapatero and the opposition leader in Catalonia, Artur Mas (CiU), which ended on the night of 21 January 2006. The event took place at the Moncloa Palace, the official residence of the president of the central government. Although the Catalan nationalists of Mas were not numerically significant in the Spanish Parliament, the PSOE did not want in any way to be left out of the agreement on the Statute. The consequent accord reached by Mas and Zapatero angered members of the government of the Generalitat, particularly ERC, which rejected the text resulting from the negotiations with Madrid; this would lead to new elections in Catalonia.

On 8 April 2006, the then vice-president of the Spanish government and deputy general secretary of the PSOE, Alfonso Guerra, who presided over the Constitutional Commission during the handling of the Statute, had declared at a PSOE youth congress that the draft was 'infumable' [untenable] and therefore had to be polished or 'cepillado' [planed down] by the Commission like wood in the hands of carpenters.[11] In addition to calling for opposition by the PP and ERC, he also asked for a no vote from the CUP (at that time an extra-parliamentary political organization). However, the Spanish Parliament, the Congress of Deputies and the Senate,

---

11   Guerra made these controversial statements during his speech at the PSOE youth congress held in Baracaldo (in the Basque Country).

after much discussion, definitively approved the draft on 10 May 2006. On 18 June, the Catalan general public were called to a referendum to approve or reject the new Statute of Autonomy, but the duration of the process, the cuts made in the text and the fatigue of Catalan society led to an abstention rate of 50.6 per cent. The text was endorsed by 73.9 per cent of the vote.

Following the referendum, there was a cascade of appeals before the *Tribunal Constitucional* [Constitutional Court] (TC), all on the grounds that the statute was excessive in terms of power granted to Catalonia and was at odds with the 1978 Spanish Constitution. The first to file an appeal was the PP, claiming that it was a parallel constitution and challenging 114 out of a total of 223 articles of the text, a good number of which are expressed in a similar way in the Andalusian Statute currently in force. The Andalusian Statute was approved in 2006 with the votes of PP and endorsed by the Andalusians in 2007. Then the Spanish Ombudsman appealed against the Catalan Statute, along with five regional communities governed not only by the PP but also by the PSOE.[12]

The debate within the TC would last until 2010. In 2009, with the imminent possibility of an unfavourable judgement, twelve Catalan newspapers published a joint editorial in defence of the Statute. The article was entitled 'La dignitat de Catalunya'/'La dignidad de Catalunya' [The Dignity of Catalonia] and warned of the historic significance of the decision that the members of the Constitutional Court had at hand. It also denounced manoeuvres to alter the balance of forces within that court and the anomalous situation in which the institution found itself. The editorial referred to the fact that the appointment of one judge had been refused, one place remained empty after the death of its incumbent, and four other judges (the TC consists of twelve seats) had continued in office after their term expired. The text warned: 'No ens confonguem, el dilema real és avanç o retrocés; acceptació de la maduresa democràtica d'una Espanya plural, o el seu bloqueig'/'No nos confundamos, el dilema real es avance o retroceso; aceptación de la madurez democrática de una España plural, o el bloqueo

---

12   These communities were autonomous regions: Murcia, La Rioja, Aragón, Valencia and the Balearic Islands.

de esta' [Let us not be confused, the real dilemma is advancement or regression; acceptance of the democratic maturity of a plural Spain, or the blocking of this].

Then it gave further information on this, evoking the agreements that made the transition from dictatorship to democracy possible in Spain:

> Estan en joc els pactes profunds que han fet possible els 30 anys més virtuosos de la història d'Espanya. I arribats a aquest punt és imprescindible recordar un dels principis vertebradors del nostre sistema jurídic, d'arrel romana: Pacta sunt servanda. Allò pactat obliga./Están en juego los pactos profundos que han hecho posible los treinta años más virtuosos de la historia de España. Y llegados a este punto es imprescindible recordar uno de los principios vertebrales de nuestro sistema jurídico, de raíz romana: Pacta sunt servanda. Lo pactado obliga.
>
> [What is at stake are the profound pacts that have made the thirty virtuous years of the history of Spain possible. And at this point it is essential to recall one of the central principles of our legal system, of Roman origin: *Pacta sunt servanda*. Pacts must be complied with.]

Finally, the editorial predicted:

> [P]erò ningú que conegui Catalunya posarà en dubte que el reconeixement de la identitat, la millora de l'autogovern, l'obtenció d'un finançament just i un salt qualitatiu en la gestió de les infraestructures són i continuaran sent reclamacions tenaçment plantejades amb un amplíssim suport polític i social./[P]ero nadie que conozca Catalunya pondrá en duda que el reconocimiento de la identidad, la mejora del autogobierno, la obtención de una financiación justa y un salto cualitativo en la gestión de las infraestructuras son y seguirán siendo reclamaciones tenazmente planteadas con un amplísimo apoyo político y social.
>
> [But nobody who knows Catalonia will doubt that the recognition of identity, improvement of self-government, obtaining a fair share of funding and a qualitative leap in the management of infrastructures are and will continue to be tenaciously defended with very broad political and social support.] (*La Vanguardia*, 26 November 2009).

When eventually, in July 2010, the Constitutional Court issued its judgement on the Statute of Autonomy, the resolution did not have unanimity among the judges. The ruling left the term 'nación' [nation] without legal validity in the preamble of the Statute. In addition, it annulled the pretensions on the Catalan language, on the establishment of an autonomous judiciary power and on improving the financing of Catalonia. In total, fourteen articles were annulled and twenty-seven were conditioned by the interpretation defined by the Constitutional Court judges. The ruling caused great consternation in most of Catalan society, with the socialist president of the Generalitat, José Montilla, addressing the Catalans to emphasize his 'indignación' [indignation], criticizing the PP's attitude and noting that the Constitutional Court was 'lamentablemente desacreditado y moralmente deslegitimado' [lamentably discredited and morally delegitimized] to issue that statement.[13]

On 10 July 2010, a protest demonstration organized by Òmnium Cultural passed through the centre of Barcelona under the slogan 'Som una nació, nosaltres decidim' [We are a nation, we decide]. This slogan can be interpreted as a direct allusion to the strange situation created since the TC substantially modified a Statute of Autonomy not only approved by the Catalan and Spanish parliaments, but also endorsed by the public. With the exception of the PP and Citizens (*Ciudadanos*), the demonstration received the support of most of the political parties of the Catalan Parliament, as well as many Catalan public figures, the unions and nearly 1,600 Catalan civil organizations. The president of the Catalan government, José Montilla, was at the front of the demonstration. The Statute that ultimately came into force was substantially different from that which the Catalan citizens had endorsed through a referendum.[14]

From Reformism to Independentism

From the restoration of Spanish democracy, Catalan nationalism had mostly opted for political reform in Spain and its economic modernization, confident that with this, acceptance of the diverse nature of the state would lead to recognition of the distinct identity of the Catalan people. Catalan nationalism, which in its political dimension has its origins in

---

[13] From the institutional statement by President Montilla on 28 June, 2010.
[14] For the independence process in Catalonia, see Minder (2017); on the contemporary history of Catalonia, see McRoberts (2001) and Dowling (2013).

the late nineteenth century (Balsells 1992; Cacho Viu 1998; Keating 1996; Solé Tura 1985; Termes 1999) has been defined by Guibernau as 'emancipatory nationalism', which she describes as 'a democratic type of nationalism emerging in nations included within larger states who do not identify with them, who do not feel represented by the states of which they are a part and who do not feel politically and culturally recognized by the state containing them'. This same author also highlighted that the will of the British government to recognize Scotland as a nation and its willingness to allow a referendum on independence contrasted with the Spanish position to ban the referendum in Catalonia (Guibernau 2013: 372).

Catalan nationalism – which has always maintained a clear pro-European stance – was constructed from the 1960s on, in one of the movements in opposition to the dictatorship of General Franco, close to the left (mainly Communists and Socialists). Since Franco's death in 1975, this would effectively contribute to the stabilization of the Spanish political situation and facilitate the advent of the new democratic regime, the Transition. And it would remain so from the restoration of the Generalitat of Catalonia and the first regional elections in 1980. Surprisingly, those elections were won by Jordi Pujol and CiU, which ousted the two main leftist parties, the PSC and the communist Partit Socialista Unificat de Catalunya [Unified Socialist Party of Catalonia (PSUC)]. Pujol would remain in power for almost twenty-three years until the arrival of the government of Pasqual Maragall hand-in-hand with the Tripartite Left. During three government terms, Pujol enjoyed an absolute majority in the Generalitat. Throughout their successive mandates, CiU laid the foundations of Catalonia today and its current welfare system (health, education, social policy, and so on). This period was also characterized by defence of the Catalan language and culture, supported by the productive economy and by better funding and investment for Catalonia.

Pujol and the CiU group in the Congress of Deputies in Madrid, always in exchange for trade-offs, provided for the necessary parliamentary support for both the PSOE and the PP when one of them did not have a sufficient majority. Similarly, they supported the governments in regard to the entry of Spain into the European Community (1986) and the Euro system (1999) and when the time came to address the crisis that erupted in Spain and Europe in 2008. Ideologically close to the Christian Democrats and a fervent pro-European, Jordi Pujol always promoted negotiation and agreement with the powers-that-be in Madrid, and opposed independence, to the extent that, as noted above, he consistently rejected reform of the Statute of Autonomy of 1979. Things changed considerably between 2003, when Pujol left power, and 2010, when judgement was pronounced on the new Statute. If we look at the opinion polls on the Catalans' position, we realize that from 2000 to 2010 the position favourable to independence became progressively stronger. For a variety of reasons, the Catalans' perception had changed in regard to the relationship between Catalonia – whose origins date back over 1,000 years – and the Spanish State.

The growth of the sovereignty and independence movement in Catalonia has multiple origins. Certainly, a significant cause has its origin in frustration and outrage that parts of the Statute already approved by Catalan citizens in a referendum were deleted or revised or differently interpreted by the Spanish Parliament and the Constitutional Court. But other origins are also particularly relevant. For example, a second element is the belief that the accumulation of very high annual fiscal deficits – which have already been discussed here – were severely damaging Catalonia and the welfare of the general public. This issue, combined with the economic crisis that erupted in 2008, undoubtedly contributed to dissatisfaction with the Spanish government's treatment of Catalonia. A third major element presents greater difficulties of definition, because there is a less tangible cause. This is the perception, widespread in Catalonia, that political and institutional Spain not only fails to recognize or appreciate its own internal diversity but in many cases treats Catalonia with contempt or worse, as evidenced by attempts to suppress key features of its identity. Among the most important of such features is the Catalan language, spoken in the regional autonomies of Valencia and the Balearic Islands, in the area of Aragon bordering Catalonia and, beyond the Spanish borders, in Andorra, in the south of France (Northern Catalonia) and in the town of Alghero on the island of Sardinia.

In relation to this, perhaps one of the issues that has caused most dissatisfaction has been the insistence of PP – and afterwards the new party, Citizens, instituted in 2006 from a general public platform – to question the linguistic model in Catalan schools. In the system of public education, children and young people use Catalan as their first language, as it is considered in need of protection. This model has been pursued with considerable success, as indicated on several occasions by the PISA Report that all children and young people know both languages. The PISA report notes that the reading comprehension in Spanish of Catalan students ranks above the Spanish average (Silió 2016). The PP has often attributed the defence of the Catalan language to a desire to obtain 'privilegios' [privileges] through 'chantaje' [blackmail] in the conviction that these accusations against Catalans are a profitable electoral weapon in the rest of Spain. Moreover, in José María Aznar's second term (2000–4) another source of dissatisfaction among Catalans was the PP's refusal to negotiate improvements to self-government by the Generalitat and its financing, together with the determination of the Spanish right to recentralize state power and convert the city of Madrid – through the concentration of economic power and huge investments in infrastructure – into a megalopolis that Barcelona could not compete with.

The Catalan draft Statute of 2006 had aimed, albeit timidly, at progress in the areas cited: identity, language and culture, as well as the economy and investment, and its failure was rejection of the different Catalonia and the different Spain it proposed. This would probably account for the fact that during the years 2000 to 2010 the independence movement gained significant ground until it stabilized at between 40 per cent and 50 per cent of all Catalan citizens.

From 2012 to the Present Day

From the 'procés participatiu' [participatory process] of 9 November 2014, which was held despite opposition from the Spanish state, many things have happened. From that date on, Catalan and Spanish policy entered a period marked by escalating pressure from the Spanish government and the state in general in an attempt to block the sovereignism and independence movements, as Culla (2017), March (2018), Martí (2018) and García (2018) explain.

CiU having been dissolved in June 2014 over separatist disagreements within the coalition, when early elections to the Catalan Parliament were held on 27 September 2015, CDC and UDC ran separate campaigns. The election was won by an electoral coalition called Junts pel Sí (JxSí) [Together for Yes]. Mas wanted to give the elections a plebiscitary character to turn them into a kind of vote on independence. However, JxSí needed the pro-independence and anti-system votes of CUP to gain control of the Catalan Parliament and, in exchange for their support, CUP demanded that Mas should withdraw from the presidency of the Generalitat. In January 2016, Carles Puigdemont became the new president and five months later, in June, announced that he would call a referendum on independence.

When, during the referendum voting on 1 October 2017 – which was to proceed in spite of opposition from the Spanish government, the Constitutional Court, and the Judiciary – agents of the National Police and Civil Guard assaulted voters in a number of polling stations, the images of police violence circled the globe. Almost 2.3 million people voted, nine out of ten in favour of an independent Catalonia. King Felipe VI, in a televised speech on 3 October, described what happened as 'deslealtad inadmisible' [unacceptable disloyalty] and warned of the 'extrema gravedad' [extreme gravity] of what was happening. He stressed that the State should ensure 'el orden constitucional' [the constitutional order] and avoided referring to the more than 1,000 people hurt and injured. That same day there was a general strike – 'aturada de país' [halting of the country] – in Catalonia to protest the violence.

Puigdemont would declare Catalan independence in the Catalan Parliament on 10 October, although in the same act it was suspended pending international mediation, something which was not going to happen. Finally, on the 27th, Puigdemont declared independence. However, it was not to be implemented. The Spanish flag on the Palace of the Generalitat in Barcelona was not even hauled down, and the statement was not published in the Official Journal of the Generalitat of Catalonia, something required if it was to become law. The reaction of the Spanish State consisted of implementing Article 155 of the Constitution, which meant the immediate suspension of all Catalan government members and the takeover of the Generalitat. At the same time, elections were also called for 21

December, in which the pro-independence parties would manage to win seventy seats in parliament, two more than required for an absolute majority. The record turnout exceeded 79 per cent, with Puigdemont once again the candidate with the greatest support.

By early 2018, the principal civil and political independence leaders were either in custody – accused of serious crimes – or refugees in various European countries. Others were free, but were awaiting Spanish judicial processes – as was the chief of the Mossos de Esquadra (Catalan regional police). Puigdemont took refuge in Belgium but was later arrested in Germany while returning by road from Finland. German judges dismissed, although they had not yet definitely denied, the order for his extradition to Spain for the crime of rebellion (punishable by a maximum of thirty years imprisonment) and said that if asked they would deliberate on the accusation of embezzlement of public funds. Puigdemont and Jordi Sánchez (leader of Òmnium Cultural, in prison for the second time) were proposed as candidates for president of the Catalan government, but their legal situation prevented their inauguration. A third candidate, Jordi Turull, failed to gain the support of the CUP. The 1 October referendum brought sharply into view the attention paid by the international press to the Catalan question, and this was also to be the case with the declarations of independence on 10 and 27 October; these events served to consolidate the Catalan situation on the international agenda, which was both the impetus for our investigation and the guide to its research processes.

Methodology

The methodology consisted in the quantitative analysis of the information appearing in the press, television, radio and internet at Catalan, Spanish and international levels. The research focused on the period from 11 September 2012 (Catalan National Day) until a few days after the elections to the Catalan Parliament on 25 November that same year. The test sample starts on 10 September and extends until

30 November 2012.[15] The quantitative analysis included a total of 4,795 journal pieces from more than 100 media sources: Catalan, Spanish and international.[16] The investigation was complemented by author interviews of members of the two different Catalan governments, including its presidents. The pieces can be characterized as follows:

- selected information published in printed newspapers;
- news programmes from selected radio and television channels;
- news distributed by selected digital newspapers;
- the main radio and television current affairs programmes including news, interviews, talk-shows and political debates.

However, the principal object of analysis was the headline for all media, whether print, radio, television or Internet.

Media Sampling

For the purpose of the investigation, and with the exception of the international press, the sample was selected for each outlet and territory according to the criterion of coverage and influence of each of these media. To maintain a certain geographical balance, a higher number of foreign newspapers was chosen.[17]

Given the territorial and political framework that the emerging pro-independence movement is articulated in, we directed our attention

---

15 This material was quantified using indicators such as time and space occupied; the pre-eminence given to this content by the media and the secondment of contributors and experts.
16 See Appendix A for the list of all media analysed.
17 Not all media reached a sample of seven in some categories: Catalan television and radio and international digital newspapers (because the number of newspaper companies representing the area in question did not reach that figure). In the case of the internet, our study included both digital newspapers without printed press – called pure players – as well as digital editions of major newspapers of global reference.

to European media, focusing the analysis on the most influential countries among the European Union (EU) founders: Germany, France, Italy, Belgium and the Netherlands. In this selection, the UK was added, although it joined the EU project later than the others, as it is still, despite the uncertainties of Brexit, a state with considerable power and influence. In addition, the Scottish case presents characteristics similar in many ways to those of Catalonia. We have considered it worthwhile to add the United States to our selection, as a traditional ally of the EU and a pre-eminent player in the international landscape. In this way, there are many of the major trading partners of Catalonia in this sample.

We also deemed it essential to give greater attention to two of the sectors: television and the printed press. While the circulation of printed newspapers is generally declining internationally, this medium still exerts a considerable influence on political, economic, social and cultural elites. As such, both media are crucial factors in shaping public opinion. As for the printed press, we thought it necessary also to include some non-generalist but nevertheless major publications specializing in economics. The leading global audio-visual channels are reference points for many media, and so have also been included. In total the sample includes 104 communication means in seven languages: twenty-four Catalan, twenty-eight Spanish and fifty-two internationals.

In the case of audio-visual programmes, the approach was to select the midday and evening television news, and the programmes with talk shows, debates, interviews, and so on of a political nature. As for the radio, we have selected information programmes, usually in the evening, together with the most relevant current affairs programmes, which are usually broadcast in the morning. With regard to digital-only newspapers, online media units were sampled using two different procedures. From the date on which the investigation began – 15 November 2012 – we proceeded to capture all the headlines studied. The capture was always carried out at 4 p.m. For the analysis of past publications, we conducted a retrospective search. We considered that employing Google for the enquiry would provide better and more homogeneous results.[18]

---

18 For Catalan media the following categories were chosen: independencia, independentisme; federalisme, federal, federalist; sobiranisme, sobiranista;

Data: Factor Analysis

Each individual piece of text information was collected and assigned the following data fields: basic identification (headline, publication, source, date and text genre) and related data on the time, place and duration, as well as the rank or position in the publication (cover or summary or home page, section, page, columns).

Among the news headlines, we differentiated between those that were referential and those that were evaluative. The referential headlines are objective and we can determine if they are true or false; the most common examples are statements such as: 'Rajoy avisa a Mas de que "se está equivocando y mucho"' [Rajoy warns Mas that 'he is making a mistake and a bad one at that'] In these headlines, we have also focused on determining the subject of the statement. For evaluative headlines we first determined whether the assessment was positive, negative or not indicated. If the news text was an interview, then we refer to the political (or ideological) affiliation of the person concerned: unionist, independentist, federalist, or not indicated.

Opinion: Factor Analysis

For opinion texts the overall objective was twofold: first, political, ideological and professional identification of the author of the text, and second, the headline analysis. For the first objective, in addition to the basic reference data – medium, date and headline – we identified the kind of opinion article – column, external pundit contribution, in-depth article, editorial, letter to the editor, and so on – and the journalist's

---

espanyolisme, centralisme, espanya, unitat. For Spanish media the categories were: independencia, independentismo; federalism, federal, federalista; soberanismo, soberanista, españolismo, centralismo, españa, unidad. For international media, the search was carried out thoroughly from the word 'Catalonia' translated into the different languages of the media studied.

credentials: author, expert, politician, and so on, as well as their ideological leaning. This part included a study of chat shows, a very popular format in Catalonia and Spain. For the second objective the headlines were classified as thematic (that is limiting themselves to the question at hand), evaluative/evaluation (issuing a judgement), or inappropriate (extremely negative or offensive). Also, as in the news elements, we indicated whether the action was presented as positive or negative, and who it was directed at or who suffered the consequences.

Results and Discussion

The first objective of our investigation was to determine whether in 2012 sovereignism had the ability to reach beyond the Spanish borders, to the extent that it was incorporated into the international public agenda. In this regard, it is significant that, of the overall total of 4,795 items analysed (see Appendix A), international media produced 233 news items through print, television and radio during our study period (4.65 per cent of the overall total), while Catalan and Spanish media published 4,562 pieces (95.35 per cent). As expected, the Catalan and Spanish media provided much more information than foreign media. From Table 11.1 (Appendix B) it can be seen that, for example, in the case of television, the total number of recorded spots was: 397 in Catalonia, 232 in Spain and twenty-five internationally – a total of 654.

In all media (print, broadcasting and digital), news items were the predominant reporting genre in Catalonia, in Spain, and in the rest of the world (Tables 11.2, 11.3, 11.4 and 11.5). Regarding opinion genres, in Catalonia and Spain many more opinions were provided by columnists than by editorials, by letters to the editor or by analyses written by experts (in-depth articles and external pundit contributions). In the international media, columnists and external pundits contributed 31.3 per cent each to the overall total (Table 11.6).

Of the headlines analysed throughout the period, internationally the subject that appears most is 'Catalonia': in printed media (Table 11.7),

'Catalonia' accounts for 29.9 per cent of the headlines, while in television (Table 11.8) this ratio is much higher – rising to 70 per cent – and in online media (Table 11.9) it was 62.5 per cent. In the case of both Catalonia and Spain the subject that dominates headlines in all three media is Artur Mas, who was the then president of the government of the Generalitat. This was to be expected, given that the perspective of the international media is more detached than that of the Catalan and Spanish.

Headlines were mostly categorized as evaluative (Table 11.10). The case of the press (General) is the most striking: evaluative headlines account for 63.1 per cent versus 33.5 per cent for referential (and 3.4 per cent where the distinction was not applicable). For international television, evaluative and referential headlines were equal at 28 per cent. In the international online media, in contrast, evaluative headlines at 42.9 per cent far exceeded referential.

The typology of international headlines (Table 11.11) was considerably more negative than positive in newspapers (44.9 per cent negative versus 17.4 per cent positive, while the rest were neutral or indeterminate). For magazines, the proportion of negative (37.5 per cent) was significantly higher than positive (25 per cent); this was even more marked in the case of online media (38.5 per cent versus 7.7 per cent). However, in TV headlines the positive (37.5 per cent) were higher than the negative (25 per cent), making international television the only outlet where positive reporting exceeded negative.

The second objective of this research was to ascertain whether the allegations of bias made by the Spanish government and unionist politicians were true. The total number of opinion pieces (column, pundit, article, etc.) analysed was 1,922. Most of these opinion headlines have an evaluative function first, then thematic thereafter. Most of the inappropriate headlines occurred in the Spanish media. This tendency was clearest in online media, given that the percentage of opinion headlines presenting an inappropriate function reached 3.4 per cent. As for the leaning of print media contributors and experts (Table 11.12), perhaps the most significant point of our analysis is the strong polarization observed, although there was a greater diversity among the Catalan media than among Spanish media. In the first case, those which can be labelled as sovereigntists take precedence at

59.5 per cent. Conversely, in the Spanish media the unionists take the first place, at 71.4 per cent. The more inappropriate opinion pieces were those of the Spanish media. In addition, and taking the strong polarization into account, we can observe that the pluralism of the Catalan media is higher than that of the Spanish.

In the case of print media contributors, Table 11.12 indicates that while sovereigntists dominated in Catalonia (59.5 per cent), in Spain it is the unionists, with 71.4 per cent of the total. Table 11.13 indicates that in the Catalan online media, sovereigntists accounted for 77 per cent versus 10 per cent of unionists and 13 per cent of federalists. In the Spanish online media, the percentages were: 54.3 per cent, unionists; 11.2 per cent sovereigntists (in favour of self-determination); 14.7 per cent federalists. In radio talk shows (Table 11.14), in the case of Catalonia nearly half the pundits were sovereigntists (49.7 per cent), and in the case of Spain 61 per cent were unionists and only 1.7 per cent were sovereigntist voices for independence. For television talk-show guest ideologies (Table 11.15), in Catalonia 45.5 per cent were sovereigntists, while on Spanish television, unionist guests accounted for 69.7 per cent; unionists among Catalonia commentators comprised 15.8 per cent while in Spain the sovereigntists (separatists) made up 5.9 per cent.

The majority opinion of the Catalans, in any media, was sovereigntist. In the Spanish media, conversely, the main point of view was unionist. The Catalan digital media and the Spanish printed media included a higher percentage of opinion contributors of the respective majority currents. The greatest balance was found in the international newspapers and magazines. As for the politicians interviewed, we should highlight the fact that the Spanish press mainly interviewed, and in this order, representatives of the PP and the PP in Catalonia, then those of PSC and Citizens, condemning representatives of political parties favourable to the self-determination of Catalonia to virtual silence.

As we have seen, during the study period, 233 pieces on Catalonia were broadcast or published in the international media we analysed (Table 11.1). Today the international presence of Catalonia is perceptibly far greater than it was then, and there can be no doubt that the independence movement has become a player in an international issue. This emergence of Catalonia on the international agenda dates from the key year of 2012 and has continued to increase and consolidate itself since. This is actually one of the principal objectives pursued by sovereigntism since 2012, the year in which, as we have seen, the movement broke out of its shell in full force. However, in that year, both Catalonia and President Mas were associated with negative actions or assessments in the international media.

In fact, after the great rally of 2012, the Generalitat government implemented a specific programme for a channel of fluid communication with international media and their correspondents in Catalonia and Spain. The programme was dubbed The Eugeni Xammar International Programme for Communications and Public Relations.[19] Additionally, in November of the same year, the Catalan government agreed to give a strong impetus to diplomatic action abroad. To do this, they created the Public Diplomacy Council of Catalonia (Diplocat) from the existing Catalonia World Board. Their goal was to explain the Catalan process internationally, including their aspirations to exercise the right to self-determination and independence. Diplocat, the Catalan *paradiplomacy*, which was abolished in 2017 by the Spanish government based on Article 155 of the Constitution, worked hard and contributed to making what was happening in Catalonia known internationally. The Catalan government also tried during the process to attract the attention of foreign correspondents, traditionally based in Madrid and therefore very exposed to the narratives on Catalonia propagated by the government of Rajoy and the Spanish media.[20]

As we noted earlier, a new analysis of the international agenda would be necessary to check to what extent the presence of Catalonia and the independence movement has increased on the international agenda. It would also need to determine whether assessment at the international level

---

19   Eugeni Xammar (1888–1973) was a notable Catalan journalist and international correspondent, besides being a diplomat and translator.
20   One of these journalists, Sandrine Morel of *Le Monde*, a critic of sovereigntism, published a book (2018) in which she exposes the pressure of a member of the Partit Democràtic Europeu de Catalunya [European Democratic Party of Catalonia] (PDECAT), the successor of the Democratic Convergence of Catalonia, to publish articles more favourable to the pro-independence movement.

remains largely negative or whether, in light of the events from 2012 to the present, the international perception has become more positive. As we have seen, the debate in Catalonia and Spain about the Catalan aspiration to decide their own future through a referendum on self-determination, took place using terms of great polarization. There is a structural explanation for this. Catalonia and Spain can consider themselves safely included in the 'Mediterranean model or polarized pluralism' (Hallin and Mancini 2004), which is characterized by a high degree of parallelism, of correspondence, between the political system and the media. However, there is less unanimity between Catalan and Spanish media. While in the former we find a greater representation of voices against self-determination and independence, the latter tend to ostensibly minimize or marginalize the voices of sovereigntism and independence.

In this section, although we do not have global studies, we do have different analyses conducted on pluralism on television both in Catalonia and in Spain. These analyses tend to confirm our results in part. El Consell de l'Audiovisual de Catalunya [The Audiovisual Council of Catalonia] (CAC), a regulator that produced different analyses, found in a study on 1 October 2017, the referendum voting day, that, in news treatment on Catalan and Spanish television channels, TV3 (the leading Catalan public television channel) 'va oferir aquell dia més pluralitat de veus en la seva programació' [offered on that day more diversity of voices in their programming] compared with the Spanish public television (TVE) and the private Spanish Telecinco, Antena 3 TV and La Sexta (CAC 2017). Another example available is the collective study on the 2017 Catalan elections by the UK Democracy Volunteers. In the 'Media Monitoring' section, the report analysed Catalan and Spanish newspapers, radio and television, noting the strong bias against independence in the Spanish media (Ault 2017).

Also in this section, we should take into consideration an important element that relates to the structure of the Catalan media market. While the Spanish media, both written and audiovisual, have a widespread diffusion and readership/audience in Catalonia, this does not happen the other way around. Without doubt, this makes it possible for the Catalan public to receive a greater diversity of points of view than the general public in the rest of the country. In a nutshell, we can say that 2012 was the year when the movement for Catalan independence became an issue that went beyond the Spanish borders for the first time in a loud and clear manner. Likewise, the international presence in 2012 became a prime objective of the independence movement and the Generalitat government redoubled its diplomatic efforts to publicize the Catalan situation to the world to garner support for holding a referendum.

While an assessment of Catalonia's presence on the international agenda may not have been a primary objective of this study, it is evident that this presence has been increasing progressively. However, we do not know whether international public opinion about the Catalan independence movement amounts to a positive assessment, although in this regard there might have been significant fluctuations throughout the different periods or stages since 2012. It also seems clear that the Spanish media were – and appear to continue to be – virtually unanimous in their position of rejecting a referendum on self-determination and promoting frontal condemnation of independence. As we have already said, the Spanish media are widely read and watched by the Catalan general public, something that does not happen on a reciprocal basis, which is to say that the Catalan media are hardly followed outside Catalonia. Our analysis has clearly shown that, for their part, the Catalan media made greater efforts to accommodate a diversity of opinions and views and provide more pluralism in their reporting.

More recent events have served to highlight the probability that the conflict between opposing views of nationhood and identity, in both Catalonia and Spain, is not likely to be resolved in the short term. This underscores the pressing need to continue the line of research that began with this study, the results and conclusions of which, drawn from a very wide spectrum of media opinion, not only shed light on the present independence movement in Catalonia and its impact on Spanish perceptions of statehood, but lead into and meld with other definitions of and aspirations towards identity worldwide. Continuing such analyses through further periods of time, following national and international opinions as they evolve and mutate, can only enhance our understanding of the issues involved.

Appendix A: Media Analysed

Catalan			
Printed press	Television	Radio	Digital newspapers (pure players)
La Vanguardia	TV3	Catalunya Ràdio	Vilaweb
El Periódico de Catalunya	TVE (the previously recorded news on Channels One and Two)	RAC1	Nació Digital
El Punt Avui	8tv	La Xarxa (COM Ràdio)	Racó Català
Ara	Barcelona TV	RNE Ràdio 4	El Singular Digital / El Món
Segre	Canal Català		E-notícies
Diari de Tarragona			Directe.cat
Regió 7			El Debat El Nacional

Spanish			
Printed press	Television	Radio	Digital newspapers (pure players)
El País	Telecinco	Cadena SER	Lainformacion.com
El Mundo	Antena 3	Onda Cero Radio	El Confidencial
ABC	La 1	RNE Radio 1	Publico.es
La Razón	Cuatro	COPE	Periodista Digital

Spanish			
Printed press	Television	Radio	Digital newspapers (pure players)
El Correo	La Sexta	ABC Punto Radio	The Huffington Post
La Voz de Galicia	La 2	Canal Sur Radio	Libertad Digital
La Nueva España	Intereconomía	Radio Intereconomía	El Plural

International			
Press	Television	Digital media	Others
Süddeutsche Zeitung (Germany)	BBC World (UK)	Huffington Post (US)	*Der Spiegel* (Germany)
Frankfurter Allgemeine Zeitung (Germany)	CNN (US)	Political (US)	*Stern* (Germany)
Le Monde (France)	Fox News (US)	Lettera 43 (Italy)	*Le Nouvel Observateur* (France)
Le Figaro (France)	Al Jazeera (Qatar)	Rue 89 (France)	*L'Express* (France)
Il Corriere della sera (Italy)	France 24 (France)		*L'Espresso* (Italy)
La Repubblica (Italy)	ZDFinfo (Germany)	Süddeutsche Zeitung (Germany)	*The Economist* (UK)
Le Soir (Belgium-Wallonia)			*Time* (US)
De Standaard (Belgium Flanders)		Le Figaro (France)	*Newsweek* (US)

International			
Press	Television	Digital media	Others
De Telegraaf (Netherlands)		Il Corriere della sera (Italy)	
Volkskran (Netherlands)			
The Daily Telegraph (UK)		La Repubblica (Italy)	
The Guardian (UK)		Le Soir (Belgium-Wallonia)	
The Times (UK)		De Standaard (Belgium Flanders)	
The New York Times (US)		De Telegraaf (Netherlands)	
The Washington Post (US)		Volkskran (Netherlands)	
USA Today (US)		Daily Telegraph (UK)	
Wall Street Journal (US)		The Guardian (UK)	
Financial Times (UK)		The Times (UK)	
		The New York Times (US)	
		The Washington Post (US)	
		USA Today (US)	
		The Wall Street Journal (US)	
		Financial Times (UK)	

Appendix B: Analyses

Table 11.1: Number of journal pieces

	Catalonia	Spain	International	Total
Printed media	1,385	914	194	2,493
Broad-casting	397	232	25	654
Online media	1,062	572	14	1,648
Total	2,844	1,718	233	4,795

Table 11.2: Number of front-page or table-of-contents pieces

	Catalonia	Spain	International	Total
Printed Media	244	175	23	442
Broad-casting	90	218	2	310

Table 11.3: Most common genres in printed press (%)

	Catalonia	Spain	International
News	79.4	91.6	70.1
Interview	8.7	2.2	3.3
Chronicle	6.5	3.6	7.1
Reportage	5.4	2.6	19.0

Table 11.4: Most common genres in broadcast media (%)

	Catalonia	Spain	International
News	91.9	100	84.0
Interview	-	-	-
Chronicle	5.5	-	-
Reportage	2.5	-	16.0

Table 11.5: Most common genres in online media (%)

	Catalonia	Spain	International
News	99.7	87.9	85.7
Interview	0.3	3.5	-
Chronicle		6.6	7.1
Report		1.9	7.2

Table 11.6: Opinion articles typology (%)

	Catalonia	Spain	International
Column	63.3	63.5	31.3
External pundit	17.3	12.9	31.3
In-depth article	6.9	12.9	18.8
Editorial	6.8	9.8	10.4
Letter to the editor	5.8	0.9	8.3

Table 11.7: Main subjects in printed press headlines (%)

Catalonia	Spain	International
Artur Mas (17.3)	Artur Mas (9.3)	Catalonia (29.9)
PSC (6.4)	Spanish gov't (6.0)	Mariano Rajoy (11.5)
ERC (6.4)	Mariano Rajoy (4.7)	Artur Mas (10.3)

Table 11.8: Main subjects in broadcasting media (%)

Catalonia	Spain	International
Artur Mas (28.7)	Artur Mas (38.1)	Catalonia (70.0)
Generalitat (7.7)	Catalonia (6.7)	ICV (10.0)
CiU (6.9)	Mariano Rajoy (6.0)	Regional gov'ts (10.0)

Table 11.9: Main subjects in online media (%)

Catalonia	Spain	International
Artur Mas (15.7)	Artur Mas (18.4)	Catalonia (62.5)
ERC (10.0)	PP (7.1)	Other (37.5)
PSC (8.0)	CiU (6.6)	

Table 11.10: Typology of headlines (%)

	General	International television	International online media
Evaluative	63.1	28.0	42.9
Referential	33.5	28.0	17.4
Inappropriate	3.4	44.0	37.7

Table 11.11: Typology of international headlines (%)

	Newspapers	Magazines	Online media	TV
Negative	44.9	37.5	38.5	25.0
Positive	17.4	25.0	7.7	37.5
Neutral	37.7	37.5	53.8	37.5

Table 11.12: Ideology of print media contributors (%)

	Catalonia	Spain	International
Sovereigntists	59.5	3	12.5
Unionists	-	71.4	18.8
Federalists	0.8	2.3	2.1
Unidentified	22	23.3	66.7

Table 11.13: Ideology of online media contributors (%)

	Catalonia	Spain
Sovereigntists	77	11.2
Unionists	10	54.3
Federalists	13	14.7
Unidentified	-	19.8

Table 11.14: Ideology of radio talk-show guests (%)

	Catalonia	Spain
Sovereigntists	49.7	1.7
Unionists	9.6	61
Federalists	13	3.8
Unidentified	27.7	33.6

Table 11.15: Ideology of television talk-show guests (%)

	Catalonia	Spain
Sovereigntists	45.5	5.9
Unionists	15.8	69.7
Federalists	23.4	5.3
Unidentified	15.3	19.1

Bibliography

Álvaro, F.-M. (2014). *Ara sí que toca! El pujolisme, el procés sobiranista i el cas Pujol*. Barcelona: Pòrtic.

Antich, J. (1994). *El virrey: ¿es Jordi Pujol un fiel aliado de la Corona o un caballo de Troya dentro de la Zarzuela?* Barcelona: Planeta.

Ault, J. (2017). 'Catalonia Regional Elections 21st December 2017 – Interim Report'. London: Democracy Volunteers <https://democracyvolunteersdotorg.files.

wordpress.com/2017/12/catalonian-regional-election-2017-interim-report1. pdf> accessed 10 November 2018.

Balsells, A. (1992). *Història del nacionalisme català: dels orígens al nostre temps*. Barcelona: Generalitat de Catalunya. Departament de la Presidència. Entitat Autònoma del Diari Oficial i de Publicacions.

Burgen, S. (2012). 'Catalan independence rally brings Barcelona to a standstill', *The Guardian*, 11 September <https://www.theguardian.com/world/2012/sep/11/catalan-independence-rally-barcelona> accessed 5 December 2018.

Cacho Viu, V. (1998). *El nacionalismo catalán como factor de modernización*. Barcelona: Quaderns Crema.

Centre d'Estudis d'Opinió (CEO) (2012). 'Baròmetre d'Opinió Política, 28' <http://ceo.gencat.cat/ca/barometre/detall/index.html?id=4308> accessed 13 November 2018.

Consell de l'Audiviosual de Catalunya (CAC) (2017). 'TV3 va respectar el pluralisme en la jornada de l'1-O i la TV pública estatal va presentar manca de pluralitat de veus' <https://www.cac.cat/actualitat/tv3-va-respectar-pluralisme-la-jornada-l1-o-i-la-tv-publica-estatal-va-presentar-manca> accessed 18 November 2018.

Corporació Catalana de Mitjans Audiovisuals (CCMA) (2012). '1,5 milions de persones demanen la independència' <http://www.ccma.cat/324/15-milions-de-persones-demanen-la-independencia-de-Catalunya-en-una-manifestacio-record/noticia/1884457/> accessed 13 November 2018.

Culla, J. B. (2017). *El tsunami. Com i perquè el sistema de partits català a esdevingut irreconeixible*. Barcelona: Pòrtic.

De Borbón, J. C. (2012). 'Carta de S.M. el Rey Don Juan Carlos' <http://www.casareal.es/ES/FamiliaReal/rey/Paginas/rey_cartas_detalle.aspx?data=51> accessed 2 December 2018.

Departament de la Vicepresidència i Economia i Hacienda de la Generalitat de Catalunya (2017). 'Els resultats de la balança fiscal amb el sector públic central els anys 2013 i 2014' <http://economia.gencat.cat/web/.content/70_analisi_finances_publiques_balanca_fiscal/arxius/resultats-BF-2013-2014.pdf> accessed 18 November 2018.

Dowling, A. (2013). *Catalonia since the Spanish Civil War: reconstructing the nation*. Eastbourne: Sussex Academic Press.

García, L. (2018). *El Naufragio*. Barcelona: Ediciones Península.

Generalitat de Catalunya (2012). 'Resultados definitivos; Eleccions al Parlament de Catalunya' <https://www.gencat.cat/governacio/resultats-parlament2012/09AU/DAU09999CM_L1.htm?d=0> accessed 10 December 2018.

Guibernau, M. (2013). 'Secessionism in Catalonia: After Democracy', *Ethnopolitics: Formerly Global Review of Ethnopolitics*, 12 (4), 368–93.

Hallin, D. C., and Mancini, P. (2004). *Comparing media systems: Three models of media and politics*. Cambridge: Cambridge University Press.

Keating, M. (1996). *Nations against the state: The new politics of nationalism in Quebec, Catalonia and Scotland*. London: Palgrave Macmillan.

La Vanguardia (2009). 'La dignidad de Cataluña' [Editorial], 26 November <http://www.lavanguardia.com/politica/20091126/53831123016/la-dignidad-de-catalunya.html> accessed 18 November 2018.

McRoberts, K. (2001). *Nation Building Without a State*. Canada: Don Mills; Oxford: Oxford University Press.

March, O. (2018). *Los entresijos del procés*. Madrid: Catarata.

Martí, J. (2018). *Cómo ganamos el proceso y perdimos la República*. Barcelona: Economía Digital.

Minder, R. (2017). *The struggle for Catalonia. Rebel politics in Spain*. London: Hurst.

Morel, S. (2018). *El huracán catalan: una mirada privilegiada al laberinto del procés*. Barcelona: Planeta.

Pujol, J. (2011). *Memòries (II). Temps de construir (1980–1993)*. Barcelona: Proa.

Pujol, J. (2012). *Memòries (III). De la bonança a un repte nou (1993–2011)*. Barcelona: Proa.

Silió, E. (2016). '¿Qué comunidades sacan mejor nota en PISA?', *El País*, 7 December <https://politica.elpais.com/politica/2016/12/02/actualidad/1480709130_114964.html> accessed 10 November 2018.

Solé Tura, J. (1985). *Nacionalidades y nacionalismos en España: autonomías, federalismo, autodeterminación*. Madrid: Alianza Editorial.

Termes, J. (1999). *Les arrels populars del catalanisme*. Barcelona: Empúries.

TV3 (2013). 'TV3 Especial Via Catalana – Les Millors imatges de la Via Catalana' [TV3 Via Catalana Special – The best images of the Via Catalana], 11 September <https://youtu.be/iffJ1TgljE0> accessed 2 December 2018.

SORINA SOARE

Romania: The Challenges of Contested Identities

ABSTRACT

The Romanian post-communist legislators rapidly implemented regulations providing facilitated access to Romanian citizenship for those former citizens who had lost their Romanian citizenship against their will or for other reasons not imputable to them – an implicit reference to the inhabitants of those territories that Romania lost to the USSR following the Molotov–Ribbentrop Pact. The current Republic of Moldova (RM) was part of these territorial losses. The chapter examines how the definition of citizenship has evolved in post-communist Romania and the impact of preferential admission to citizenship upon the Romanian-speaking community originating from the RM. The focus of the analysis is the interplay between the demand side (the procedural elements codifying the existence of ethno-national ties) and the supply side (the substantive outcomes of preferential access to citizenship within a specific community).

Since the early days of Romanian post-communism, references – explicit and implicit – have been made to the need to invest in formal and informal relations with the territories of the current Republic of Moldova (RM), which once belonged to the so-called Greater Romania (1918–40). The case of Romania–Moldova is fascinating not only with respect to its Soviet-era and post-Soviet definitions of national identities but, more widely, in the light that its contrary views, implementations and failures may throw on the present escalation of nationalisms evident very clearly in the precarious union of European states. The extent to which its story is their story is a matter for discernment, as the account may serve as a stand-alone review of evolving Moldovan–Romanian relations as well as a pointer to arguments and resolutions relevant to other current and potential nationhood and identity disputes. In the Romanian context, beyond the rhetoric of the slogan 'Basarabia e Romania' [Bessarabia is Romanian land][1] few projects or

1   All translations are my own.

deadlines for unification have been publicly produced over the last two decades.[2] In Moldovan society, competing nation-building plans have blossomed, filtered by divergent nationhood projects and trajectories for regional integration. Meanwhile, *the Moldovan issue* has maintained its relevance in Russian politics as illustrated by the well-known scenario drafted in 2004 by Stanislav Belkovski, which referred to a possible unification of Bessarabia with Romania, endorsed by Russia in exchange for Transnistria's independence. Surprisingly, the Belkovski plan received a degree of positive assessment in Romanian politics, although not officially endorsed (Pop et al. 2005: 86–7). Since then, both in Romania and the RM, several demonstrations in support of the unification have been organized, but without any significant impact. The most recent was organized on 1 December 2018, on the occasion of the centenary of Romanian Unification. Meanwhile, in March 2018, the Romanian parliament had organized a special session dedicated to the anniversary of the unification with Moldova after the First World War. The official statement endorsed the position Romania has taken on the topic of re-unification over recent decades: 'We underline that such an act would depend on their will and we declare that Romania and its citizens are, and will always be, ready to welcome any organic move to reunification by Moldovan citizens as an expression of their sovereign will' (reuters.com 2018). All in all, while the Romanian population has regularly testified its interest in a project of unification, popular endorsement in the RM has not taken off and the Russian position has remained sceptical.[3]

---

2   Among the very limited concrete examples, there is the so called 'Country Project – The Unification with the Republic of Moldova' endorsed by the People's Movement Party (PMP) (Program PMP 2016), echoed by different 2018 declarations of support among the central and local elites of the PMP.

3   According to a March 2018 survey conducted by the Moldovan Center for Sociological Research, among Moldovan citizens, 35 per cent would cast their vote in favour of a project of unification with Romania and 47 per cent against (Adevarul 2018). Note that, in the summer of 2015, endorsement among the Romanian population was 68 per cent (Agerpres 2015).

In this context, the Romanian post-communist legislators rapidly implemented regulations providing facilitated access to the status of Romanian citizens (reacquisition – *redobândire* – of citizenship) for those former citizens who had lost their Romanian citizenship against their will or for other reasons not imputable to them – an implicit reference to the inhabitants of those territories that Romania lost to the USSR following the Molotov–Ribbentrop Pact (Dumbrava 2015; Iordachi 2009; Knott 2018). The Romanian post-communist legislators, endorsed by all the main parties, institutionalized the extension of Romanian citizenship entitlements beyond the circle of national residents, to specifically include those who were no longer residents or nationals but who were historically included within a national definition of the Romanian state (Iordachi 2009). The post-1991 legal changes targeted *in primis* citizens of the current RM, territory lost by Romania in the Second World War. Initially a subject of academic research, with limited public impact, these provisions were to become a topic of Europe-wide debate. News about Moldovans exploiting their Romanian passports in order to gain access to the privileges enjoyed by Romanians as citizens of an EU Member State multiplied in line with widespread immigration concerns among national and European representatives (Knott 2017). In this context, the literature focused intensively on national identity as a particularly useful lens for interpreting the relations between the two countries. Initially, scholars focused on the legal provisions linking specific ethno-national claims and preferential acquisition of citizenship. Progressively, this has been integrated with bottom-up interpretations underlining the motivations of both individuals and their communities for taking advantage of these provisions (Chinn and Roper 1995; Danero 2015; Dumbrava 2014, 2015; Heintz 2008; Iordarchi 2009, 2013; King 2000; Knott 2015; Negură 2013; Waterbury 2014). To my knowledge, there have been no systematic attempts to explore the interplay between the demand side (the procedural elements codifying the existence of ethno-national ties) and the supply side (the substantive outcomes of preferential access to citizenship within a specific community). This chapter is an attempt to fill this gap. The analysis relies on the literature of the complex evolutions in the institution of citizenship, with a special focus on the different impacts of the facilitated practices (and connected experiences) pertaining to the acquisition of a citizenship in line with Brubaker's (1996) triadic nexus (i.e. kin-state, kin-community abroad and home state). It also deals with the implications of these practices for the literature on national identities and, partially, the study of migration (i.e. the literature on the enfranchisement of citizens residing abroad).

In relation to case studies, the premise of this chapter is that an in-depth case study can be more rewarding analytically, as it not only enables the specification of the conditions under which particular outcomes may occur, but also identifies the mechanisms through which they arise (George and Bennet 2005; Yin 2014). A caveat has to be mentioned. While a case study has the advantage of providing an in-depth and multi-layered analysis, a major weakness is connected to its limited capacity to produce scientific generalization. However, a recent scan of the literature reveals a considerable number of scholars who acknowledge that case studies can contribute to scientific development by generating hypotheses and building theory (Flyvbjerg 2006; Steinberg 2015; Yin 2014). The utility of thoroughly executed case studies is connected to the need for a systematic production of exemplars, considering that a discipline without exemplars is ineffective (Steinberg 2015).

In light of the above, the focus on Romanian–Moldovan relations can be justified on various levels. It is a particularly challenging research argument, considering the geopolitical implications of an ongoing process of state-building, as illustrated by the 2014 Crimean crisis or the enduring Transnistrian question, with theoretical inputs for the more general debate on existing kin-relations identity politics in the region. The process of extra-territorialization of the Romanian citizenry in relation to the Moldovan kin-community is, however, far from being a unique case in the post-communist area. Forms of facilitated citizenship acquisition for kin-communities living outside the confines of the national state have been amply documented across the region (Croatia, Bulgaria, Hungary and Serbia) (Ragazzi and Balalovska 2011). The extension of citizenship rights varies greatly: Romanian and Croatian laws entitle their kin-communities to vote; others privilege quasi-forms of citizenship. Accordingly, a focus on Romanian-Moldovan kinship seems to be particularly appropriate, considering the complexity of the institutional relations and their tortuous evolutions over the last twenty-eight years. Initially synchronized, the positions of the institutional actors in Bucharest and Chișinău have remained more or less divergent up to the present day. In parallel, the level of allegiance of the community to the varied offer of citizenship-based practices developed in Bucharest has remained relatively low, if one excludes their participation in parliamentary and presidential elections in Romania in 2009 and 2014. Considering the above, this chapter is based on qualitative material, desk research and primary sources (official statements, public discourses, legal texts, transcriptions of parliamentary debates, official statistics), and the case selection is pragmatically motivated by access to reliable in-depth data covering the perspectives of both supply and demand.

Last but not least, there is a quantitative criterion of relevance. According to international statistics, Romania experienced its highest-ever levels of emigration between 2000 and 2015, and emigration from Romania is considered to be increasing at a faster rate than from any other state not facing a conflict (World Migration Report 2018). Meanwhile, Romania also figures among the European Member States with the lowest levels of immigration, if one excludes the number of citizens 'reacquired' since 1991. Indeed, according to various estimates, the number of Moldovan citizens who 'reacquired' Romanian citizenship reached 800,000 between 1991 and 2017 (Adevărul 2017), of which 175,339 gained Romanian citizenship between 2015 and 2017 (Romanian National Agency for Citizenship statistics quoted by Ziarul National 2018). Beyond the regular caveats when it comes to suspect round figures, different reports insist on a potential underestimation of the number of Romanian citizens with Moldovan origins. This underestimation is due to the fact that the Romanian Agency in charge of the management of the applications of citizenship does not include children in its statistics, but includes them within the individual files of their parents. Considering these caveats, if we refer to the 2014 census, out of the 2,998,235 Moldovans, those with Romanian citizenship would represent approximatively 27 per cent of the population. This explains why the community of Romanians in Moldova represents a central element in the statutory missions of the wide constellation of diaspora-focused institutions covering ministry, inter-ministry and sub-ministry levels since 1995.

With these things in mind, the case of the Moldovan community is treated as representative for post-communist settings (Yin 2014). It is well known that, in the last three decades, the entire area has witnessed a proliferation of policies concerning the integration of diaspora/kin-communities. From the early 1990s, these policies and practices have become central across the region due to the relevant percentages of ethnic-kin communities living in the territory of a neighbouring country or nearby host countries. Across the region also, these policies have challenged the traditionally conceived sovereignty of nation-states and strengthened the diffusion of ethnic political identities. Exploration of the historical background presents the core-elements for the existence of sizeable kin-communities beyond the frontiers of the home-state.

Considering the relevance of these policy interventions (home-states and kin-states; kin-majorities and kin-minorities), this case study has a double theoretical purpose. First, it aims at a better understanding of the dynamics between the supply side and the demand side. More specifically, it aims to identify the practical and symbolic aspects of the policies incorporating kin-communities within the majority society. It also aims to take into account the relevance of additional incorporated benefits such as education, travel, labour aspects. Second, and more modestly, it aims to contribute to the most recent literature, with a focus on the strategic-instrumental approach to citizenship. As such, the main empirical contribution of this text is related to providing an updated overview of the legal provisions for the reacquisition of Romanian citizenship targeted at ethnic Romanians from Moldova.

From a methodological point of view, the analysis contributes to the literature by exploring the interplay between the demand side and the supply side, through providing a more nuanced understanding of the dynamics behind the processes of renationalizing communities. All in all, the conclusions complement the existing solid research in the field by offering, hopefully, new insights in relation to what Harpaz and Mateos (2018: 1–2) call 'the instrumental-strategic attitudes to nationality' (see also Joppke 2018; Knott 2018).

This chapter seeks to map the motives for both providing and seeking Romanian citizenship by focusing on how and why experiences and practices associated with Romanian citizenship located outside the boundaries of the territorial nation-state have evolved into an incomplete equivalence between the status of citizenship and the perception of belonging to an ethnically homogeneous community. All in all, the case under scrutiny provides additional evidence for the current academic debate related to the multiplication of forms of non-exclusive and controversial national memberships. The Romanian citizenship provisions (*redobândire*) echo the symbolic attempt to reproduce a homogeneous national community with close ties of allegiance to the (Romanian) home-state, and hence regularly focus on a narrative praising an ethnically homogeneous group tied to the Romanian state by a primordial identity; on the demand-side, however, the citizenship policies implemented by the Romanian side are less about symbolic resonance and re-inclusion in an organic community, and more about practical outputs such as the rights and privileges connected with access to EU citizenship.

The analysis is structured as follows. Section one specifies the main theoretical framing for the identity politics analysis. Section two examines the historical relations between Romania and the current RM, presenting the different meanings of identity politics across history. Section three presents an analysis of the causal mechanisms connecting nation and citizenship in the Romanian–Moldovan case. The final section concludes with a summary of the main findings.

State under Siege: Kinship and Citizenship in Post-communist Societies – a Theoretical Overview

Following the dismantling of the communist regimes, nationalism has been very much at the forefront of politics. Highly sensitive concepts like nation and national identities have been used in order to rebuild kinship-communities by mobilizing groups that were perceived as sharing historical, ethnic, religious and cultural identity features, even though their members had their residence and legal citizenship in other states (Brubaker 1996). In the wider context of the post-1989 diffused globalization, the traditional understanding of citizenship as the connection between an individual and a polity has been fine-tuned (Nussbaum 1998; Smith 1997; Turner 2000). The literature has pinpointed post-nationalized forms of citizenship in line with the multiplication of forms of (quasi-)citizenship outside the territory of the (national) state's sovereignty (Soysal 1994). One consequence of the extra-territorialization of these forms of citizenship is the fact that ethnicity was not only an issue of domestic policies, but rapidly became a matter of international relations, with consequences ranging from radical and violent resolutions to more accommodative economic relations and cultural policies. While research focused on Western democracies illustrates that post-Second World War disputes between states have generally been resolved in a peaceful manner (Kornprobst 2008), in the post-communist area this complex web of identity affiliation has sown the seeds of discord between sovereign states (Laitin 2001; Saideman and Ayres 2008). Unsurprisingly, scholars have interpreted these ethnicized forms of citizenship as potential sources of violence, due to attempts to achieve congruence between the members of the nation and the borders of the state (Brubaker 1996; Smith 2002). In parallel, the relocation of elements of citizenship outside the national state has also transformed the boundaries of the demos. With increasing immigration, the transformation of the practices of citizenship has become a key element of the literature on the enfranchisement of citizens living abroad (Bauböck 2006; Ellis et al. 2007; Knott 2017; Kostelka 2017; Lafleur 2015). However, the de-territorialization of state has not always been accompanied by a cosmopolitan and de-ethnicized account of citizenship. This is starkly illustrated in relation to the post-Yugoslav case by Ragazzi and Balalovska (2011). From a different perspective, scholars like Fowler (2004) or Knott (2015, 2018) argue that the classic assumption that territoriality and citizenship go together has radically changed. Together with the transformation of international norms on dual citizenship, increased international migration and minority rights regimes, the ability of states to claim exclusive juridical authority in their own territories has diminished (Fowler 2004: 186–7). The upshot is interpreted as 'fuzzy citizenship' (ibid. 205–6). On this basis, scholars like

Joppke (2010, 2018) have chronicled a strategic instrumentalization, and/or 'lightening of citizenship'.

The perspective adopted by the literature has primarily focused on top-down institutional relations (Dumbrava 2014; Iordachi 2009, 2013), and, for a while, little was known about the bottom-up perspective. Few analyses are available on the impact of bottom-up dynamics (Danero 2015; Knott 2015, 2018). The pioneering work of these authors in this field reveals the different perceptions of the kin-group members regarding both their homeland and the kin-state. In addition, Knott (2015) emphasizes the differential demographic and power status of the kin-group: a kin-majority, she rightly argues, cannot relate to the home state as a 'host-state' in the same way that a kin-minority does; in my view, the kin-majority is, at least putatively, the founding political community in the homeland territory.

Drawing on the available literature, from the demand-side perspective, I suggest that a commitment to providing preferential access to citizenship is influenced by both domestic and international inputs. The more consensus there is on the topic in the domestic arena, both in relation to political competition and the population, the more the co-ethnics are targeted as the strategic community to focus on for the preferential acquisition of citizenship. Still, this endeavour can be influenced by the kin-state's engagement in alternative and strategic international socialization projects (e.g. NATO or the EU). Intensive ethno-nationalistic policies for kin-minorities/majorities would most likely not be a reasonable option *vis-à-vis* those international actors with a significant capacity to sanction a widely supported trans-partisan objective such as the EU/NATO project in the Romanian case. At the same time, we can expect that, after achieving the main objective, a change would occur in both the intensity and the content of policies towards kin-majorities/minorities, considering the limited range of post-accession leverages. From the demand-side perspective, one might expect that the desirability of preferential access to citizenship among kin-populations living abroad would depend on the kin-state's capacity to push the targeted population to accept the kin-state not only as pragmatically appealing but also as trustworthy. Moreover, the attractiveness of preferential access to citizenship should increase when the rights regarding the new status are not just combined with political and social entitlements in the kin-state, but also with limited losses in the original community.

Competing Identities: An Historical Perspective on Romanian–Moldovan Relations

Prior to the 1991 declaration of independence the RM had never been an independent state (Chinn and Roper 1995: 293). Situated in a territory with variable geography, its inhabitants have been subjected to various changes and contestations of identities and loyalties. These identity-shaping projects have been interpreted, among others, as proof of an unrealized nation-state (Brubaker 1996), of a weak state and uncertain citizenship (Heintz 2008), and of a territory with no strong and unifying national idea, but a conglomerate of different competing nationalizing agendas acting at separate levels (Negură 2013). Along with redrawing borders and population transfer, a historical overview can illustrate not only the tortuous relationship between Romania and the RM, but also the continuities and discontinuities in various national identity processes with a direct impact upon the different senses of belonging and membership.

Conflicting Processes of Identity-Building (1812–1991)

The historical origins of the medieval provinces covering the territory of Romania and the RM have been blurred by a complex sequence of historical events. First, there is the delayed 'awakening' of the Romanian national consciousness and the nineteenth-century creation of a national and unitary Romanian state, following the union of Wallachia and Moldova. Meanwhile, the Eastern part of the Moldovan territory had been annexed by the Tsarist Empire (1812). In order to increase the allegiance of the new territories to St Petersburg, a process of modernization, urbanization and industrialization backed the tsarist rhetoric of a distinct Moldovan identity (King 2000; Vahl and Emerson 2004; Van Meurs 1994). After 1918, an intensive process of Romanianization was implemented through a top-down nationalizing agenda based on industrialization and schooling/literacy campaigns. Still, the allegiance of local communities to the nationalization process remained partial, while stronger differences arose between the old elite, loyal to Bucharest and the younger generation of elites who supported greater autonomy for Moldova (Negură 2013). By the end of the 1940s, the Soviet-Romanian border was restored on the line agreed after the Molotov–Ribbentrop pact and the 1947 Peace Treaty had confirmed the international recognition of Soviet sovereignty in Bessarabia. The Moldovan Soviet Socialist Republic (MSSR) was created; its inhabitants lost their Romanian citizenship rights and instead received Soviet citizenship.

Meanwhile, in communist Romania, the newly established Popular Republic exhibited strong anti-nationalist principles, stemming from its rigid interpretation of the Universalist-Leninist model, tacitly accepting the annexation of Bessarabia and northern Bukovina by the Soviet Union. As of the late 1950s, the communist regime in Romania progressively adopted policies and symbolic gestures of independence from Moscow. In pursuing an ethnicization of the Communist Party, national variations were introduced and encouraged in public discourses and legal regulations. In line with the nationalist discourse implemented since the early 1970s, the communist Romanian president, N. Ceaușescu, for instance, criticized not only the tsarist annexation of Bessarabia, but also the official position towards the Soviet annexation in the 1940s (King 2000; Van Meurs 1994). However, prior to the fall of the regime in December 1989, the nationalistic rhetoric on Bessarabia was never translated into official talks with Moscow aiming to challenge the post-Second World War frontiers and endorse a project of territorial unification.

Meanwhile, throughout the communist period, the newly established MSSR underwent a modernization process which impacted not only the social structure but also its ethnic composition, while failing, however, to solve the different interpretations of national identity which had coexisted since the nineteenth century. In short order, the MSSR became one of the most Sovietized republics, characterized by high rates of linguistic assimilation towards Russian and high levels of inter-ethnic marriage (Panici 2003). The Moldovan identity crisis re-emerged in the context of Soviet liberalization, as testified by the 20th Congress of the Moldovan Communist Party in 1988, which debated the ethnic problem. The language dispute was eventually solved in favour of recognition of the Latin alphabet and Romanian cultural heritage, as well as the symbolic adoption of a flag similar to the Romanian tricolour, and the Romanian national anthem. From the beginning, reunification was endorsed almost exclusively by urban intellectual elites, while the prevalently rural society was rather sceptical (Negură 2013). Among the weaknesses of the early 1990s project there was also the implicit exclusion of other ethnic and linguistic minorities. Significantly, tensions multiplied in relation to the Turkic-speaking minority (the Gagauz) and the Slavs (mostly of Russian and Ukrainian origins). While the issue of the Republic of Gagauzia was rapidly solved, tensions exploded on the bank of the Dniester River and degenerated into armed confrontations. Romanian-oriented politics was to be progressively dismantled.

Post-Communist Evolutions (1990–2015): Romanian Perspectives

By declaring that 'România este stat național, suveran și independent, unitar și indivizibil' [Romania is a sovereign, independent, unitary and indivisible National State] (art. 1) the post-communist constitution indirectly excluded the significant percentage of the population made up of ethnic minorities (10.53 per cent in the 1992 census). The debates preceding the adoption of the Constitution are highly evocative of this understanding of the nation. Beyond ideological differences, there was a strong consensus among the MPs representing the Romanian majorities (Preda 2001: 745). The only discordant voices belonged to the representatives of the ethnic minorities, in particular the Hungarian MPs. On these grounds, the choice of 1 December as the date for the post-communist national holiday is both a symbolic message to the Hungarian minorities by marking the unification of Transylvania with the Romanian Kingdom in 1918 and an emblematic recollection that this union included the lost provinces of Bessarabia and Bukovina. The organic nature of the Romanian state was further reinforced by the provisions of art. 7 of the Constitution:

> Statul sprijină întărirea legăturilor cu românii din afara frontierelor țării și acționează pentru păstrarea, dezvoltarea și exprimarea identității lor etnice, culturale, lingvistice și religioase, cu respectarea legislației statului ai cărui cetățeni sunt.
>
> [The State shall support the strengthening of links with the Romanians living abroad and shall act accordingly for the preservation, development and expression of their ethnic, cultural, linguistic and religious identity, under observance of the legislation of the State of which they are citizens.]

Although no specific references are made to who 'the Romanians living abroad' are, the article implicitly refers to those kin-groups (e.g. kin-minorities in Ukraine, Bulgaria, Serbia or Hungary and kin-majorities in the RM) that the post-communist state aimed to invest in by fostering historical ethno-cultural, linguistic and religious bonds. Without any attempt to challenge the frontiers and the regional status quo, Romanian international affiliations became an increasingly significant factor in determining not only the diplomatic relations with the home states of these kin-groups, but also the different social and political policies provided by the Romanian state.

The Institutional Level

Since the end of the post-communist period the Romanian position on the Moldovan issue has remained hesitant. The relationship between Romania and the RM was rapidly framed by the complex regional arrangements and Bucharest's westward-oriented foreign policy (Ivan 2009). The risk of ethnic conflict, as well as the complex Russian-Romanian relations and widespread support for European integration, led to a 'bell curve' in the relations with Chișinău (Angelescu 2011: 130). In the early 1990s, official relations were marked by symbolic gestures such as the Bridges of

Flowers,[4] the condemnation of the Molotov–Ribbentrop Pact, and recognition of the RM within two hours of its proclamation of independence on 27 August 1991, all of them leading to a leitmotiv: the celebration of 'the emancipation from the tutelage of Moscow and a first step towards reunification with Romania' (Cebotari and Ejova 2014: 43). In order to catch up with the other Central and Eastern European Countries (CEEC, mostly ex-communist), starting in 1994, national politics voluntarily adapted to the EU requirements and controlled so-called 'politically unfit' behaviour (Gherghina and Soare 2016). In this context, Romanian politicians laid emphasis on the endeavour to promote 'friendly and good-neighbourly relations' and to limit 'the risks of ethnic conflicts to future EU/NATO members (Bulgaria, Hungary) and non-EU/NATO members (Russia, Ukraine and Serbia)' (Angelescu 2011: 131).

The relations with the RM represented a particularly thorny issue, openly exploited by the Transnistrian conflict (Angelescu 2011). The activism of the early 1990s was to be replaced by a pragmatic position. The symbolic involvement of the Moldovan pro-unionist former prime minister in the 1992 Romanian presidential elections and his electoral agenda – the restitution of the Romanian treasure deposited in Moscow during the Second World War or endorsement of the restoration of Romanian citizenship for all Romanians from abroad (Miclescu 2002: 65) – had a limited effect, given that his candidacy received 2.75 per cent of the vote.

The attempts to negotiate a basic treaty between the two countries echoed the complexity of the situation. Neither Romania nor the RM could agree on how to define the nature of their relations, hesitating between the symbolic adjective 'brotherly', compliant with the politics of two Romanian states (favoured among the pan-Romanists) and the neutral 'neighbourly' (widespread among the Moldovanists) (Ivan 2009). The 'two brotherly Romanian states' concept was to be abandoned after the Moldovan 1994 parliamentary elections in favour of a vaguer concept of 'privileged relations'

---

4   The first event was organized by the 'București – Chișinău' Cultural Association and the Popular Front, with an estimated attendance of 1.2 million people (6 May 1990). Romanian inhabitants were allowed to cross the USSR border without a passport or visa. The second event allowed 150,000 Moldovan citizens to cross the Romanian border (6 June 1991).

(Ivan 2009: 123). With the aim of Romania becoming a credible partner for NATO, in the 1996–2000 period, Romanian foreign policy advocated the need for trilateral relations, with the RM being included in a regional cluster with Ukraine (Angelescu 2011). Starting in the early 2000s, the accession negotiations put additional pressure on the Romanian authorities to manage the unsolved problem of a bilateral treaty on good neighbourly relations and friendly co-operation. As of 2001, Romania introduced a visa requirement for citizens of the RM, who had previously been able to enter Romanian territory with just ID cards. While these provisions came into force immediately for all ex-Soviet states, it was postponed in the case of RM citizens until 2005, when a preferential bilateral agreement regulating the visa regime was signed.[5]

Over the last decade, the relevance of Moldovan issues in Romanian politics has remained constant, although, with the exception of the People's Movement Party (PMP), founded in 2013 by supporters of President Băsescu, no parliamentary party has endorsed concrete unification projects. The Moldovan issue occupies a major place in strategic government documents such as the 2016 Foreign Affairs Ministry partnership with the Diaspora or the 2018–20 Program of Government. In terms of the projects managed by the Foreign Affairs Ministry for the diaspora, 22.7 per cent of the available budget was implemented in Moldova. These strategic investments have become a routine aspect of Romanian foreign policy.

During this period, Romania undertook to support the RM through a wide range of instruments such as 100 million euro of non-refundable financing covering infrastructure, education and training (e.g. annual training programs at homologous governmental institutions for prison affairs, diplomats, civil servants and so on), and emergency humanitarian assistance, including, for example, reconstruction of houses flooded in 2010 (Roaid 2016).[6] Economic relations also multiplied. By 2014, there were

---

5   The visa issue was fully resolved, as part of EU visa liberalization, on the eve of the EU Association Agreement signed by the RM in June 2014.
6   Roaid, the International Development Cooperation Agency, is 'the national institutional mechanism devoted to Official Development Assistance, set up by Law 213/2016, under the co-ordination of the Ministry of Foreign Affairs'.

4,500 Moldovan companies in the Romanian capital (Adevarul 2014) and Romania became the RM's prime commercial partner (Relații bilaterale 2016). After fulfilling the goal of becoming an EU member state, Romania invested in advocating the Moldovan cause in Brussels.

In parallel, in terms of party politics, while – with the exception of the national-populist Greater Romania Party (PRM) – all the parliamentary parties endorsed the Moldovans' Romanian identity, no party raised the Moldovan question openly until around the middle of the first decade of the new century. Even in the case of the PRM, the nationalistic rhetoric was dominated more by the Magyar issue in Transylvania than by unification with Moldova. It was mainly under the Băsescu presidency (2004–9, 2009–14) that the union with Moldova became an open topic of discussion. After the 2007 enlargement, Romania was actively involved in providing political, diplomatic and economic support to the Moldovan European project. The thesis of a reunification between Romania and the RM was boosted during President Băsescu's second mandate when, in 2013, he declared that, after the achievement of the first two strategic objectives, namely membership of NATO and the EU, the next goal should be union with the RM within the EU (Angelescu 2011). By the 2016 parliamentary elections, with differences of intensity, all the parliamentary parties had focused on the special Romania–Moldova relationship, and the topic of unification has become one of the flagship issues for the PMP.

The Bottom-up Perspective

In direct connection with the above, although Romania has recognized the electoral rights of its citizens living abroad since the 1990s, it is in the context of the 2008 electoral reform that Romania has allowed external voters to form separate constituencies to elect their representatives. The system of reserved seats implemented in 2008 and maintained after the 2016 amendment of the electoral law gave a major weight to Romanian voters abroad. In this context, as demonstrated by Knott (2017), Bădescu and Burean (2016) and Popescu (2012), Romanian voters in RM provide the most relevant part of Romanian diaspora voters in terms of absolute numbers. This element, coupled with the impact of these votes in extremely tight elections (2008, 2009 and 2014), has induced the main parties to open local offices in Chișinău, the capital of Moldova (Bădescu and Burean 2016). However, beyond the unanimous assessment that Moldovan votes are important electoral capital, the involvement of Romanian parties across the Prut has remained underdeveloped in comparison with the professionalized organizations in Romania.

However, the capacity of a home-state to implement engagement policies for its kin-communities cannot be exclusively connected with an institutional approach conducted through foreign service or business-focused initiatives. The Romanian state's constant interest in reinforcing claims of shared national identities fails to mobilize the home-community. Ghinea et al. (2011) identified a rather complex landscape when it comes to the way Romanians relate themselves to RM. While Romanians strongly endorsed a project of unification with the RM, they had limited contact with the Moldovan community, either through travel or within forms of socialization (Ghinea et al. 2011: 11–12). Significantly, over 64 per cent of Romanians considered that unification would be more beneficial to the interests of Moldovans than Romanians, and their endorsement of a unification project waned significantly when they were asked questions on the financial costs (Ghinea et al. 2011: 88). All in all, symbolic references have surfaced during electoral campaigns or public speeches, emblematic official visits have been organized, and pro-unionist groups launched but, to date, close to thirty years after the fall of the Berlin Wall, the project of unification is far from capturing the public imagination.

Post-Communist Evolutions (1991–2015): Moldovan Perspectives

Since the late 1980s, Moldovan politics has been torn between contradictory feelings about relations with Romania. Definition of the ethnic composition of the RM is a significant contributor to this issue. Using the same ethnic categories as in the communist period, according to the official data Moldovans constitute the largest declared ethnic group, accounting for 63.9 to 75.8 per cent of the population. The other major ethnic groups are Ukrainians, Russians, Gagauz and Bulgarians. The Romanian ethnic group accounted for less than 1.0 per cent of the population under the communist regime and 2.2 per cent in the 2004 census (*Recensamantul populatiei* 2004: 30). Notable also is the presence of small numbers of Jews, Belarusians, Poles and Roma. Despite the methodological bias identified in relation to ethnic identity, the categories were maintained in the 2014 census. The issue of this complex ethnicity must be integrated with what King (1997) called the politics of language. Since the early 1990s, the complex linguistic debate on the distinctiveness of the Moldovan language corpus after the abandonment of the Cyrillic alphabet in 1989 has been politically driven. While for the Romanian scientific community it has been largely taken for granted that the idea of a distinct Moldovan language was and still is a political construction, lacking scientific or linguistic foundation given the limited differences in terms of vocabulary or grammar between the two languages, in 1994 the Constitution of Moldova enshrined its distinctiveness: 'Limba de stat a Republicii Moldova este limba moldovenească, funcționând pe baza grafiei latine' [The State language of the Republic of Moldova is the Moldovan language, and its writing is based on the Latin alphabet] (art. 13 (1)). Up to this point, in recent years, the 1991 declaration of independence took precedence over the constitutional codification.

However, and more specifically, in December 2013, the Moldovan Constitutional Court ruled that the official language is Romanian, based on detailed references to the historical context and technical expertise (The Constitutional Court, 2013). With no implementation of this constitutional amendment, the pro-European Liberal Democratic Party in 2017 initiated a proposal to amend Article 13 of the constitution in favour of Romanian. Once again the Constitutional Court of Moldova delivered a positive opinion in favour of Romanian, considering the legal changes from Moldovan to Romanian a mere 'technical' matter. However, President Igor Dodon vocally criticized the initiative and proposed instead to handle the language issue through a referendum. In a tense climate, the project of change to Romanian was blocked by the Parliament in Autumn 2018.

Considering the different fault lines established over time around specific interpretations of Moldovan identity, in the early 1990s the pan-Romanianist discourse lost public support and the balance of power shifted to a soft-Moldovanism (1994–8). The 1994 non-binding national identity referendum confirmed the prevalence of the sovereigntist view: 95.4 per cent of the participants voted against union with Romania. A short-lived soft Romanianism characterized Moldovan politics from 1998 to 2001. The Moldovanist discourse was permeated by radicalism under the Communist Party of Moldova (2001–9) in line with widespread Soviet-era symbolism and an emphasis on a U-turn on economic reforms (Tudoroiu 2011: 240). After the electoral victory of the Pro-Democratic alliance in 2009, a soft Romanianism became the reference point for politics in Chișinău. In 2014, the legislative elections maintained a weak pro-European parliamentary majority, which was rapidly destabilized by the events of 2015 and early 2016.[7] The 2016 presidential elections marked a turnabout in the RM's relations with Romania when the first election by direct vote in two decades resulted in the victory of the pro-Russia candidate, Igor Dodon. A former Minister of the Economy in two communist cabinets (from 2006 to 2009), Dodon placed emphasis on the need to strengthen ties with Russia and expressed his opposition to the trade deal signed with Brussels in 2014, endorsing instead RM membership of the Eurasian Economic Union. In parallel, Romania was openly targeted as the enemy, particularly in relation to elements of soft-power deployed on the RM territory (e.g. scholarships, funds for NGOs, etc.), which were considered to be part of a strategy of unionism. The same interpretation was applied to the conflict in Transnistria. According to President Dodon, the conflict

---

7   Moldovan society had been progressively inflamed by a banking scandal involving the disappearance of 1 billion dollars and the falsification of his diplomas by the Prime Minister, Chiril Gaburici, who was eventually obliged to resign in June 2015. The difficulties faced by the pro-European parties in forming a government were partially solved by the minority government backed by the Communist Party in July 2015. By the beginning of 2016, new tensions had emerged following a controversial ruling of the Constitutional Court, which cancelled the constitutional amendments that, since 2000, had allowed parliament to elect the Head of State.

broke out only because of Moldova, because Moldova wanted unification with Romania:

> Totul a început din cauza faptului că la Chișinău au existat minți fierbinți, care au dorit unirea cu România. [...] Eu înțeleg că în primul rând vina este a conducerii Moldovei, eu asta recunosc. Eu de nenumărate ori am spus că noi trebuie să recunoaștem asta și să ne cerem scuze, deoarece au murit sute, mii de cetățeni. Desigur asta nu se uită, eu pe ei îi înțeleg foarte bine, dar trebuie să privim în viitor.
>
> [It all started because of the hot minds in Chișinău who wanted to unite Romania and Moldova. [...] In my understanding, it is first the fault of the Moldovan leadership, I recognize that. I have repeatedly said that we must recognize this and apologize for the deaths of hundreds, thousands of citizens. Of course, they cannot simply forget, I understand them very well, but we have to look to the future.] (I. Dodon quoted by Adevarul 2016)

In direct connection with this statement, Dodon expressed his intention to amend the Education Law by changing the subject 'Romanian History' to 'Moldovan History'. All in all, Romania is presented as a threat to RM's security and, in his understanding, people holding double citizenship should not hold leading positions (TRM 2016).

Today, close to thirty years after independence, three major political interpretations of the Moldovan identity coexist. The Moldovanists advocate the consolidation of Moldovan statehood and a balanced East-West orientation in foreign policy; within this perspective two main subtypes coexist: an exclusive Moldovanism which promotes the existence of Moldovan ethnicity distinct from Romanian identity, and an inclusive civic interpretation, based on a stand-alone agenda, which attempts to integrate other ethnic and linguistic groups. The pan-Romanianists adopt a different stance: they deny the existence of a Moldovan identity, militating in favour of a common Romanian history and culture. This agenda has an openly Western orientation and endorses projects of unification with Romania, ranging from an accommodative and elastic interpretation of Romanianism to an exclusivist and radical pro-unionist position. The third group refers to a Euroasianist vision, widespread among supporters of reintegration into the zone of Russian influence, who are consistent promoters of anti-Romanianism. The most recent political evolutions in Chișinău have increased the relevance of the Moldovanist supporters. This change of perspective in Moldovan politics is a direct result of President Dodon's critical voice regarding alleged Romanian irredentism. Symbolically, in March 2017, President Dodon stripped the former Romanian president, T. Băsescu, of his recently obtained Moldovan citizenship.[8] Tensions with Bucharest multiplied, as illustrated by reactions to the publicized gift received by president Dodon from President Putin during a visit to Moscow in January 2017. The object of controversy was a 1790 map, drafted during the Russian-Ottoman war, representing Greater RM, including the current homonym Romanian province, northern Bukovina and a part of the Romanian Dobrogea region.[9] President Dodon's insistence on signing a Border Treaty with Romania has further stressed the relations with Bucharest. This treaty has been regularly postponed by the Romanian authorities, who consider it a *de jure* recognition of the aggressive 1939 Molotov–Ribbentrop Pact, which became the basis of the current RM. Pro-Russian forces in Moldova have regularly interpreted Romania's refusal to sign the treaty as proof of their commitment to a strategy of reunification.[10]

It is noteworthy that Moldovan citizens have not actively reacted to these controversies, which are for the most part elements of party competition and less socially relevant. As illustrated by Knott, the prevalence of socio-economic issues linked to the process of democratization (employment, corruption, migration, etc.) account for the limited impact of the identity issue on society. After so many years since the RM declaration of independence, not only does Moldovan national identity remain a political object with blurred origins in line with the competing interpretations fed by systematic alternations in power and politicized surveys, but the Romanian position continues to be lost in an equilibrium of strategic diplomacy and in ambiguous ethno-nationalistic relations with its kin-majorities/minorities.

---

8   Traian Băsescu became a Moldovan citizen on 3 November 2016.
9   On this occasion, President Dodon declared: 'Half of today's Romania is actually Moldova' (balkaninsight.com 2017).
10   A detailed account is available at moldovanpolitics.com (2016).

Romanian Kin-state Policies: Co-optation through Citizenship

Following Brubaker, citizenship can be described as 'a universal feature of the modern political landscape. Every state formally attaches to the status of citizenship certain rights, including usually political rights, and certain obligations' (Brubaker 1989: 30). Given this, the citizenship debate in post-communist Romania not only refers to the rights and obligations of political and social membership, but also to (symbolically) belonging to a nation-state with distinctive identity features that are supposed to reinforce the in-group amity within and beyond the current frontiers. The importance of delineating membership of the post-communist state is illustrated by the adoption of the succinct decree law no. 7, nine days after the fall of Ceauşescu's regime. The main focus of the decree is to guarantee the right of repatriation to all Romanian citizens residing abroad (art. 1) and the reacquisition of citizenship by former Romanian citizens living abroad (art. 2). Beyond the symbolic investment in bridging the gap with (former) Romanians living abroad during the communist regime and rebuilding a post-communist community, the importance of this 12-article decree relates to the implicit recognition of dual citizenship (Iordachi 2013; Muraru and Tănăsescu 2011).

Modelled on the traditional *ius sanguinis* principle, active since its first codifications in the nineteenth century (Iordachi 2009), the new citizenship legislation was defined in March 1991. Within the transitory and final dispositions, the legal text included provisions regulating the situation of former Romanian citizens who had lost Romanian citizenship for various reasons before 22 December 1989, who may reacquire it on request, even if they have a different citizenship and do not wish to establish residency in Romania. Those from whom Romanian citizenship was withdrawn against their will or for other reasons – as well as their descendants – are held blameless in this regard. Though apparently redundant, an important difference is put forward by Iordachi (2013: 11): the first paragraph refers to cases of individual losses of citizenship, whereas the second covers denaturalization *en masse* following territorial changes. By allowing these new citizens to retain the citizenship of their current homeland, a new legal category was produced: non-resident dual citizens living in neighbouring countries (Iordachi 2013: 11). It is precisely this category of citizenship that allows us to evaluate the Romanian state's interest in bridging the gap between the autochthonous community and kin-communities, tantamount to the manifestation of an attempt to undo the unjust deprivations brought about by communist rule (Dumbrava 2014; Iordachi 2013).

By 2000, the provisions on the reacquisition of citizenship were clarified. Romanian citizenship could be granted to persons who had lost it and to their descendants to the second degree. The reacquisition of citizenship applied to minors too, while it did not have any direct consequences upon the citizenship of a spouse. In direct connection with the agreement on Romanian citizens' visa-free travel in the Schengen space, these provisions were temporarily suspended in 2001 before being implemented again in 2003. Meanwhile, a significant change was introduced through emergency ordinance no. 62/2002: this single article unified the previous provisions on the reacquisition of citizenship with the restoration. Emergency ordinance no. 43/2003, however, brought further changes. Former Romanian citizens who had lost their Romanian citizenship against their will, or for reasons that could not be imputed to them, before 22 December 1989, as well as their descendants up to the second degree, could reacquire it, but they had to comply with almost all the conditions for the naturalization of foreign citizens, including command of the Romanian language. Considered to be an indicator of ethnic selectivity, this specific provision was to be removed by emergency ordinance no. 36/2009. In response to criticisms formulated by different EU Member States against pragmatic reacquisitions of citizenship – the Romanian passport was seen as a key, giving access to the EU labour market – a new provision introduced a limitation on freedom of movement for former citizens during their first four years of citizenship (Iordachi 2013). Numerous non-governmental organizations from Romania and Moldova criticized this provision as a form of open discrimination, leading to its cancellation by emergency ordinance no. 52/2007. The legal text issued in 2007 openly declared its aim was to speed up procedures for dealing with the high number of applications for restoration of citizenship, which were taking an average of three and a half months to process (Iordachi 2004: 254). Between 2007 and 2017, thirteen amendments were produced that redefined the citizenship framework. Among the most relevant changes is the simplified citizenship restoration procedure. Most of the following changes focused on correcting deficiencies in the administrative procedures or speeding up the bureaucratic process.

In brief, three main stages can be identified in the process of post-communist regulation of citizenship. The early 1990s regulation delineated a permissive frame of reference with a symbolic focus on the restoration of citizenship, motivated by the aim of repairing the injustices of the past. In parallel with the criticisms raised by EU member states in relation to the opportunistic reacquisition of citizenship incentivized by the 2001 visa-free agreement, a temporary closure of the system occurred. In the years that followed the first manifestation of dissent over application of the regulation on an inclusive basis, Romania modified the terms of reference as a response to potential criticisms from Brussels. Filtered by new provisions such as command of the Romanian language or limitations to freedom of movement, the attitude of the Romanian legislator from 2001 until 2007 was mainly guided by rational cost-benefit calculations. On the eve of accession, the rewards of EU membership triggered a restriction in the application of principles formally still motivated by the moral obligation to repair the injustices of the past. It is only after 2007 that the system progressively reopened. Pressure from civil society and increased awareness among legislators themselves of the deficiencies of the bureaucratic process led to multiple amendments aimed at rationalizing the efficiency of the reacquisition process. The pace of the changes further increased following the personal involvement of President Băsescu in managing the content of the necessary amendments.

Lost in Dual Citizenship Practices and Experiences

By the end of the 1990s, Romania's investment in maintaining relations with kin-minorities/majorities based on the facilitated reacquisition of citizenship had raised numerous criticisms of hidden nationalism and irredentism from within the RM, in particular after 1994. The timing of these criticisms was in line with the profusion of the Moldovanist vision in local politics. Political investment in the sovereigntist option for Moldova explains the virulence of criticisms of the provisions for restoring citizenship. In parallel with the imposition of a radical Moldovanism between 2001 and 2009, the reactions of criticizing and voicing discontent shifted to boycotting such things as educational agreements that promoted student mobility to Romania.

From 1994 until 2009, rhetoric focused on two principal issues: dual citizenship in Moldova and an 'expansionist' Romania. Apart from the legal incompatibilities, debates on the first issue focused on the consequences of dual allegiance in terms of loyalty and sovereignty. The partial amendment of the Moldovan constitutional provisions on citizenship in 2002, together with the consequent changes in the Law on Citizenship, helped to ameliorate the issue (Gasca 2012). The alleged attacks on sovereignty remained a leitmotiv of the argument. President Lucinski judged the proliferation of dual Moldovan-Romanian citizens to be a strategic attempt to increase Bucharest's control throughout the lands of the former Greater Romania (Iordachi 2004: 253–4). Indeed, following the 2000 Moldovan law on citizenship, the foreign minister was charged with identifying and denaturalizing all persons who held dual citizenship, in an indirect reference to Romanian-Moldovan citizens. The virulence of these attacks increased under the Voronin presidency. In order to counterattack against Romanian interests, Chișinău invested in strengthening Moldovan identity by symbolically supporting the publication of a Moldovan-Romanian dictionary and a history of Moldova. The 2004 census further illustrated the politicization of the ethnic dimension, as the Moldovan Institute of Statistics included two distinct options of ethnic affiliation: Moldovan and Romanian. The fact that only 2.2 per cent of the population chose to identify as Romanian (compared with 75.8 per cent as Moldovan) was used by the authorities as proof of the weakness of the unionist project, while Romanian and other pro-Romanian local intellectuals accused the census of methodological bias (Negură 2013).

By 2009 the range of reactions had diversified. The authorities in Chișinău imposed a visa regime on Romanian citizens. In a public statement, President Voronin declared that Moldova would lift the visa requirements when the EU, of which Romania is a member, did so for Moldovans (rferl. org 2009). Such criticisms targeted an implicit collusion between Bucharest and Brussels. Within this context, the incompatibilities maintained by the amended version of the law prohibiting people with dual citizenship from holding certain categories of public office triggered criticisms not only from institutions such as the Commission against Racism and Intolerance of the Council of Europe and the Venice Commission, but also from Romanian members of the European Parliament, who asked the Council and the European Commission to examine its conformity with EU norms (Gasca 2012: 19). The European Court of Human Rights upheld the complaint of two leading Moldovan politicians, both holders of dual Romanian and Moldovan citizenship, who claimed that these provisions infringed their human rights (Gasca 2012: 19). Beyond the court's decision, this claim is particularly relevant in illustrating the European ramifications of the tensions generated by applying the restoration of citizenship to former Romanian citizens at an international/European level. It is also an important heuristic for assessing the different fault lines dividing Moldovan politics.

In 2009, President Vladimir Voronin spoke about a new 'iron curtain' raised by the EU against Moldovan citizens. Speaking on national television, he said: 'What the European Union is doing to Moldova is not good. To open Europe only for those Moldovan citizens who hold Romanian passports is humiliating for the Moldovan people. They should not insult us and make us travel to Europe via Romania' (euobserver.eu 2009). In the same period, E. Boc, the Romanian Prime Minister, publicly rejected allegations by the Voronin presidency that facilitating acquisition of Romanian citizenship by Moldovan citizens had strategic value in Romanian foreign policy (euobserver.eu 2009). The atmosphere became particularly heated on the occasion of the 2009 elections; protesters demanded repeat elections.

But the citizenship issue was becoming almost peripheral by the time that President Voronin, with backing from Russia, accused Romania of an attempted *coup* through manipulation of the emotions of its young people. Meanwhile, Bucharest denied all the allegations and its Foreign Minister declared that Romania continued support for closer ties between Moldova and the EU. After 2010, in line with the pro-European synergies between Bucharest and Chișinău, the level of tension diminished.

By 2014, it was further reduced by the abolition of the visa regime for Moldovan citizens travelling in the EU. Still, the potential for tensions remained latent, given the diplomatic incident linked to the expulsion of a Romanian citizen, the leader of the Action 2012 platform at the gathering of Moldovan and Romanian NGOs for the union of the RM with Romania (balkaneu.com 2015).

The frontiers of these institutional clashes are somewhat porous. The complexity of the kinship issue and its impact on citizenship status is illustrated by the case of Ilie Ilascu, a former member of the Moldovan Popular Front known for his opposition to the creation of a Transnistrian Republic.[11] Arrested and sentenced to death by a Transnistrian court, he became a symbol for national identity both in the RM and Bucharest. Imprisoned in Tiraspol, Ilascu became a Moldovan MP in 1998 and, two years later, was elected to the lists of the national-populist PRM in the Senate of Bucharest. His fast-track acquisition of Romanian citizenship put him in clear breach of both Romanian and Moldovan law: President Luchinski's rejection of Ilascu's renunciation of Moldovan citizenship put the newly elected Romanian senator in breach of Moldovan law; similarly, according to the Romanian Constitution, non-resident citizens could not stand in national elections. But the Romanian parliament validated his mandate (Iordachi 2004: 251). Given his notoriety, both the Romanian and Moldovan authorities treated the violation of their legal framework as an exceptional situation. Accorded such special status, he received the highest order of Romania, 'The Star of Romania', on 10 May 2001, and, together with other colleagues charged by Tiraspol with terrorist allegations, 'The Star of Moldova' on 2 August 2010. Ilascu was to regain public attention in both countries when, in 2013, threatened with the loss of public housing granted by the Romanian authorities, he received wide press coverage and eventually retained his state housing privileges.

In the wider European context, alarmist news about the impact of the facilitated reacquisition of citizenship by former citizens had multiplied immediately after the Commission recommended opening negotiations with Romania in March 1999. Various other international actors intervened. The

11   A detailed account of the case is provided by Iordachi (2004).

'expansionist' power of Bucharest was used by the Kiev authorities as a reason to criticize the implementation of a permissive citizenship restoration policy. In this context, various Western cabinets voiced their concern that double citizenship was an opportunity for Moldovan citizens to bypass the visa system for the Schengen area. Despite the temporary suspension of the procedures for the restoration of citizenship in Bucharest, the Western media estimated that between 650,000 and 1 million people would migrate within the EU's borders after the accession of Romania (Dumbrava 2013). President Băsescu himself contributed to the diffusion of these estimates and conspiracy theories.[12]

If we change perspective and look at the direct beneficiaries, Moldovan citizens, the first difficulty concerns the unavailability of official statistics. The various estimates available in the press or in different statements tend to clash with figures provided by NGO reports or the official figures of the National Authority for Citizenship (NAC). According to data provided by the NAC (2016), there were over half a million requests for the reacquisition of Romanian citizenship, including applications from Moldavans, over a period of fourteen years (2002–April 2016). A major increase in the number of applications received and processed was observed after 2009, in the aftermath of the implementation of simplified procedures, with an overall 54.6 per cent of the applications received being registered in the three years 2010 to 2012. The lifting of the last restrictions in 2014 led to a slight increase in the number of applications registered between 2015 and 2017 (NAC 2017).

Note that the National Authority does not collect data on applicants' motivations. It is, therefore, difficult to provide an assessment of the relationship between strategic and symbolic acquisition of Romanian citizenship. The pioneering work of Panainte et al. (2013) identified a mix of pragmatic and idealistic motivations. Job market requirements after graduation were the main motivation, while the need to legally confirm Romanian identity was mentioned exclusively in relation to stories told by acquaintances. For other scholars, the pragmatic dimension prevails too: Gasca's

---

[12] In 2009, president Băsescu voiced his support for speeding up the process of restoration of citizenship, given that, according to him, over 1 million Moldovans, a quarter of the population, 'would become, not from a moral, but a legal point of view, members of the European family' (www.euractive.com 2009).

analysis suggests that 'the acquisition of dual citizenship does not make Moldovan citizens less patriotic' (2012: 15). Other scholars maintain that citizenship applications have an instrumental dimension, allowing applicants to enjoy the benefits of citizenship of an EU Member State, while claiming a Romanian national attachment (Danero 2015). These interpretations are in line with surveys on the issue, considering that fewer than 25 per cent of Moldovans endorse the unification project (BPO 2018). Knott (2015) provides a more nuanced interpretation by identifying motivations for the reacquisition of Romanian citizenship according to five types of identification with Moldova and/or Romania: organic Romanians; cultural Romanians; ambivalent Romanians; Moldovans; and Linguistic Moldovans. With the exception of Linguistic Moldovans, all categories expressed their interest in, or had already engaged in, processes of reacquisition of citizenship for complex and intricate reasons (e.g. security, benefits of EU citizenship, etc.) and symbolic motivations.

Analyses focusing on the issue of migration in Romania support these observations. Alexe and Păunescu depict a nuanced landscape, although no specific differences are made between Moldovans with and without Romanian passports. They observe that unlike immigration from China and Turkey, Moldovan migrants are attracted more by education and employment opportunities than by entrepreneurial activities (Alexe and Paunescu 2010). The focus on education is in line with other studies. Moldovan beneficiaries of scholarships for secondary, university and post-university education funded by the Romanian state justify their interest mainly in relation to the quality of the education system or the opportunities provided by the job market in Romania. Interviewees quoted by Gamurari et al. declared: 'Toată lumea din Chișinău reacționează pozitiv când știe că tu ai făcut facultatea în România' [People in Chișinău react positively when they know that you went to college in Romania]; 'Niciodată nu m-am gândit la posibilitatea de a face facultatea în Moldova. Pentru că știam din start cum stau lucrurile acolo. Nu există oportunități de dezvoltare, nu există piață de muncă, nu putem vorbi de transparență și corectitudine' [I never thought about the possibility of going to college in Moldova. I knew from the very start how things work here. There are no opportunities for development, no job market, there is no transparency or fairness] (Gamurari et al. 2013: 6).

Despite the emphasis on the opportunities provided, scholarships in smaller Romanian towns are less attractive, and sizeable percentages of the budget are not allocated (6 per cent in the 2007–8 academic year, 10 per cent in 2008–9, 4 per cent in 2009–10, 18 per cent in 2010–11 and 36 per cent in 2011–12). Moldovans complain about limited financial resources and suggest a reorganization of the system, with fewer scholarships and more funding. Owing to these financial limitations, most students are obliged to work illegally, as the administrative procedures for the legal employment of residents are considered complex (Gamurari et al. 2013: 7–8). Still, 80 per cent of foreign citizens studying in Romanian universities come from Moldova; the attractiveness of the Romanian higher education system is increased not only by the numerous scholarships but also by potential access to the EU higher education system. In relation to the job market, the Moldovan community is mainly employed in the building sector, clothing, commerce, banking and financial services, as well as agriculture.

If we focus on Romanian society, behind symbolic support for the project of unification, the relationship with the kin-community from the RM is more complex. Ghinea et al. (2011) show that the RM is not a territory of major interest for Romanian citizens; not only do they not travel regularly to the RM (only one in four has ever visited the RM) but they declare relatively few direct personal contacts with people originating from the RM and the eastern bank of the Prut. When it comes to perceptions of the Moldovan community, Romanians are more likely to designate the inhabitants of the RM as Moldovans or as citizens of the RM than to refer to them as Romanians, or as Romanians of Moldova, or Russified Romanians or Bessarabians (Ghinea et al. 2011).

Conclusions

As Angelescu notes (2011: 131), 'the question of identity affected not just the talks about a possible reunification, but more general relations between Moldova and Romania'. The competing, and sometimes conflicting, questions of identity have had an impact on the meaning of state sovereignty. More specifically, the complex politics of identity have challenged the international sovereignty of the RM, considering that various groups in Romania, including the former Prime Minister Druc, interpreted the 1991 recognition of the RM's independence as a strategic mistake. Following the same logic, the former president Băsescu depicted the reunification of the two territories as a reparatory act for the abuses of the Molotov–Ribbentrop Pact. In relation to domestic sovereignty, the implementation of a permissive regulation on the reacquisition of Romanian citizenship was considered a voluntary infringement of the loyalty due from Moldovan citizens to their home state. In 2007, while simultaneously raising territorial claims to Romania's province of Moldova, President Voronin accused Romania of being the last European empire (Iordachi 2009). Signs of tense relations multiplied, including the 2009 declaration that the Romanian ambassador in Moldova was *persona non grata*, while Romanian officials laid emphasis on the non-reciprocal expulsion of the Moldovan ambassador. Chișinău imposed a visa regime on Romanian citizens, making Romania the only EU member state whose citizens required a visa (euobserver.eu 2009).

At a general level, the principal conclusion is that the analysis of Romanian–Moldovan relations reveals an emblematic case of the prevalence of diplomacy over confrontation, demonstrating that, beyond the Crimean case, radical forms of ethnic-derived politics are far from being the only political solution in the region. At an institutional level, the case under scrutiny illustrates that a kin-state can influence domestic politics in relation to the kin-community outside its borders, particularly through material aid (e.g. structural investments, grants, etc.) and political support (e.g. lifting visa requirements, relations with the EU, etc.). However, the position of the kin-state, Romania, as a key actor within Moldovan politics is limited by its unstable relations with the relevant parties in power, as well as by its weak capacity to mobilize support within the kin-community as a whole. The heart of the matter is that co-ethnicity is not fully recognized by the kin-community in RM and this weakness has been fully exploited by pro-Russian political parties since 1994 (Knott 2015, 2017, 2018). Indeed, Romania's portfolio of programmes and policies for RM has been regularly used as proof of an attempt to cultivate disloyalty to their state among Moldovan citizens.

Given all this, the present analysis contributes to theoretical work on nations and national identities by providing a more nuanced understanding of the dynamics behind the processes of renationalizing communities. Beyond these observations, the analysis points to the fact that Romanian legislation promoted a distinct, territorially defined citizenship (Knott 2016; Waterbury 2014); the definition of a particular case of restored citizenship, seen as a reparatory act for historical injustices, was based on proofs of descent from citizens living in former Romanian territories. Accordingly, Moldovan citizens are perceived as natural members of the national Romanian community, since they are direct descendants of the original inhabitants of a Romanian province. Proof of linear descent includes elements that pull together the members of the same ethnic group beyond current borders: having language, religion, history, myths and symbols in common. Within Moldovan politics, rejection and/or reticence prevails over unification projects. These conclusions join previous research on the puzzling synchronization between the deterritorialization of the state and the continued ethnicization of citizenship in the Balkans (Ragazzi and Balalovska 2011). Indeed (from the demand side) in Romania, as in Croatia or Serbia, it is possible to equate the practices of citizenship for kin-communities with forms of post-territorial nationalism, in which potential irredentism is hermetically controlled by the constant adherence of the parties in government to recognition of the sovereignty of the Moldovan state. As in Croatia (Knott 2017), emotive and reparative justifications have provided the core elements of Romanian law on Citizenship since 1991. However more pragmatic logics increasingly prevail, particularly when it comes to the relevance that the 'electoral capital' of the kin-community represents for the parties in Bucharest. From the perspective of the supply side, heterogeneity is the key word, with instrumental-strategic attitudes cohabitating with both emotional investments and hostility towards Romanian citizenship.

At the beginning of this chapter, I suggested that preferential access to citizenship is influenced by both domestic and international considerations. With regard to the home-state, it is intuitive that if the definition of who belongs to the kin-community is consensually assessed by both political parties and the citizenry, the easier it is for co-ethnics to be considered as strategic investments in rebuilding an organic community. However, this consensual assessment could be fine-tuned by the kin-state's engagement with international socialization projects (e.g. those of NATO and the EU). Meanwhile, we expect the desirability of preferential access to citizenship among kin-populations living abroad to depend on the kin-state's capacity to push the targeted population to accept it not only as pragmatically appealing, but also as trustworthy. In parallel, I suggested that the level of attractiveness of preferential access to citizenship among the kin-population should increase when the rights regarding the new status are combined not just with political and social entitlements in the kin-state, but also with limited losses in the original community. In relation to these assumptions, the analysis has illustrated that in Romania, since the early 1990s, privileged relations with the RM have been unanimously and consistently endorsed by both the political community and civil society. Because of this consensus, the Moldovan issue has never been a divisive topic in the political arena. Scholars like Waterbury have nevertheless identified a potential domestic outcome: the incentives for a wide incorporation of new Romanian citizens of Moldovan origins are instrumental to a change in the demography of Romania and, more specifically, to diluting the impact of the ethnic Hungarians (Waterbury 2014: 40). However, until the 2007 enlargement and even afterwards, Romania voluntarily aligned with European benchmarks not only on such matters as an accelerated rate of transformation on delicate issues like the market economy or justice reform, but also on foreign policy. In brief, in order to secure EU accession, Romanian parties in power refrained from any 'politically unfit' behaviour. The endeavour to promote positions that could be interpreted as irredentist was particularly obvious in the early 2000s. The intensity of involvement in relations with the RM increased in the aftermath of EU integration and has been a pillar, particularly, of the second mandate of President Băsescu. Turning to the supply-side perspective, the desirability of Romanian citizenship among the Moldovan community is difficult to assess. According to the limited data available, a complex pragmatic dimension prevails, although symbolic motivations are particularly important for certain groups. Prior to the 2014 visa-free agreement, the desire to have access to the free circulation area increased the appeal of a Romanian passport. Similarly, elimination of transitional restrictions on migrant workers in Romania should maintain the high pragmatic interest in joining the Romanian community. More detailed and structured information on the motivations is needed. Knott's illuminating ethnographic research on the Moldovan kin-majority is a major contribution to this open space of analysis, and more in-depth research into this would provide additional impetus to current theoretical debates on post-territorial citizenship.

Bibliography

Adevarul (2014). 'S-a creat o nouă Cameră de Comerț și Industrie Republica Moldova–România', 19 July <http://adevarul.ro/moldova/economie/s-a-creat-noua-camera-comert-industrie-republica-moldova-romania-1_53ca169f0d133766a8905047/index.html> accessed 28 August 2018.

Adevarul (2016). 'Dodon: De războiul civil din Transnistria este vinovat Chișinăul, fiindcă și-a dorit unirea cu România. Trebuie să ne cerem scuze! [Dodon: The war in Transnistria is Chisinau's fault, because Chisinau wanted the union with Romania. We have to apologize]', 16 December, <https://adevarul.ro/moldova/politica/dodon-razboiul-civil-transnistria-vinovat-chisinaul-fiindca-si-a-dorit-unirea-romania-trebuie-cerem-scuze-1_5853e4005ab6550cb87c4a4b/index.html> accessed 28 August 2018.

Adevarul (2017). 'Un milion de Moldoveni cu cetățenia Română', 1 April <http://adevarul.ro/cultura/patrimoniu/un-milion-moldoveni-cetatenia-romana-1_58df4b7e5ab6550cb8de564a/index.html> accessed 28 August 2018.

Adevarul (2018). 'Sondaj: 35 % din cetățenii Republicii Moldova ar vota pentru unirea cu România', 4 April <http://adevarul.ro/moldova/politica/sondaj-35-cetatenii-republicii-moldova-vota-unirea-romania-1_5ac4b858df52022f75686fce/index.html> accessed 28 August 2018.

Agerpres (2015). 'Sondaj IPP Chișinău: Doar 21 % din cetățenii R.Moldova ar vota pentru unirea cu România la un referendum', 8 December <http://www.agerpres.ro/externe/2015/12/08/sondaj-ipp-chisinau-doar-21-din-cetatenii-r-moldova-ar-vota-pentru-unirea-cu-romania-la-un-referendum-15-22-41> accessed 28 August 2018.

Alexe, I., and Păunescu, B. (eds) (2010). *Studiu asupra fenomenului imigrației în România. Integrarea străinilor în societatea românească*. Bucharest: Fundația Soros România & Asociația Română pentru Promovarea Sănătății.

Angelescu, I. (2011). 'New Eastern Perspectives? A Critical Analysis of Romania's Relations with Moldova, Ukraine and the Black Sea Region', *Perspectives*, 19 (2), 123–41 <http://www.fundatia.ro/proiectul-%E2%80%9Estudiu-asupra-fenomenului-imigra%C5%A3iei-%C3%AEn-rom%C3%A2nia-integrarea-str%C4%83inilor-%C3%AEn-societatea-rom%C3%A2n> accessed 28 August 2018.

Bădescu, G., and Burean, T. (2016). 'Migrant political culture and voting behavior in Romania', Paper presented at the ECPR General Conference, Prague <https://ecpr.eu/Events/PaperDetails.aspx?PaperID=31191&EventID=95> accessed 11 July 2019.

balkaneu.com (2015). 'Romania seeks explanations after unionist militant expelled from Moldova', 16 May <http://www.balkaneu.com/romania-seeks-explanations-unionist-militant-expelled-moldova/#sthash.1KQeBXu2.dpuf> accessed 28 August 2018.

balkaninsight.com (2017). 18 January. <http://www.balkaninsight.com/en/article/putin-s-old-moldova-map-alarms-romania-01-18-2017#sthash.fr7aeBJV.dpuf> accessed 28 August 2018.

Bauböck, R. (2006). 'Citizenship and Migration – Concepts and Controversies'. In R. Bauböck (ed.), *Migration and Citizenship: Legal Status, Rights and Political Participation*, IMISCOE Report, pp. 15–31. Amsterdam: Amsterdam University Press.

BPO (2018). Barometer Public Opinion (Barometrul Opiniei Publice), November. Institutul pentru Politici Publice. <http://ipp.md/wp-content/uploads/2018/05/BOP_05.2018_sondaj.pdf> accessed 11 July 2018.

Brubaker, R. (1989). 'The French Revolution and the Invention of Citizenship', *French Politics and Society*, 7 (3), 30–49.

Brubaker, R. (1996). *Nationalism Reframed: Nationhood and the National Question in the New Europe*. Cambridge: Cambridge University Press.

Cebotari, S., and Ejova, C. (2014). 'The Evolution of Republic of Moldova Relations with Romania (1991–2013)', *Studia Universitatis Moldaviae*, 3 (73), 43–9.

Chinn, J., and Roper, S. D. (1995). 'Ethnic Mobilization and Reactive Nationalism: The Case of Moldova', *Nationalities Paper*, 23 (2), 291–325.

Constituția Republicii Moldova (1994) <http://lex.justice.md/document_rom.php?id=44B9F30E:7AC17731> accessed 28 August 2018.

Constitution of Romania. (1991) <http://www.cdep.ro/pls/dic/act_show?ida=1> accessed 28 August 2018.

The Constitutional Court. (2013). Judgment on the interpretation of Article 13, par. (1) of the Constitution in correlation with the Preamble of the Constitution and the Declaration of Independence of the Republic of Moldova (Applications No. 8b/2013 and 41b/2013). <http://www.constcourt.md/public/ccdoc/

hotariri/en-Judgment-N036-of-5122013-on-Romanian-Language-eng82ea4. pdf> accessed 27 February 2019.

Danero, I. J. (2015). 'Ukraine, Romania and Romanians in Ukraine', *Südosteuropa: Journal of Politics and Society*, 62 (3), 372–83.

Dumbrava, C. (2013). 'Rolling back history: the Romanian policy of restoration of citizenship to former citizens', *CISEE*, 15 April <http://www.citsee.eu/citsee-story/rolling-back-history-romanian-policy-restoration-citizenship-former-citizens> accessed 28 August 2018.

Dumbrava, C. (2014). *Nationality, Citizenship and Ethno-Cultural Belonging: Preferential Membership Policies in Europe*. Basingstoke: Palgrave Macmillan.

Dumbrava, C. (2015). 'Super-Foreigners and Sub-Citizens. Mapping Ethno-National Hierarchies of Foreignness and Citizenship in Europe', *Ethnopolitics*, 14 (3), 296–310.

Ellis, A., Navarro, C., Morales, I., Gratschew, M., and Braun, N. (2007). *Voting from Abroad: The International Idea Handbook*. Stockholm: International Institute for Democracy and Electoral Assistance (IDEA); Mexico City: Instituto Federal Electoral (IFE), <https://www.idea.int/publications/catalogue/voting-abroad-international-idea-handbook> accessed 11 July 2019.

euobserver.eu (2009). 'No more than 30,000 Moldovans to receive EU citizenship', 30 April <https://euobserver.com/political/28039> accessed 28 August 2018.

euractive.com (2009). 'Romania offers citizenship to Moldovans', 15 April <http://www.euractiv.com/justice/romania-offers-citizenship-moldo-news-221728> accessed 28 August 2018.

Flyvbjerg, B. (2006). 'Five Misunderstandings About Case-Study Research', *Qualitative Inquiry* 12 (2), 219–45.

Fowler, B. (2004). 'Fuzzing citizenship, nationalising political space: A framework for interpreting the Hungarian Status law as a new form of kin-state policy in Central and Eastern Europe'. In Z. Kántor, B. Majtényi, O. Ieda, B. Vizi, and I. Halász (eds), *The Hungarian status law: nation building and/or minority protection*, pp. 177–238. Sapporo: Slavic Research Center.

Gamurari, L., Ganea, O., and Ghinea, C. (2013). 'Perspective pe termen lung ale bursierilor din Republica Moldova', *CRPE Policy Memo*, n.50 <http://www.crpe.ro/perspective-pe-termen-lung-ale-bursierilor-din-republica-moldova-experienta-si-oportunitati-de-cariera> accessed 28 August 2018.

Gasca, V. (2012). 'Country report: Moldova', EUDO citizenship observatory <http://eudo-citizenship.eu/docs/CountryReports/Moldova.pdf> accessed 28 August 2018.

George, A. L., and Bennet, A. (2005). *Case Studies and Theory Development in the Social Sciences*. Cambridge, MA: The MIT Press.

Gherghina, S., and Soare, S. (2015). 'A Test of the EU Post-Accession Influence: Comparing Reactions to Political Instability in Romania', *Democratization*, 23 (5), 1–22.
Ghinea, C., Horváth, I., Popescu, L., and Stoiciu, V. (2011). *Republica Moldova in constiinta publica romaneasca*. Bucharest: Fundaţiei Soros România.
Harpaz, Y., and Mateos, P. (2018). 'Strategic citizenship: negotiating membership in the age of dual nationality', *Journal of Ethnic and Migration Studies*, 45 (6), 843–57 <https://www.tandfonline.com/doi/full/10.1080/1369183X.2018.1440482> accessed 21 March 2019.
Heintz, M. (2008). 'State and citizenship in Moldova: a pragmatic point of view'. In M. Heintz (ed.), *Weak state, uncertain citizenship: Moldova*, pp. 1–18. Frankfurt am Main: Peter Lang.
Iordachi, C. (2004). 'Dual Citizenship and Policies toward Kinminorities in East-Central Europe: a Comparison between Hungary, Romania and the Republic of Moldova'. In Z. Kantor, B. Majtényi, O. Ieda, B. Vizi, and I. Halász (eds), *The Hungarian status law: nation building and/or minority protection*, pp. 239–69. Sapporo: Slavic Research Center.
Iordachi, C. (2009). 'Politics of citizenship in post-communist Romania: Legal traditions, restitution of nationality and multiple memberships'. In R. Bauböck, B. Perchinig, and W. Sievers (eds), *Citizenship policies in the new Europe*, pp. 177–210. Amsterdam: Amsterdam University Press.
Iordachi, C. (2013). 'Country report: Romania', EUDO citizenship observatory <http://eudo-citizenship.eu/admin/?p=file&appl=countryProfiles&f=2013-19-Romania.pdf> accessed 28 August 2018.
Ivan, R. (2009). *La politique étrangère roumaine (1990–2006)*. Bruxelles: Editions de l'Université de Bruxelles.
Joppke, C. (2010). *Citizenship and Immigration*. Cambridge: Polity Press.
Joppke, C. (2018). 'The instrumental turn of citizenship', *Journal of Ethnic and Migration Studies*, 45 (6), 858–78 <https://www.tandfonline.com/doi/abs/10.1080/1369183X.2018.1440484> accessed 21 March 2019.
King, C. (1997). 'The Politics of Language in Romania and Moldova', Wilson Centre <https://www.wilsoncenter.org/publication/147-the-politics-language-romania-and-moldova> accessed 28 August 2018.
King, C. (2000). *The Moldovans. Romania, Russia, and the Politics of Culture*. Stanford, CA: Hoover Institution Press.
Knott, E. (2015). 'What does it mean to be a kin majority? Analyzing Romanian identity in Moldova and Russian identity in Crimea from below', *Social Science Quarterly*, 96 (3), 830–59.
Knott, E. (2016). 'The extra-territorial paradox of voting: the duty to vote in extra-territorial elections', *Democratization*, 24 (2), 325–46.

Knott, E. (2017). 'Contesting regimes of post-communist citizenship restitution: analysing UK media coverage of "paupers' passports"', *Central and Eastern European Migration Review*, 6 (1), 75–97.
Knott, E. (2018). 'Strategy, identity or legitimacy? Analysing engagement with dual citizenship from the bottom-up', *Journal of Ethnic and Migration Studies*, 45 (6), 994–1014 <https://www.tandfonline.com/doi/abs/10.1080/1369183X.2018.1440494> accessed 21 March 2019.
Kornprobst, M. (2008). *Irredentism in European Politics: Argumentation, Compromise and Norms*. Cambridge: Cambridge University Press.
Kostelka, F. (2017). 'Distant souls: post-communist emigration and voter turnout', *Journal of Ethnic and Migration Studies*, 43 (7), 1061–83.
Lafleur, J.-M. (2015). 'The Enfranchisement of Citizens Abroad: Variations and Explanations', *Democratization*, 5 (22), 840–60.
Laitin, D. D. (2001). 'Secessionist Rebellion in the Former Soviet Union', *Comparative Political Studies*, 34 (8), 839–61.
Miclescu, C. (2002). Cotroceni gară pentru doi. Politici electorale comparate în campaniile prezidențiale de la televiziune 1990, 1992, 1996, 2000. Bucharest: All.
Moldovanpolitics.com (2016). 'Moldovan-Romanian Relations Under a Dodon Presidency: Off to a Rocky Start' 2 December <https://moldovanpolitics.com/2016/12/02/2200/> accessed 11 July 2019.
Muraru, I., and Tănăsescu, E. S. (2011). *Drept constitutional și instituții politice*, vol. I, Bucharest: Editura C. H. Beck.
NAC (2016). 'Official data citizenship 2002–2016' (Response to written query. Nr.8056/ANC/25.03.2016).
NAC (2017). *Annual Report of Activity, Year 2017 – National Authority for Citizenship* (Raport anual de activitate, anul 2017 – Autoritatea Națională pentru Cetățenie), <http://cetatenie.just.ro/images/raport_anual_activit__ANC_2017_pentru_MJ_2.pdf> accessed 11 July 2019.
Negură, P. (2013). 'Competing nation-building projects in Bessarabia, Transnistria, and the Republic of Moldova: Deconstructing a Plural Identity', Paper presented at Leipzig University on the invitation of Leibniz-Institut für Länderkunde, Leipzig, 28 October. <http://petrunegura.blogspot.it/2013/11/competing-nation-building-projects-in.html> accessed 28 August 2018.
Nussbaum, M. C. (1998). *Cultivating Humanity: A Classical Defense of Reform in Liberal Education*. Cambridge, MA: Harvard University Press.
Panainte, S., Nedelciuc, V., and Voicu, O. (2013). *Redobândirea cetățeniei române: o politică ce capătă viziune?* Fundația Soros <http://fundatia.ro/sites/default/files/ro_125_Raport%20Cetatenie.pdf> accessed 28 August 2018.
Panici, A. (2003). 'Romanian Nationalism in the Republic of Moldova', *The Global Review of Ethnopolitics*, 2 (2), 37–51.

Pogonyi, S. (2011). 'Dual citizenship and sovereignty', *Nationalities Papers*, 39 (5), 685–704.
Pop, A., Pascariu, G. C., Anglițoiu, G., and Purcăruș, A. (2005). 'Romania and the Republic of Moldova – between the European Neighbourhood Policy and the prospects of EU enlargement', European Institute of Romania – Pre-accession impact studies III. <http://ier.gov.ro/wp-content/uploads/publicatii/Pais3_studiu_5_en.pdf> accessed 27 February 2019.
Popescu, B. (2012). 'Out-of-Country Voting – Participation in Elections of Romania Diaspora', *Studia Politica*, 9 (1), 94–110.
Preda, C. (2001). 'La nation dans la Constitution', *Studia Politica*, 1 (2), 733–62.
Ragazzi, F., and Balalovska, K. (2011). 'Diaspora Politics and Post-Territorial Citizenship in Croatia, Serbia and Macedonia', *CITSEE Working Paper*, No. 2011/18 <http://dx.doi.org/10.2139/ssrn.2388857> accessed 28 August 2018.
Recensamantul populatiei (2004). 'Caracteristicile demografice, nationale, lingvistice, culturale, Biroul Național de Statistică al Republicii Moldova' <http://catalog.ihsn.org/index.php/catalog/4272/download/56169> accessed 28 August 2018.
Relații bilaterale (2016). <http://www.mae.ro/bilateral-relations/1677> accessed 28 August 2018.
reuters.com (2018). 'Romanian parliament says would back reunification with Moldova', 27 March. <http://www.reuters.com/article/us-romania-moldova/romanian-parliament-says-would-back-reunification-with-moldova-idUSKBN1H32CS> accessed 27 February 2019.
rferl.org (2009). 'Moldovan President Praises Russia, Accuses Romania of "Revisionism"', 24 June <http://www.rferl.org/content/Moldovan_President_Praises_Russia_Accuses_Romania_Of_Revisionism/1761999.html> accessed 28 August 2018.
RoAid (2016). <http://www.roaid.ro/page/republica-moldova-66> accessed 28 August 2018.
Saideman, S. M., and Ayres, R. W. (2008). *For Kin or Country: Xenophobia, Nationalism, and War*. New York: Columbia University Press.
Smith, D. J. (2002). 'Framing the national question in Central and Eastern Europe: a quadratic nexus?', *The Global Review of Ethnopolitics*, 2 (1): 3–16.
Smith, R. M. (1997). *Civic Ideals: Conflicting Visions of Citizenship in U.S. History*. New Haven, CT: Yale University Press.
Soysal, Y. N. (1994). *Limits of Citizenship: Migrants and Post-national Membership in Europe*. Chicago: University of Chicago Press.
Steinberg, P. F. (2015). 'Can We Generalize from Case Studies?', *Global Environmental Politics*, 15 (3), 152–75.

TRM (2016). 'Igor Dodon presents part of electoral program', 5 October <http://trm.md/en/electorala-2016/igor-dodon-si-a-prezentat-o-parte-din-programul-electoral/> accessed 28 August 2018.

Tudoroiu, T. (2011). 'Structural factors vs. regime change: Moldova's difficult quest for democracy', *Democratization*, 18 (1), 236–64.

Turner, B. S. (2000). 'Liberal citizenship and cosmopolitan virtue'. In A. Vandenberg (ed.), *Citizenship and Democracy in a Global Era*, pp. 18–32. Basingstoke: Macmillan.

Vahl, M., and Emerson, M. (2004). 'Moldova and the Transnistrian Conflict', *Journal of Ethnopolitics and Minority Issues in Europe*, 1, 1–29 <http://www.ecmi.de/fileadmin/downloads/publications/JEMIE/2004/1-2004Chapter4.pdf> accessed 28 August 2018.

Van Meurs, W. P. (1994). *The Bessarabian Question in Communist Historiography: Nationalist and Communist Politics and History-Writing*. New York: East European Monographs.

Waterbury, M. A. (2014). 'Making Citizens Beyond the Borders', *Problems of Post-Communism*, 61 (4), 36–49.

The World Factbook 2016–17. Washington, DC: Central Intelligence Agency. <https://www.cia.gov/library/publications/the-world-factbook/index.html> accessed 27 February 2019.

World Migration Report. (2018). <https://www.iom.int/wmr/world-migration-report-2018> accessed 28 August 2018.

Yin, R. K. (2014). *Case Study Research Design and Methods*. Thousand Oaks, CA: Sage.

Ziarul National. (2018). 'Numărul cetățenilor R. Moldova care obțin cetățenia României, în CREȘTERE permanentă: Peste jumătate de milion de basarabeni și-au redobândit identitatea românească', 14 April <http://www.ziarulnational.md/numarul-cetatenilor-r-moldova-care-obtin-cetatenia-romaniei-in-crestere-permanenta/> accessed 28 August 2018.

IÑIGO URRUTIA

The Constitutional Crossroads in Spain

ABSTRACT
Since the Constitutional Court ruling (31/2010) – which included the declaration that interpretation of references to Catalonia in the 2006 Statute of Autonomy as 'a nation' and to its 'national reality' were devoid of legal effect – the Spanish central government has taken approaches to territorial power distribution which have had increasingly severe negative impacts on the autonomy of the Basque Country and Catalonia. Specifically, while the Basque and Catalan Autonomous Communities have begun to question why the current model cannot adapt to some of the more ambitious expectations of self-government, in the Spanish State the present model of devolution has been questioned precisely for the opposite reason: a perception that the model has gone too far. Facing such a complex panorama, this chapter examines the characteristics of the current Constitutional crossroads in Spain, proposing a new constitutional consensus based on the development of democracy and deepening of human rights.

The Starting Point

Throughout recorded history, Spain has been subject to the acquisition and the imposition of so many 'identities', ethnic, religious and social, that their reconciliation under the banner of a single 'State' remains to this day one of the most difficult problems faced by any government. It is little wonder, then, that the model of political decentralization in Spain has suffered constant political tensions since its inception.

Although the Basque nationalist parties did not take part in the constitutional consensus, the 1978 Constitution acknowledged the uniqueness of the Basque provinces, on the basis of historical rights. The first Additional Provision of the 1978 Constitution states as follows:

> La Constitución ampara y respeta los derechos históricos de los territorios forales. La actualización general de dicho régimen foral se llevará a cabo, en su caso, en el marco de la Constitución y de los Estatutos de Autonomía.
>
> [The Constitution protects and respects the historic rights of the territories with traditional charters (fueros). The general updating of historic rights shall be carried out, where appropriate, within the framework of the Constitution and of the Statutes of Autonomy.]

The historical rights of the Basque territories engage directly with claims of a right to special status for the Basque territories, based on the idea of the constitutional recognition for a subject: the Basque people.[1] The constitutional recognition of the forality (Basque ancient legal order) means the legal recognition of the existence of a Basque Country, which has the capacity to govern by itself and for itself (Lasagabaster 2014: 129). The recognition by the 1978 Constitution of these historical specialties was considered by the Basque nationalist parties and the supporters of the ancient law of Navarre as a tool that allowed the Southern Basque territories (the Autonomous Community of the Basque Country and Navarre) a greater degree of autonomy than other regions in Spain. Through this recognition, the Basque territories could design and implement public policies in education, public safety, economic development, and environmental protection, along with a full taxation and financial capacity. Over time, however, this interpretation was challenged legally by the restrictive view of the Constitutional Court in several judgements on the legal scope of the historical status.[2] Consequently, this has reduced the possibility for an asymmetric development of the self-government system, allowing the central state to define the extent of regional powers. Likewise, taxation and financial autonomy, which was initially considered to be a full power of the Basque territories to finance their competencies, has been subjected to central State supervision and control.

---

1. See also the Additional Provision of the Statute of Autonomy of the Basque Country, and the first Additional Provision of the Statute of Autonomy of Navarre (so called LORAFNA).
2. See Constitutional Courts' Decision no. 76/1988 (2 and 4 legal basis); no. 76/1988 (4 legal basis); no. 140/1990; no. 148/2006; and no. 208/2012.

At the very same time as the Spanish Constitution of 1978 was approved, the problem of the territoriality of the Basque Country arose.[3] Two separate autonomous communities were created, one for Navarra and another for the rest of the Basque provinces. The territorial configuration was rigidly established, and also consolidated by the constitutional prohibition of federations between autonomous communities.[4] In any case, the 1978 Constitution introduced a special clause for an eventual territorial integration of all the Basque territories.

Following the fourth Transitional Provision of the Spanish Constitution:

> En el caso de Navarra, y a efectos de su incorporación al Consejo General Vasco o al régimen autonómico vasco que le sustituya, en lugar de lo que establece el artículo 143 de la Constitución, la iniciativa corresponde al Órgano Foral competente, el cual adoptará su decisión por mayoría de los miembros que lo componen. Para la validez de dicha iniciativa será preciso, además, que la decisión del Órgano Foral competente sea ratificada por referéndum expresamente convocado al efecto, y aprobado por mayoría de los votos válidos emitidos.
>
> [In the case of Navarre, and for the purpose of its integration into the General Basque Council or into the autonomous Basque institutions which may replace it, the procedure contemplated by section 143 of this Constitution shall not apply. The initiative shall lie instead with the appropriate historic institution (órgano foral), whose decision must be taken by the majority of its members. The initiative shall further require for its validity the ratification by a referendum expressly held to this end and approval by the majority of votes validly cast.]

This clause has never been implemented.

The Statute of Autonomy of the Basque Country was passed in 1979, and then approved by a referendum.[5] In Navarre, the Statute of Autonomy was approved in 1992 by a unique procedure, as an Improvement of the Ancient Legal Charter, and without a referendum.[6]

---

3   With regard to the precedents see the Statute of Autonomy for the Basque Country of 1936.
4   See article 145.1 of the Spanish Constitution.
5   Organic Law 3/1979, of 18 December, on the Statute of Autonomy for the Basque Country.
6   Organic Law 13/1982 of 10 August, on Reintegration and Improvement of the Historical Regime of Navarre.

The Statute was drafted with a view to attributing to the Autonomous Community of the Basque Country (ACBC) all the powers and competencies not reserved by the 1978 Constitution to the central state. It also recognizes the right of the ACBC and of Navarre to almost full financial autonomy through the system of economic agreement or 'covenant'. Also recognized were the powers of the ACBC to manage essential public services such as education and health, welfare and public safety as well as a number of powers in economic matters, such as in agriculture, fisheries, transport and communications, housing, industry and energy.[7]

The major political parties in Spain (minor parties in the Basque Country) have consistently tried to impose conditions on Basque self-government. This was reflected in the Autonomy Agreements signed by the major political parties, which we will refer to below. All the self-government reforms prior to 2004 had been promoted and largely controlled by the central government with the support of both the party in office and the main nation-wide opposition party. In 1981, the two major political parties agreed on the first (so-called) Autonomy Agreement. That Agreement closed the definitive map of autonomous communities in Spain and determined the competencies of each one. It also established the internal organization of the autonomous communities, recognizing legislative powers to all of them, and created a homogenous system of relations between the central state and the autonomous communities, to the detriment of the bilateral relationship established in the Statute for the Basque Country. In short, the agreement was designed to control the timing and the process by which the Autonomous Community would acquire greater powers.[8]

---

7   See Articles 9, 10, 11, 12 of the Statute of Autonomy of the Basque Country.
8   On the basis of this first Autonomy Agreement, the Organic Law for Harmonization of the Autonomy Process was adopted, regulating aspects of the management of the autonomic process, and also developing the scope of the powers of the State. The Constitutional Courts' Ruling no. 76/1983, of 5 August, overturned much of the content of this law, saying that it contained merely an interpretation of the Constitution, intruding upon the jurisdiction of the Constitutional Court. Since then, the definition of the power-sharing system has been fixed by the Constitutional Court through numerous rulings.

In 1992, the second Autonomy Agreement came into force as a result of a new pact between the two major nation-wide political parties. The aim of this second agreement was to make equal the competencies of all autonomous communities.[9] At the end of the 1990s, and as a result of these top-down reforms, the Statutes of Autonomy of all the autonomous communities formally reached similar levels of power. This egalitarian approach would adversely affect the historical autonomous communities, which would be limited to levels of powers not exceeding the standards accepted by the state parties, also limiting bilateral agreements to strengthen their autonomy. Autonomy was hence homogenized.

The Proposal to Reform the Statute of Autonomy of the Basque Country of 2004: A Missed Opportunity

In December 2004, the Basque Parliament passed a proposal to reform the Statute of Autonomy of the Basque Country (entitled Proposal for a New Political Statute of the Community of the Basque Country). Any reform of a Statute of Autonomy, although formally initiated and proposed by the Autonomous Community's Parliament, had to be submitted to the Spanish Parliament for approval.[10] The proposal was adopted by the Basque Parliament, by absolute majority. In January 2005, it was sent to the Spanish Parliament to be debated and voted on.[11]

---

9   This was performed firstly by a Transfer Law (authorized by Article 150.2 of the Constitution) on the basis of which some state powers were transferred to the Autonomous Communities – Law 9/1992 of 23 December; and secondly, the Statutes of Autonomy were reformed in 1994, accommodating their content to the competencies previously transferred to the Autonomous Communities.
10 See article 147.3 of the Spanish Constitution.
11 In Spain the Statutes of Autonomy are finally adopted by an Organic Law of the Spanish Parliament (Cortes Generales) requiring the favourable vote of the absolute majority of the Congress of Deputies (the lower chamber).

On 1 February, the consideration of the proposal for a new Statute for the Basque Country was refused by the Spanish Parliament. The Basque proposal was firmly rejected at the initial stage of submission. The reason for the rejection was the proposed new scheme for the relationship between the Basque Country and the Spanish state, based on a free association status, on the grounds that it was not in line with the Constitution. The central state tried by every means to avoid any discussion on the merits of the proposal approved by the Basque Parliament, using arguments of legitimacy and legality, thereby avoiding a democratic debate (Lasagabaster 2005: 1035). The Spanish Parliament thus prevented an actual debate on the quality of Basque autonomy and the will of the Basque institutions as representatives of the Basque people (Lasagabaster 2005).

In fact, the three pillars of the new proposal were the following: first, the recognition that the Basque people have their own identity; second, the legal acknowledgement of the right to decide the community's own future and its relations with the Spanish state; and third, the statute of autonomy would turn the Basque Country into a community freely associated with the Spanish state, with the potential for further change according to the principle of self-determination.

Article 13.3 of the Proposal for a New Political Statute of the Community of the Basque Country contained a clear expression of the democratic principle, harnessing the future legal status of the Basque Country to the popular will. On the basis of this democratic legitimacy, the Political Statute prescribed that, in the case of a clear majority vote of the Basque people in favour of sovereignty or independence, both the Spanish State and the Autonomous Community would be compelled to start a negotiation process. This system was based on the doctrine established by the Supreme Court of Canada to which we will refer later.

Two further features of the proposed reform that also aimed at preserving areas of exclusive competence for the Basque institutions were the mechanisms for power distribution and the system of self-government guarantees. The distribution of powers was set on the basis of 'public policies' rather than on a functional division of competences. The objective was to avoid unilateral interference by the central government in areas attributed to the Basque Country (Jauregi 2005: 1010). Thus, in those areas in which the proposal determined that the Community of the Basque Country could develop public policies, the central state would have no power to intervene without the consent of the Basque institutions. The new system of legal guarantees was based on the principles of mutual institutional loyalty, co-operation and balance of powers (Article 14 of the proposal). Two mechanisms for conflict resolution were proposed: the Basque Country–Spanish State Bilateral Commission (Article 15) and a special chamber in the Constitutional Court (Article 16).

After the proposal's rejection by the Spanish Parliament, the Prime Minister of the ACBC in 2008 promoted the approval of a Basque law regulating a public consultation for the purpose of ascertaining opinion in the ACBC on starting negotiations in order to achieve peace and political normalization. In June 2008, the Law was finally passed by the Basque Parliament.[12] However, the president of the Spanish government brought an unconstitutionality appeal against it, which was approved by the Constitutional Court in its Ruling no. 103 of 2008, declaring the Basque law unconstitutional:

> La Ley recurrida presupone la existencia de un sujeto, el 'Pueblo Vasco', titular de un 'derecho a decidir' susceptible de ser 'ejercitado' [art. 1 b) de la Ley impugnada], equivalente al titular de la soberanía, el Pueblo Español, y capaz de negociar con el Estado constituido por la Nación española los términos de una nueva relación entre éste y una de las Comunidades Autónomas en las que se organiza. La identificación de un sujeto institucional dotado de tales cualidades y competencias resulta, sin embargo, imposible sin una reforma previa de la Constitución vigente.
>
> [The appealed law presupposes the existence of a subject, the 'Basque people' holder of a 'right to decide' likely to be 'exercised' [art. 1 b) of the contested law] equivalent to the holder of sovereignty, the Spanish people, and able to negotiate with the State constituted by the Spanish nation the terms of the new relation between the state and one of the Autonomous Communities in which it is organized. The identification of an institutional subject provided with such qualities and authorities is, however, impossible without a previous reform of the current Constitution.][13]

12 See <http://parlamento.euskadi.net/pdfdocs/leyes/y20080009_f_cas.html> accessed 16 August 2018.
13 Constitutional Court Ruling no. 103/2008 of 11 September, 4th legal basis (English translation by the services of the Constitutional Court).

The argument of the Court reveals the existence of different conceptions of the democratic principle. For the Basque institutions, the law was considered to be a tool to channel popular will and popular legitimacy, to start a process for changing the current sharing of power. In contrast, the Spanish government understood the Constitution as non-negotiable, as it was so considered by the Constitutional Court.[14]

True to the Spanish state's traditional aspiration to uniformity, the only holder of sovereignty, the Spanish state, interprets territorial unity in the strictest possible sense. In short, Spanish institutions were unwilling to increase self-government as an acknowledgement of the right to decide. However, as we shall see later, the Constitutional Court has recently ruled again on the constitutionality of the right to decide, loosening its previously rigid interpretation.

The Crossroads

After a 2010 ruling in the Constitutional Court (31/2010), the central powers of the Spanish state have taken a recentralization approach to power distribution, with an increasingly severe impact on the quality of autonomy in the Basque Country and Catalonia. Specifically, some communities (especially the Basque and Catalan Autonomous Community) have begun to question why the current model cannot adapt to some of the most ambitious expectations of self-government; in the Spanish state, the present model of decentralization has been questioned precisely for the opposite reason, with arguments that the current model of political decentralization has gone too far. For the first time since the transition to democracy, representatives of the central powers of Spain favoured self-government involution, with the preference now for centralism and cuts in the self-government powers of the current autonomy framework.

14 This was the term used by the Supreme Court of Canada in the Reference re Secession of Quebec, [1998] 2 S.C.R. 217.

As a result of the current crisis of territorial organization in Spain, several scenarios can be discerned.

First, some legal scholars are in favour of a constitutional reform in order to centralize de jure the Spanish state. They argue that the distribution of power between the state and autonomous communities is obscure, inefficient and inadequate (Muñoz Machado 2012: 125; Fernández Rodríguez 2013). In fact, a rethinking of the relationship between the central state and autonomous communities is proposed, giving advantage to the former. The use of harmonization laws is also proposed as a means of reconciling the rulemaking provisions of autonomous communities. The ability of central legislature to enact harmonization laws is provided for in Article 150.3 of the Constitution:

> El Estado podrá dictar leyes que establezcan los principios necesarios para armonizar las disposiciones normativas de las Comunidades Autónomas, aun en el caso de materias atribuidas a la competencia de éstas, cuando así lo exija el interés general. Corresponde a las Cortes Generales, por mayoría absoluta de cada Cámara, la apreciación de esta necesidad.
>
> [The State may enact laws laying down the necessary principles for harmonizing the rulemaking provisions of the Self-governing Communities, even in the case of matters over which jurisdiction has been vested to the latter, where this is necessary in the general interest. It is incumbent upon the Cortes Generales, by overall majority of the members of each House, to evaluate this necessity.]

In addition, the legislative power of the Autonomous Community is called into question.

Second, more nuanced positions can be observed, suggesting that the decentralized system has worked reasonably well, serving to both encourage political participation and also to foster the development of each region in Spain (Quadra-Salcedo 2012; Sánchez Morón 2013).

Third, there is another view, also characterized by dissatisfaction with the current political development, but arguing for the breaking up of the constitutional agreement. These critics claim that the political autonomy of autonomous communities serves only to manage the policies of the central state (Viver 2011). This view leads to political positions demanding constitutional reform aimed at federalizing the state, and even to political positions supporting full sovereignty on the basis of the right to decide (Lopez 2015: 35).

All in all, there are different political options, increasingly far-removed from one another, and giving rise to difficulties when it comes to reaching a new constitutional consensus. In fact, we really are at a crossroads where we are witnessing two opposing processes of nation-building.

There has been an economic crisis, and also a constitutional and values crisis in Spain. In this context, there is a need to rethink the current system of distribution of powers between the central government and the autonomous communities.[15] Beyond purely jurisdictional issues, new perspectives are needed to cope with questions about the territorial configuration of the state, and address the claims for a greater degree of sovereignty raised by Catalonia and the Basque Country. The recent legal reforms driven by the central government are moving along another road, that of a nation-building process, with the aim of centralizing the Spanish state and making it uniform. From the opposite perspective, there is clear dissatisfaction with the current development of power sharing and the decrease in regional powers, giving rise to proposals for a very different constitutional reform, in a federal direction (Seijas 2013: 24) or towards the full sovereignty of autonomous communities. The latter involves a second process of nation building, of a constituent character.

Adapting the Legal Frame of Reference to Political Changes

The right to self-determination is a constantly evolving right which will continue to develop in the future. We should note that this right has not undergone the same development in all geographical or historical contexts, and the conditions governing it are still debated, with a range of views regarding its scope and the validity of this right when applied to

---

15   See Muñoz Machado (2012: 45) and Quadra-Salcedo (2012) for the view that the regional model and the territorial distribution of power have worked reasonably well; also Sánchez Morón (2013: 35).

non-colonial contexts.[16] The international community is divided about this, and the International Court of Justice has not yet ruled openly on this matter.

Even though decolonization may be considered a common expression of the right to external self-determination, there have been many developments thereof outside the colonial context. To name just a few, apart from the Bangladeshi example, we could consider the reunification of Germany, the international scenario after the breakup of the Soviet Union, Yugoslavia or Czechoslovakia as well as Eritrean secession from Ethiopia.[17]

In the Advisory Opinion of the International Court of Justice on the Legal Consequences of the Construction of a Wall in the Occupied Palestinian Territory[18] there is a clear statement that the right to self-determination is a right that can be applied outside contexts of decolonization. The right to self-determination implies freedom of peoples to decide their political status.[19] Self-determination is simply the right to live in a democracy.

In the view of some, secession is seen just as a remedial measure, and a remedial right, whereby if a mother-state fails to permit a people forming

---

16   See Hannum (1996: 28).
17   Generally, international practice has established the right to self-determination to be achieved principally through so called 'internal self-determination', by means of autonomy arrangements enabling a people to attain a certain degree of political, social, cultural etc. independence within the framework of an existing state. To what extent the notion of self-determination implies a right to 'external self-determination', and thus enables minorities to secede in order to become independent or associate with a new state, however, remains controversial. See Crawford (1998: 86).
18   ICJ Advisory Opinion of 9 July 2004, on the Legal Consequences of the Construction of a Wall in the Occupied Palestinian Territory, paragraph 88, page 39, and paragraph 122, page 184. This clearly states that today self-determination is an erga omnes (i.e. universally applicable) right (cf. East Timor (Portugal v. Australia), 1995 I.C.J., page 102, paragraph 29). See also Case Concerning East Timor (Port. v. Austl.), 1995 I.C.J. 90, 102–3 (30 June) (characterizing East Timor as a 'non-self-governing territory,' whose people 'has the right to self-determination').
19   In the case of the Western Sahara the court of justice stated that the right to self-determination 'requires a free and genuine expression of the will of the peoples concerned' (paragraph 32).

part of it to develop freely, or systematically blocks its development, it is legitimate for that people to have recourse to secession.[20] Remedial secession is seen as an option for special cases. Although neither the principle of self-determination nor the remedial character has been formally resorted to in many secession processes that have taken place in Europe, the international community has recognized such states.

The practice of the international community suggests that there can be other methods or ways for achieving independence. In this regard the Quebec case[21] and especially the ruling of the Supreme Court of Canada concerning Quebec's secession is of particular interest.[22]

The Supreme Court of Canada, after finding that Canadian domestic law did not support a right to unilateral secession,[23] explained that under international law, 'the right to self-determination of a people is normally fulfilled through internal self-determination within the framework of an existing state.'[24] After that, the Court went a step further, drawing on 'the principles of federalism, democracy, constitutionalism and the rule of law, and respect for minorities' enshrined in the Canadian Constitution to outline a process of negotiated secession. Following the Supreme Court of Canada: although Canadian domestic law does not condone unilateral secession, 'a clear majority vote in Quebec on a clear question in favour of secession would confer democratic legitimacy on the secession initiative which all of the other participants in Confederation would have to recognize.'[25] The democratically expressed will of the people of Quebec to secede would oblige the Canadian state to engage with Quebec in negotiations

---

20 See Buchanan (2007: 331–400) presenting a comprehensive argument that '[i]nternational law should recognize a remedial right to secede' where 'secession is a remedy of last resort against serious injustices'.
21 An approach to the context can be found in Dodge (1999: 287). For an in-depth consideration of the possible contours and consequences of Quebec's secession, see Young (1998: 34–40).
22 Reference re Secession of Quebec, [1998] 2 S.C.R. 217.
23 Ibid., paras 32–108.
24 Ibid., para. 127.
25 Ibid., para. 150.

concerning possible separation, at least as a way of obtaining the acceptance of the result by the international community.

From its wording two important conclusions can be drawn: first, the Supreme Court of Canada proclaimed the 'democratic legitimacy' of a hypothetical secession process, provided that a clear majority[26] of Québécois support it by answering a clear referendum question. Second, based on that legitimacy, a negotiated process is required.

Bearing this in mind, let us underline the non-univocal nature of the relationship between secession and the right to self-determination. Secession may come about as a result of self-determination, but not only in that way. Secession can also be based on democratic principles without using the right to self-determination.

In the same way, the International Court of Justice considers that there is not an emerging prohibition of secession arising from the principle of territorial integrity. The conclusion of the International Court of Justice in the Advisory Opinion of 22 July 2010 on the Accordance with International Law of the Unilateral Declaration of Independence in Respect of Kosovo[27] is that '[t]he scope of the principle of territorial integrity is confined to the sphere of relations between States'.[28]

There are no provisions in international law that regulate secession. The secession will be legal if it is an effective political fact. International law does not recognize the right to secession as such, but neither can it be affirmed that international law denies its existence. Despite the international community being extremely reticent with regard to secession, this

---

26   The Court did not answer the question of what a clear majority is. In 2000, the Canadian government passed the Clarity Act, which obliges Canada to negotiate with Quebec over the terms of a possible separation only in the case of a vote on a question that sets forth a stark choice between either full separation or continued inclusion in the Canadian state. Clarity Act, 2000 S.C., Chapter 26 (Can.). In 2006, based on a proposal made by the EU, Montenegro held a referendum on separation from Serbia that required a majority of 55 per cent to succeed. See Office of Security and Co-operation in Europe, Office for Democratic Institutions and Human Rights, Serbia and Montenegro Referendum 21 May 2006, 14 March 2006, at 3–4.
27   General List No. 141, International Court of Justice (ICJ), 22 July 2010.
28   Kosovo AO, supra note 29, at paragraph 80 (in fine).

is not prohibited by international law, based on the fact that the principle of territorial integrity applies to States.

Things seem clearer, in this regard, if secession is founded upon the right to self-determination as this will provide a more straightforward motivation for recognition by third states. If, on the other hand, secession is not linked to the right to self-determination, international law cannot be said to prohibit making it effective (Summers 2010: 16). In this case secession is not forbidden, it is merely not privileged; and the privilege will be even less forthcoming if the mother-state refuses to recognize the secession. Even so, in cases where secession is not privileged, third states may still recognize the entity that has seceded as a state on the basis of the democratic legitimacy of the process (Urrutia 2012: 138; 2014).

Following Ralph Wilde's approach here, for sub-state groups who aspire to independence the central matter is not so much what the international-law position is on the legality of declarations of independence, but rather their prospects for enjoying the support of at least the kind of critical mass of other states that will make their claim practically viable (Wilde 2011: 153).

Thomas M. Franck contends that '[i]t is wrong, to say there is no right of secession if by that one seeks to convey the impression that any secession is prohibited by international Law' (2000: 335). Malcolm Shaw opines in the same sense:

> It is true that the international community is very cautious about secessionist attempts, especially when the situation is such that threats to international peace and security are manifest. Nevertheless, as a matter of law the international system neither authorizes nor condemns such attempts, but rather stands neutral. Secession, as such, therefore, is not contrary to international law. (Shaw 2000: 136)

Approaching Secession?

In Spain a pro-independence vision is emerging. The right to decide, whose first normative expression was contained in the Draft of the Political Statute for the Basque Country, has become the hub of the sovereignty claim. In Catalonia, the social push in favour of the right to decide has given way to political statements made by the Parliament of Catalonia on the sovereignty of the Catalan people and their right to decide.

The Parliament of Catalonia Resolution 5/X of 23 January 2013 adopted the *Declaració de sobirania i el dret a decidir del poble de Catalunya* [Declaration of sovereignty and right to decide of the people of Catalonia] which asserted that Catalonia 'sea un ente soberano y "acuerda iniciar el proceso para hacer efectivo el ejercicio del derecho a decidir para que los ciudadanos y ciudadanas de Cataluña puedan decidir su futuro político colectivo"' [is a sovereign entity and 'marks the beginning of a process by which the citizens of Catalonia will be able to choose their political future as a people'].[29]

The Constitutional Court, reaching a unanimous decision,[30] declared the first part of the text, which stated that 'El pueblo de Cataluña tiene, por razones de legitimidad democrática, carácter de sujeto político y jurídico soberano' [The people of Catalonia are, for reasons of democratic legitimacy, a sovereign political and legal subject] to be 'unconstitutional and void' (3rd legal basis).[31] However, it added that the people of Catalonia have 'the right to decide', though not the 'right to self-determination' (4th legal basis).[32] The Court recognized that 'Catalan citizens' right to

---

29   The Declaration was approved with eighty-five votes in favour, forty-one against and two abstentions.
30   See Ruling of the Constitutional Court of 25 March 2014.
31   See Ruling 25 March 2014, 3rd legal basis ('Se declara inconstitucional y nulo el denominado principio primero titulado "Soberanía" de la Declaración aprobada por la Resolución 5/X del Parlamento de Cataluña' [The unconstitutionality and nullity are hereby declared of principle one, entitled 'Sovereignty', in the Declaration approved by Resolution 5/X of the Parliament of Catalonia]).
32   See Ruling 25 March 2014, 4th legal basis ('Estos principios, como veremos, son adecuados a la Constitución y dan cauce a la interpretación de que el "derecho a decidir de los ciudadanos de Cataluña" no aparece proclamado como una manifestación de un derecho a la autodeterminación no reconocido en la Constitución, o como una atribución de soberanía no reconocida en ella, sino como una aspiración política a la que solo puede llegarse mediante un proceso ajustado a la legalidad constitucional' [These principles, as seen below, conform to the Constitution and enable an interpretation that 'the right to decide held by citizens

decide'[33] fits into the Constitution, if it does not imply self-determination. Such a right is

> una aspiración política a la que solo puede llegarse mediante un proceso ajustado a la legalidad constitucional con respeto a los principios de 'legitimidad democrática', 'pluralismo', y 'legalidad'. De hecho, el Tribunal destaca que la Constitución puede ser reformada a través de los procedimientos previstos para ello, incluso cabe 'modificar el fundamento mismo del orden constitucional.'

> [a political aspiration which can only be achieved through a process totally in line with the Constitutional order, following the principles of 'democratic legitimacy', 'pluralism' and 'legality'. In fact, the Court points out that the Constitution can be reformed according to legal procedures, including 'to modify the fundamental grounds of the Constitutional order'.][34]

Moreover, the Court urged the political powers to talk and find agreements, and pointed out that all parts of the current Constitution can be reformed.

The Court wrote that the problems that arise when a particular territory wishes to change its legal status cannot be solved by the Constitutional Court. It could only check that the applicable legal procedures to organize this dialogue are properly complied with. The Court invoked also the principles of institutional co-operation and loyalty to the Constitution, and held that if a region submits a proposal to change the Constitution, the Spanish Parliament should take it into account.

---

of Catalonia' is not proclaimed as a manifestation of a right of self-determination not recognized in the Constitution, or as an unrecognized attribution of sovereignty, but as a political aspiration that may only be achieved through a process that conforms to constitutional legality]).

33 See Ruling 25 March 2014, Ruling point 2 ('Las referencias al "derecho a decidir de los ciudadanos de Cataluña" […] no son inconstitucionales' [the references to 'the right to decide of the citizens of Catalonia' […] are not unconstitutional]).

34 See Ruling 25 March 2014, 4th legal basis 'El planteamiento de concepciones que pretendan modificar el fundamento mismo del orden constitucional tiene cabida en nuestro ordenamiento' [Any approach that intends to change the very grounds of the Spanish constitutional order is acceptable in law (lit. 'has a place in our law')].

There is, definitely, a cry here for the political branches to assume the burden of negotiating a political solution to a deeply problematic meeting of opposing views at a constitutional crossroads.

This judgement reveals a new and positive approach to the issue, to the extent that it urges political powers to talk and find an agreement. However, the judgement reveals again a clash of legitimacies: on the one hand, the legitimacy of the constitutional legal order and, on the other, the political legitimacy of the Parliament of Catalonia.

It does not follow from denying a people a certain way of exercising a right that this right does not exist in and of itself. The core question is not whether the Spanish Constitution allows the Catalan people to exercise their right to decide through a referendum, but rather whether the Catalan people is vested with such a right (see Turp 2017: 60).

Definitely, the way opened up by the Supreme Court of Canada leaves open the possibility of a negotiated secession. The approach taken by the Supreme Court of Canada seems to have been assumed, perhaps in a more nuanced way, by the Spanish Constitutional Court when it demanded a negotiation between the Spanish central state and the representatives of the people of Catalonia, or of the Basque Country.

Conclusion

The current recentralization process in Spain presents novel characteristics. In a context of the economic downturn, a constitutional mutation of the horizontal relationships occurred in the exercise of public power. A constitutional mutation or transformation of the nature of political decentralization in Spain emerged which affects the regional capacity to establish public policies on key areas of the welfare state, cultural areas and self-government. Also, we can observe the weakening of social and cultural rights, which are mainly provided by the Autonomous Communities.

This imbalance has produced a situation that makes it difficult to accommodate the national realities and the desires for greater self-government within the Spanish state, and has seen new approaches emerging that promote a constitutional rupture and are in favour of creating new constitutional legitimacies. We are facing two opposing processes of nation building, working face to face from opposite perspectives.

The unilateral recentralization process breaks the statutory consensus upon which the Autonomous Communities were created and prevents the Basque Country from fully exercising the tools and powers provided by the autonomous institutions. As a result, the capacity for self-government is weakened and opportunities for building up an adequate level of well-being and the sustainable development of its territory are limited within the current legal framework. The self-government model seems to be exhausted due to a de facto constitutional mutation, which lacks the necessary consensus.

At this stage the major unresolved issues relating to the Basque Country include its future relationship with the state, the recognition of the right to decide and the territorial articulation of all the historical Basque territories in order to ensure an appropriate welfare system. In this situation, priority should be given to ensuring the transition to a new phase without violence, thus ensuring opportunities to all policy options that can be defended by democratic means. Basque society is becoming aware of the important role it has in this new phase. The final outcome will depend solely on an accord between the central state and the democratically expressed will of the Basque people. We are facing a constitutional crossroads at which a negotiated democratic solution is needed.

Bibliography

Albertí Rovira, E. (2013). 'El impacto de la crisis financiera en el estado autonómico español', *Revista Española de Derecho Constitucional*, 98, 63–89.

Aparicio Perez, M. A. (2011). 'Posición y funciones de los Estatutos de Autonomía en la STC 31/2010', *Revista d'Estudis Autonòmics i Federals*, 12, 16–43.

Buchanan, A. (2007). *Justice, Legitimacy, and Self-Determination: Moral Foundations for International Law*. Oxford: Oxford University Press.

Corretja i Torrens, M. (2013). 'El sistema competencial español a la luz de la eficiencia: indefinición, duplicidades, vulnerabilidad de las competencias autonómicas y conflictividad', *Cuadernos Manuel Giménez Abad*, 5, 35–44.

Crawford, J. (1998). 'State Practice and International Law in Relation to Secession', *British Yearbook of International Law*, 69 (1), 85–117.
Dodge, W. J. (1999). 'Succeeding in Seceding? Internationalizing the Quebec Secession Reference Under NAFTA', *Texas Journal of International Law*, 34, 287–96.
Fernández Rodríguez, T. R. (2013). 'La España de las autonomías: un estado débil devorado por diecisiete estaditos', *Revista española de derecho administrativo*, 158, 27–54.
Franck, T. M. (2000). 'Experts Report', reproduced in A. F. Bayefsky (ed.), *Self-determination in International Law: Quebec and Lessons Learned*. The Hague: Kluwer Law.
Hannum, H. (1996). *Autonomy, Sovereignty, And Self-Determination: The Accommodation of Conflicting Rights*. Philadelphia: University of Pennsylvania Press.
Jauregi, G. (2005). 'Estatuto de Autonomía del País Vasco y autogobierno'. In P. García-Escudero, J. Lerma, M. Roca, and M. Balado (eds), *La España de las autonomías: reflexiones 25 años después*, pp. 1009–26. Barcelona: Bosch.
Lasagabaster, I. (2005). 'Legalidad y legitimidad en la reforma del Estatuto de Autonomía del País Vasco: un análisis en torno a la propuesta de reforma aprobada por el Parlamento Vasco el 30 de Diciembre de 2004'. In P. García-Escudero, J. Lerma, M. Roca, and M. Balado (eds), *La España de las autonomías: reflexiones 25 años después*, pp. 1033–48. Barcelona: Bosch.
Lasagabaster, I. (2014). 'La propuesta de reforma del Estatuto de Autonomía del País Vasco: del Parlamento Vasco al Congreso de Diputados. El final de un ciclo (2000-2006)', *Iura Vasconiae*, 12, 120–253.
Lluch, J. (2013). *The Moral Polity of the Nationalist: Sovereignty and Accommodation in Catalonia and Quebec (1978–2010)*. Barcelona: Institut d'Estudis Autonòmics.
Lopez, J. (2015). 'A Right to Decide: On the Normative Basis of a Political Principle and its Application to the Catalan Case'. In K. J. Nagel, and S. Rixen (eds), *Catalonia in Spain and Europe*, pp. 28–42. Baden-Baden: Nomos.
Muñoz Machado, S. (2012). *Informe sobre España: repensar el estado o destruirlo*. Barcelona: Crítica.
Nogueira, A., Ruiz Vieytez, E., and Urrutia, I. (2012), *Shaping language rights: commentary on the European charter for regional or minority languages in light of the committee of experts' evaluation*. Strasbourg: Council of Europe.
Prott, V. (2016). *The politics of Self-Determination*. Oxford: Oxford University Press.
Quadra-Salcedo, T. (2012). 'El federalismo español ante la crisis económica y el debate estatutario', *Sistema Revista de Ciencias Sociales*, 224, 3–20.

Sánchez Morón, M. (2013). 'Reformar el Estado: ¿Modificar la Constitución? Apuntes para el debate', *El Cronista del Estado Social y Democrático de Derecho*, 34, 32–9.

Seijas, E. (2013). 'Crisis, federalismo, cultura federal y federalismo asimétrico: odisea constitucional 2013', *Revista General de Derecho Constitucional*, 16, 1–25 <https://www.iustel.com/v2/revistas/detalle_revista.asp?id_noticia=413124> accessed 1 July 2019.

Shaw, M. (2000). 'Re: Order in Council P.C. 1996–1497 of 30 September 1996'. In A. F. Bayefsky (ed.), *Self-Determination in International Law: Quebec and Lessons Learned*. The Hague: Kluwer Law.

Summers, J. (2010). 'Relativizing Sovereignty: Remedial Secession and Humanitarian Intervention in International Law', *St Antony's International Review*, 6 (1), 16–36.

Turp, D. (2017). 'Catalonia's Right to Decide under International, European, Spanish, Catalan and Comparative Law'. In D. Turp, N. Caspersen, M. Qvortrup, and Y. Welp (eds), *The Catalan Independence referendum: An Assessment of the Process of Self-Determination*. Montreal: IRAI.

Urrutia, I. (2012). 'Territorial integrity and self-determination: the approach of the International Court of Justice in the advisory opinion on Kosovo', *Revista d'Estudis Autonòmics i Federals*, 16, 107–40.

Urrutia, I. (2014). 'Derecho de autodeterminación y creación de nuevos estados europeos a partir de la Opinión Consultiva de la Corte Internacional de Justicia sobre Kosovo'. In *Fòrum sobre el dret a decidir (I): Dret comparat i context internacional*, pp. 29–68. Barcelona: Institut d'Estudis Autonòmics.

Viver Pi-Sunyer, C. (2011). 'El impacto de la crisis económica global en el sistema de descentralización política en España', *Revista d'Estudis Autonòmics i Federals*, 13, 146–85.

Waters, T. W. (2016). 'A World Elsewhere: Secession, Subsidiarity and Self-Determination as European Values', *Revista d'Estudis Autonòmics i Federals*, 23, 11–45.

Wilde, R. (2011). 'Self-Determination, Secession, and Dispute Settlement after the Kosovo Advisory Opinion', *Leiden Journal of International Law*, 24, 149–54.

Young, R. A. (1998). *The Secession of Quebec and the Future of Canada*. Montreal: McGill-Queen's University Press.

ERIC VANDERHEYDEN

Ethical Nationalism: Social Citizenship in Multi-National States

ABSTRACT
This chapter explores the role social policy plays in sub-state nationalist politics in Scotland and Flanders by analysing the political discourse framing social policies as well as the policies themselves. Regional social policies are examined to ascertain whether they diverge from the national status quo and thus might alter the nature of social citizenship. In order to understand how these social policies relate to sub-state nationalism, the manifestos and parliamentary discourse of sub-state nationalist parties are analysed. The chapter concludes that in pursuit of congruence between national and political units, political actors may, where possible, use social policy at a regional level in order to foster national solidarity or convey understanding and assumptions about people and their needs.

Introduction

Over the past two decades we have seen a major shift of political authority away from the national level towards both sub-national (devolution) and supra-national bodies (European integration). In the case of devolution, the transfer of political authority to sub-state entities was, in part, meant to assuage concerns over language rights, cultural policy and education as well as representation vocalized by nationalist parties active in regions of Spain, the United Kingdom and Belgium. However, despite the status upgrade of minority languages, far-reaching devolution and proportional representation, sub-state nationalism has continued to persist in several European regions.

In fact, in cases such as Scotland, Flanders and Catalonia, nationalist parties have increased their voter share and are leading regional governments. In Scotland we even witnessed a referendum on independence, and Catalan politicians organized a plebiscite regardless of objections from Madrid while, in Flanders, nationalists garnered the largest voter share in federal, regional and local elections. In light of the many concessions made by their respective states, the enduring surge in sub-state nationalist mobilization seems inconsistent with expectations. As such, the search for what drives and makes nations and nationalism has continued unabated since Renan, Gellner, Anderson and Smith.[1]

Over the past two decades, studies aimed at explaining and understanding sub-state nationalism have focused on a wide variety of factors, ranging from European integration (Hepburn and McLoughlin 2011; Hepburn and Elias 2011; Jolly 2015) and national identity (Kymlicka and Norman 2000; Moreno, Arriba and Serrano 2007; Boonen and Hooghe 2013; Dodeigne, Gramme, Reuchamps and Sinardet 2016), to federalism (Swenden 2006; Máiz 2007) and regional interest groups (Keating 2014; Keating and Wilson 2014).

An avenue of scholarship which has received some, though not always sufficient, attention is that of the relationship between nationalism and social policy.[2] This, despite the fact that the strategic importance of social policy in territorial politics and nation-building has been pointed out repeatedly:[3]

> Where power rests with central government, social policy can be utilized to mediate regional conflicts and reinforce national integration, strengthening the authority and legitimacy of the state in the face of challenges from territorial minorities. Conversely, where social programmes are developed and managed at the sub-state level, they can strengthen regional cultures and enhance the significance of regional governments in the everyday lives of their citizens. (Banting 1995: 270–1)

---

[1] That is to say, since the best-known general theorists of nations and nationalism. For a comprehensive overview see Özkirimli (2010).
[2] For the purposes of this chapter we understand social policy to mean the entirety of public policy and practice in the areas of healthcare, social services, inequality, education and labour.
[3] See also: Béland and Lecours (2007), Taylor and Francis Online (publishers' database) <https:/www.tandfonline.com/> accessed January 2016.

Although I do not claim that social policy is the sole, or even the most relevant, force driving nationalism and nationalist mobilization, this chapter will argue that part of the reason some sub-state nationalist struggles persist is not only that social policy has become a new focal point of contention since the development of the welfare state in the second half of the twentieth century but that it has come under considerable pressure at the start of the twenty-first century.

Many of the works on social policy and nationalism consider this relationship in terms of the effects territorial politics may have on social policy (McEwen and Moreno 2005; McEwen 2006; Greer 2006; Birrell 2009; Mackinnon 2015). They describe and theorize the implications of devolution for social policy making, yet tend to dwell only briefly on what this means for the nature of nationalism and the nation. To be sure, certain students of nationalism have looked into social policy's role in nation-building (Mooney and Scott 2011; Law and Mooney 2012), though their analyses have tended to deal with the issues of policy divergence and electoral support rather than address the question of how social policy questions are intrinsically linked to the nation and nationalism. Scott L. Greer and Margitta Mätzke (2009) do much to flesh out the connection between social citizenship and the nation in Greer's edited volume on devolution and social policy in the United Kingdom; however, the contributions following the introduction soon revert to political and policy analysis.

Only a small number of works have bucked the trend of remaining in the realms of policy analysis and political economy when exploring the relationship between social policy and sub-state nationalism. One such work is Daniel Béland and Andre Lecours' 2008 book *Nationalism and Social Policy: The Politics of Territorial Solidarity*, which examines this relationship in Belgium, Scotland and Canada. In this comparative study the authors delve deeper into what they call the nexus between nationalism and social policy than most before them. They explicitly theorize the role social policy plays in the contest for citizens' allegiance to one nation or another. Indeed, Béland and Lecours do more than theorize as they delve into the historical development of nationalist movements and their respective socio-economic and institutional contexts. This way they examine how social programmes play a central role in national identity building and territorial mobilization, as well as study how nationalist movements can affect social policy making through the territorial structuring of policy reform and implementation (Béland and Lecours 2008: 40). That being said, the authors do not engage in a systematic analysis of nationalism and its discursive and policy-based manifestations in the three cases they present.

This chapter endeavours to theorize what lies behind social policy's rise to prominence in territorial politics and nationalist mobilization since most traditional concerns over language, culture and representation have been assuaged. The chapter argues that this aspect of nationalism's continuing push and pull on politics can be captured and understood in an integrated theory of ethical nationalism, combining communitarian ethics and social citizenship.

I intend to achieve this by exploring the notion that many nations' national identities and representations of national identity do not merely include the traditionally described linguistic, cultural and territorial elements; but in some cases can also be said to include ethical elements. These ethical elements describe distinctiveness in an ethical dimension. That is to say that they represent the nation as an ethical community as explained by David Miller (1995). After an elaboration of Miller's ideas on the nation as an ethical community, we will go on to illustrate how we can see ethical considerations and representations at work today in disputes surrounding Marshallian social citizenship[4] in the form of political discourse and social policies. Conceptions of social citizenship form the bridge which allows political actors to translate their ideas of the nation as a particular kind of ethical community into concrete policy-talks and social policies, thus reproducing and reinforcing these ideas on the nation's public culture and engaging in nationalist mobilization on the basis of social policy issues. Aside from relying heavily on Miller and Marshall's conceptual work, the chapter will employ empirical examples drawn from two cases – Scotland and Flanders – to illustrate what the proposed notion of

---

4   T. H. Marshall's take on social citizenship will be explored later in the chapter. For his original work, see Marshall (1950).

ethical nationalism looks like in practice, and how we might better understand where it originates.

The Nation as an Ethical Community

David Miller (1995) argues that nations can be viewed as ethical communities in the sense that aside from deriving distinctiveness from common cultural practices (such as language), shared belief and mutual commitment, from being extended in history, being active in character, and occupying a particular territory, nations may also mark themselves off from other communities through sharing particular interpretations of what we owe our fellow nationals. Miller describes the nation as an ethical community in which members 'recognize duties to meet the basic needs and protect the basic interests of other members' (Miller 1995: 83).

Indeed, in Miller's view, each nation has a distinct public culture which determines 'a set of ideas about the character of the community which also helps to fix responsibilities' (Miller 1995: 68). Miller describes this public culture as being the product of political debate and therefore as having an ideological coloration (Miller 1995: 69). More specifically a nation's public culture is formed by political debate held in the past as well as in the present. This debate is characterized as a process of reflection on equal footing by all members of the community. The public culture and consequent obligations that emerge from this historical debate are not merely traditional, but instead 'bear the imprint of the various reasons that have been offered over time in the course of these debates' (Miller 1995: 70). Depending on the public culture resulting from this historical process, a nation's public opinion may attach more importance to, for example, individual freedom and self-sufficiency or to collective solidarity. These values and preferences would then, in turn, inform the community's obligations towards fellow members; such obligations would include providing the minimum levels of security and infrastructure necessary for individuals to shape their own lives in the first case; or providing a wider array of public goods in the second case.

Furthermore, Miller describes public culture as resilient and open to interpretation. This allows public culture to 'serve as a source of ideas that may then be used to justify or criticize the policies of a particular government' (Miller 1995: 70). In other words, citizens or political actors may appeal to public culture or invoke public culture values when arguing in favour of or against policies or engaging in electoral campaigning. Miller illustrates this idea using the example of a national health service. He argues that if, in a democratic society, one has the obligation to contribute to the functioning of a national health service, this obligation is 'grounded in the reasons given for having the health service when it was first introduced, and reaffirmed from time to time when the health service is debated' (Miller 1995: 70). What this might look like in the case of sub-state nationalist politics will be illustrated with a number of examples in the later stages of this chapter.

In a national community (unlike in face-to-face communities), despite the guiding light of public culture, there is no clear understanding of what or how we are expected to contribute towards the welfare of other members in a practical sense. This reminds us of Benedict Anderson's reflection that the nation is still, essentially, an imagined community (Miller 1995: 68). In order to bring Miller's view of the nation as an ethical community well and truly into the world of politics and policy, we need to look at how obligations owed to co-nationals can be fulfilled. In the past such obligations have often included 'serving one's country' by way of civil or military service or simply paying one's taxes. However, in modern industrialized countries, ever since the development of the welfare state in the second half of the twentieth century, obligations are most commonly fulfilled by means of different social policies. After all, what better means are there to fulfil one's duty 'to meet the basic needs and protect the basic interests of other members' (Miller 1995: 83) than social policy which entails the actions that affect the well-being of members of a society through shaping the distribution of and access to goods and resources in that society (Cheyne, O'Brien, and Belgrave 2005). The gap between the nation as an ethical community and a set of social policy rights and obligations can be bridged best by the concept of social citizenship.

From Imagined Community to Material Community: Social Citizenship

The most commonly recognized *conditio sine qua non* for participation in the rights and duties that come with group membership is citizenship. Thomas Humphry Marshall divides citizenship into three elements: civil, political and social. The civil element includes the rights that are vital to individual freedom such as liberty of the person, freedom of speech, thought and faith, property rights, freedom of contract and the right to a fair trial. The political element entails the right to political participation and organization, thus involving the rights to stand for election and hold office (Marshall 1950). In the aftermath of the Second World War he formulated social citizenship as a third set of rights that exist aside from basic political and civil rights, acquired gradually over the period between the seventeenth and twentieth centuries.

Social citizenship, as it was coined by Marshall, means: 'the whole range from the right to a modicum of economic welfare and security to the right to share to the full in the social heritage and to live the life of a civilized being according to the standards prevailing in society' (Marshall 1950: 14). More concretely, this entails the set of socio-economic rights and obligations held by members of the community which pertain to socio-economic instruments such as taxation, redistributive programmes such as unemployment benefits and family allowances, all manner of social services, pensions, education, healthcare, criminal justice and public transport. In short, the aspects of policy primarily concerned with human well-being and welfare.

Marshall's definition of social citizenship consists of two important parts. The first is the so-called 'what', namely a modicum of economic welfare and security and the right to share in the social heritage and to live the life of a civilized being. The second element is a qualifier for the first, captured in the phrase 'to the standards prevailing in the society'. Or, in other words, what the container of economic security ought to include. In order to vindicate the compatibility of our two theoretical protagonists, we will now proceed to demonstrate how these two elements tie in with David Miller's idea of the ethical community.

The first element of the definition, what constitutes 'a modicum of economic welfare and security', is shaped, in Miller's words, by interpretations of what obligations are owed. Obligations towards co-nationals thus determine conceptualizations of social citizenship which, in turn, inform concrete social policy preferences. More concretely, they help shape – among other things – different nations' ideas on social policy and the limits of the welfare state. As we have seen, these obligations are usually fixed through public culture, for which we move on to the second element of social citizenship: standards prevailing in the society.

The second element in Marshall's definition, as mentioned earlier, concerns the 'prevailing standards' qualifier, an important proviso which allows for the existence of diverse interpretations of what one member of a national community owes another. After all, different societies may well have gone through different political debates conditioned by diverging historical paths, thus leading to different public cultures which help fix the rights and obligations of co-nationals, and so resulting in different ideas of what a 'modicum of economic welfare and security' entails in practical terms.

For example, public opinion in different nations may have a distinct idea of when a jobless person should receive unemployment benefits; or of the extent to which a richer co-national's income should be taxed. To mention two examples, US public opinion seems to prefer limited government interference in the social economy and emphasizes individual freedom and private initiative; whereas in a country such as France public opinion favours strong government regulation and involvement in society and the economy as a way of ensuring equality. Thus, it can be said that the theories of both Marshall and Miller include provisos allowing for or, indeed, elucidating variation in social policy preferences between national communities. The matter of how we might trace the origins of public cultures will be addressed more elaborately in the section of this chapter preceding the conclusion.

Sub-state Nationalism and the Ethical Community

With the provisos allowing for divergence in obligations and social citizenship, we move ever closer to our specific cases of sub-state nationalism. How do the theories of the ethical community and social citizenship interact with the sub-state nationalists' drive for congruence between the national and the political unit?

As we have seen so far, rights and obligations which stem from nationality are generally systematized through codification of these rights and obligations into the more practical terms of citizenship. People's rights and obligations as enshrined in citizenship *sans plus* are based upon 'their participation in a practice from which they stand to benefit' (Miller 1995: 71). In other words, as citizens they are entitled to the use of public goods such as social assistance, infrastructure and education, and in return they are obliged to pay their dues, obey the law and sustain the co-operative arrangement.

Indeed, the majority of rights and obligations of nationality are discharged through the state and citizenship, in which enforcement mechanisms exist to induce compliance. However, it would be wrong to think that nationality ceases to be relevant the moment such a practice of state-citizenship co-operation is established (Miller 1995).

After all, this kind of co-operation would be based on the principle of fairness. A rational citizen would demand rigorous reciprocity from the other participants. Indeed, they would expect their benefit from the arrangement to be equal to their contribution. Miller illustrates the limitations of such an arrangement using the example of redistributive taxation:

> So, for instance, redistributive taxation would be agreed to only in circumstances in which each person thought it was rational to insure him- or herself through the state against the possibility of falling below a certain level of resources. Given the possibility of private insurance, we would expect states that lacked a communitarian background such as nationality provides to be little more than minimal states, providing only basic security to their members. In particular, it is difficult to explain why states should provide opportunities and resources to people with permanent handicaps if one is simply following the logic of reciprocity. (1995: 71)

According to Miller, the reason we find arrangements considerably more generous than this one in the world today is thus due to the prior obligations of nationality – which do include obligations to contribute to the provision of benefits beyond those that serve rational self-interest, for in a national community one's own interests tend to be viewed as inter-twined with the interests of the group as a whole to some extent or another. Hence, one has less trouble recognizing and fulfilling Miller's duties regarding basic needs and interests of co-members (1995: 83). Where mutuality of recognition fails, however, the character of the community to which one thinks one belongs is put in question. This could mean that there exist fundamentally different views between members of what obligations are owed, leading to the possible collapse of the co-operative arrangement of social citizenship.

As such, there exists the potential for an ethical motive to drive the pursuit of national and political units to coincide. After all, when obligations of citizenship are informed by obligations of nationality, redistributive arrangements can go well beyond what rational self-interest would otherwise allow. When two or more conceptions of obligations clash, on the other hand, at least one of the groups in question is likely to feel they are being cut a 'bad deal'. Indeed, they might even feel they need increased political autonomy in order to satisfy their conception of social citizenship, or, in Gellner's words, to obtain congruence between the national and political unit (Gellner 1983); which in this case means: congruence between the ethical and the political unit, in order to determine the rights and obligations of citizenship based on their views on obligations of nationality. This is when the connection between ideas of social citizenship and nationality and the expression thereof becomes particularly relevant. In other words, this is when we might see the occurrence of ethical nationalism.

Ethical Nationalism and Where to Find It

Now, in order to ascertain whether our theory of ethical nationalism helps us understand why and how nationalism persists in our two cases of sub-state nationalism, we must look at territorial politics in each region. Nationalism may be manifested through discourse but also in policy. Therefore, to establish whether elements of ethical nationalism are present we will, after explaining how they may be used in nation-building, analyse both nationalist discourse and regional social policy. In the case of discourse we would expect to see political actors making claims about different public cultures being dominant in their respective regions as opposed to the 'state's' public culture. They will evoke these distinct public cultures when arguing for region-specific social policy and increased autonomy or independence. Where regional social policy is concerned, we would expect to see attempts at reterritorializing the focus of national solidarity through unique and diverging social policies only available in the region in question and in line with the proclaimed public culture.

First, however, we must explore the historical development of each case to trace the development of a possibly distinct public culture. After all, as we have seen, public culture lies at the heart of the obligations that we now acknowledge. Considering that these obligations 'bear the imprint of the various reasons that have been offered over time in the course of these debates' (Miller 1995: 70), we must examine history to identify those developments and consequent political debates which shaped public culture – we cannot view nationalism's contemporary manifestations independently from history – and only then can we engage in the analysis of discourse and policy to establish whether ethical nationalism is present or not.

Historical Development and Public Culture Formation

As mentioned earlier, the conditions and preferences underlying the surfacing of ethical nationalism do not materialize overnight. They are the result of a historical process of socio-economic development and political debate. Therefore, in order to understand how ethical nationalism may develop in cases of sub-state nationalism we must examine the historical development of the nation in question and identify critical junctures or evolutions that have helped shape the community's public culture.

In the case of Scottish public culture, one critical juncture is the welfare retrenchment under the consecutive Conservative governments of John Major and Margaret Thatcher. In places like Scotland, where an alternative identity existed, Britishness was particularly wedded to the universal benefits and protection provided by the welfare state. After all, Scotland was comparatively reliant on national heavy industries and social programmes; and ever since the demise of the British Empire, the welfare state and National Health Service had replaced it as the main source of utility and prestige attached to Britishness. Hence, the Thatcherite policies of welfare retrenchment and privatization 'weakened the foundation of this implicit "social contract" and simultaneously presented a strong challenge to Scotland's societal and administrative autonomy' (Béland and Lecours 2008: 95). As the Conservative Party did not obtain a majority in Scotland throughout this period, the Labour Party put itself forward as the defender of Scottish interests and values. This also meant that Scottish voters were underrepresented in the Westminster government.

At the same time, centralizing policies were viewed as a grave threat to the administrative and societal autonomy of Scotland. This enraged Scottish civil society. Organizations such as professional groups, labour unions, churches and cultural associations mobilized support for the defence of Scottish particularism; and later on for devolution (Greer 2007).

This potent mixture of welfare retrenchment and centralization made up the context which shaped the resurgence of the movement towards home rule. The imminent threat to Scottish household incomes across the region meant that this time potential support for home rule was to be much broader. The argument was that in order to protect Scotland from Thatcherite neo-liberalism, political autonomy was needed. Then, Scotland could formulate the progressive social policies Scots needed and wanted. This dynamic caused two major political shifts. First, Scottish Labour, until then a strictly unionist party with social democratic policies, shifted to supporting devolution as a way of seizing the mood and regaining power after eighteen years out of office (Béland and Lecours 2008).

The second shift pertains to the Scottish National Party. The SNP had always steered clear of ideology so as not to lose any nationalist voters; however, throughout the 1970s and 1980s the party moved clearly towards the left (Béland and Lecours 2008). Its rhetoric transformed from Scottishness being 'somewhat ethnic and occasionally exclusive to being now civic and inclusive' (Leith 2008): a fresh focus was placed on Scotland's ideological distinctiveness, rather than on linguistic or ethnic markers. In brief, it was to be a crucial period in the formation of Scotland's public culture. The Thatcher era remains a point of reference to this day, for the threat that Westminster and the Union may pose to Scottish livelihoods and values.

In the Flemish case, the example of public culture formation is somewhat more gradual in nature, although there are some political crises that spurred on public debate in a particular direction. One such event is the so-called school struggle (*schoolstrijd*) that gripped Belgium throughout the 1950s. The issue is an excellent example of how a pre-existing traditional marker of identity – in this case the dominance of Catholicism among the Flemish population – had an influence on political debates and, in turn, went on to influence social policy preferences and shape public culture. The school struggle is the term generally used to indicate the competition for the government's favour and the public's preference for the secular or the Catholic education establishments. After the Second World War, state schools and Catholic schools across Belgium were struggling to cope with the sharp increase in students. The former had a structural problem as there were considerably fewer state schools in the country, whereas the latter had a financial problem as Catholic schools did not receive subsidies, and therefore had to hike their tuition fees.

The Christian-Democrat governments in power from 1950 to 1954 allocated subsidies to Catholic schools, which were significantly more popular in Flanders. However, in 1955 the new minister for education, the Francophone socialist Leo Collard, attempted to pass reforms slashing subsidies for Catholic schools, tightening conditions required for the acquisition of these subsidies and vastly increasing the number of state schools. The public's reaction was intense. A concerted mobilization effort by schools and Christian unions resulted in a protest of around 100,000 people on 26 March 1955 in Brussels alone. Newspapers reported that

Catholic Flanders had marched into Brussels and laid peaceful siege to the capital, despite the government's best efforts to obstruct the influx of protesters. Although Walloon Catholics had also participated in the movement, the episode was most commonly depicted as a moment of solidification of Christian-Democrat and centre-right support in Flanders. The intermittent protests continued until the re-election of a Christian-Democrat government in 1958, which consolidated the subsidy system. Thus the place of Christian values and institutions together with a preference for right-of-centre policies in public culture was confirmed and reinforced. Overall, the school struggle is a prime example of the 'Flemish right' versus 'Walloon left' dynamic that was to intensify in the years to come with the 1960–1 strikes and would eventually be part of the reason for the split of political parties along linguistic lines (Béland and Lecours 2008). This split and the subsequent establishment of regional constituencies for federal elections are factors that congealed the ideological division between north and south. It is a division visible in voting patterns and social policy preferences to this day.

Ethical Nationalist Mobilization: Political Discourse

What does all this mean for nationalist politics in practical terms? How can we recognize politics of ethical nationalism and tell them apart from other forms of nationalist politics? By connecting traditional elements of nationality such as territory, history, culture, or language to understandings of social citizenship, nationalist actors may add an ethical element (what obligations one should fulfil towards other group members within this territory) into the definition of nationality. They are representing the nation as an ethical community. And, as we have seen, we expect this to be accompanied by evocations of a shared public culture, described as different from that of the state.

How might political actors mobilize support based on ethical nationalist grounds? If interpretations of obligations owed to co-nationals in the shape of a specific conceptualization of social citizenship can be said to be part of national identity, and this element of national identity is compromised (or perceived as being compromised), sub-state nationalist politicians may be able to mobilize support on this basis, just as this has been done in the past based on threats to other elements of national identity such as language, culture, or territory. Ethical nationalist arguments can be viewed as just another way of saying: 'Our way of life is under threat!' Only that, in this case, the aspect of this 'way of life' is not cultural or linguistic *per se*, but is that part which deals with how to take care of the elderly in society, who should be responsible for a child's education, or whether healthcare is a right or a privilege.

The theme of nationalist mobilization based on socio-economic issues is present in Béland and Lecours' work (2008). In their study the authors examine several central claims about the nexus between nationalism and social policy by looking at three case studies: Quebec, Scotland and Flanders. Several of their claims are useful for the objectives of this chapter. We will use two of these claims as a means of testing the nationalist discourse and employ them as a barometer to indicate the presence or absence of arguments relating to conceptualizations of social citizenship, and thus the representation of the nation as an ethical community. This will allow us to identify whether elements of ethical nationalism are present and to provide one or two brief examples of discourse to illustrate the point more concretely.

A first indication of ethical nationalism would be social policy becoming 'a major component of the effort of nationalist movements to build and consolidate national identity, and an important target for nationalist mobilization' (Béland and Lecours 2008: 23). As national identity is a constructed concept, it takes place mainly in the discursive sphere. What we are looking for concretely in this case are statements linking the national identity in its traditional sense – language, history, culture, religion, territory, traditions – to social policy preferences. Usually, in order for the connection to be stronger, we would expect these statements to ascribe to the nation such characteristics as 'progressive', 'compassionate', 'hardworking', or 'entrepreneurial'.

A striking example of this value-ascription comes from the 1999 Scottish Parliamentary Elections campaign of the Scottish National Party, wherein the election manifesto's social policy chapter is introduced with the phrase: 'Traditionally Scots have believed in the values of compassion, community and the common weel' (Scottish National Party 1999: 19).

The values of compassion and community are said to be things Scots have 'traditionally' believed in. National identity – represented by 'tradition' or 'traditional beliefs' – is connected to values which inform a distinct socio-economic outlook. Furthermore, the use of the phrase 'the common weel' (also spelt 'weal') is tremendously relevant. The common weal is an old Scots phrase meaning both 'wealth shared in common' and 'for the wellbeing of all'. The use of a phrase embodying a distinctively Scottish concept to describe a set of social policies including public housing and free healthcare and education, evidently illustrates an attempt to establish a link between ideas of social citizenship and national identity.

In the Flemish case, too, we can find interesting examples of such discourse. In their election manifesto for the 2007 federal elections the *Nieuw-Vlaamse Alliantie* [New Flemish Alliance] or N-VA for short, Flanders' largest sub-state nationalist party, put forward a similar argument. After explaining how the Flemish prefer initial medical care to be provided by local general practitioners, before referral, while the Francophones prefer seeing specialists at public hospitals immediately, the conclusion frames the public healthcare debate in national terms: 'In Belgium there is a clear 'care-border'. A 'care-border' which coincides with a cultural border: the language border' (Nieuw-Vlaamse Alliantie 2007: 50).

The implication of this argument is that the language border is also an ideological border. North of the border, in Flanders, people prefer centre-right policies focusing on subsidiarity – a Catholic political concept – with limited state intervention through subsidies; south of the border, large-scale publicly provided uniform social and health care is preferred.

Béland and Lecours identify a second indicator of ethical arguments: '[T]he focus of nationalist movements on social policy is not simply the product of economic self-interest, yet references to the fairness of financial transfers between territorial entities become effective mobilization strategies' (2008: 25). Although some nationalist discourse may refer to actual structural differences, the differences in economic interest are not necessarily the sole driving force behind nationalist politics. Although we cannot, here, engage in an analysis in the interests of individual political actors, references to fairness and justice in nationalist discourse would be indicative of an ethical characterization.

A telling example here would be that in their 2003 election manifesto for the Federal Elections the N-VA attempt to redefine solidarity from a Flemish perspective when denouncing the inter-regional transfers in Belgium flowing from Flanders to Wallonia and Brussels. After describing how Flemings and Walloons have different preferences regarding public transport, healthcare and employment, the manifesto goes on to refer to 'Real solidarity with Wallonia instead of transferring billions' and states:

> Every year Flemings pay around 10 billion euros for Wallonia. This boils down to 5.000 euros per year for every average Flemish family with one child. But the average Walloon is not served by all this money [...]. The stream of money to Wallonia is not solidarity, but injustice. And that has to end [...]. Solidarity means giving money voluntarily and knowing what this money will be used for. Not the unnoticed and unsolicited taking money from your wallet. (Nieuw-Vlaamse Alliantie 2003: 7, 19)

This argument does not represent an outright rejection of the idea of fiscal inter-regional transfers — that would make for a much shorter quotation — but what we see here is rather the breakdown of the co-operative scheme because it is not, according to the N-VA, based upon shared and mutually recognized nationality. In other words, since the scheme is based purely on obligations stemming from citizenship, that is to say, a connection based on the principle of fairness, then strict reciprocity is demanded. The quotation indicates that the N-VA subscribes to a different idea of what obligations Flemings owe Walloons than what current citizenship arrangements impose.

To reiterate, based on the theoretical understandings above, this chapter suggests that the presence of these three claims in sub-state nationalist discourse points to the presence of ethical nationalism in some shape or form. This, of course, does not mean nationalist mobilization is driven exclusively by ethical nationalist arguments, but it does suggest that it plays a role. This, together with their substantial electoral support, would seem to signify that some nations may view their national identity as incorporating an ethical element, or at least respond to political mobilization based on ethical nationalist arguments. Moreover, this would seem to suggest that even if the traditional markers of national identity have already been safeguarded, the fact that the ethical aspect of national identity is compromised allows for nationalist mobilization.

Social Citizenship beyond Discourse: Policies Reproducing the Ethical Community

Ethical nationalism goes beyond discourse, however. As Marshall's definition suggests, social citizenship is more than just policy-talks: it includes actual policies which provide the aforementioned 'modicum of economic welfare and security'. In pursuit of congruence between national and political units, political actors may, where possible, use social policy at a regional level in order to foster national solidarity (McEwen 2002) or convey understanding and assumptions about people and their needs (Mooney and Williams 2006: 610). In this dynamic, regional governments may represent autonomy as a prerequisite for the 'right' socio-economic policies or represent themselves as guarantors of social protection where the central state fails (McEwen 2002). This dynamic ties back neatly to the theory of nationalist mobilization based on a perceived threat to an element of national identity or 'way of life' – in this case the so-called ethical element.

The idea behind ethical nationalism in the form of social policy is that when regional governments, especially when led by autonomist or nationalist parties, enact social policies that diverge considerably from the status quo on the national level, they alter what 'modicum of economic welfare and security' citizens in their region are entitled to. In other words, they are implementing different citizenship rights and obligations, based on regional variations of nationality rights and obligations, informed by what they view as the predominant public culture, or indeed 'the standards prevailing in the society'. Of course, regional governments are limited in what they can achieve by the constitutional arrangement of the state. Though social policy often remains largely in the hands of central governments, some regions have been known to test the limits of their legislative and executive prerogatives where social policy is concerned. To illustrate what I mean by this, I will provide examples of policies in concrete cases.

In the United Kingdom the Scottish programme introducing universal free personal care for the elderly is such an example. In 2000 planning for the programme was initiated by the Scottish Labour–Liberal Democrat government after the Sutherland Report on long-term care had made recommendations in that direction. The Westminster government, also led by Labour, favoured a means-tested programme, unlike the Scottish Executive, which leaned towards cradle-to-grave universalism.

In fact, the UK Labour Party raised objections to the Scottish plans to fully implement the Report's recommendations for free personal care, as they considered it an act of defiance by its Scottish arm, and as it would effectively mean British citizens living in Scotland would enjoy different social rights based purely on territorial parameters. Scottish Labour was torn and the decision was postponed. Meanwhile, the Scottish National Party was free to campaign vigorously for the full implementation of the Sutherland Report's recommendations, as they were 'delighted at having found an issue on which to open up a divide between Edinburgh and Westminster' (Marnoch 2003: 258). The episode clearly illustrates the dynamic between party competition and the quest for national distinctiveness in post-devolution Scotland, which led to a game of social policy chicken.

Eventually, as Liberal Democrats, Scottish nationalists and even Scottish Conservatives colluded to vote in favour of universal coverage, at the end of June 2001 the Scottish Executive made an unambiguous commitment to funding free personal care for the elderly. The policy is clearly in line with the claims made surrounding Scottish public culture, and the public discussion at the time reflected this as Scottish values and preferences were regularly invoked throughout the affair. In the end the policy took Scottish public culture and Scottish society as the relevant reference point for solidarity. As such, the programme brought Scottish social citizenship closer to the proclaimed Scottish ideas on obligations owed to co-nationals.

A policy that had a similar effect on social citizenship in Flanders is the Flemish Insurance for Non-medical Care. It is an additional mandatory insurance scheme for non-medical aid and service provision to individuals that have been assessed as in need of such help. The scheme came into being on 1 October 2001 by Flemish Parliamentary decree. Individuals residing in the Flemish Region are obligated to join whereas residents of Brussels have the option to do so. Residents of Wallonia, on the other hand, cannot join unless they fulfil a number of stringent requirements such as being signed up to the Belgian social security system as a result of employment in Flanders, and having lived in a third member state of the EU, the EEA or Switzerland immediately prior to or during their employment in Flanders. Unsurprisingly, these are conditions a marginal number of Francophone Belgians fulfil. The insurance scheme is meant as one element of the overarching Flemish Social Protection. There is no doubt that the Flemish Care Insurance Act, both in content and framing, could be regarded as a clearcut example of a policy initiative which influences what is entailed in the rights and obligations that come with citizenship. The invariable mention of the adjective – Flemish – is aimed at creating a bond with the region (Beyers and Bursens 2010). In practical terms, the rights and obligations are affected in one specific region: Flanders. After all, the implementation of the Flemish care insurance programme is changing the nature of social citizenship insofar as it implies a very concrete difference in what the 'right to a modicum of economic welfare and security' entails. In Flanders (and Brussels to a lesser extent) it now includes the right to financial support for non-medical care, whereas in the rest of Belgium it does not.

The fact that throughout the insurance scheme's life and inception no fewer than five legal cases seeking to annul or alter it have been brought against the Flemish government further serves to illustrate its relevance for territorial politics. After all, four of these originated with Francophone or Walloon regional governmental bodies, whereas one was brought by a federal organ. The regions and the federal government are thus clearly locked in a struggle for the prerogative to determine the relevant national community for social solidarity, and what that solidarity ought to look like. Politically this was played off by nationalist and even moderate autonomist parties in Flanders as being a clear case of the central government – and, more importantly, Francophone politicians – threatening Flemish policy priorities.

Conclusion

In this chapter we have attempted to formulate an answer to the question of why and how sub-state nationalism persists in some European regions today. We have done so by positing that national identity and its representations may not only include traditional markers such as language, religion and culture; but may also include ethical elements which determine what obligations we owe co-nationals. Using the tool of social citizenship, governments attempt to realize their ideas of what co-nationals owe one another. Sub-state nationalist mobilization focused on social policy may occur if a community is forced to accept a set of social citizenship obligations they do not subscribe to, or if they are engaged in a co-operative arrangement with one or more groups they do not consider co-nationals. Should attempts at mobilization include references to national identity in function of social policy and references to the fairness of inter-regional transfers, this chapter argues that we are dealing with a specific type of nationalism: ethical nationalism. In order to better understand where ethical nationalism comes from, we have looked at the historical development of public culture as a source of ideas about the character of the community which also helps to fix responsibilities. Finally, we illustrated what all this might look like in practice, by going through historical public culture formation, nationalist discourse analysis and regional social policy-making in the cases of Scotland and Flanders. In the process, it has become somewhat more clear why and how nationalism persists in these regions and, although it is not claimed that ethical nationalism is the only force at play, we believe that it may also help us to better understand the dynamic of sub-state nationalist politics in other cases.

Bibliography

Banting, K. G. (1995). 'The Welfare State as Statecraft: Territorial Politics and Canadian Social Policy'. In S. Leibfried, and P. Pierson (eds), *European Social*

Policy: Between Fragmentation and Integration, pp. 269–300. Washington, DC: The Brookings Institute.
Béland, D., and Lecours, A. (2007). 'Federalism, Nationalism and Social Policy Decentralisation in Canada and Belgium', *Regional and Federal Studies*, 17 (4), 405–19.
Béland, D., and Lecours, A. (2008). *Nationalism and Social Policy: The Politics of Territorial Solidarity*. Oxford: Oxford University Press.
Beyers, J., and Bursens, P. (2010). 'Towards a multilevel welfare state? On the relative autonomy of regional social policy'. In *Politicologenetmaal 2010*, pp. 1–23. Leuven: KU Leuven.
Birrell, D. (2009). *The Impact of Devolution on Social Policy*. Bristol, UK: Policy Press.
Boonen, J., and Hooghe, M. (2013). 'Do Nationalist Parties Shape or Follow Subnational Identities? A Panel Analysis on the Rise of the Nationalist Party in the Flemish Region of Belgium, 2006–2011', *Nations and Nationalism*, 20 (1), 56–79.
Cheyne, C., O'Brien, M., and Belgrave, M. (2005). *Social Policy in Aotearoa New Zealand*. South Melbourne, Victoria: Oxford University Press.
Dodeigne, J., Gramme, P., Reuchamps, M., and Sinardet, D. (2016). 'Beyond Linguistic and Party Homogeneity: Determinants of Belgian MPs' Preferences on Federalism and State Reform', *Party Politics*, 22 (4), 427–39.
Gellner, E. (1983). *Nations and Nationalism*. Ithaca, NY: Cornell University Press.
Greer, S. L. (2006). 'The Politics of Divergent Policy'. In S. L. Greer (ed.), *Territory, Democracy and Justice: Federalism and Regionalism in Western Democracies*, pp. 157–74. 1st edn. New York: Palgrave Macmillan.
Greer, S. L. (2007). *Nationalism and Self-government: The Politics of Autonomy in Scotland and Catalonia*. New York: State University of New York Press.
Greer, S. L., and Mätzke, M. (2009). 'Introduction: Devolution and Citizenship Rights'. In S. L. Greer (ed.), *Devolution and Social Citizenship in the UK*, pp. 1–20. 1st edn. Bristol: Policy Press.
Hepburn, E., and Elias, A. (2011). 'Dissent on the Periphery? Island Nationalisms and European Integration', *West European Politics*, 34 (4), 859–82.
Hepburn, E., and McLoughlin, P. (2011). 'Celtic Nationalism and Supranationalism: Comparing Scottish and Northern Ireland Party Responses to Europe', *The British Journal of Politics and International Relations*, 13 (3), 383–99.
Jolly, S. K. (2015). *The European Union and the Rise of Regionalist Parties*. Ann Arbor: University of Michigan Press.
Keating, M. (2014). 'Rescaling Interests', *Territory, Politics, Governance*, 2 (3), 239–48.
Keating, M., and Wilson, A. (2014). 'Regions with Regionalism? The Rescaling of Interest Groups in Six European States', *European Journal of Political Research*, 53 (4), 840–57.

Kymlicka, W., and Norman, W. (eds) (2000). *Citizenship in Diverse Societies*. 1st edn. Oxford: Oxford University Press.
Law, A., and Mooney, G. (2012). 'Devolution in a "Stateless Nation": Nation-building and Social Policy in Scotland', *Social Policy & Administration*, 46 (2), 161–77.
Leith, M. (2008). 'Scottish National Party Representations of Scottishness and Scotland', *Politics*, 28 (2), 83–92.
McEwen, N. (2002). 'State Welfare Nationalism: The Territorial Impact of Welfare State Development in Scotland', *Regional & Federal Studies*, 12 (1), 66–90.
McEwen, N. (2006). *Nationalism and the State*. Brussels: P.I.E.-Peter Lang.
McEwen, N., and Moreno, L. (eds) (2005). *The Territorial Politics of Welfare*. 1st edn. London: Routledge/ECPR Studies in European Political Science.
MacKinnon, D. (2015). 'Devolution, State Restructuring and Policy Divergence in the UK', *The Geographical Journal*, 181 (1), 47–56.
Maiz, R. (2007). 'Federalismo multinacional: una teoría normativa', *Revista d'Estudis Autonomics i Federals*, 2007 (3), 43–85.
Marnoch, G. (2003). 'Scottish devolution: identity and impact and the case of community care for the elderly', *Public Administration*, 81 (2), 253–73.
Marshall, T. H. (1950). *Citizenship and Social class*. Cambridge: Cambridge University Press.
Miller, D. (1995). *On Nationality*. Oxford: Clarendon Press.
Mooney, G., and Scott, G. (2011). 'Social Justice, Social Welfare and Devolution: Nationalism and Social Policy Making in Scotland', *Poverty & Public Policy*, 3 (4), 1–21.
Mooney, G., and Williams, C. (2006). 'Forging new "ways of life"? Social policy and nation building in devolved Scotland and Wales', *Critical Social Policy*, 26 (3), 608–29.
Moreno, L., Arriba, A., and Serrano, A. (2007). 'Identidades múltiples en la España descentralizada: El caso de Cataluña'. In M. Escobar (ed.), *El análisis de segmentación: técnicas y aplicaciones de los árboles de clasificación*, pp. 199–224. Madrid: Centro de Investigaciones Sociológicas.
Nieuw-Vlaamse Alliantie (2003). *Waarom N-VA? 18 Redenen voor 6 Miljoen Vlamingen*. Brussel: N-VA.
Nieuw-Vlaamse Alliantie (2007). *Voor een Sterker Vlaanderen*. Brussel: N-VA.
Özkirimli, U. (2010). *Theories of Nationalism: A critical introduction, 2nd Revised and Extended Edition*. Basingstoke: Palgrave Macmillan.
Scottish National Party (1999). *Enterprise, Compassion, Democracy*. Edinburgh: SNP.
Swenden, W. (2006). *Federalism and Regionalism in Western Europe*. Basingstoke: Palgrave Macmillan.

Notes on Contributors

FRANCESC-MARC ÁLVARO VIDAL is a professor at the Blanquerna School of Communication and International Relations, Ramon Llull University (Barcelona) and former director of the Degree in Journalism. His main areas of interest are political journalism, public opinion, and the relations between collective memory and the media. He is a political analyst for the newspaper *La Vanguardia*, RAC1 and the Catalan public television station TV3-Televisió de Catalunya. He was awarded the National Prize for Journalism of Catalonia.

LEYRE ARRIETA ALBERDI, PhD in Modern History, is a professor in the Faculty of Social and Human Sciences at the University of Deusto. She has lectured in Universal History II, Modern History, Modern Social Thought, History of Scientific and Philosophical Thought, and Today's World. She has worked on individual and team research projects involving areas such as Basque nationalism and its symbols, and exile and integration within Europe, as well as the history of Basque nationalist radio. Her most noteworthy publications are *Estación Europa. La política europeísta del PNV en el exilio (1945–1977)* (2007), *La historia de Radio Euskadi* (2009), *Fondo Gobierno de Euzkadi: historia y contenido* (2011), *Diccionario ilustrado de símbolos del nacionalismo vasco* (2012, with others) and *Estudio introductorio y edición de La causa del pueblo vasco de F. J. Landaburu* (2017).

SUSANA BAYÓ BELENGUER is a former Head of the Department of Hispanic Studies, Trinity College, Dublin University, where she obtained her PhD and where she teaches contemporary Spanish politics and history, and the representation of history in literature, journalism and visual media. Her publications have centred on the writer and intellectual Manuel Vázquez Montalbán and on the Spanish Civil War. She is a member of the editorial board of Ediciones Alfar (Spain) and of a Research Network, officially recognized by the Spanish Ministry of Education, on the International Brigades.

NICOLA BRADY is a research associate with the Department of Hispanic Studies, Trinity College, Dublin University. Her PhD examined the response of the political hierarchy to political violence in Northern Ireland (1921–73) and the Basque Country (1936–75). She is currently General Secretary to the Irish Council of Churches where her work has a particular focus on the contribution of Christian churches to peace, reconciliation and social justice in Ireland, as well as in a wider European and global context. In 2019 she was awarded an Eisenhower Fellowship to examine the role of churches and faith communities in overcoming political polarization and social exclusion in the United States. She is a Director of Christian Aid Ireland and of the Maximilian Kolbe Foundation.

EMMANUEL DALLE MULLE is a post-doctoral researcher at the Graduate Institute of International and Development Studies, where he co-ordinates a project entitled 'The Myth of Homogeneity: Minority Protection and Assimilation in Western Europe, 1919–1939'. He previously worked at the Catholic University of Leuven and the Universitat Pompeu Fabra (Barcelona), and held visiting researcher positions at the London School of Economics, Boston University and the Vrije Universiteit Brussels. His book *The Nationalism of the Rich: Discourses and Strategies of Separatist Parties in Catalonia, Flanders, Northern Italy and Scotland* won the 2018 Latsis Prize for the University of Geneva. He is specialized in nationalism and ethnic politics. His research interests include Western European nationalist parties, welfare nationalism, minority–majority relations, and separatism.

GORKA ETXEBARRIA DUEÑAS is a researcher in the University of the Basque Country whose field includes the relation between national identities, ideologies, cultural references and scenarios of the everyday. He has published several works on national identity analysis and recent history in the Basque Country.

KATERINA GARCIA, PhD, is an assistant professor in the Department of Hispanic Studies, Trinity College, Dublin University. Her principal research interests and current areas of publication are Judeo-Spanish and Hispanic linguistics; the historical and socio-cultural contexts of Judeo-Spanish language use and Judeo-Spanish literary creation; contemporary interpretations of Judeo-Spanish secular song.

RICHARD GOW completed his PhD in Hispanic Studies at Trinity College, Dublin University in 2018. His doctoral research, funded by an Irish Research Council Government of Ireland Postgraduate Scholarship, explored the ideals of citizenship in Spain during the dictatorship of General Primo de Rivera (1923–30) through an analysis of more than 100 official correspondences maintained between ordinary individuals and the Spanish State. He has contributed chapters on military and civil relations in Spain during the First World War and on the denunciation of political corruption under Primo de Rivera to volumes published by Brill and by Marcial Pons respectively. He works in the Irish justice sector.

MARK FRIIS HAU is a PhD candidate in European Studies, Aarhus University, who has worked with the pro-independence movement in Catalonia since 2011. A trained anthropologist, his doctoral research is a comparative 'party ethnography' of activism and European attitudes among members and politicians of the Scottish National Party and Esquerra Republicana de Catalunya. His research interests include (minority) nationalism, the anthropology of Politics (capital P), social movements, and political party activism. He is currently exploring the use of social media as a tool to study online activism.

CARLES JOVANÍ GIL holds a PhD in International Relations from the University of Valencia and an MA in EU Diplomacy Studies from the College of Europe. He has been a Visiting Scholar at Columbia University and at the London School of Economics, and has also gained work experience at several EU institutions. Among other honours, he obtained the Spanish National Award for Excellence in Academic Performance and a Ramón Areces Foundation scholarship.

JOAQUÍN MARTÍN CUBAS is Professor of Political Science and Administration at the University of Valencia. Currently he is Director of the Department of Constitutional Law and Political Science and Administration. Among his publications are studies on democracy and political institutions. He has studied the institutions of the Valencian Community and local governments.

JOSEP-LLUÍS MICÓ-SANZ is a professor and Chair of Journalism at the Universitat Ramon Llull (Barcelona). He is the Academic Vice-Dean of the Blanquerna School of Communication and International Relations, where he directs the Degree in Journalism, the Master's Degree in Advanced Journalism (Blanquerna-Grupo Godó), the Master's Degree in Fashion Communication (Blanquerna-080 Barcelona Fashion), and the Master's Degree in Sport Communication (Blanquerna-F. C. Barcelona). He is a technology analyst in media for the newspaper *La Vanguardia* and for Radio Nacional de España-Ràdio 4.

XOSÉ M. NÚÑEZ SEIXAS obtained his PhD at EUI Florence and is Full Professor of Modern History at the University of Santiago de Compostela. Between 2012 and 2017 he was also Professor of Modern European History at the Ludwig-Maximilian University (Munich), and has been a visiting professor at the College of Europe (Natolin), as well as at Stanford University, City University of New York and Verona University. He has published widely on the comparative history of nationalist movements and national and regional identities, as well as on overseas migration from Spain and Galicia to Latin America, and the cultural history of war in the twentieth century. Among his latest books are *Suspiros de España. El nacionalismo español, 1808–2018* (Barcelona, 2018; German edition, Hamburg, 2019) and (coedited with E. Storm) *Regionalism and Modern Europe. Identity Constructions and Movements from 1890 to the Present Day* (London, 2018).

DANIEL PURCELL gained his PhD at Trinity College, Dublin University, where he held a Long Room Hub Early Career Fellowship and was awarded a Postgraduate College Research Studentship. His research focuses on the Ulster Protestant community in Cavan, Monaghan and Fermanagh during the years of the Irish Revolution. He is particularly interested in how different national and cultural communities navigated and were changed by the stresses of the Irish Revolution and the partition of Ireland. He has published articles in the *Breifne Historical Journal* and has contributed a chapter to the forthcoming volume *Southern Loyalism and its Discontents*, edited by Brian Hughes and Conor Morrissey.

JUAN ROMERO is Professor of Human Geography at the University of Valencia and a member of the Interuniversity Institute of Local Development. He has also been Visiting Scholar at the School of Geography at the University of Leeds. Recently he has focused his teaching and research activity within the fields of political geography, social geography, state structure and new forms of territorial governance. He is the author or editor of twenty-nine books and almost a hundred articles and book chapters.

MARGARITA SOLER SÁNCHEZ is Professor of Constitutional Law at the University of Valencia and a member of the Institute of Studies of Women. Currently she is President of the Legal Advisory Council of the Generalitat Valenciana. She is the author of numerous publications related to the study of political institutions and, especially, gender equality.

ROBERT SAUNDERS, PhD, is a professor in the Department of History, Politics, and Geography at Farmingdale State College, a campus of the State University of New York (SUNY). His geographic area of specialization is post-Soviet Eurasia and his research explores various intersections of popular culture, geopolitics, nationalism, and religious identity. He is the author of five books, one of which, *Ethnopolitics in Cyberspace: The Internet, Minority Nationalism, and the Web of Identity* (Lexington Books, 2017), examines the role of the internet in shaping national identity.

MARÇAL SINTES OLIVELLA is a professor and researcher in the Blanquerna School of Communication and International Relations, Ramon Llull University (Barcelona), where he is Director of the Research

Institute on Communications and International Relations, the Master's Programme on Comprehensive Corporate Communication and the postgraduate course on Data Journalism and Visualization. His principal research areas include public opinion, political journalism and freedom of speech. As a political analyst he contributes to various newspapers, such as *El Periódico de Catalunya*. In 2010, he won the Ramon Trias Fargas Award for Political Essay.

SORINA SOARE is Lecturer in Comparative Politics at the University of Florence. She holds a PhD in political science from the Université libre de Bruxelles and has previously studied political science at the University of Bucharest. In the area of comparative politics, her research interests lie primarily in the field of post-communist political parties and party systems, democratization and institutional development. Her most recent publications include (coedited with S. Gherghina and A. Iancu), *Party Members and Their Importance in Non-EU Countries. A Comparative Analysis*; and (with C. Tufis) 'Phoenix Populism', *Problems of Post-Communism*, 2018.

IÑIGO URRUTIA is currently Full Professor of Administrative and Constitutional Law at the University of the Basque Country (UBC) and the University Ombudsperson. He earned his Master's degree in Public Law in 1994 and his doctorate in Law, with honours, awarded Magna Cum Laude and the 2004 Extraordinary Prize. His current research projects focus on power decentralization, language rights, rights of minorities and environmental law. He is the author of ten books, one of which has been published by the Council of Europe, and over ninety articles on fundamental rights, constitutional and administrative law, EU law, cultural, ethnic and linguistic diversity, protection of minorities and self-determination.

ERIK VANDERHEYDEN, from Flanders in Belgium, completed his undergraduate education at the University of Leuven. He holds an MA in International Relations from National Chengchi University in Taiwan, and is completing a PhD on social policy and nationalist politics in

Scotland and Flanders at the University of Leipzig's Graduate School for Global and Area Studies.

JOSÉ Mª VIDAL BELTRÁN is Professor of Constitutional Law at the University of Valencia. Currently he is the *Secretario Autonómico* of Communication of the Generalitat Valenciana. He is the author of numerous publications related to constitutional law, especially in the field of public and territorial administrations, as well as the law of communication.

Index

A
accession 66, 70, 73–6, 79, 81–2, 84, 287, 293, 297, 347, 362, 366, 371
Albania 297, 299
America *see* United States
Andalusia 37, 313
Anderson, Benedict 4–5, 183, 400, 404
Arana, Sabino 32, 34, 44, 95
army 65, 99, 107, 108, 148, 150, 157, 158, 165, 167, 170, 209, 288
  see also military
Austria 8, 9, 284, 287, 293
authority 18, 23, 55, 110, 170, 211, 212, 257, 346, 399, 400
autonomous community 103–4, 266, 386, 387
  Basque Autonomous Community 38, 91, 101–2, 105, 106, 107, 111, 113, 380, 382, 383–4
autonomy 33, 37, 39, 43–4, 46, 49, 68, 96–101, 180, 193, 259, 261, 265, 273, 274, 285, 290, 293, 294, 297, 298, 349, 379–85, 386–7, 408, 409, 410, 416

B
Balkans 120, 134, 142, 286, 297, 370
Basque Country 29–50, 91–113, 189, 261, 262, 263, 265, 267, 269, 276, 379–96
  Basque identity 29–31, 34–36, 91, 95, 98, 100–1, 384
  Basque nationalism 30, 45–6, 49, 92–113, 260, 267, 269, 379
  see also Euskadi

Basque Nationalist Party *see* PNV (*Partido Nacionalista Vasco*)
Belgium 276, 291, 298, 320, 399, 401, 411, 414–15, 418
belonging 2–3, 8, 21, 23, 55, 177, 178, 345, 348, 360
Billig, Michael 93–5, 103, 111, 181, 186, 189
Bosnia 297
Brexit 1, 8, 11, 12, 15, 22, 78, 80, 81, 83, 219, 223, 299
Britain 9, 11, 12, 67, 79, 95, 153, 227, 241, 287
  British identity 14, 410
Brubaker, Rogers 285, 342, 360

C
Canada 276, 384, 390–1, 395, 401
Catalonia 37, 56, 58, 61–2, 64–67, 68, 81–2, 84, 100, 179–81, 191, 192–4, 195, 197–9, 256, 261, 262, 263–7, 269, 270, 276, 286, 294, 298, 303–20, 327, 379, 386, 388, 393–5, 399–400
  Catalan identity 177, 178–181, 183, 188, 189, 195, 315
  Catalanism 21, 183, 185–6, 187–91, 194–7, 200
Catalunya *see* Catalonia
Christian Democrats 45, 48, 316, 411–12
citizenship 149, 159, 167, 274, 341–5, 345–7, 360–2, 370–2, 407–8
  European Union citizenship 73–4, 76–7, 367
  Moldovan citizenship 364–5

Romanian citizenship 339, 341–5, 352, 360–2, 362–7, 369–72
social citizenship 399, 401–2, 405–6, 407–8, 412–19
civil society 13, 18, 19, 57, 91, 171, 362, 371
community 3, 5, 21, 23, 29, 33, 37–9, 119, 132, 150, 161, 166, 179, 180, 189, 345, 402–8, 410, 412–14, 418–19
  Basque community 41, 44, 104
  Jewish community 120, 122, 128–9, 137, 140–3
  political community 4, 270, 347, 371
conflict 3, 7, 16, 23, 81, 108, 111, 177–8, 199, 215, 230, 259, 264, 283–4, 292, 293, 294, 296, 329
  see also ethnicity, ethnic conflict; identity, identity-based conflict
constitution 37, 40, 41–3, 65, 68, 71, 101–2, 107, 211, 253–4, 256, 259–66, 267–9, 270–2, 274, 275–6, 350–1, 379–96
  Constitutional Court 68, 210, 256, 262–3, 264, 313–5, 317, 319, 356, 379, 380, 385–6, 393–5
CiU (*Convergència i Unió*) 64, 190, 259, 265–6, 306, 309, 311–12, 316, 319
corruption 148, 154, 157, 163, 169, 208, 218, 359
Crimea 20, 203–19, 289, 299
Crimean Tatars 210, 289, 299, 342, 369
Croatia 15, 296, 342, 370
culture 4, 37, 47, 159, 180, 188, 205, 261, 276, 400, 402–4, 406–13, 416–17, 419
  political culture 55, 99, 255
currency 76, 80, 100
Cyprus 79, 293
Czech Republic 300
Czechoslovakia 284, 285, 287, 288, 290, 292, 295, 297, 389

D
democracy 19, 57, 72, 183, 194–7, 219, 258–9, 295, 379, 389, 390
devolution 19, 70, 297, 299, 307, 379, 399, 401, 410
dialogue 56–7, 91, 95, 199, 253, 255, 394
diaspora 123, 128, 141, 143, 343–4, 353, 354
diplomacy 213, 327, 359, 369
diversity 57, 169, 194, 258, 270, 271, 317
Donbas (Donbass) 20, 203, 206, 218–19, 283, 287, 299, 300

E
ECJ (European Court of Justice) 70, 73–4, 77
economic crisis 11, 13, 263–4, 308, 317, 388
education 100, 122, 148, 273, 283, 296, 316, 344, 353, 358, 367–8, 380, 382, 399, 405, 407, 411, 413, 414
elites 5, 8, 14, 57, 58, 93, 102–3, 151, 153, 205, 208, 257, 283, 322, 349–50
empire 12, 204, 206, 284, 285, 369
  British Empire 286, 410
  Ottoman Empire 120, 122, 124, 127
England 10, 67, 80
equality 22, 72, 107, 187, 269, 406
ERC (*Esquerra Republicana de Catalunya*) 64, 179, 306
Estonia 15, 290, 294, 295, 300, 310
ETA (*Euskadi Ta Askatasuna*) 32, 96, 293
ethics 183, 199, 244, 402
ethnicity 4, 124, 182, 293, 296, 346, 356, 358, 369
  ethnic conflict 290, 296, 351–2
EU (European Union) 6–17, 22–3, 58, 59, 61–6, 70–84, 208, 213, 215, 219, 275–6, 293, 297, 299, 306, 341, 345, 347, 352, 354, 361–2, 364, 371, 418

Eurasian Economic Union 208, 214–15, 217, 357
Europe 4–17
    European identity 6–7, 9, 11, 17
Euskadi 34, 37, 45, 47–8, 49
    see also Basque Country

F
family 19, 21, 95, 137, 155, 189
federalism 60, 254–6, 269, 390
Finland 297, 298
flags 158, 181, 350
    Basque flag (*ikurriña*) 44, 92–113, 166
    Catalan flag (*estelada*) 181, 305
Flanders 59, 298, 399–400, 402, 411–12, 413–19
France 8, 9, 17, 46, 49, 128, 153, 195, 255, 287, 291, 292, 300, 317, 406
Franco, Francisco 29–33, 45, 48, 95–8, 99–100, 106, 107, 286, 294, 316
    Franco dictatorship 95–6, 100
Francoism 58–9, 94, 98, 107
freedom 72, 140, 178, 193, 198, 218, 269, 292, 305, 389, 403, 405, 406
Frisia 59, 291, 299
fueros 30, 34, 41, 380

G
Galicia 37, 50, 59, 100, 261
Gellner, Ernest 3, 400, 408
Generalitat 187, 308–10, 311–12, 315, 316, 318, 319, 327, 329
Germany 9, 10, 12, 17, 46, 258, 284, 286–7, 290–1, 292, 300, 320, 389
    German reunification 63, 71, 389
globalization 7–8, 12–14, 59–60, 254, 346
Great Britain *see* Britain

Greece 9, 10, 12, 15, 127–8, 134, 291, 292, 293
Greenland 63, 71, 298

H
HB (*Herri Batasuna*) 43, 99, 104–5, 107, 109, 110–12
history 4, 9, 23, 35, 56, 150, 151, 180, 188, 189, 190, 223, 243, 245, 255, 256, 358, 363, 370, 403, 409, 412–13
Holocaust (*Shoah*) 6, 123, 124, 143, 287
Hungary 8, 9, 284, 288, 300, 342, 351, 352
hybridity 4, 57, 211, 261, 285, 296, 300

I
identity v 1, 2, 3, 8, 12, 329
    collective identity 133
    cultural identity 345
    identity crisis 132, 254, 350
    identity formation 1, 19, 226
    identity markers 132, 411, 416
    identity politics 1, 7, 9, 12, 203, 291, 294, 342, 369
    identity-based conflict 1, 23
    national identity 4, 7, 19, 55, 58, 95, 184, 188, 270, 285, 288, 400, 401, 402, 413–14, 416, 419
    political identity 245, 255
    regional identity 5–6
ideology 55, 148, 184, 187, 192, 204, 234, 285, 411
ikurriña see flags, Basque flag (*ikurriña*)
integration 6–13, 23, 167, 206, 208, 253, 256, 261, 340, 344, 351, 381, 400
international law 20, 66, 67–74, 82–3, 212, 390–2
Ireland 19, 20, 67, 223–5, 227, 232, 235, 241, 242, 245
    Irish border 223, 237, 249, 299
    Irish Free State 67, 235, 236

Irish identity 225
Irish independence 235, 286
irredentism 284, 289, 297, 299, 359, 370
Italy 8, 9, 12, 153, 255, 258, 292, 293, 297, 299

J
Jewish identity 121, 124, 126
Judeo-Spanish language 119–26, 135–40, 143

K
kin 342, 344, 347, 351, 359, 371
  kin-community 342, 344, 355, 361, 370
  kin-state 342, 344, 347–8, 369, 371
Kosovo 68, 79, 84, 212, 216, 290, 297, 391

L
language 3–4, 37, 119–121, 132–134, 180, 194, 259, 261, 291, 293, 294, 350, 356, 402, 403, 412–14, 419
  Basque language 39, 44
  Catalan language 188–9, 200, 314, 316, 318
Latvia 290, 294, 295, 300, 310
Linz, Juan J. 257, 259, 276
Lithuania 284, 290, 294, 295, 310

M
Mas, Artur 64, 305–6, 308–9, 312, 319, 325, 327
media 19, 44, 208, 211, 233–4, 265, 268, 303–7, 321–9, 366
  social media 17, 125
memory 121, 123, 133, 142
  collective memory 119, 124, 127, 141, 143
  cultural memory 127, 132,
migration 13–17, 22–3, 292, 359, 367
  emigration 128, 288, 343

immigration 11, 59, 197, 341, 343, 346
military 6, 101, 102, 105, 107, 147–8, 151, 154–8, 164, 166, 169, 171–2, 209, 211, 213, 216, 260, 287, 295
  military service 154, 159, 404
  see also army
monarchy 94, 100, 102–3, 106–7, 308
Moldova 337–72
  Moldovan identity 357, 358, 359
Montenegro 69, 76, 127, 391
multiculturalism 7, 12, 13–16, 59

N
nationalism 1–6, 13–17, 55–6, 59, 60, 181, 185–6, 192
  banal nationalism 93–5
  ethical nationalism 402–3, 408–9, 412–13, 415, 416, 419
  sub-state nationalism 59, 399–403, 407–8, 419
nation-building 181, 257, 340, 388, 396, 400
nationhood 157–8, 169, 172, 189, 192, 203, 329, 339–40
NATO (North Atlantic Treaty Organisation) 210, 213–15, 297, 347, 352, 353, 354, 371
Navarre 35, 38, 40, 91, 101–8, 113, 127, 261, 380–2
Netherlands, The 9, 291, 300, 322
Northern Ireland 20, 67, 223–5, 236, 237, 238, 243, 244, 246–7, 249, 250, 293, 297

P
passports 178, 189, 200, 298, 341, 361, 364, 372
patriotism 147, 186, 212, 258, 268
peace v 6, 22, 108, 168, 235, 244, 349, 385, 392
pluralism 57, 394

PNV (*Partido Nacionalista Vasco*) 29–50, 95, 97, 101, 104–5, 107, 109–11, 112, 259
Poland 8, 9, 219, 287, 288, 291, 295
police 44, 61, 96, 99, 106, 108–12, 199, 208, 319
populism 7, 10, 14
PP (*Partido Popular*) 179, 191, 262, 263, 266, 267–8, 308, 312–13, 315, 316–8, 326
Primo de Rivera, Miguel 147–8, 152, 154–8, 159, 167, 169, 171–2
propaganda 65, 167, 227, 300
PSOE (*Partido Socialista Obrero Español*) 42–4, 49, 97, 102–12, 191, 259, 262, 266, 267, 269, 272, 306, 311–12, 316
public opinion 209, 265, 322, 329, 403, 406
Puigdemont, Carles 62, 305, 319–20
Pujol, Jordi 179, 266–7, 310–11, 316–17
Putin, Vladimir 208–13, 216–19, 298, 359

Q
Quebec 390–1, 413

R
Rajoy, Mariano 65, 265, 306, 308, 309, 310, 312
reconciliation 100, 379
referendum 56, 75, 102, 104, 107, 210, 291, 356–7, 381, 391
  on Brexit 78
  on Catalan independence 61, 81, 199, 266, 270, 305, 307, 308–10, 313, 315–17, 319–20, 328–9, 395
  on Crimea 207
  on Scottish independence 61, 63, 64, 78, 316, 400
  on Spanish Constitution 42, 43
regeneration 150, 152, 154, 155, 171

regionalism 5, 47
religion 2, 184, 297, 370, 413
Renan, Ernest 2, 8, 400
rights 4, 33–9, 50, 62, 70, 73–4, 75–7, 225, 274
  citizenship rights 342, 416
  human rights 72, 82, 84, 211, 261, 364, 379
  minority rights 288, 346
Rodríguez Zapatero, José Luis 264, 311, 312
Romania 79, 285, 291, 295, 337–72
  Romanian identity 366
Russia 6, 210, 211, 215–19, 284–5, 295–6, 340, 352, 357, 364
  Russian nationalism 204–6
Russian Federation *see* Russia

S
Salonika 119–22, 126–8, 141–3
Scotland 56, 59, 61, 63–4, 67–8, 71–2, 74, 78–81, 82–4, 293, 298, 410, 417, 419
  Scottish independence 68, 75, 78, 83, 299
secession 7, 56, 61–84, 207, 236, 270, 284, 288, 296, 299–300, 389–395
security 15, 205, 213, 215, 217, 273, 358, 392, 403
self-determination 42, 50, 61–2, 65, 69, 77, 81–2, 99, 127, 192, 212, 259, 285, 306, 307, 308–10, 326–9, 384, 388–94
self-government 29, 180–1, 260–1, 379–86, 395–6
separatism 191, 283–4, 287, 288–93, 296–300
Sephardim 119–143
Serbia 69, 84, 127, 216, 284, 290, 297, 342, 351, 352, 370
Shoah see Holocaust (*Shoah*)

Slovakia 79
Slovenia 296
Smith, Anthony D. 3, 4, 55, 400
SNP (Scottish National Party) 63–4, 69, 78, 411, 413–14, 417
social citizenship 399, 401–2, 405–8, 412–14, 416–17
social cohesion 15, 212, 270
social policy 316, 399–419
solidarity 5, 73, 91, 107, 217, 234, 247, 257, 260, 272, 399, 403, 409, 415, 416–18
sovereignty 23, 41, 55, 67, 91, 95, 203, 207, 284, 285, 317, 344, 363, 369, 386, 387
    national sovereignty 10, 94, 260, 262, 295
Soviet Union *see* USSR
Spain 2, 9, 18, 40–4, 57–8, 65, 79–80, 94, 100, 104, 107–8, 147–8, 150–5, 171–2, 196, 253–76, 286, 307–8, 311, 314, 315–18, 379–83, 386–8, 392–6
    Spanish Civil War 95–6, 172
    Spanish identity 94, 99–100, 111, 181, 188, 253, 263
    Spanish nationalism 58, 94–5, 99–101, 104, 150, 258, 267–8
    Spanish transition to democracy 57, 256
State of Autonomies 18, 253, 268
statute 58, 169–70, 261, 262, 263–4
    Basque Statute of Autonomy 39, 41–4, 263, 380–6, 392
    Catalan Statute of Autonomy 68, 178, 256, 263–5, 305, 310–15, 317–18, 379
Sweden 9, 80, 298
Switzerland 77, 418

T
terrorism 14, 22, 217, 292, 299
tradition 56, 123–4, 132
treaty 64, 67, 71–3, 207, 210, 349, 352–3, 359
Turkey 127, 128, 134, 284, 285, 298, 367

U
UK (United Kingdom) 9, 12, 22–3, 46, 56, 63–4, 67–70, 74, 77–81, 223–4, 255, 276, 297, 322, 399, 401, 417
Ukraine 203–19, 283, 288, 291, 294, 300, 351, 352, 353
Ulster 223–37, 240–2, 243, 245–7, 248–50, 297
    Ulster identity 224, 231, 246, 249
Ulster Unionism 223–44, 249–50
    Ulster Unionist identity 225, 226–7, 233, 236, 237–8
UN (United Nations) 69, 75, 211, 212
unification 340, 349, 351, 353, 355, 358, 367, 368, 370
    reunification 350, 352, 354, 359, 368–9
    see also German re-unification
US (United States) 128, 152–3, 211, 213, 215, 217, 219, 255, 294, 295, 299, 406
USSR (Union of Socialist Soviet Republics) 69, 203–5, 207, 212, 216, 285–90, 294–6, 339, 341, 349, 389

V
values 9, 21, 23, 72, 102, 103, 148, 162, 178, 182–3, 185, 186, 187, 190, 193, 197, 199–200, 208, 270, 388, 403–4, 410–2, 414, 417
violence 7, 98, 110, 199, 211, 242, 254, 265, 293, 295, 297, 319, 346, 396
    political violence 94, 283, 292

Index

W
Wales 293
Wallonia 298, 415, 418
war 5, 6, 216, 219, 292, 296
    Balkan wars 127
    Cold War 203, 204, 205, 216, 290, 292, 294
    culture war 7, 196
    First World War 119, 126, 128, 147, 154, 227–8, 284, 286, 340
    Great Patriotic War 290
    Great War *see* war, First World War
    Inter-war Europe 148
    Irish War of Independence 232
    Second World War 46, 142, 286–7, 295, 341, 346, 349, 352, 405
    Spanish–American War 152
welfare 57, 272–3, 274, 316, 382, 395–6, 401, 404, 405–6, 410, 416, 418

Y
Yugoslavia 69, 288, 290, 295, 389

NATIONALISMS ACROSS THE GLOBE

Although in the 1980s the widely shared belief was that nationalism had become a spent force, the fragmentation of the studiously non-national Soviet Union, Yugoslavia and Czechoslovakia in the 1990s into a multitude of successor nation-states reaffirmed its continuing significance. Today all extant polities (with the exception of the Vatican) are construed as nation-states, and hence nationalism is the sole universally accepted criterion of statehood legitimization. Similarly, human groups wishing to be recognized as fully fledged participants in international relations must define themselves as nations. This concept of world politics underscores the need for open-ended, broad-ranging, novel and interdisciplinary research into nationalism and ethnicity. It promotes better understanding of the phenomena relating to social, political and economic life, both past and present.

This peer-reviewed series publishes monographs, conference proceedings and collections of articles. It attracts well-researched, often interdisciplinary, studies which open new approaches to nationalism and ethnicity or focus on interesting case studies. The language of the series is usually English, with authors/editors of proposed volumes responsible for meeting the Peter Lang standards of copy-editing. Book proposals for *Nationalisms Across the Globe* and queries should be emailed to either, or both, of the series editors:

Dr Tomasz Kamusella (University of St Andrews, Scotland, UK), tomek672@gmail.com

Dr Krzysztof Jaskułowski (University of Social Sciences and Humanities, Poland), krzysztofja@interia.pl

The series is affiliated with the Institute for Transnational and Spatial History at the University of St Andrews (http://standrewstransnational.wp.st-andrews.ac.uk/), headed by Bernhard Struck and Tomasz Kamusella. The Institute gathers scholars with a strong interest in the comparative, entangled and transnational history of modern Europe and the globalized world.

Vol. 1   Tomasz Kamusella and Krzysztof Jaskułowski (eds):
         Nationalisms Today. 334 pages, 2009.

Vol. 2   Cezary Obracht-Prondzyński and Tomasz Wicherkiewicz (eds):
         The Kashubs: Past and Present. 307 pages, 2011.

Vol. 3   Sabelo J. Ndlovu-Gatsheni and James Muzondidya (eds):
         Redemptive or Grotesque Nationalism? Rethinking
         Contemporary Politics in Zimbabwe. 446 pages, 2011.

Vol. 4   Blessing-Miles Tendi:
         Making History in Mugabe's Zimbabwe. Politics, Intellectuals
         and the Media. 304 pages, 2010.

Vol. 5   Pavlos I. Koktsidis:
         Strategic Rebellion. Ethnic Conflict in FYR Macedonia
         and the Balkans. 279 pages, 2012.

Vol. 6   Janusz Sawczuk:
         Turbulentes 1989. Genese der deutschen Einheit. 327 pages, 2011.

Vol. 7   Chris Kostov:
         Contested Ethnic Identity. The Case of Macedonian
         Immigrants in Toronto, 1900–1996. 330 pages, 2010.

Vol. 8   Alexander Maxwell (ed.):
         The East–West Discourse. Symbolic Geography and its
         Consequences. 237 pages, 2011.

Vol. 9   Agnieszka Bielewska:
         Changing Polish Identities. Post-War and Post-Accession
         Polish Migrants in Manchester. 208 pages, 2012.

Vol. 10 Anders E. B. Blomqvist, Constantin Iordachi
         and Balázs Trencsényi (eds):
         Hungary and Romania Beyond National Narratives.
         Comparisons and Entanglements. 855 pages, 2013.

Vol. 11 Olesya Khromeychuk:
         'Undetermined' Ukrainians. Post-War Narratives
         of the Waffen SS 'Galicia' Division. 217 pages. 2013.

Vol. 12 Michael Leach, James Scambary, Matthew Clarke, Simon Feeny and Heather Wallace: Attitudes to National Identity in Melanesia and Timor-Leste. A Survey of Future Leaders in Papua New Guinea, Solomon Islands, Vanuatu and Timor-Leste. 232 pages. 2013.

Vol. 13 Ephraim Nimni, Alexander Osipov and David J. Smith (eds): The Challenge of Non-Territorial Autonomy. Theory and Practice. 285 pages. 2013.

Vol. 14 Virve-Anneli Vihman and Kristiina Praakli (eds): Negotiating Linguistic Identity. Language and Belonging in Europe. 354 pages. 2014.

Vol. 15 Ilir Kalemaj: Contested Borders. Territorialization, National Identity and 'Imagined Geographies' in Albania. 285 pages. 2014.

Vol. 16 Martina Neuburger and H. Peter Dörrenbächer (eds): Nationalisms and Identities among Indigenous Peoples. Case Studies from North America. 261 pages. 2015.

Vol. 17 Dorota Szeligowska: Polish Patriotism after 1989. Concepts, Debates, Identities. 309 pages. 2016.

Vol. 18 Pedro Ibarra Güell and Åshild Kolås (eds): Basque Nationhood. Towards a Democratic Scenario. 326 pages. 2016.

Vol. 19 Jule Goikoetxea: Privatizing Democracy. Global Ideals, European Politics and Basque Territories. 280 pages. 2017.

Vol. 20 Alim Baluch: The Disintegration of Bosnia and Herzegovina. From Ethnic Cleansing to Ethnified Governance. 316 pages, 2018.

Vol. 21 Susana Bayó Belenguer and Nicola Brady (eds): Pulling Together or Pulling Apart? Perspectives on Nationhood, Identity and Belonging in Europe. 446 pages, 2019

www.ingramcontent.com/pod-product-compliance
Lightning Source LLC
LaVergne TN
LVHW021754060526
838201LV00058B/3086